God, the World, and Hope

God, the World, and Hope

An Introduction to Christian Dogmatics

HARALD HEGSTAD

WIPF & STOCK · Eugene, Oregon

GOD, THE WORLD, AND HOPE
An Introduction to Christian Dogmatics

Copyright © 2018 Harald Hegstad. All rights reserved. Except for brief quotations in critical publications or reviews, no part of this book may be reproduced in any manner without prior written permission from the publisher. Write: Permissions, Wipf and Stock Publishers, 199 W. 8th Ave., Suite 3, Eugene, OR 97401.

Wipf & Stock
An Imprint of Wipf and Stock Publishers
199 W. 8th Ave., Suite 3
Eugene, OR 97401

www.wipfandstock.com

PAPERBACK ISBN: 978-1-5326-1953-3
HARDCOVER ISBN: 978-1-4982-4587-6
EBOOK ISBN: 978-1-4982-4586-9

Manufactured in the U.S.A. 10/24/18

Originally published in Norwegian: *Gud, verden og håpet: Innføring i kristen dogmatikk* (Oslo, Norway: Luther, 2015). Translated by Brian McNeil.

Unless marked by an asterisk, Scripture quotations are from the New Revised Standard Version, copyright © 1989 National Council of the Churches of Christ in the United States of America. Used by permission. All rights reserved worldwide.

Contents

Preface | xiii

1 What Is Dogmatics? | 1

1.1 Dogmatics as a Field of Study | 1

The study of the intellectual content of the Christian faith | 1

Dogmatics as an academic discipline | 2

The question of truth: four models | 5

  A. Theology as purely descriptive | 5

  B. Theology based on positions of faith | 6

  C. Theology as the grammar of faith | 6

  D. A theology that seeks to establish the truth of faith | 7

Dogmatics as academic work on a Christian interpretation of life | 8

1.2 Dogmatics and the Church | 10

Ecumenical convergence | 11

Religious primary language and dogmatic secondary language | 14

Other arenas for dogmatics | 18

1.3 Dogmatics and Context | 18

1.4 The Material and Methodology of Dogmatics | 20

The Bible as source for dogmatics | 20

Church history as source for dogmatics | 21

Contemporary sources | 22

Dogmatics as a work of interpretation | 23

1.5 Basic Elements of a Christian Interpretation Of Life | 24

2 How Can We Know Anything about God? | 26

2.1 Revelation | 26

The general revelation: Traces of God in the creation | 27

The special revelation: God's revelation to bring salvation | 29

    Law and gospel | 31
    The relationship between the general and the special revelation | 34

2.2 The Bible as a Testimony to God's Revelation | 37
    The apostolic tradition | 38
    The formation of the canon | 39
    The biblical texts as witness and interpretation | 40
    The Old Testament as part of the Christian canon | 42
    A Lutheran view of the Bible | 44
    The Bible as norm | 45
    Historical-critical biblical scholarship | 46
    Is the Bible free of error? | 47
    The inspiration of the Bible | 49

2.3 Scripture and Tradition | 50
    Bible and confession | 53
    Bible, tradition, reason, and experience | 55

3 Who Is God? | 57

3.1 Christian Belief in God and Other Theistic Belief | 57
    Christian belief in God and belief in God in other religions | 58
    Christian belief in God and the philosophical concept of God | 59
    Christian belief in God and other forms of monotheism | 60
    The challenge from atheism | 61

3.2 God as Triune | 62
    The biblical foundations of the doctrine of the Trinity | 63
    The development of the doctrine of the Trinity | 65
    Differences between East and West | 68
    Trinitarian doctrine in recent theology | 70
    The relationship between God in himself and God in his relationship to the world | 71
    The structural significance of the doctrine of the Trinity | 72

3.3 What Is God Like? | 72
    How is it possible to talk about God? | 73
    God and gender | 74
    Two types of affirmation about God | 76
    God revealed in history | 76
    God is love | 78

God's freedom and faithfulness | 79
God's wrath and judgment | 80
God as holy | 81
Law and gospel | 82
When we do not understand God | 82
Faith in God as an existential question | 84

4 The World, the Human Being, and Evil | 85

4.1 God and the Creation | 85
God's continuing creation | 87
The relationship between God and the world | 88
God and the freedom of the world | 89
The possibility of miracles | 91
Communication between the human person and God: prayer | 92
The world as finite | 93
Belief in the Creator and the natural sciences | 94
Heaven and earth | 96
The angels | 97

4.2 The Human Being—Created for Fellowship with God | 97
Made in the likeness of God | 98
Human dignity | 100
Society and gender as constitutive of the human being | 101
Body and soul | 103
The human being and nature | 104

4.3 Sin and Evil | 105
The concept of sin | 106
Original sin | 108
The human being as created and as sinner | 110
Various views of original sin and original guilt | 110
Where does sin come from? | 112
Evil as demonic | 113
The problem of theodicy | 114

5 Jesus | 116

5.1 Jesus—How Can We Know Who He Was? | 116
The significance of this question | 116
The question of the historical Jesus | 118

5.2 True God and True Human Being | 120
    The confession of Jesus as Christ | 122
    Jesus as the Son of God | 123
    The development of Christology in the early church | 126
    The doctrine of two natures | 127

5.3 The Significance of Jesus' Life, Death, and Resurrection | 130
    Conception and birth | 131
    Kenosis and sinlessness | 133
    Life and work | 135
    Suffering and death | 136
        The theological significance of Jesus' suffering and death | 137
        Jesus' death as a sacrifice | 139
        Other perspectives on Jesus' death | 140
        Theories of atonement | 141
        Jesus' death as answer to the world's injustice | 145
    He was buried and descended into the realm of the dead | 146
    The resurrection | 147
        A disputed event | 148
        The resurrection as transformation | 148
        The resurrection as a historical event | 149
        Jesus' death and resurrection belong together | 149
        Resurrection as anticipation | 150
    Ascension and exaltation: he sits at the right hand of the Father | 151
    He will return in glory | 153

6 Receiving Salvation—the Work of the Holy Spirit | 155

6.1 What Is Salvation? | 155
    Creation and salvation | 156
    Various dimensions of salvation | 157
    The relationship between biblical and dogmatic concepts | 160
    Salvation as already now, but now yet | 161

6.2 The Holy Spirit: Giver of Life | 162
    The role of the Spirit | 163
    The Spirit as the power of God | 164
    The Spirit as a person in the Trinity | 165
    The appropriation of salvation as the work of the Spirit | 166

6.3 Justified by Faith | 167
  The concept of justification | 167
  Luther's doctrine of justification | 169
  The forensic or the effective understanding? | 172
  The Lutheran and the Catholic understanding | 173
6.4 The Divine and the Human Roles in Salvation | 175
  Election and predestination | 176
6.5 Life in the Spirit | 182
  Sanctification | 182
  The Christian's relationship to sin | 184
  How far is it possible to come in sanctification? | 186
  The Christian and the law | 187
  Christ dwells in the believer | 189
  The fruit of the Spirit and the gifts of the Spirit | 189

7 The Means of Grace | 192

7.1 Word and Sacrament | 192
  The Word as a means of grace | 193
  The concept of sacrament | 194
  The relationship between the Word and the sacraments | 197
  An ecumenical topic | 198
7.2 Baptism | 198
  The baptism of John and Christian baptism | 199
  Baptism and salvation | 200
  Baptism and faith | 201
  The significance of baptism for the Christian life | 201
  Infant baptism | 203
  Rebaptism as an ecumenical problem | 206
  The form of baptism | 208
  Baptism as an event and as one stage in a process | 209
  What about the unbaptized? | 210
7.3 The Eucharist | 211
  The eucharist in the New Testament | 211
  The real presence | 212
  The dispute between Lutherans and Reformed | 214
  Ecumenical developments | 215

The eucharist as a sacrifice? | 217
   What does the eucharist give? | 218
   Who can take part in the eucharist? | 219
   The eucharist and the Trinity | 220
   Eucharistic theology and eucharistic praxis | 221

8 The Church—the Fellowship of Salvation | 223

8.1 The Church and the Human Race | 223
   The one human race and the people of God | 224
   A church of Jews and Gentiles | 225
   The church, the world, and the kingdom of God | 227

8.2 The Church as God's Church | 229
   The church as a theme for faith | 229
   The church's unity | 230
   The church as catholic | 232
   The church as apostolic | 233
   The church as local congregation | 233
   The relationship between the local and the universal church | 234

8.3 Mission and Ministries | 236
   The ministries of the church | 236
   Sent to the world | 238

9 Hope | 240

9.1 The Question about the Future | 240
   Hope that the world will be saved | 241
   How are we to speak of a new reality? | 242
   Life after death, or a newly created world? | 243

9.2 What Is to Happen at the End of the World? | 244
   Expectations about the last days in the Old Testament | 244
   The last days according to the New Testament | 246
   The interpretation of the millennium | 248
   Dispensationalism | 249
   When does the end come? | 250

9.3 The Intermediate State: What Happens after Death? | 253
   The intermediate state in the Bible | 253
   What becomes of the dead? | 254

9.4 Judgment | 256
>Judgment as settling accounts with evil | 256
>Judgment in accordance with faith or works? | 257
>The definitive salvation | 258
>The possibility of eternal damnation | 260
>Will all be saved at the end? | 262

9.5 Hope as the Perspective for the Christian Interpretation of Life | 264

Glossary | 265
Bibliography | 271
Name Index | 273
Scripture Index | 275

Preface

ALTHOUGH THE CORE OF the Christian message always remains the same, each generation is obliged to rethink and express in words its understanding of the gospel. This is constantly done in the preaching and witness of the church. Academic theology too has an obligation to interpret the content of Christian faith. As Robert Jenson puts it: "Theology is thinking what to say to be saying the gospel."[1] Such a systematic reflection is the core task of the theological discipline of dogmatics. The present book is a contribution to this discipline, introducing the reader to the various questions that arise when one tries to express what Christian faith in God is all about.

The book is primarily written as an introduction to dogmatics for theological students at a beginner's level. Hopefully, it will also find readers among others interested in the basic content of Christian doctrine.

Many previous attempts have been made to give a holistic presentation of the contents of the Christian faith. The present book differs from many of its predecessors through two conscious strategies. First of all, I have endeavored to apply a consciously ecumenical perspective in my presentation. Although I write from a Lutheran standpoint, I also illuminate the various topics on the basis of other church traditions, asking what we can agree about, and what continues to divide us.

Secondly, my presentation employs the perspective of an interpretation of life. This means that dogmatics is not presented as a closed system that merely answers its own questions. Rather, it attempts to show how the Christian faith is one particular interpretation of reality, and how it answers questions that are generated by the experience of reality that we all share.

I would especially like to express my thankfulness for the excellent cooperation with the translator, Dr. Brian McNeil, in the translation process. The fact that Dr. McNeil in his daily work is the pastor of a Catholic parish in Munich, Germany, speaks for the ecumenical potential of the book.

For good reasons, many theological authors avoid using masculine pronouns in speaking about God, as God is clearly beyond human gender differences. As English translations of the Bible consistently use masculine pronouns about God, this becomes

---

1. Jenson, *Systematic theology*, vol 1, 32.

Preface

stylistically very complicated in a book that makes heavy use of biblical material. The translator has therefore chosen to stick to the traditional use of pronouns.

I have refrained from giving extensive references to relevant sources and literature, in order not to overload the text. References are therefore mainly limited to direct quotations and works explicitly mentioned in the text. Further introductions to persons and theologies mentioned in the book are easily available elsewhere. I myself have found Bengt Hägglund's *History of Theology* to be an important frame of reference. For an introduction to the works of more recent theologians, I would recommend *Key theological Thinkers,* edited by Kristiansen and Rise.

Quotations from the Bible are mostly taken from the New Revised Standard Version. Occasionally, the translator has given his own translation, for the sake of greater accuracy. These passages are marked with an asterisk.

Quotations from the Apostolic, Nicene and Athanasian creeds, the Augsburg Confession, and Martin Luther's Small Catechism are taken from Kolb and Wengert's translation of the Book of Concord. Quotations from the Augsburg Confession are taken from the translation of the Latin version of text.

Basic biographical information about persons mentioned in the text can be found in the index of names at the end of the book, together with a glossary of some technical terms.

Harald Hegstad
Oslo, July 2018

1

What Is Dogmatics?

1.1 DOGMATICS AS A FIELD OF STUDY

WHAT IS THE MEANING of existence? Is there a higher power behind everything, or did the world come into being by chance? Do humans occupy a special position in relation to other living beings? How do we cope with evil and suffering, and is there any salvation from evil? Is death the end, or is there a life after this life?

People have asked such questions in every age, and the various religions and worldviews give a variety of answers. But even if the answers are different, it is often the same fundamental human experiences that one attempts to interpret and to make meaningful. This means that the various religions and worldviews can be seen as various proposals of an interpretation of human life. On some points, these various proposals can overlap; on other points, they can be very different. This applies both to the answers that are given and also to how one understands the questions that are to be answered.

The Study of the Intellectual Content of the Christian Faith

When religions and worldviews are understood as *interpretations of life*, this focuses primarily on their intellectual content. This book is about the intellectual dimension in one particular religious tradition: namely, Christianity. It is, however, important to remember that religions and worldviews also have other dimensions than the intellectual, and that the various dimensions are all closely connected. Religion and worldview are also concerned with the conduct of life and morality, with societal fellowship and institutions, and with rituals. Religions and worldviews can also mediate experience, and they can be given a material expression. In the concrete religions and worldviews, the various dimensions interact and contribute reciprocally to sustain each other.

The fact that the Christian faith has a social dimension has consequences for how we understand the intellectual content of faith. This is not a free-floating philosophical system. Nor is it merely an expression of the personal conviction of the individual believer, because the intellectual content of faith is also something that is shared in the community of believers—in other words, in the church. This fundamental starting point does not prevent the various Christian communities from having different views of the content of faith, nor does it preclude the existence, within one and the same community, of different interpretations of the shared faith of that community. We shall return to these questions later; they do not alter the fact that the Christian faith is a faith that exists in a community. In this presentation of the intellectual content of the Christian faith, therefore, the primary theme is not what the individual Christians believe, but what can count as an expression of *the church's faith*.

One concept that is often used to designate the content of the church's faith is *teaching*. On the basis of a Greek word that can mean "a doctrinal proposition," *dogma*, we use the technical expression *dogmatics* in this context. On the basis of what I have said, we can understand dogmatics as an exposition and synthesis of the content of the church's teaching. Another concept that is often used to denote the church's teaching is *doctrine*, a word with a Latin root (*doctrina*) that means "the teaching of the faith."

In many contexts, words such as "dogmatics" or "dogmatic" do not evoke positive associations. They are often used to signify something rigid and authoritarian. But a rigid and authoritarian dogmatics is a bad dogmatics. Although dogmatics is obliged to relate to the current teaching in Christian churches, it must discuss the content of this teaching in a nuanced and critical manner. Dogmatics must ask how this teaching can be interpreted, what it is based on, and how it relates to alternative views. A critical and interpretative perspective of this kind is especially important when one works in dogmatics in the framework of academic research and education. A certain tension can be seen here between an ecclesiastical theology and an academic theology; this tension is resolved in various ways in the ecclesiastical and the academic setting.

In order to grasp this question more precisely, we must first look more closely at how we can understand dogmatics as an academic discipline.

Dogmatics as an Academic Discipline

The attempt to employ academic means to understand the Christian faith is not a new phenomenon. Already in the second century, several of the church fathers sought to understand the faith on the basis of the philosophy of their age. This had a clear theological justification: since the God in whom the Christians believed was the one who had created both the world and human thought, there was no antithesis between what one could discover with the help of faith and what one could discover with the help of thinking. This is why theology had a central place in the development of philosophy and science throughout the Middle Ages. When the first universities were founded towards the close of that period, theology was a central discipline.

The foundation of the universities, however, also entailed a greater measure of institutional autonomy vis-à-vis the church. In earlier times, theology had been located primarily in an ecclesiastical context, not least in monasteries. Now, it became a discipline at institutions that gradually became more and more independent of the church.

The Enlightenment in the eighteenth century posed a powerful challenge to the understanding of what theology is and of its relationship to the church. This discussion goes on today too; it is far from being concluded. In the wake of the Enlightenment, there occurred a secularization of the universities, where belief in God was no longer a shared presupposition. On the one hand, this meant that theology lost its privileged position. It was no longer taken for granted that a university had a theological faculty and the principal reason why theology was retained as a university discipline (with specific faculties of theology) was its role in the formation of the clergy. In Europe, clergy in many of the largest churches are still educated at state universities.

On the other hand, this led to changes in the perception of theology. Many parts of theology acquired a strong historical orientation, not least the biblical disciplines, which concentrated primarily on the genesis of the biblical texts and on what they had meant in their original historical context. In many cases, church teaching too was studied first and foremost historically, in the form of the history of dogma.

At the same time, systematic theology emerged as a discipline that sought to take a position on the content of faith from a more up-to-date and normative perspective. Dogmatics has often been understood as a sub-discipline of systematic theology, together with theological ethics and the philosophy of religion. Whereas it was held in earlier times that theology spoke rather directly about God (the word "theology" means "doctrine about God"), it was now increasingly held that the theme of systematic theology is human beings' *belief* in God, that is to say, faith and religion as human phenomena.

The dominance in theology of this kind of "anthropological turn" is due not least to the great German theologian Friedrich D. E. Schleiermacher. In his arguments in support of theology's place at the newly founded university in Berlin, he proposed an understanding of theology as something anchored in the human being's feeling of dependence. In such a perspective, the task of systematic theology is to unpack the content in the human being's religious consciousness and experience. As a reaction to this kind of anthropological anchoring of theology, the Swiss theologian Karl Barth claimed that theology is about God, not about the human being, and that it must take its starting point in God's revelation.

Another factor that influences the understanding of theology is the competition it has received from the discipline of religious studies as an academic investigation of human religiosity. As a general historical and empirical science, it studies religion without discussing, or adopting a position on, the content of truth in what is studied. Nor is religious studies restricted to one particular religion. It studies all the forms of human religiosity. The fact that both theology and religious studies are engaged in research into religion as a human phenomenon makes it necessary to ask about the relationship between the two, and what it is that is attended to by theology but not by religious studies.

In describing this difference, it is important to draw attention to two basic differences. While religious studies seeks to take a neutral and descriptive attitude to the content of truth in the religiosity it investigates, theology is concerned to treat the question of truth. It is not a question only of describing what people believe about God and the world, but also of asking about the truth in what people believe.

In this way, theology has much in common with philosophy, which likewise discusses the big questions about the meaning of existence. But while philosophy seeks to do this on a general basis, theology takes its starting point in one particular religious tradition. For Christian theology, this is the Christian tradition. Theology thus not only looks at the religious interpretation of life "from the outside" (as in religious studies); it can also be understood as a perspective "from the inside" in which one investigates one particular religious tradition and its claims to truth, with the starting point in this tradition itself.

Barth's formulation of what dogmatics is is based on an understanding of theology along these lines: "As a theological discipline dogmatics is the scientific self-examination of the Christian Church with respect to the content of its distinctive talk about God."[1] On the basis of such an understanding, dogmatics investigates the Christian faith as this is found in the Christian tradition, with its starting point in this tradition itself. This does not entail an uncritical parroting of what tradition or the church teaches. On the contrary, it entails a critical examination of the content of this faith. To speak of a "*self*-examination" means that its starting point lies in some fundamental presuppositions that are given in the Christian tradition. At the same time, Barth takes it for granted that this examination will be *scientific*, and this means that theology has its due place among other sciences.

As a scientific, academic branch of study, theology and dogmatics share some fundamental ideals that form the basis of all the sciences. These characteristics include:

- The ideal of seeking truth for the sake of truth itself
- The ideal of elaborating methods that are relevant with regard to the object that is being studied
- The ideal of operating with clear concepts and definitions
- The ideal of being consistent in one's methodologies and one's argumentation

---

1. Barth, *Church Dogmatics*, vol. 1, pt. 1, 3.

- The ideal of openness and checkability
- The ideal of being open to criticism and revision

The Question of Truth: Four Models

This, however, does not settle the question of the scientific character of theology and its relationship to other sciences, because this also involves the content of theology in relation to the content in other branches of study. How can a tradition that takes its point of departure in one particular tradition of faith defend its place within a general scientific context, and thus at public universities? Various answers have been given to this question. I will indicate four possible positions here.

A. Theology as Purely Descriptive

First, it has been claimed that theology must be a purely describing and descriptive discipline, if it is to be regarded as scientific. This means that one can only investigate and describe what people *de facto* believe, without taking a position on the question whether one form of faith is more valid or true than another. This makes theology scientific in the sense that it has the same historical and empirical base as all the other sciences. Nor does theology demand any particular belief or conviction on the part of those who practice it. It is, therefore, "presuppositionless" in the sense that its work is not based on any presuppositions other than those found in other sciences. This also means that theology does not have a normative tie to one particular church or confession. When theology in practice gives priority to the investigation of one particular part of the Christian tradition, this has more pragmatic reasons, such as the training of clergy for one particular church. But it is this church itself that must take care of the more normative and praxis-oriented parts of the preparation for ordained ministry.

This way of understanding theology has been dominant at Swedish universities for many years, not least in the wake of the philosopher Ingemar Hedenius' criticism of theology as unscientific. One consequence was that dogmatics changed its name in some places to the "science of faith and worldviews," a discipline that investigates what people *de facto* believe, but without taking a position on the validity of different forms of faith. For pragmatic reasons, priority is given to the study of one particular religious tradition—the Christian Lutheran tradition—but otherwise, such an understanding of theology is very close to religious studies.

B. Theology Based on Positions Of Faith

A second understanding of the scientific character of theology criticizes the understanding of the presuppositionlessness of science that we have seen in the first position.

It is pointed out that, in reality, there are no sciences without presuppositions, and that the scientific character lies, not in denying the presuppositions, but in clarifying them and applying them as consistently as possible. Apart from the formal requirements for a scientific character (objectivity, the search for truth, methodological consciousness, and so on), there is no basis that is common to all the sciences. Ultimately, every understanding of reality builds on some fundamental positions of belief that cannot be demonstrated. It is impossible to take a neutral position with regard to what one is studying, and this is all the more true in the case of religion and worldviews. A characteristic of Christian theology and dogmatics is thus that it has its starting point in the fundamental premises of belief that are distinctive of the Christian tradition it studies.

The Norwegian theologian John Nome calls such premises the "axioms" on which theology (in the same way as other sciences) builds. These axioms cannot themselves be demonstrated, but they presuppose one particular standpoint of faith. The scientific character of dogmatics consists, not in the attempt to demonstrate its axioms, but in the investigation of how what is asserted is related to the fundamental axioms. This understanding of the scientific character of theology makes possible a close relationship between the church and theology, since they both share the same fundamental presuppositions of faith. This does not mean that theology cannot speak critically about how the church *de facto* gives expression to its faith. There may be a price to be paid, however: theology can risk being isolated in relation to other academic disciplines, since they operate on the basis of completely different presuppositions.

One representative of this way of understanding the scientific character of theology is Karl Barth, whom I have mentioned above. For Barth, the Christian faith in God is incompatible with the attempt to justify this faith on any other basis than God himself and his self-revelation.

C. Theology as the Grammar of Faith

The American theologian George Lindbeck has proposed what he calls the "cultural-linguistic model" for understanding Christian doctrine. He argues that Christian doctrine can be seen as a form of "language," as a way of talking about reality. The task of dogmatics is to describe the structure in this way of speaking about existence—to describe the "grammar" of Christian faith. Theology has a normative function here, since it can assess to what extent one is in accordance with the fundamental Christian grammar. It is, however, outside the mandate of theology to state whether there is also an objective reality that corresponds to this language of faith, that is to say, whether what the doctrine affirms is objectively true.

On this point, Lindbeck's position differs from that of Nome and Barth, who very clearly assume that what the doctrine affirms is objectively true, even if one cannot argue for this truth on the basis of general presuppositions.

D. A Theology That Seeks to Establish the Truth of Faith

In the present book I will take as a point of departure a fourth position on how theology should relate to the question of truth in a scientific context. This position agrees with the second position, that Christian theology must work on the basis of the presuppositions that are given in the Christian tradition. This, however, does not mean that these presuppositions themselves are exempt from critical examination, nor that there is no common basis for discussions with other academic disciplines. Since the Christian faith holds that it is saying something true about reality, it is also theology's task to specify and elucidate this demand for truth, in relation to what we otherwise know about reality.

One influential representative of this way of thinking is the German theologian Wolfhart Pannenberg, who argues that since God, who creates and perfects the world, makes himself known through history, it must be possible to integrate affirmations about God into what we otherwise know about reality. This means that theology must argue for the truth of the Christian faith on the basis of other knowledge that is accessible to us. This does not mean that the Christian faith can be proved definitively in a scientific way. Pannenberg sees the basic presupposition of theology in epistemological terms as a *hypothesis* that will not be definitively proved until the end of history. Although the end of history is anticipated in and through the resurrection of Jesus, it remains just as much the object of the faith of the individual and of the Christian community.

For Pannenberg too, the fundamental presuppositions of theology are given through the biblical and Christian tradition. Theology, in other words, is not constructed on a presuppositionless basis. Its task is to interpret and establish the fundamental presuppositions that are given in the tradition.

Even with such a starting point, one can have differing views about how far it is possible to get in elucidating the truth of the Christian faith with the aid of academic argumentation. Pannenberg has been criticized for undue optimism on this point; others would emphasize more strongly faith's character as a personal choice or decision, while attempting to give reasons for such a choice.

For theology as an academic discipline, this means *both* that it builds on presuppositions that are given through one particular religious tradition *and* that these presuppositions are open to discussion in the light of all the types of accessible knowledge about existence. This also makes possible a discussion of theological questions both with other forms of Christian theology and with various forms of non-Christian theology. It is therefore perfectly conceivable that theologies building on different premises can live side by side in the same institutions, as is the case at German universities that have both a Catholic and a Protestant theological faculty. In such a perspective, one can envisage that a theology based on other faith traditions, for example a Jewish or Islamic theology, can also have its place at the same universities.

The relationship between theology and other academic disciplines was much more strained several years ago than it is today. One reason was a much greater optimism on the part of science: many people thought that a scientific investigation of existence would make religious explanations superfluous. Today, there are fewer and fewer people who share the notion of an all-encompassing science of this kind. A science that believes it can give such an explanation has in reality itself become a worldview, and it must be evaluated on the same terms as other worldviews.

This does not mean that theology is assigned to work on those aspects of reality about which other sciences cannot say anything. On the contrary, we can affirm that Christian theology, as an expression of the interpretation of the Christian faith, is an attempt to do justice to the totality and the interconnections in existence. In other words, the theme of theology is the Christian faith, understood as an *interpretation of life*.

Dogmatics as Academic Work on a Christian Interpretation of Life

I began this chapter by indicating some fundamental questions that human beings have asked in every age, and that are given different answers in different religions and worldviews. Taking his starting point in the fourth position set out above, Norwegian theologian Peder Gravem has developed the concept of the *interpretation of life* to do justice to the relationship between faith/theology and people's experience of reality. Gravem defines the interpretation of life as "the understanding of ourselves and of our experience of reality in the light of a holistic context of meaning."[2] It is thus a way to order and interpret experience. It may be implicit, or expressed more explicitly; but in an academic study of the interpretation of life, one attempts to formulate it in words. The interpretation of life is partly an understanding of the totality, and partly an understanding of individual phenomena in the light of this totality. The understanding of oneself and the understanding of reality coalesce in a person's interpretation of life, thereby forming his or her *identity*. In many cases, interpretations of life are related to the same phenomena and experiences, while they interpret them differently in the light of different total contexts. This also means that elements of one interpretation of life can be taken over by another interpretation.

Since the interpretation of life deals with a totality that is not directly accessible, it is possible only through an element of *trust* or *faith*, in a general sense. There is no unambiguous path from the parts to an ordered whole, and this means that all we can do is to take hold proleptically of the totality of meaning and organize our life on this basis. That a certain interpretation of life is based upon trust and faith is not something specific to religious worldviews; it applies to every attempt to understand one's life in the light of a holistic interpretation.

---

2. Gravem, "Livstolkning," 249. Translated from Norwegian.

What Is Dogmatics?

In a situation with several competing outlines of a holistic interpretation of life, Gravem looks for criteria to test the various holistic views with regard to their truth. He indicates two fundamental criteria: First, there must be an inherent connectedness in the understanding of the totality. This means that the totality must consist of parts that are mutually compatible (consistency) and that the parts are linked to a pattern (coherence). Secondly, an understanding of the totality must be able to integrate, and thereby interpret, our whole experience of reality in a convincing way. This means that an interpretation of life that lays claim to truth must not be a closed system. It must be as open as possible to reality and to the variety of experience.

Against the background of a general description of the concept of interpretation of life, Gravem then asks what it is that characterizes a *Christian* interpretation of life. In order to bring out the specific content in a Christian interpretation of life, he defines it as "the understanding of ourselves and of our experience of reality in the light of the Bible and of the history of its reception in church teaching, tradition, and piety."[3] In Gravem's perspective, systematic theology (including dogmatics) is a contribution to defining the content of a Christian interpretation of life and to arguing in support of this. He writes that systematic theology has a double task here: First, it must present the inherent connectedness in the Christian faith, taking its starting point in faith in the triune God as the one who creates, redeems, and perfects, which is the central point that gives meaning to a Christian interpretation of life. Secondly, it must show how the human experience of life falls into place within faith in God as the framework that bestows meaning. This means that theology must not only present the content in a Christian interpretation of life. It must also show how it can be *true*.

As Gravem understands it, a Christian interpretation of life is not a closed system, but an understanding of reality that must relate both to other alternative interpretations of life and to general human experiences of life and the world.

It is important in this context not to interpret the concept of "experience of reality" too narrowly, reducing it to a matter of phenomena that the individual can experience directly. For a Christian interpretation of life, historical persons and events are decisively important both in order to understand the content of a Christian interpretation of life and in order to understand how it can lay claim to be true. At the center of a Christian interpretation of life stands the belief that God has acted in a special manner through the history of the people of Israel (as the Old Testament relates) and that he has revealed himself through Jesus of Nazareth (as the New Testament relates). The Christian faith thus presupposes one particular interpretation of historical events, in which Jesus' death and resurrection play a central role. As Pannenberg in particular has argued, this is not a special Christian history in a narrow sense: rather, these events belong to history as a whole, with which they are woven together. This also means that Christian theology must discuss the Christian interpretation of

---

3. Gravem, "Livstolkning," 263. Translated from Norwegian.

these events in comparison with alternative interpretations that may exist in other interpretations of life (for example, an alternative understanding of Jesus in Islam).

The double task that Gravem assigns to systematic theology means, on the one hand, that the presentation of a Christian interpretation of life must be identifiably *Christian*. In other words, one must be able to support it with evidence from the basic sources of the Christian faith, and it must agree with the basic structures of this faith. On the other hand, theology must be able to point to arguments for the *truth* of a Christian interpretation of life. In other words, it must show that it is possible to defend it as a good interpretation of our experience of reality.

Although there is no antithesis in principle between these two aspects of the tasks of systematic theology, they are often understood and emphasized somewhat differently, as we often see in the relationship between more conservative and more liberal interpretations of Christianity. In a more conservative interpretation, the greatest weight tends to be attached to theology's agreement with the sources of the faith, as these have been understood in the tradition to which one belongs. At the same time, there has not been the same concern to show how theology is related to general experiences of life. This has often been linked to the view that there is a fundamental opposition between faith and general experience; and this perspective has made work on the general validity of theology less relevant. But there are also many examples of a conservative theological approach that argues in more general terms for what are perceived as central truths of the faith. Such a tendency is also common in Catholic theology, where the idea of a universally accessible natural law leads to the use of general arguments, not least in ethical questions (see chapter 2).

In a more liberal interpretation of Christianity, the tendency has been to attach greater weight to how the Christian faith can appear relevant in a broader cultural context and can attend to a general experience of life. In many cases, this has prompted an extensive reinterpretation of a traditional Christian doctrine; sometimes, this has gone so far that it comes into conflict with essential ideas in the Christian tradition.

When we speak of the Christian faith as an interpretation of life, it must be underlined that this does not mean that everything in existence can be given a logical and rational explanation. Existence also contains things that appear meaningless and inexplicable—not least, phenomena such as death, suffering, and moral evil. A Christian interpretation of life seeks to integrate such phenomena within the framework of a holistic understanding of existence, without claiming to have understood these phenomena completely (see the treatment of the problem of evil in chapter 4).

1.2 DOGMATICS AND THE CHURCH

I have already mentioned that dogmatics' work on the intellectual content of the Christian faith does not primarily deal with the individual understanding of this content; it is linked to the *church's* faith. This raises a fundamental question: *Which church's faith* are we talking about? There are many various churches, which differ doctrinally from each other to a greater or lesser extent. There are many reasons for the existence of so many churches, but one important reason is divisions on doctrinal questions. The division into various churches has traditionally also had an impact on dogmatics, to a much larger degree than in other branches of theology. As a rule, dogmatics has dealt with the teaching of one particular church, and it has therefore tended to be presented as Lutheran dogmatics, Reformed dogmatics, Catholic dogmatics, and so on. Some churches have been less concerned than other traditions about doctrinal formulations. This is why (to take one example) there were few works on Pentecostal dogmatics before very recently.

Accordingly, presentations of dogmatics have tended to be markedly *confessional*, with their starting point in the confessional basis of one particular church. When they referred to the doctrinal stances of other churches, this was often with a polemical undertone, with the aim of showing that the stance taken by one's own tradition was more appropriate to the facts than the stance of other traditions. For example, it was not uncommon for text books in Lutheran dogmatics to present Lutheranism as the golden *via media* between the Catholics on the one side and the Reformed on the other.

Ecumenical Convergence

Recent decades have seen a convergence between the various churches that is unparalleled in church history. This has taken place both through practical cooperation and through doctrinal discussions, both through ecumenical organizations such as the World Council of Churches and through bilateral processes between churches. In some cases, the convergences have led churches to unite, but in most cases, the primary outcome has been a greater degree of recognition and cooperation. One important aspect in these convergences has been doctrinal conversations, with results that have been published in a long series of dialogue documents.

In the past, interchurch relations were more strongly marked by the principle that "We are right, and they are wrong," but the ecumenical processes have taught us to appreciate more positively the differences between the traditions. In many instances, conversations have revealed that they were not so far apart as they had thought. Perhaps there had been mutual misunderstandings, and earlier condemnations lacked sound foundations; or else different concepts were employed, but there was agreement on the matter itself; or it was more a case of differing emphases. Where agreement had still not yet been achieved, one was obliged to ask how fundamental a continuing disagreement was. In the convergences between the churches, it has been necessary to inquire into the relative weight and importance of the various points of doctrine, and to ask what we must agree on, in order to have unity with each other.

One of the most sensational breakthroughs in ecumenical convergence came in 1999, when representatives of the Catholic Church and the World Lutheran Federation signed the document *Joint Declaration on the Doctrine of Justification*. The sensation is due to the fact that it was thought that the division between Catholics and Lutherans was greatest precisely in their understandings of justification. We shall return in greater detail to the content of the Joint Declaration in chapter 6.3. The important point here is the methodological approach to doctrinal conversations on which the Declaration builds, namely, the idea of a *differentiated consensus.*

The Joint Declaration affirms that a demonstrable "consensus in basic truths of justification exists between Lutherans and Catholics." This does not mean that they agree on every point, but they believe that "the remaining differences of language, theological elaboration, and emphasis in the understanding of justification . . . are acceptable."[4] This is expressed in the structure of the Declaration: each main section begins by saying something about what Lutherans and Catholics "confess together." Only then does the text speak of the differing emphases and expressions that nevertheless exist.

The idea of a differentiated consensus presupposes that it is possible to identify a basic unity in central matters, while recognizing continuing differences in forms of expression and in less central questions. While thus retaining the goal of a fundamental unity in faith and teaching, one opens the door to an understanding of legitimate ecclesial plurality that also includes differences in how one speaks of doctrinal questions. Traditional antitheses are laid aside, because there is a consensus about what is central and agreement that continuing differences concern the use of concepts and emphases, or else that a genuine continuing disunity is not so great that it affects the unity in what is central. This is why it has been possible to declare that the mutual condemnations from the past no longer apply.

One difficulty in such conversations between churches is that the understanding of what is central can vary. In a Lutheran context, this supremely central content in faith and theology has been characterized with the aid of the concept of *gospel*, that is to say, the message that God saves people by grace on the basis of Jesus' death and resurrection. In the Augsburg Confession, therefore, the following conditions for church unity are stipulated in article 7:

> And it is enough for the true unity of the church to agree concerning the teaching of the gospel and the administration of the sacraments. It is not necessary that human traditions, rites or ceremonies instituted by human beings be alike everywhere.

Support for this approach can be found in the Letter to the Galatians, where Paul makes unity about the gospel the decisive test of true or false doctrine: "If anyone proclaims to you a gospel contrary to what you received, let that one be accursed!" (Gal

---

4. *Joint Declaration on the Doctrine of Justification*, par. 40.

1:9). There is no disagreement between Lutherans and Catholics that it is precisely here that the core lies, although the Catholic Church has emphasized that other factors too must be taken account of, if full unity is to be achieved—not least, agreement about ecclesial ministries.

The approach on which the idea of a differentiated consensus is based has important consequences not only for the relationship between the churches, but also for theology in general, and for dogmatics in particular. When one discusses the intellectual content in the church's faith, it is not sufficient to work with the doctrine of one individual church or one specific confession: one must investigate the content in the faith in an ecumenical perspective, identifying what is common, but also what causes separation. The point of demonstrating differences is not, however, primarily a matter of showing that one church is right and the other wrong, but rather of seeeing how the different positions are seeking to express the central content in the faith. When one encounters differences, one must ask whether these involve different uses of concepts and emphases, and what significance the differences have for understanding what is central.

It is impossible to write a purely ecumenical dogmatics, as if one could rise above the doctrinal differences between the churches. In order to be ecumenical, one must have one's starting point in one particular tradition. The author of this book is a Lutheran, and the presentation will naturally be influenced by this fact. In addition, I am writing in a Norwegian context, where Lutheranism is still numerically the dominant form of Christianity. This does not mean that I shall restrict myself to presenting the content in Lutheran doctrine, nor that I shall show that other churches are wrong where they do not think like the Lutheran church. The point I am making is that, in order to understand others, one must have a starting point from which to approach them.

Some readers of this book share the author's starting point, while others are in a different Christian tradition, or have their starting point in another religion or worldview. These readers too can take part in the process of reflection to which the book invites them. My starting point and the context in which I am writing mean that there will be a more consistent account of the Lutheran perspective than of other perspectives; sometimes, the Lutheran perspective will have the final word. Here, the reader is challenged to introduce more perspectives from other traditions and to bring the arguments to a different conclusion.

Although I include perspectives from various church traditions, there is no complete overview of the positions that are taken on the various topics. For a more complete review of what the various Christian churches teach on these questions, I refer to introductions to denominational studies.

The fact that dogmatics has one particular confessional starting point and that it is practiced in an ecumenical framework means that it cannot be content to give an account of the doctrine of one particular church, or to argue one-sidedly on the basis of what can be accepted within one particular church. It is not enough to be able to show that something is "Lutheran" or "Catholic." The Lutheran, the Catholic, and other positions anchored in one particular confession are, each in its own way, attempts to interpret "that which is Christian." The different confessions are not expressions of different truths, but are attempts to express the one truth or the one gospel. Dogmatics must discuss critically various attempts to express this truth. This means that it must also discuss where the *boundaries* for that which is Christian lie, that is to say, what can, and what cannot, count as legitimate expressions of Christian doctrine. But positions that can be understood as expressions of Christian doctrine must also be critically evaluated in relation to each other. In some cases, they will more or less overlap, and will be compatible (see what I have written above about differentiated consensus), while in other cases they will in fact contradict each other.

The various versions of Christian doctrine must thus be evaluated in terms of how they express that which is fundamentally Christian. The problem with a criterion of this kind, however, is that that which is fundamentally Christian is not found in pure form, but only in and through the various interpretations of the common basis. In addition to comparing and combining the various interpretations, therefore, one must go back to the biblical writings, which are the historical starting point common to all the churches. It is true that the Bible is interpreted in various ways, and that not all ascribe the same importance to it, but it remains an inescapable common starting point. Participants in many ecumenical processes have experienced that joint work on biblical texts has made it easier for them to come to terms with doctrinal differences. Other historical texts also unite the churches, not least some confessional texts from the early church. The Nicene Creed has a special position, since most churches recognize it as a binding expression of the Christian faith. Also the reading of such confessional texts will therefore also be a starting point for a critical evaluation of Christian doctrine today. (I shall speak in greater detail about the understanding of the Bible and the confessional texts in chapter 2.2 and 2.3.)

Religious Primary Language and Dogmatic Secondary Language

Dogmatics is concerned primarily, not with what the individual Christian believes, but with the content of the faith as this is understood in the Christian community in the church. Since dogmatics is an academic and critical activity, it is also necessary to distinguish between dogmatics' work on the church's faith and this faith itself. One way to formulate this is to distinguish between the religious primary language and dogmatics, understood as a secondary language.

According to this distinction, *the religious primary language* is what happens in the church's worship or in the individual believer's practice of his or her faith. Examples are prayer, adoration, preaching, witnessing, and so on. These tend to include statements about God, the human being, and the world in the form of address or confession. The religious primary language is not a purely cognitive language. It is woven together with experience, rites, and religious community.

Dogmatics, on the other hand, represents a *secondary language*, where one takes a step back and analyzes the content of the religious primary language: what is the meaning of what is expressed or presupposed in the religious primary language, and what is this based on? These are two distinct phenomena, and although they are closely connected, it is nevertheless necessary to keep them distinct.

The two languages tend to be spoken in two different contexts. While the religious primary language is expressed in acts of worship and the personal life of faith, the dogmatic secondary language belongs in the academic sphere, in theological research and teaching. This can be conducted in academic institutions and within the church itself, but it has a different character from the primary language. This book is an example of dogmatic secondary language: although it relates to the religious primary language, it is neither a prayer nor a sermon. One consequence of these differing locations is that it is possible to engage in Christian dogmatics without necessarily sharing the Christian faith and taking part in the Christian primary language. In many cases, it can be an advantage to share the faith one is studying, although it may perhaps be easier for those who come from outside to establish critical perspectives. At any rate, it is important to underline that dogmatics, as an academic discipline, does not demand a personal faith on the part of the one who practices it.

One possible parallel might be the relationship between being a performing musician and studying musicology as an academic discipline. In many ways, musicology is a kind of academic secondary language (in contradistinction to the primary language of a musical performance), in which one makes an academic analysis of what happens in the music that is performed. It is certainly no disadvantage to be a performer, but it is perfectly possible to study musicology without this.

Although it is necessary to draw a distinction between the religious primary language and the dogmatic secondary language, there will also be a close connection between them. This is not a one-way street where the secondary language builds on the primary language: the secondary language is also significant for the primary language. The academic theological discussion is often very important for what happens in church praxis. For example, the reflexive element that characterizes an academic perspective can often be found in a sermon, although this does not turn the sermon into a lecture in dogmatics. And in many churches, the clergy and other leaders have an academic theological training that, naturally enough, leaves its mark on their ministry.

The way in which the relationship between the church and academic theology is structured will vary from one country and one church to another. In some churches, academic theological work is more closely integrated into the church itself, or is subject to a stricter church control; this is often the case in a Catholic context. In a

Lutheran context, there has tended to be a more independent university theology. Both models have their strengths and weaknesses.

Although dogmatics must have a close relationship to what is going on in the church, it must nevertheless preserve a critical distance. It is not meant to be an uncritical parroting or defense of whatever happens to be the dominant view at any time—even if this is the dominant view of the church leaders. On the contrary, it is the task of dogmatics to submit such views to a critical examination and discussion. This *critical* task also includes a *constructive* task, namely, to attempt to express how the Christian faith can best be formulated today. In both tasks, dogmatics will naturally be influenced by the one who formulates the critical and the constructive proposals, so that these often have a strongly personal character; but they must not be understood as the dogmatic theologian's own personal view of the Christian faith. Dogmatic proposals are not primarily an expression of personal opinions, but an attempt to formulate what can count as an expression of the church's faith; and their success will depend *inter alia* on how far they are accepted by the church community. History shows that some dogmatic theologians have been very influential in the church, while others have had a more limited impact.

The secondary language of dogmatics differs from the religious primary language not only because it has another *location*, but also through its *form*. When dogmatic theologians work on the content of the Christian faith, they seek to formulate this content with the help of concepts and the discussion of the various problems. In this way, dogmatics has much in common with philosophy, which also seeks to formulate the connections in human existence with the help of a theoretically and conceptually precise language.

Religious language often has a strongly narrative element: it speaks of events or experiences. Such narratives can also have the form of exemplary stories or myths. The language of dogmatics is more concerned to analyze in a more conceptual vocabulary what such narratives and experiences mean. For example, one central element in religious language is the story of how God intervenes and gives human beings a new life. Such narratives are found both in the Bible and in the experiences of individuals. Instead of simply retelling such stories, dogmatics aims to express such experiences with the help of concepts like "salvation" or "justification."

This does not mean that dogmatics works only with abstract concepts that are detached from concrete experience. Understood as an expression of the Christian interpretation of life (see chapter 1.1), dogmatics seeks to interpret concrete human experience. Some experiences and events are more central in the Christian faith than others—especially those connected with Jesus' life, death, and resurrection. This anchoring in concrete historical events prevents Christian dogmatics from ever becoming a purely philosophical system. When the Apostolic Creed attempts to sum up the central content of the faith, it includes an account of specific events: ". . . who was conceived by the Holy Spirit, born of the Virgin May, suffered under Pontius Pilate

What Is Dogmatics?

. . ." The question of the significance of these events for the Christian faith and interpretation of life today is therefore a central element in the work of dogmatics on the content of the Christian faith.

The use of narratives is not the only difference between religious language and a more philosophical language. Another difference is the use of *metaphors* in religious language. It is obvious, for example, that when God is spoken of as "light" (see 1 John 1:5), or Jesus as "the way" (see John 14:6), these are not statements meant to be understood literally; nevertheless, their intent is to express something essential. Dogmatics will attempt here to formulate what the various metaphors want to express, and to discuss the relationship between the metaphor and the reality itself. It is impossible to get completely "behind" the metaphors, or to elaborate a dogmatic language wholly devoid of metaphorical elements. This is because the reality to which the Christian faith refers is not directly accessible to human experience; this applies both to God himself and to the future state of perfect salvation. In order to take hold of this type of reality in language, we need to employ concepts from the known world of our experience, and to use these in a metaphorical or transposed sense. This is why dogmatic language cannot get by without metaphorical elements. For example, when we speak of the first Person in the Trinity as "the Father," this is indubitably a concept with metaphorical elements, but it is not easy to replace it with any other concept. The important thing is that one is aware of the metaphorical character of the concepts, and that one discusses the relationship between the metaphor and the reality it refers to.

The difficulty in capturing in unambiguous, non-metaphorical concepts the reality that dogmatics describes is closely connected to the understanding of God and of God's reality. The idea that God cannot be captured in human statements about God is a fundamental notion in the Christian tradition. This does not prevent statements about God from being true, but it means that God is always *more* than what is captured by such statements. It is indeed possible to know something about God, but it is not possible to know *everything*. God is also a *mystery*. Accordingly, the statements dogmatics makes about God and God's reality always entail the reservation that they are provisional and imperfect. A well-known expression of this idea is Paul's statement that "we know only in part" and "see in a mirror, dimly" (1 Cor 13:9, 12).

On the one hand, dogmatics aims to create the greatest possible conceptual clarity and coherence in the Christian faith in God. It attempts to understand this faith as a totality that is as free as possible from contradictions, and to demonstrate how it relates to what we otherwise know about reality. On the other hand, there will always be elements in faith that *cannot* be completely explained or integrated into a system. In the encounter with the mystery, dogmatics sometimes ends up with paradoxes (apparent contradictions) that we cannot get behind. Paradoxes have often been important, not least in Lutheran theology. A theology that tidily resolves everything in a unified system often does so at the expense of important truths or concerns. For example, when Trinitarian doctrine speaks of God as both one and three, this cannot be fully explained. This is not strange, since it is a question of God's own reality. Although it is the task of dogmatics to explain and justify Trinitarian doctrine as far as possible, one cannot get behind the fundamental paradox of this doctrine. The history of theology shows that attempts to abolish the paradox tend to end up either emphasizing the three at the expense of the one, or the one at the expense of the three. But the recognition that, in some contexts, dogmatics cannot get any further than statements that look paradoxical must not dispense us from taking seriously the work of reflection on the content of faith. Nor must we elevate every contradiction into a genuine paradox.

Other Arenas for Dogmatics

I have pointed out the close connection between dogmatics and the church, but the church is not the only context in which dogmatics' work on presenting the content of the Christian faith is relevant. Since dogmatics is a part of theology, which is an academic discipline, it is related to other academic disciplines and to the academic milieu. Theology and dogmatics draw on insights and methodologies from other disciplines, while theology too can contribute academic insights to other disciplines.

As an introduction to the content of Christian faith the study of dogmatics is an important resource for religious education in schools. Depending on the distinctive character of this subject in various school systems, dogmatics might provide an important insider's perspective on Christian faith for both teachers and students.

Dogmatics also has a task in society in general. It is important that the content in the Christian faith is presented and explained in an academically defensible manner. It is also important to contribute thereby to the understanding of the Christian faith as an interpretation of life. The Christian faith is not merely a "closed system" that one must either accept or reject; it also contributes to the general debate about important questions in human life, such as those about meaning, human dignity, evil, guilt, and so on.

1.3 DOGMATICS AND CONTEXT

There has been an increasing awareness in recent theology that all theology is *contextual*. In other words, it is conditioned by the context within which it is practiced. This insight has not always been taken for granted; often, the aim has been to give a universally valid presentation of theology, independent of the time and place where it is written. In reality, however, such theology too is marked by the context in which it is written, including not least the culture and the historical situation. Much theological literature came into existence in a Western, European and North American context, which naturally has left its traces on what was produced. Contextual theologies such as African theology, Asian theology, or indigenous theology elaborate theology in a way that takes account of other cultural and geographical conditions than those of the West.

The gender or the social status of those who elaborate theology is also significant. The fact that men have dominated the theological tradition has obviously been a factor in how it is elaborated. It is also important whether the one who formulates theology is rich or poor. In response to men's dominant position, various forms of feminist theology seek to be a contextual theology that includes women's experiences in the theological work. In a similar way, liberation theology wants to give a prominent place in theological work to the experiences of the poor and the underprivileged.

When we read the history of theology, we should also be conscious of the context within which theology came into existence. If, for example, we want to understand the theology of the Reformation period correctly, we must see it in the light of the historical, societal, and cultural situations in which it was produced. And if we wish to profit from insights in Reformation theology, we must bear in mind that our own context is different from that of the Reformers.

We must have the same awareness when we read and interpret the Bible, since it too is marked by the context of its genesis—or more correctly, by the many different contexts in which it came into being. We see differences that are linked to their contexts even in writings that are chronologically close to one another, for example in the relationship between the four Gospels. While Matthew seems to belong in a Jewish context, the context and the addressees of Luke are primarily Gentile.

The fact that there are contextual differences already in the New Testament tells us something important about the Christian message. First of all, it means that there is no acontextual version of the Christian message. There is no pure and timeless formulation of the message, independent of any particular context. Every formulation of the Christian faith will be marked by the context in which it is expressed. Secondly, it means that there is a fundamental identity in the message, as it finds expression in the various contexts. Although it can be formulated in different ways, it is nevertheless basically the same message. This is also the reason why Christians from different contexts can acknowledge each other's faith as an expression of confessing the same Christ and the same gospel.

Throughout history, the Christian faith has shown a remarkable ability to adapt to a variety of cultures while retaining its fundamental identity. Through mission, the faith has moved from one context to another. In a situation of mission, the awareness of the contextual character of the Christian faith and of its cross-cultural identity is especially important. The strength of the Christian faith is that it can both speak to people across different contexts and take root in one particular context.

For dogmatics, this entails the necessity of being aware that one is always formed by one's own context, and that there is no acontextual theology. At the same time, dogmatics must always aim to formulate the Christian faith in a way that is not *limited* to one particular context. It must be possible for Christians from other contexts too to acknowledge that what we write is an expression of the shared Christian faith.

1.4 THE MATERIAL AND METHODOLOGY OF DOGMATICS

The way in which we understand the material and methodology of dogmatics is, naturally enough, linked to how we understand dogmatics itself. I have emphasized in the preceding sections an understanding of dogmatics as a critical investigation of the intellectual content of the Christian faith. The fact that the investigation is critical means that one cannot be content with a simple description of how the content of the faith is understood *de facto* in various churches today. Dogmatics works critically, in the sense that it must inquire into the basis and the anchoring of doctrine, and must discuss alternative interpretations and understandings. While dogmatics is related to historical sources, it has a *contemporary* perspective, since it asks how faith can serve as an interpretation of life for people today.

The Bible as Source for Dogmatics

Since the fundamental source for Christian faith and theology is found in the Bible, dogmatics must relate to the biblical texts in its work. The themes that dogmatics treats will be touched upon and treated in one way or another in the Bible. This means that work on a dogmatic theme involves investigating how the questions we are treating are related to the biblical texts. This does not mean that the answers to the various dogmatic questions can be read straight out of individual passages in the Bible. Like all other texts, the biblical texts must be interpreted on the basis of their context in the Bible and of their historical context. And dogmatics must continually ask in what way the biblical texts can have something to say for people in another time.

A fundamental principle in every interpretation of a text is that it must be understood on the basis of its context. This means that one cannot draw dogmatic conclusions directly from one or more passages in the Bible. It is necessary to see how what is expressed in one particular passage is related to the rest of the text, or to the group of writings to which it belongs. It is also necessary to see how what is expressed is related to other parts of the Bible.

It goes without saying that dogmatics will have a close relationship to biblical scholarship here. This applies not least to the part of biblical scholarship that is often called *biblical theology*, which investigates the theological ideas that mark the individual writing and the individual group of writings, and that may also compare the theology in the various writings. This applies both to an Old Testament and to a New Testament biblical theology. Presentations of this kind are very important for dogmatics, but we must underline that the task of dogmatics is not ended once a biblical-theological investigation has been carried out. This is because the principal object of biblical scholarship and biblical theology is the biblical texts and their theological content from a historical perspective. While biblical scholarship primarily investigates what the texts meant in the historical period and context of their genesis, dogmatics must ask what the texts mean for the understanding of the Christian faith today.

Nevertheless, the work of dogmatics cannot be carried on in isolation from biblical scholarship and its results. Nor can the biblical texts, even when they are regarded as a source for what faith entails today, be understood in isolation from the historical context of their genesis. This is due not least to the fact that the Christian faith is linked to very specific historical events, and that the biblical writings are our primary sources for these events. Theological differences within the Bible are not irrelevant to dogmatics, because they display a breadth in the understanding of the Christian faith that dogmatics must take into account. The fact that the biblical texts express things in different ways and with varying emphases reminds dogmatics not to make things more unambiguous than the sources themselves warrant. Dogmatics must not succumb to simple harmonizations. At the same time, dogmatics must assume that there is a fundamental unity in the biblical message, and that each of the biblical writings in its own way contributes to our understanding of this message.

The idea of such a unity lies behind the understanding of the various writings as parts of a common *canon*, that is, a delimited collection of writings that have a normative character for the understanding of the Christian faith. A dogmatic reading of the biblical writings thus means reading them, not as isolated individual writings, but as a part of the totality that these writings constitute together. We shall return in the next chapter to the understanding of the Bible and its normative character, including the understanding of the concept of canon.

Church History as Source for Dogmatics

Dogmatics is related not only to the biblical texts *per se*, but also to the way in which the Bible has been interpreted down through the church's history. When we say that the task of dogmatics is to interpret the content of the church's faith, this is not restricted to the church as it exists today, but also includes how the church has interpreted its faith in the course of history. There are various opinions about the normative weight that should be attached to this history. While some churches (not least the Orthodox churches and the Catholic Church) go a long way in the direction of ascribing a central role to one particular interpretative tradition in determining how the faith is to be understood today, other churches (especially Protestant churches) seek to go back more directly to the Bible. Irrespective of how one sees this question, it is clear that when the Christian faith is interpreted today, one cannot avoid relating to how the faith has been interpreted in the past.

This is necessary for at least two reasons. First, our way of understanding the Christian faith today did not come into existence in a vacuum: it is the result of a historical process. In order to understand the faith today, we are obliged to relate to this history. Most of the concepts, problems, and perspectives that mark today's understanding of Christianity were formed in various ways in the course of history. To relate to history does not mean that one should accept it uncritically. But precisely in order to relate critically to history, it is necessary to know history. Secondly, it is necessary to relate to history in order to get a richer and deeper picture of what the Christian faith is. Interpretations of the faith that emerged in other periods of church history can also prove significant for the interpretation of the faith today.

Not all historical material is equally interesting or valuable. Certain periods in church history were particularly significant for doctrinal development. When one works on Trinitarian doctrine and Christology, one cannot avoid studying the development in the patristic period. When one works on the understanding of salvation, one cannot avoid studying the conflicts in the Reformation period. This does not mean that these questions were settled once and for all in those historical periods, so that all we would have to do would be to repeat historical positions.

In this context, some sources are more significant than others. This applies not least to confessional texts and other church documents, such as those of councils. But while the Nicene Creed is acknowledged by most churches, other texts will occupy the most important position in particular ecclesial traditions. When various dogmatic themes are treated in a Lutheran context, one will usually refer to the Lutheran confessional texts from the Reformation period.

Some individual theologians have left larger traces on history than others, and might still be of importance. While theologians from the patristic age have been important for most churches, others are more strongly linked to particular confessions. In a Lutheran context, it is naturally Martin Luther who continues to play an important role, while John Calvin has been important for Reformed theology and John Wesley for Methodist theology. One expression of the ecumenical convergence in our own days is the discovery of the significance of theologians from other traditions than one's own.

We see above all in modern theology that the impulses often cross confessional boundaries: theological currents and tendencies make an impact on more than one church. One example from the twentieth century is the influence that the Reformed theologian Karl Barth had in many different contexts, in both Protestant and Catholic theology. Theological currents such as liberation theology, charismatic theology, feminist theology, and so on, make their impact across the ecclesial spectrum.

Contemporary Sources

Dogmatics' material is not, however, limited to church tradition alone. As an interpretation of life, the Christian faith seeks to say something about life and reality as such, and this means that dogmatics must investigate how the understanding of

God and the world in the Christian faith is related to what we otherwise know—or suppose—about reality. Dogmatics must thus relate to philosophy, to the natural sciences, and to various forms of sociology and cultural studies, and indeed to various cultural expressions that can help it to understand the reality within which the faith is to be interpreted. This means that various forms of empirical research and empirical knowledge are also relevant to dogmatics.

Dogmatics as a Work of Interpretation

As this survey shows, the material for dogmatics is almost unlimited, although the church tradition that one relates to, and the concrete situation that one faces, will lay down certain guidelines. This is why it is important to underline that the work of dogmatics does not consist primarily in collecting and assembling different kinds of material; such material is only an aid for the *work of interpretation* that is the core in every presentation of dogmatics. This is not merely a description of what people believe or have believed, but an independent interpretation of the content of the Christian faith. In other words, dogmatics is a hermeneutical (interpretative, from hermeneutics = the theory of interpretation) activity. In purely methodological terms, this means that one is guided by the particular questions and problems that are to be discussed and answered. Since dogmatics is a contribution to a Christian interpretation of life today, contemporary questions about human life will also be included in the interpretation of biblical and other historical texts.

This interpretative perspective may sound to some people like a way of relativizing the content of the Christian faith. Can one not simply present the biblical message "as it stands," without also interpreting it? Such a point of view does not do justice to the fact that every presentation of the Christian faith entails one or other form of interpretation—even a presentation that thinks its interpretation is completely "literal." We see this already in the New Testament itself, where the various writings and groups of writings give a somewhat different presentation of the same events and the same message. For example, the four Gospels give rather different presentations and interpretations of Jesus and his work, and the first Christians seem not to have found this a problem. In the same way, various theologians in the church's history have attempted to interpret the same message for their own age, in dialogue with other theologians and with the interpretative tradition to which they belonged. Nor can today's dogmatics be content to repeat old interpretations. We must ourselves formulate the content of the Christian faith for our own age, for it is only in this way that the Christian message can be seen as a contribution to people's interpretation of life today—and not only as historical information.

The fact that the content of the faith must be continually interpreted does not mean that every interpretation is equally good. Much of the discussion in dogmatics concerns precisely the investigation of which interpretations are tenable and which are not, and which are better than others. In many cases, it also involves showing how differing interpretations do not necessarily exclude one another, but actually promote a richer understanding of the matter (see what was said above about differentiated consensus).

The task of interpreting the content of the Christian faith also includes finding the inner coherence in the faith and presenting it as a whole. This means that the various parts cannot be treated in isolation; they must be seen in the context and in the light of a holistic interpretation. This ideal of totality and system is also expressed in the technical term "systematic theology," to which dogmatics belongs. This, however, does not mean that the ideal for dogmatics is to present a system without inner tensions and antitheses (see the discussion of paradoxes, above).

1.5 BASIC ELEMENTS OF A CHRISTIAN INTERPRETATION OF LIFE

Before we take up the individual partial themes in dogmatics, I would like to sketch some of the fundamental characteristics in a Christian interpretation of life. My intention here is to say something about the totality that each of the following chapters will attempt to elaborate.

- The Christian interpretation of life has its starting point in faith in God. The Christian faith involves seeing one's own life, and the world in which one lives, in the light of the conviction that God has created the world and acts in relation to the world. The Christian faith understands God as triune, as Father, Son, and Holy Spirit. At the center of the understanding of God is the idea of God as love, both in the relations between the divine Persons and in relation to created things.

- A basic pair of concepts in a Christian understanding of God and of his relationship to the world is *creation* and *salvation*. This is a fundamental distinction that characterizes most forms of Christian theology, although the relationship between the two concepts can be understood somewhat differently. In this context, the understanding of God as Creator means that he is the origin of the world and that he acts in relation to the world, without himself being a part of the world. A Christian interpretation of life means seeing life and its good things as a gift from God. In a Christian interpretation of life, the understanding of God as savior is connected to the insight that the world as we know it is not completely in accord with God's creative will. Evil leaves its imprint on the world, but evil is not created or willed by God. Since God is love, God seeks to save the world and to bring his work of creation to perfection.

- According to the Christian faith, God's salvific action takes place in history, first through the election of the people of Israel (as the Old Testament relates), and then when the Son of God becomes a human being in Jesus of Nazareth (as the

New Testament bears witness). Through his life, death, and resurrection, Jesus overcame the power of evil and reconciled the world with God.

- God's salvific action has an individual, a collective, and a universal dimension. On the individual level, salvation is mediated by the Holy Spirit to the individual, through faith in Jesus. Through baptism, the individual becomes a part of the Christian church, which is the community of all believers.

- On the universal level, one day, at the end of history, the whole of creation will share in salvation. At the close of history, God's creative will will be perfected. This involves God's definitive settling of accounts with evil, and the new creation of the world.

- Faith in God as Creator is not only an affirmation about something that happened at one point in the past, but is a starting point for understanding life here and now. In the same way, faith in God as the one who brings everything to perfection is not only an affirmation about something that will happen at some point in the future, but is a basis for interpreting life today. This happens when the encounter with God's saving presence here and now is understood as an anticipation of the definitive salvation.

This basic structure in a Christian interpretation of life makes it natural to organize the rest of this book as follows. After looking at how we can know anything about God (the question of revelation, chapter 2), we discuss in chapter 3 the understanding of God. The next theme is the world and the human being as created by God (chapter 4). In chapter 5, we begin the discussion of God's salvific action, first by looking at how Jesus Christ is understood (Christology); this is continued in chapter 6 by seeing how Jesus' life, death, and resurrection bring salvation for human beings. In chapter 7, we discuss the Word and the sacraments as the means God uses to give people salvation. In chapter 8, we treat the understanding of the church as the community of salvation. In the concluding chapter 9, we treat questions about God's perfecting of the world and of salvation (eschatology).

2

How Can We Know Anything about God?

2.1 REVELATION

EVERY RELIGION AND EVERY worldview must in some way take a position on the question how one can know what one believes or holds to be true. Worldviews that do not believe in any supernatural reality will tend to point to experience and science, although here too, it is necessary to take some decisions about values that cannot be demonstrated empirically. New Age movements would claim that there exists a spiritual dimension that can be experienced, for example by searching within one's own self. For a Christian interpretation of life, the object of faith is not immediately accessible to human experience. God created the world, but God himself is not a part of the world. A fundamental idea in Christian theology is therefore that knowledge of God builds on the fact that God makes himself known, that he *reveals* himself. Accordingly, the understanding of God's revelation is a central theme of theology.

The idea of revelation is something that Christianity shares with other religions of revelation such as Judaism and Islam, but it takes a very specific shape in Christian theology, not least because of faith in Jesus Christ, who in his person reveals God himself. This is why there is a close link in Christian theology between the understanding of revelation and Christology (the doctrine about Christ).

The concept of "revelation" (literally: "unveiling") means that something that was concealed becomes visible. Theology often employs the concept of "transcendence" to express the fact that God is initially hidden from human experience. His transcendence means that his reality is not immediately accessible to human experience. In this context, transcendent/transcendence is the antithetical concept to immanent/immanence, which designates that which is accessible to human experience. When God reveals himself, this is his own initiative: God chooses to make himself known.

Although God makes himself known in the world of human experience, this does not mean that his transcendence is abolished. The fact that God makes himself known does not mean that we receive a total insight into the reality of God. God remains the transcendent one who can be known only partially and imperfectly. Theologians have given somewhat various answers to the question of the relationship between the revelation of God and God himself—that is, how directly God makes himself known, and how much of God's reality remains hidden. This is a fundamental theme in Martin Luther, who went very far in his distinction between the revealed God (Latin: *deus revelatus*) and the hidden God (*deus absconditus*). In the former, he discovered the loving God of grace, but in the latter, he found the wrathful God who judges. In modern times, it was especially Karl Barth who was concerned to safeguard the idea of God's transcendence, and who consequently underlined the *indirect* character of revelation: although revelation genuinely shows us God, Barth claimed that it does not give a direct access to God's reality.

Irrespective of how one envisages the relationship between the revelation of God and God himself, it is important to affirm that the most important content of revelation is *God himself*. Revelation in the Christian sense is not the communication of knowledge about this and that, but about God and God's will and actions in relation to the world.

One fundamental distinction that characterizes Christian theology on this point is between "the general revelation" (the way in which God makes himself accessible to all human beings) and "the special revelation" (the way in which God makes himself accessible through salvation history and in Jesus Christ). As we shall see, there are differing views about how these two forms of revelation are to be understood, and about the relationship between them.

The General Revelation: Traces of God in the Creation

The fact that God himself is not a part of the creation does not make it impossible to reach a knowledge of God on the basis of the creation. This also explains the similarities that may exist between statements about God on the basis of the special revelation and views about God that are not based on this source (*inter alia*, in other religions). When we speak about a revelation that is "general," this means that it accessible to everyone, independently of any link to the Christian tradition. At the same time, we insist that this involves "revelation": we affirm that although God himself is not directly accessible in the world, certain phenomena point to something that *per se* is hidden. Knowledge of God through knowledge of created things is possible because God himself has chosen to deposit some "traces" of himself there.

What is the content of the general revelation? The first point is that two different matters are involved here. On the one hand, it is a question of the *knowledge of God*, in the sense of the knowledge that behind the world, there is a God. We see above all in the Old Testament how the greatness and complexity of the creation are interpreted as a testimony to God and his power. One example is Psalm 19:1, "The heavens are telling the glory of God, and the firmament proclaims his handiwork" (see also Ps 8).

We find a very important expression of such an understanding in Paul's Letter to the Romans, where he presupposes that it is possible to acquire knowledge of God on the basis of the creation. For Paul, however, this is not the starting point for a positive evaluation of human religiosity, but on the contrary for criticism of a religiosity that is taking the wrong path: although they had the possibility of knowing God, they chose to worship idols:

> For what can be known about God is plain to them, because God has shown it to them. Ever since the creation of the world his eternal power and divine nature, invisible though they are, have been understood and seen through the things he has made. So they are without excuse; for though they knew God, they did not honor him as God or give thanks to him, but they became futile in their thinking, and their senseless minds were darkened. Claiming to be wise, they became fools; and they exchanged the glory of the immortal God for images resembling a mortal human being or birds or four-footed animals or reptiles (Rom 1:19–23; see Acts 17:27).

On the other hand, the idea of the general revelation entails a general *moral knowledge*, in the sense of a knowledge of God's will. In the biblical context, God's will for human life is often described with the help of the idea of *God's law*. This law of God is revealed through salvation history (see below), but the moral demands of the law are accessible also to those who have not had the law revealed in this way. This is why persons who do not know the biblical revelation can do what is good, and can be called to account when they do what is evil. The classical expression of this idea is found once again in Paul's Letter to the Romans:

> When Gentiles, who do not possess the law, do instinctively (Greek *phusei*, literally: "by nature") what the law requires, these, though not having the law, are a law to themselves. They show that what the law requires is written on their hearts, to which their own conscience bears witness, and their conflicting thoughts will accuse or perhaps excuse them (Rom 2:14–15).

Other passages in the biblical writings likewise presuppose a certain basic shared unity among human beings on fundamental moral questions (Matt 5:16; Phil 4:8; 1 Pet 2:12). This is due to the belief that God, as the Creator of the world, has deposited in the creation knowledge of himself and of his will.

In the passage from Romans 2, Paul writes that the Gentiles do "by nature" what God's will demands. The concept of nature designates here that which is created, the world and human life as God created them. This led, in the course of the history of theology, to a tendency to speak of the general revelation as "the natural revelation" and the moral law that is present in every human being as "the natural law."

Knowledge of God that is anchored in the natural revelation can thus also be called "natural theology."

The understanding of what we have called the general or natural revelation is much disputed among theologians, who ask how this can be said to be a reliable source of knowledge about God and his will, and what relationship exists between the knowledge about God that is deposited in the creation and that which God has revealed about himself through salvation history.

The Special Revelation: God's Revelation to Bring Salvation

Although account has been taken in various ways of the possibility of knowing about God on the basis of the creation, it is the idea of God's revelation through salvation history that is fundamental to the Christian theological understanding of God. This has been called the "special revelation," in the sense that it is not present everywhere and always, but has taken place at specific times and specific places in history. This revelation has its historical beginning and its close within the framework of what is often called "salvation history." While the *beginning* of salvation history can be identified with the call of Abram (Gen 12), its high point is the revelation in Jesus. The first chapter of the Letter to the Hebrews gives us a condensed summary of this understanding:

> Long ago God spoke to our ancestors in many and various ways by the prophets, but in the last days he has spoken to us by a Son, whom he appointed heir of all things, through whom he also created the worlds (Heb 1:1–2).

Apart from the prehistory in Genesis 1–11, we can say that salvation history is delimited by the Bible's narrative, and this also shapes the understanding of the Bible's role as witness to revelation. The idea of a salvation history binds together the Old and the New Testaments within the Christian Bible.

Christian faith shares with Judaism the understanding that God reveals himself through the history of the people of Israel. Judaism's prophets are also the prophets of the Christian church. At the same time, however, the perspective is different. From a Jewish point of view, the high point in the history of revelation was the revelation of the law through Moses; in the Christian context, the events described in the Old Testament are understood as a preparation for the revelation in Jesus Christ, as this is described in the New Testament.

Revelation, as the biblical writings present it, means, on the one hand, that God speaks through specific human beings. The words of the prophets and of other special persons are thus perceived in a particular way as words from God. On the other hand, revelation also involves actions: God not only *speaks* to human beings, he also *acts* in relation to them. These actions are not merely meant to serve as illustrations of timeless truths about God; they are themselves a part of what is revealed. The revelation of

God is thus not only a revelation of God as he is in himself, but also of God as he acts in history. What God does in history is itself a part of what is revealed.

When God reveals himself in Jesus, revelation takes on a further dimension, since Jesus not only represents God or speaks on behalf of God, but *is* himself God. It is only in the light of Trinitarian doctrine (see chapter 3) that we can grasp how he can simultaneously be both God and sent by God. Through the incarnation, God enters the world in human form. Jesus not only speaks on behalf of God; he *is* himself the Word from God. In his person, therefore, Jesus is a revelation from God. This is expressed, for example, in the prologue to the Gospel of John: "And the Word became flesh and lived among us, and we have seen his glory, the glory as of a father's only Son, full of grace and truth" (John 1:14).

The use of the concept of "salvation history" with regard to this trajectory from Abraham to Jesus points here to the content of this history, namely, God's action to bring salvation. In the Old Testament, this salvation concerns primarily the people of Israel and the concrete circumstances of their life as a people. The greatest saving act in this context is the liberation from slavery in Egypt, which is described in the Book of Exodus. In the New Testament, the perspective on salvation is widened to include all human beings, and it is given an ever broader content.

While God's actions in history aim at salvation, they also have an element of settling accounts and judgment. This is expressed with particular clarity in the Old Testament narrative of God's relationship with the people of Israel, where he seeks to save them, but also judges them when they rebel against his will (see, e.g., Deut 30:15–20). Judgement also occurs so that God can save the people later on—we can say that its whole aim is salvation (Isa 14:1; 54:7–8). In the New Testament too, the idea of God's demands and God's judgment forms a part of the background to the understanding of salvation as salvation from judgment (see John 3:17–18).

The idea that what God has done in Jesus represents the high point in God's revelation also entails that the revelation in Christ is the close of God's revelation. It is not merely a "provisional high point," so that we could expect new revelations at a later date—not even smaller, "supplementary" revelations. According to the New Testament, the church's primary task is therefore to proclaim the message that had already been received. And the content of this message was what God has done in Jesus.

In this way, the Christian faith differs from Islam, which sees Jesus as one in a long sequence of prophets, with Mohammed as the end point. It is also necessary to undertake a similar drawing of boundary lines vis-à-vis groups that seek to place themselves within the Christian tradition, but that claim new revelations as the basis for their theology. This applies to groups such as the Mormons, who base their teaching not only on the Bible, but also on alleged revelations to their founder, Joseph Smith.

The fact that revelation is closed does not exclude the possibility and indeed the necessity of attempting to understand better its content and meaning. In this connection, Jesus' words to his disciples are often quoted: "When the Spirit of truth comes, he will guide you into all the truth" (John 16:13). This promise has been understood in the Christian tradition to mean, not that the Holy Spirit will give completely new knowledge, but that the understanding of what has already been given in and through Jesus will be developed and deepened, and will be applied in new situations. The various Christian traditions do not completely agree about what this means in practice, and especially about how far one can argue on the basis of matters that are "implicit" in revelation, with a content that is grasped fully by the church only at a later date. While the Catholic Church has tended more strongly to envisage such a "development" of revelation through the church's tradition, the Protestant tradition has been more restrictive about such an idea (see chapter 2.3).

The fact that revelation is closed does not exclude the possibility that people can tell of special experiences of contact with God or with Jesus. Sometimes, special experiences of this kind can be called "revelations"; and they can often provide divine guidance in particular situations. In the framework of dogmatics, it is impossible to say anything general about the genuineness of this type of experiences, but it is important to underline that each individual experience must be examined carefully, and that they cannot be used as a decisive argument in doctrinal questions.

The only thing that can supersede the revelation that is linked to Jesus' life, death, and resurrection is his own coming at the end of history. At present, our knowledge of God has a provisional and indirect character; but then, it will be replaced by a more direct experience of God himself. One text that shows us this understanding of revelation is 1 John 3:2, "What we do know is this: when he is revealed, we will be like him, for we will see him as he is." But not even this revelation when Jesus returns will be a "new" revelation, in the sense that it would concern anything else than what was revealed in and through Jesus' life, death, and resurrection, because it is the same Jesus who revealed himself to disciples who will also come back (Acts 1:10), and the same Jesus who through his resurrection anticipates the definitive victory over death (1 Cor 15:20–23).

Law and Gospel

The duality in God's actions, as these are revealed in salvation history, the fact that both judgment and salvation are involved, is often expressed by means of the conceptual pair "law and gospel." In a Lutheran context, this conceptual pair has traditionally played an important role in understanding the various dimensions of God's revelation. In other traditions, these concepts do not play the same central role, or else they are understood differently. Nor is there, even within Lutheranism, complete agreement about the use of this distinction. In order to understand the debate, we must understand what is indicated by this pair of concepts.

In this context, *law* is an expression of God's will in relation to the human being and the world. In Judaism, there is a stronger tendency to identify the law (torah) with what was revealed to the people of Israel through Moses, but in Lutheranism, law is a more general designation of God's will in relation to all human beings. The content of the law can be summarized in particular texts (such as the Ten Commandments or the double commandment of love), but it is not restricted to these concrete texts. In this context, God's law functions to provide guidance by telling us what is good and right in society, while it also has an accusatory and judging function by unmasking the human being's failures to meet God's demands—and thereby driving the human being to Christ. In the Lutheran tradition, these two aspects of the law are often called the first and second use of the law; they are also known as the "civil use" of the law (Latin: *usus civilis* or *politicus*) and the "pedagogical or accusing use" of the law (Latin: *usus paedagogicus* or *elenchticus*). (On the question of whether there is a "third use of the law," see under 6.5 below.)

In this context, the *gospel* is understood as the message of salvation in Jesus Christ. While the law expresses God's demands, the gospel is about God's gift. While the law is about what the human being is to do, the gospel is about what God has done to save the human being.

Both the law and the gospel are found in the Old and in the New Testaments. This is a duality that permeates the entire Bible, not something that is to be thought of as divided between the two Testaments.

One central concern in the Lutheran tradition is that law and gospel belong together, while at the same time they must be distinguished from each other. If they are blended together, either the demands of the law will lose their radicality, or else the gospel will no longer be a message about God's unconditional grace.

The question is how we understand the distinction between law and gospel in relation to the distinction between the general and the special revelation. It is not difficult to grasp that the gospel and the special revelation belong together, not least because the core in the gospel is what God has done in and through Jesus' death and resurrection. Since the gospel is linked to salvation history and to God's action in Jesus Christ, it is impossible to say that the gospel belongs to the general revelation.

There is, however, much greater disagreement about how we are to understand the law in relation to the two forms of revelation. The idea "that what the law requires" as "written on" people's "hearts" from the beginning of creation (Rom 2:15) leads some to claim that the law is given through the general revelation, while the content of the special revelation is exclusively the gospel. This view has played an important role in Scandinavian Lutheran theology, for example in K.E. Løgstrup and Gustaf Wingren. According to Wingren, the law is accessible through creation, and the revelation of Christ is therefore not a revelation of the law.

The consequence of such a position is that there is no specifically Christian ethics, since Christians have no different access from anyone else to what is right. Ethical argumentation must therefore be carried out on a general basis, not with reference to the Bible. The Bible does *de facto* contain much ethical material, but this is to be understood as the revelation of an ethical content that was indeed not known previously, but that actualizes and makes concrete what is already present in the general moral knowledge. On this view, the new element that the special revelation brings would be the message of forgiveness and new life for human beings who do not live up to the demands of the law, as well as the inspiration given by Jesus' life to act in accordance with God's will.

A completely antithetical position on this question claims that the general revelation does not give any certain knowledge of God's will; this knowledge is erroneous or, at best, fragmentary. This means that the special revelation is understood as revelation *both* of the law *and* of the gospel. One argument for this view is that the human being's sinfulness makes it impossible to have certain knowledge about the content of the law on the basis of what is deposited in creation. Another argument is that the special revelation, as this is presented in the Bible, does in fact contain a large amount of ethical material, since God reveals the law through Moses, and both Jesus and the prophets give various types of ethical instructions and admonitions.

The view that insight into God's will must be built exclusively on the special revelation is held for example by Karl Barth. In Barth, however, this standpoint is combined with a different understanding of the relationship between law and gospel: Barth protests against the tendency to divide the content in revelation into two parts—a tendency implied by the traditional distinction between law and gospel. He therefore emphasizes that revelation is primarily a revelation of the gospel, and that the law is to be understood as subordinate to the gospel, as a form of gospel. Instead of speaking of "law and gospel," Barth prefers to speak of "gospel and law." One consequence is that he integrates the treatment of ethics into dogmatics.

An intermediary position affirms that while it is possible to gain insight into God's will (the law) both through the general revelation and the special revelation, it is the special revelation that gives the most certain and most unambiguous insight into it. This is a possible reading of Luther's understanding of the relationship between the natural law and the ethical guidance that is formulated by Jesus and the apostles in the New Testament. Although the knowledge of God's will is deposited in our hearts, we often go wrong in our understanding of it, and this is why we find the most certain formulation of the natural law in Jesus and the apostles. This way of understanding the law means that Christian ethics can argue both more generally and on the basis of the Bible. (For a more precise discussion, I refer to books that give an introduction to theological ethics.)

God, the World, and Hope

The Relationship between the General and the Special Revelation

We have already touched on the question of the relationship between the general and the special revelation, in our discussion of the relationship between law and gospel. This is only one part of a more general problem that has been answered in very different ways in the history of theology. The question of the relationship between the general and the special revelation is closely connected to the question of the relationship between faith and reason, faith and experience, the specifically Christian and the general, and between theology and philosophy.

We find clear positions at both ends of the spectrum, as well as a number of intermediate positions. Already in the early church, we find very various attitudes to this relationship. The so-called apologists in the second century (including Justin Martyr) envisaged a close relationship between the Christian faith and Greek philosophy, where Christianity was the true philosophy that answered philosophy's questions. The idea was that, even independently of the biblical revelation, elements of the divine reason (Greek: *logos*) were present in all human beings, and that these were confirmed and reached their full meaning through Christ.

On the other hand, Tertullian claimed around 200 that there was an absolute antithesis between theology and philosophy, and between faith and reason. A well-known quotation expresses such an understanding: "What, then, do Athens and Jerusalem have in common? What do the academies and the churches have in common? What do heretics and Christians have in common?"[1]

Unlike Tertullian, mediaeval theology is marked to a greater degree by an understanding of a more harmonious relationship between theology and philosophy, and between the natural knowledge of God and that which is bestowed through the Christian faith. For Augustine, this means accepting faith, and the revelation on which it builds, as the starting point for rational understanding (as in the words of Anselm of Canterbury: "I believe in order to understand").[2]

Thomas Aquinas, the great theologian and philosopher of the High Middle Ages, has a positive view of the possibilities of a natural knowledge of God. He represents in this context what we could call a "two storeys model" of the relationship between the knowledge of God that is given in the general revelation and that which is given in the special revelation. He is rather optimistic about the possibility of a valid natural knowledge of God and of morality, although this has a clear limitation. This means that the knowledge of God and of his will that is built on the special revelation does not replace the natural knowledge. Rather, it represents a *supernatural* knowledge that supplements the natural knowledge and builds on it. To take one example: on the basis of the natural knowledge, one can know that there is a God who is the highest perfect being and the source of all that exists. Thomas indicates, by means of various

---

1. Terrtullian, *Praescriptione Haereticorum*, 7.
2. Latin: *credo, ut intellegam*. Anselm, *Proslogion*, ch. 1.

forms of proofs of the existence of God, the grounds for such a natural knowledge of God. Other aspects of the being of God, for example, that God is triune, lie outside the range of the natural knowledge of God, and must be revealed through the supernatural revelation. One can argue rationally for the content of the natural revelation of God, but the supernatural knowledge is the object of faith.

It is important to know about Thomas' model of the relationship between the general and the special revelation because it has been, and still is, extremely significant within Catholic theology, and it forms the background for the idea of the natural law as the basis of a universally binding ethics.

While Catholic theology continues to be influenced by Thomas, Lutheran theology bears the imprint of Luther's position on this question. Like Thomas, Luther acknowledges the possibility of a natural knowledge of God and of morality, but he does not think in terms of a similar "two storeys" model. Luther's thinking about this relationship contains a greater degree of tension, since the revelation in Christ is not merely a further development and supplement to the natural knowledge of God: it is also antithetical to it. Luther holds that the two forms of knowledge possess their primary validity within different spheres of life. On the secular level, in life in society, reason is a sufficient instrument to know what is right and good. In the church and in the spiritual life, however, reason has no competence at all to indicate the path to God. This distinction finds expression *inter alia* in the doctrine of the "two kingdoms" where the secular and the spiritual are understood as two relatively autonomous ways in which God acts in relation to the world.

In later Protestant theology, we find various ways of understanding revelation. Some tend strongly to emphasize the possibilities of a natural knowledge of God, while others tend strongly in the other direction, dismissing the significance of the general revelation.

In the Enlightenment period, in the eighteenth century, many theologians were extremely optimistic with regard to the natural knowledge of God, and many even held that it made superfluous the idea of a supernatural revelation. According to Gotthold Lessing, a religion built on a special revelation was a stage that had been overcome, and ought to be replaced by a religion that was based purely on reason.

In the so-called Neo-Protestant theology of the nineteenth and early twentieth centuries, many theologians endeavored to demonstrate how Christian theology was a development of the universal human religiosity. Unlike the rationalism of the Enlightenment, however, they were not so much concerned about faith as an expression of rational knowledge. They underlined more strongly the emotional and moral aspects of faith and religion.

We find a diametrically opposite position in Karl Barth and in the theology that is similar to his or influenced by him. For Barth, God's revelation in Jesus Christ is God's only revelation, and he does not reckon on any general revelation at all. This means that whatever human beings may think about God on the basis of reason and experience is merely a false knowledge of God, which must be corrected by revelation. Accordingly, one cannot speak of any connection between human ideas of God and what God reveals about himself through Jesus Christ.

But although Barth strongly emphasizes that the revelation in Christ is the only source of knowledge of God and of his will, this does not mean that his theology lacks any place for a discussion of the more general existential experiences of human beings. We see this above all in his treatment of the theology of creation, where Barth takes up several aspects of human life, but always does so in the light of the revelation in Jesus Christ. We find a similar line of thinking in Eberhard Jüngel. Like Barth, Jüngel finds his orientation in the Word of revelation. At the same time, he is concerned to show that faith is relevant and viable in the encounter with modern human beings and their way of experiencing reality. The general revelation is thus not a source of the knowledge of God, independently of faith; it must first be interpreted in the light of faith and the gospel.

Wolfhart Pannenberg represents an alternative to the thinking of Barth and Jüngel on this point. Like them, he too accepts the traditional distinction between the general and the special revelation, but instead of saying that the knowledge of God is accessible only through the revelation in Christ, Pannenberg claims that God reveals himself through history as such. This does not lessen the importance of what God does in Christ, but this cannot be isolated as a special salvation history. Pannenberg argues that it must be understood as a part of "universal history," of history as a whole. Accordingly, he emphasizes that God reveals himself not only through his *words*, but also through his actions. Since history is not yet finished, and our standpoint is in the midst of history, it is impossible for us to have an unambiguous knowledge of the meaning of history. It is only at the close of history that universal history will appear as an unambiguous revelation of God. God's action in Jesus is the key to the revelation of God, because the close of history is anticipated in Jesus' resurrection. But what happens through Jesus must not be understood as an isolated event; it must be seen in connection with the history of the people of Israel. This gives a special importance to that part of history to which the biblical writings bear testimony, even though this does not amount to a delimited salvation history.

The way in which one understands the relationship between the general and the special revelation has also consequences for how one understands the relationship between the Christian faith and other religions. At the cost of some simplification, we can say that the more positively one evaluates the possibility of a natural knowledge of God, the more positively will one evaluate the content of truth in non-Christian religions. Similarly, a negative view of the possibility of a natural knowledge of God leads to a negative view of those religions, as we see not least in Karl Barth, who regards the relationship between religion and the Christian faith as an absolute antithesis. Barth writes that while the religions are human beings' attempts to draw closer to God, the revelation in Christ is what God does with human beings. The theologians of the Enlightenment period tended to think in a developmental perspective, with Christianity as the zenith in a progressive process of development. For Pannenberg, the religions are an important part of the universal history through which God reveals himself. He understands them as human attempts to understand the God who becomes visible by means of history. In this context, the Christian faith is to be understood as a religion, but it differs from other religions because it also builds upon God's revelation in Jesus Christ.

All these various models of understanding the relationship between the general and the special revelation have one point in common, namely, that they all attempt to see the connection between the Christian faith and the general experiences of life, although they relate them to each other somewhat differently. This is not always the case in Christian thinking and praxis, since one can often find a tendency to isolate the Christian part of life from the rest of life.

One question that arises here is what is actually meant by the term "general" when we speak of general experiences of life and of a general revelation. It refers basically to realities that are not limited to persons who have a special faith, or who belong to one special tradition. But one should avoid using this concept as if it referred to a reality that could be understood independently of faith and tradition. Nothing is "general" in the sense that it exists independently of interpretation. No experience is a "pure" experience; it is formed by specific patterns of interpretation that are supplied in and through the traditions of religions and worldviews.

Despite their almost antithetical starting points in their understanding of the general revelation, Barth/Jüngel and Pannenberg share a common concern, namely, the wish to understand the general experience of life in the light of God's action in Jesus Christ, but without isolating the understanding of "the general" from what God does in Christ. Barth/Jüngel begin in the revelation in Christ, and Pannenberg holds that the general knowledge acquires its ultimate meaning in the light of what God does in Christ. In both cases, it is clear that a Christian interpretation of life is something that comes, not "in addition" to something that is purely general, but as a starting point for understanding and interpreting the reality to which all human beings belong. According to a Christian interpretation of life, God is present in all aspects of reality and in every human being's life. One receives the definitive understanding of who this God is, and of how he acts, when one interprets reality in the light of what God does in Christ.

2.2 THE BIBLE AS A TESTIMONY TO GOD'S REVELATION

The fact that God's revelation (that is to say, the special revelation) takes place in history, from the election of Abraham to Jesus' death and resurrection, means that this revelation is not directly accessible to us who live today, but is given as events in the past. Although God is still present and acts in the world, the self-revelation that forms the basis of Christian faith and doctrine is finished in and through Jesus. If we are to gain access to the content of the revelation, it must be mediated or transmitted to us, and this takes place through the Bible.

The Old Testament tells us how God revealed himself in the history of the people of Israel. This revelation took place through historical events that are interpreted as expressions of God's action (see the summaries of these events in texts such as Deut 26:5–10 and Ps 78). But revelation also occurs when God speaks directly to human beings, not least to the prophets (Isa 38:4; Jer 1:2). These events and words were first transmitted orally. Later, they were written down in the books of the Old Testament.

The New Testament shows that the first Christians were concerned to communicate the message of what God had done in Jesus. According to Acts 1:8, the risen Jesus commissions the disciples to be his "witnesses in Jerusalem, in all Judea and Samaria, and to the ends of the earth." The rest of the Acts of the Apostles relates how this command was followed by means of a wide-ranging activity of preaching and mission, with the foundation of Christian communities across large areas of the Roman Empire. What they preached was precisely the Good News of what God had done through Jesus as a foundation for human beings' salvation (see, for example, the account of Peter's speech at Pentecost, in Acts 2:14–36).

The Apostolic Tradition

Although the proclamation of the message was not reserved to only a few persons, it appears that Jesus' original disciples ("the twelve," Acts 6:2; also called "the apostles," Acts 2:37; 1 Cor 15:7) had a special role in watching over the message and interpreting it, thanks to two factors. First of all, they themselves had been with Jesus and had witnessed what he had said and done, and they had also met him after his resurrection. This function as eyewitnesses is underlined in the introduction to the First Letter of John: "We declare to you what was from the beginning, what we have heard, what we have seen with our eyes, what we have looked at and touched with our hands, concerning the word of life" (1 John 1:1). Secondly, the apostles could appeal to a special commission from Jesus to go out and speak on his behalf. (This is expressed, for example, in Luke 10:16, "Whoever listens to you listens to me, and whoever rejects you rejects me.")

Paul was subsequently accorded a status on the same level as the other apostles, although his conversion took place only at a later date. He too underlines that he is not preaching anything else than what he had himself received from the other apostles. (See 1 Cor 15:3, "For I handed on to you as of first importance what I in turn had received.")

Paul's reference to what he himself had received points to an important aspect of the earliest Christian tradition, namely, that it is not merely the communication of information, but the preaching of a message that leads to faith and salvation. In the same section where he states that he is handing on something that he himself has received, he says that the readers are saved through the gospel he has preached to them (1 Cor 15:1–2). In the Letter to the Romans, he speaks of the gospel in a similar way, as "the power of God for salvation to everyone who has faith" (Rom 1:16). The gospel that is preached thus not only communicates historical information about Jesus. It makes Jesus present in the lives of those who hear it and believe it.

Initially, the message was transmitted only by word of mouth, but it gradually came to be put down in writing. This happened already while the first apostles were still alive; in some cases, this was done by the apostles themselves. The oldest written expressions of the Christian faith are probably to be found in Paul's Letters (although the authorship of some of them is a matter of dispute). A number of writings are also traditionally ascribed to the apostles Peter and John, although here too, the authorship is a matter of discussion in recent historical scholarship. But even where an apostle is not himself the author, there are reasons to assume that these writings contain traditional oral material that goes back to the apostles and that was written down by their fellow workers or successors.

The Gospels, which give continuous accounts of Jesus' public ministry and narrate his death and resurrection, occupy a special position. The Synoptic Gospels, which have the character of edited collections of traditional oral material, are probably the oldest. The background and the intention of the Gospels are summed up as follows in the introduction to the Gospel of Luke:

> Since many have undertaken to set down an orderly account of the events that have been fulfilled among us, just as they were handed on to us by those who from the beginning were eyewitnesses and servants of the word, I too decided, after investigating everything carefully from the very first, to write an orderly account for you, most excellent Theophilus, so that you may know the truth concerning the things about which you have been instructed (Luke 1:1–4).

This emphasizes that what is being written down goes back to the eyewitnesses (the apostles) and that the author has tried to render it as exactly as possible. The text shows that what the author is presenting here is not new and unknown material. He is writing down material that already existed in Christian preaching and teaching.

The Formation of the Canon

As the first generation of eyewitnesses gradually left the scene, these writings took on an increasingly important role in the church, both because they were used in worship and because they were regarded as authoritative sources of the apostolic tradition. Over time, boundaries were drawn between those writings that belonged to the collection (the canon) of the authoritative texts and those that did not belong to it. It was only towards the end of the fourth century that the total collection of texts that gradually came to be called the "New Testament" was fixed at twenty-seven.

There were above all three criteria that played a central role in the evaluation of the writings that were to be included in the canon. First, a text had to come from an apostle or from his closest circle. Secondly, the contents of the text had to agree essentially with the content of the apostles' message about Jesus. These two criteria of origin and contents underline, each in its own way, the *apostolic* character of the writings: in other words, their value consists in their handing on the tradition from the earliest eyewitnesses. Thirdly, texts that were to defend their place in the canon had to show that they were already read and used in the church.

In our own days, early Christian texts that were not included in the New Testament canon attract a considerable degree of attention. Several of these texts, such as the Gospel of Thomas, claim an apostolic origin, but there is no historical basis for this. Some of these writings also have contents that deviate strongly from the message in the canonical writings; above all, many of them are influenced by ideas from gnostic currents, ideas against which the early church put up a vigorous fight.

The Biblical Texts as Witness and Interpretation

One important insight into what we know about the genesis of the biblical writings is that revelation, in the Christian sense, was not primarily something that happened in writing. The writings that form part of the biblical canon did not come into existence as a result of direct divine communication. They are testimony to God's actions in history and to his personal presence in Jesus. This is the dividing line between the Christian faith and scriptural religions that regard a sacred writing as itself the divine revelation. The most obvious example is Islam, which regards the Koran as itself the divine revelation: in other words, God reveals his will by means of a text. According to Islamic thinking, the Koran is a copy of a heavenly Koran; this, of course, makes historical questions about the genesis of the Koran less relevant to Islamic theology.

In contradistinction to such an idea, revelation in Christian thinking is not a book, but something that takes place when God acts and speaks in history. This means that the content of revelation is not exalted above history; it is about what happens in history. The biblical writings are not in themselves the revelation, but they *bear witness* to the revelation. Since we are not contemporaries of the historical events that are involved here, we are dependent on this testimony, if we are to share in the revelation. This is why the biblical writings are completely necessary for Christian faith and Christian theology, as the written record of the testimony to revelation.

Since the written records go back to people who were primary witnesses of the revelation, and who had been charged to hand the message on to others, these writings also possess a special authority as communicators of the revelation. The same evaluation is expressed in the name "sacred scripture" (or "Scripture") for the Bible, and in the fact that the Bible as a whole, or individual biblical texts, can be called "the Word of God" in a theological and liturgical context. This term does not mean that the Bible itself is the actual revelation. It indicates the role of the Bible as a unique witness to the revelation, both as the Word about God and as the Word that God himself uses.

Another important factor here is that the biblical texts are not direct reports of the events to which they refer, but are rather testimonies that bear the mark of specific perspectives and interpretations. The various biblical texts have one common characteristic, namely, that they are written from a standpoint of faith. All the New Testament texts that write about Jesus' life, death, and resurrection are marked by the belief that he was the Son of God and the Messiah promised to Israel. In other words, the biblical texts are not the expression of a neutral historiography. We also see that they represent somewhat differing interpretations, in the sense that they attach different weight to the various aspects of what they tell us. The most concrete expression of this situation is the fact that the New Testament canon includes four different Gospels, which narrate the events in different ways. This was obviously not a problem for those who gave the Gospels their place in one and the same collection of texts. The various versions of the gospel were not so different that they contradicted one another; nevertheless, they were so different that, taken together, they could give a richer picture than each one on its own.

This observation is important for dogmatics, because it reminds us that every presentation of the content of the Christian faith is the expression of one particular interpretation. The biblical texts are no exception here: they are the attempt by the first witnesses to interpret what they have seen and heard. We see this, for example, when Paul points to the statement "that Christ died for our sins in accordance with the scriptures" (1 Cor 15:3) as expressing the core in the Christian tradition. Here, a historical event (Jesus' death) is linked to two fundamental theological interpretations: that Jesus' death took place "for our sins" and that this was "in accordance with the scriptures," that is to say, in agreement with what the Old Testament had foretold.

When we read the texts, we must read them as *interpretations*. At the same time, when we read the texts, we ourselves are obliged to interpret—both in the sense that we interpret the texts, but also that we, together with the texts and through our interpretation of the texts, interpret the events that the texts relate. In this context, dogmatics can never dispense with the biblical texts, since one has no access, independently of the texts, to the events to which they refer. But dogmatics cannot be content only to give a simple report of the content in the various texts, or to compare one text with another. It is required to interpret the matter about which the texts speak, with a view to the time in which we live. There will therefore always be a certain difference between a purely historical and a theological interpretation of the biblical texts, although the latter can never be independent of the former.

The Old Testament as Part of the Christian Canon

While it took some time for the message about Jesus to be given a written form, the first Christians regarded the Old Testament writings from the very outset as the testimony to God's revelation in the history of the people of Israel. According to the Gospels, Jesus shared the Jewish understanding of these writings as authoritative, and he saw his own activity as a fulfillment of these writings (see, for example, Matt 5:17). The New Testament also contains many references to the Old Testament. One central element in the proclamation by the first Christians of the message about Jesus was precisely that what had happened was a fulfillment of the "scriptures" (see, for example, 1 Cor 15:3–4). In its understanding of God and in its anthropology, the New Testament builds on the Old.

Since the Old Testament was something the church took over from the Jews, there was no discussion about the extent of the Old Testament canon that was comparable to the discussion about the New Testament canon. The extent of the Old Testament canon was not, however, completely fixed in Jesus' time; it was only towards the end of the first century that the extent of the Hebrew canon was definitively clarified. Since Greek was the principal language in the early church (as we see in the fact that all the New Testament texts were written in Greek), they mostly used Greek translations of the Old Testament, especially the Septuagint. The difference between the Hebrew canon and the Septuagint was, however, not only a matter of language. The Septuagint contained writings that were not found in the Hebrew canon, and this led to a discussion in the early church (for example, between Jerome and Augustine) about whether one should follow the Hebrew canon or also include texts that were found only in the Septuagint. The result was that, in addition to the thirty-nine books of the Hebrew canon, the seven so-called deuterocanonical books (Tobit, Judith, Wisdom, Sirach, Baruch, and 1 and 2 Maccabees) were also regarded as canonical, and this is still the official canon in the Catholic Church and the Orthodox churches today.

One consequence of the desire in the Reformation period to take up anew the original tradition was the argument that one should keep to the Hebrew canon and to the Hebrew text as the basis for new translations. This was the collection of texts that Jesus, as an Aramaic-speaking Jew, knew. This line of thought led Protestant churches to accept only thirty-nine texts in the Old Testament canon. The fact that they do not accept the deuterocanonical writings—which Protestants often call the Old Testament apocrypha—as canonical does not mean that they are regarded as empty of value. According to Luther, the deuterocanonical texts are "books that are not considered equal to the Holy Scriptures, but are useful and good to read."[3]

There is also a large measure of agreement among the various churches that the Hebrew text is the basic text of the Old Testament (just as the Greek text is for the New

---

3. Translated from Luther, *Übersetzung des Apocryphenteils*, 2.

Testament), and that this is the basis both for doctrinal discussions and for translations into other languages.

The Old Testament's place in the Christian canon has, of course, consequences for the interpretation and understanding of the Old Testament writings. Their special characteristic is that they not only form part of the Christian canon, but are also sacred scriptures for Judaism. Although the same texts are involved, these two different contexts mean that the same texts are used in very different ways. The name "Old Testament" is a Christian name; in a Jewish context, other designations are employed. The adjective "Old" presupposes, naturally enough, that there is also a "New" Testament.

The presence of both Testaments in the same (double) canon affects the understanding of the Testaments, each in its own way. On the one hand, this means that the Old Testament is a necessary interpretative background for the understanding of the New, where the latter is understood as the fulfillment of what is prepared and foretold in the Old Testament. On the other hand, a Christian reading of the Old Testament means that it is understood in the light of its context in salvation history, as a preparation for God's definitive revelation in Jesus. A quotation from Augustine expresses a Christian understanding of the relationship between the two bodies of texts: "The New Testament is concealed in the Old, and the Old lies open in the New."[4]

For a Christian interpretation of the Old Testament, this means that one is interested in how the Old Testament points ahead to a fulfillment that is not found within the Old Testament itself. This is often described as a Christological reading of the Old Testament, where the texts are read in the light of what God does in Jesus. This also means that some texts have a limited validity, because of their place in salvation history. This applies to all the laws about sacrifices, purity, and the Temple service. It does not entail that such texts are uninteresting from a Christian or theological point of view; on the contrary, they acquire a central Christological significance by being interpreted as models of Jesus' definitive sacrifice (this is elaborated in the Letter to the Hebrews, for example). The Old Testament is also theologically important in its understanding of God as Creator, and in its understanding of the world and the human being. These are themes that are not much developed in the New Testament, because the New Testament takes belief in the Creator for granted. The Book of Psalms has been decisively important for the language of Christian prayer.

A Christological reading of the Old Testament does not render superfluous a historical reading in which one investigates the intention and meaning of the various texts when they were written down. This is, to a large extent, the problem studied by historical biblical scholarship, a discipline where Jewish and Christian researchers collaborate without any great problems. The interpretation of the Old Testament texts in their historical context is of very great theological relevance, precisely because God's revelation is something that happens in history. A historical reading of the texts has

---

4. Latin: *Novum testamentum in vetere latet, et in novo vetus patet.* Augustine, *Quaestiones in Heptateuchum* 2.73.

often shown that numerous Christological readings of individual passages in the past were solely a "reading into" the texts. In addition to understanding the texts in their historical context, a theological use of the texts requires that they be interpreted on the basis of their place in the Christian canon.

A Lutheran View of the Bible

The question of the Bible's role in the church and in theology became a central topic during the Reformation in the sixteenth century. When the Reformers criticized parts of contemporary church theology and praxis, their starting point was in the Bible. While the Catholic theologians claimed justification for their standpoints in the ecclesial tradition, the Reformers held that it must be possible to criticize tradition too on the basis of the Bible. The principle that theology ought to build on the Bible as its highest norm is often called *sola scriptura* ("Scripture alone"). This basis for the Reformation understanding of Christianity is summarized as follows in the Formula of Concord: "We believe, teach, and confess that the only rule and guiding principle according to which all teachings and teachers are to be evaluated and judged are the prophetic and apostolic writings of the Old and New Testaments alone."[5]

This so-called "scriptural principle" was not only central to the Reformation; it has also been central in the various forms of Protestant theology, and has often been seen as one of the decisive dividing lines between Protestant theology on the one hand and Catholic and Orthodox theology on the other, where tradition has been accorded a more autonomous role as a theological norm. However, the understanding of what the scriptural principle means in practice can vary. In order to grasp what it can entail, let us first look more closely at Luther's view of the Bible and of its role in theology.

One fundamental perspective in Luther's understanding of the Bible is that it is both sufficient and clear. He opposes contemporary views that the Bible was both insufficient and unclear, and that it therefore had to be supplemented by the tradition and the church's magisterium. The fact that the Bible is sufficient means that it contains all that we must know in order to be saved. It does not necessarily have answers to every question, but that about which it has something to say is sufficient for human beings to be saved, and also as a foundation for the church's theology. The fact that the Bible is clear means that it is possible to read this central message of salvation out of the Bible without the aid of other authorities. This does not mean that everything in the Bible is clear, but that its central content is clear. The principle that "Scripture is its own interpreter" applies here. In other words, unclear passages in the Bible must be interpreted in the light of the passages that are clear.

The idea of the Bible's clarity also means that Luther denies that allegorical interpretations can be accorded the same status as literal interpretations (as often happened

---

5. Kolb and Wengert, eds., *Book of Concord*, 486.

in the Middle Ages). Luther insisted on the literal and straightforward meaning of the biblical text, with the starting point in an understanding of the authors' own line of thought and their use of concepts.

When Luther identifies the center of the Bible, he does so by pointing to Jesus Christ. It is the gospel about Christ that is the substantial midpoint of the Bible, and the Bible must be interpreted from this midpoint. For Luther, this is not only an interpretative principle, but also a *critical* principle, which he applies in his discussion of the New Testament canon. In principle, the extent of the canon is for him an open question, and Luther sets specific question marks against the Letters of James and Jude, the Letter to the Hebrews, and the Revelation of John. Only writings that proclaim faith in Jesus as the basis for salvation can be accepted as apostolic, and thus as part of the canon.

It is important to emphasize that when Luther employs as his critical principle the idea of Christ as the midpoint of the Bible, this is something he believes he finds in the Bible itself, not a principle that comes to the Bible "from the outside." This also means that the extent of the biblical canon is decided by the Bible itself. Nor does the Bible receive its authority from any source exterior to the Bible itself. It is through the encounter with the Bible's message about Christ that human beings—with the help of the Holy Spirit—are convinced that it is God's Word.

In his insistence that the Bible is clear when it is understood on the basis of Christ as its center, Luther is arguing not only against contemporary Catholic theology, but also against the radical Reformers (whom Luther called "enthusiasts") who made a correct understanding of the Bible dependent on the individual's possession of the Spirit.

The Bible as Norm

The idea of the gospel about Christ as the center of the Bible would be accepted by almost all theologians and churches, but there is less unity about what such a starting point entails for the interpretation of the Bible, and for the authority that is ascribed to its various parts. Although one can agree that one thing is more central than another, this does not mean that there is agreement about how the central element is to be interpreted, or about how one should understand that which does not belong directly to the center.

On the one hand, there is a theology that emphasizes the gospel about Jesus as the only truly normative element in the Bible. This means that texts that speak about anything other than the gospel are only of limited theological interest. And this in turn means that, with one's starting point in the gospel, one can criticize parts of the Bible that appear to contradict the gospel.

On the other hand, there is a theology that is less willing to distinguish between what is more important and what is less important in the Bible. Such an attitude is often referred to as *biblicism*. A biblicistic way of relating to the Bible takes little account of the fact that the various parts of the Bible came into existence in different historical situations, and individual texts tend thus to be applied in a rather direct manner to today's situation. One may also pay little heed to how central the individual texts are in relation to the center of the biblical message. Many forms of biblicism draw little distinction between revelation as something that happens in history and the Bible as a testimony to this revelation. The Bible is seen instead as a direct expression of revelation, often in combination with one particular theory of inspiration (see below).

We find examples of a biblicistic approach to the Bible not least in the treatment of eschatology (for more details, see chapter 9), where there are many detailed sequences of what will happen in the last days, built on a compilation of texts from various parts of the Bible. The content in the detailed pictures of the last days is not always set in relation to the central message of the Bible.

Each of these approaches is one-sided. Against a biblicism that wants to put everything on the same level, it is necessary to point out that the Bible has a center, and that everything else is to be understood in the light of this center. Against those who want to limit the normative content of the Bible to the gospel alone, it must be pointed out that the gospel is to be understood in the light of the total context in which it stands. There is indeed a difference between the center and the periphery, but both belong to the totality.

One expression of the distinction between center and periphery is Luther's understanding of the relationship between law and gospel. Although the message of salvation is the center of the Bible, the Bible's ethical teaching is a necessary background to the gospel. The gospel cannot be understood if the human being does not grasp that he or she is a sinner and in need of salvation. The law too points (indirectly) to Christ.

Historical-Critical Biblical Scholarship

The breakthrough of historical-critical biblical scholarship from the close of the eighteenth century onwards was in many ways a crisis for the church's traditional interpretation of the Bible. Although Luther too had insisted that it was necessary to see the individual texts in the light of their authors and their historical contexts, this was now done in a much more radical way. While Luther in his interpretation of the Bible presupposes that the Bible must be understood as the expression of God's revelation, and that it has one principal subject (namely, the gospel about Christ), historical-critical scholarship treated the Bible as an expression of human religiosity in various periods. Scholars also wanted to demonstrate the plurality and the contradictions in the biblical material. They also wanted to show that the biblical texts had not necessarily come into being in the way that previous generations had believed, and that the events that are narrated in the biblical texts are not always recorded correctly.

Theologians reacted variously to the crisis that was caused by historical-critical research. On the basis of a new historical reading of the biblical texts, some proposed that what had been regarded as central truths of the faith should now be reviewed—for example, belief in the miracles or in Jesus' resurrection, which many considered unhistorical.

Alongside more radical approaches of this kind, there has always existed a biblical scholarship with a more conservative orientation, which sought to a greater extent to give an account of the unity in the biblical message, in the conviction that a historical-critical understanding of the biblical texts could be compatible with a traditional ecclesial reading.

A central concern of the pioneers of the historical-critical approach was to establish a dividing line between historical and dogmatic theology. This means that historical theology should be carried out without paying heed to dogmatic interests and consequences. This led within dogmatic theology to a tendency to attempt to make it as independent as possible of the results of historical exegesis, *inter alia* by referring to church confessional texts as the key to a theological reading of the Bible. In the Norwegian Lutheran context, Leiv Aalen advocated such an approach. In purely structural terms, this line of thought is strongly reminiscent of a Catholic position in which tradition and the magisterium became the key to a correct understanding of the Bible. The primary difference is that Aalen held that it was possible in principle to examine the confession critically on the basis of the Bible, whereas it is in principle impossible in a Catholic context to overrule the tradition and the decisions of the magisterium.

Is the Bible Free of Error?

In addition to such attempts to adapt to the historical-critical method, we also find attempts to reject it completely. This negative attitude was official in the Catholic Church until 1943. A negative attitude of this kind is found today primarily among more conservative Protestant circles, not least in the USA. One example is the Missouri Synod, the second-largest Lutheran church in the USA, where the official position is that the Bible does not contain any errors or contradictions: in all its individual details, it contains an infallible truth, even when it speaks of historical and geographical circumstances.

This position can entail (for example) that the creation narrative in Genesis is to be taken literally. In other words, the earth was created in six days, and this happened roughly six thousand years ago; this makes it necessary to reject insights from modern biology (not least the theory of evolution) and geology (theories about the age of the earth). In many cases, this understanding of the Bible's inerrancy has led to alternative theories about the origin of life that have claimed to be scientific, such as so-called creationism. But not all those who hold such a view of the Bible draw the same consequences in their view of the age of the earth and other questions.

Sometimes, apparent errors and contradictions in the Bible are explained by asserting that the original version of the biblical texts is inerrant (free of error), but that this does not exclude the possibility that errors may have crept in during the transmission of the texts.

Such an understanding of the Bible as inerrant has often been called a *fundamentalist* view of the Bible, with its starting point in a movement in the USA in the early twentieth century. Today, "fundamentalism" has largely become a designation of a political extremism that is given a religious justification, and this makes it unsuitable as a description of a way of understanding the Bible.

The problem with understanding the Bible as inerrant in all its details is that this corresponds badly to the Bible as it *de facto* exists. There are many instances of contradictory accounts of the same sequences of events, where it is impossible to harmonize them. This applies, for example, to the relationship between the Books of Kings and Chronicles in the Old Testament, or to the relationship between the Gospels in the New Testament. In other cases, the texts presuppose a picture of how the universe is constructed that is untenable today (Ps 104:5). And clear errors on points of detail can also occur, as when Matthew 23:35 says that that the martyr Zechariah was the son of Barachiah, whereas according to 2 Chronicles 24:20, he was the son of Jehoiada.

Such contradictions were obviously not a problem for those who brought the various writings together to form one and the same canon, and this shows that the view of the biblical texts as inerrant does not simply reproduce the self-understanding of the biblical texts themselves. First of all, the understanding of "errors" and of historical correctness that the defenders of the Bible's infallibility work with is not exactly the same that characterizes the texts and the period in which they came into being. On the contrary, the understanding of infallibility is a modern construction that makes specific demands of a text, if it is to be regarded as trustworthy—whereas such demands were not customary in the pre-modern period. Secondly, the different genres of the biblical texts are often overlooked. When the creation narrative is used as an argument for the creation of the earth in six days, this overlooks its metaphorical and poetic character, and one also forgets that it exists in two versions, with rather different sequences of events (Gen 1:1—2:3 and 2:4–25). In other texts too, the point is not necessarily that something happened in precisely this or that manner.

A more serious objection to the view of the Bible as inerrant in all its details is that this position does not draw a distinction between the central message and other kinds of material in the Bible. The church has understood the Bible as its authoritative sacred scripture because it mediates the message of God's salvation in Jesus. But there is no reason to see the Bible as the highest authority in every question about which it speaks. The reliability of the Bible is linked to its role as the communicator of the gospel, not as a source of insights into history or natural science.

This does not mean that the Bible's accounts of historical events are theologically irrelevant. This is because the gospel concerns, not timeless truths, but God's salvific actions in history. And thus it is not irrelevant whether Jesus did in fact live, whether he rose from the dead, or whether the people of Israel were in fact rescued from Egypt.

Nor does it mean that the historicity of such events is exempt from investigation by historians. And it does not mean that something is true merely because the Bible says so, because that easily leads to a circular argumentation: it is true because the Bible says so, and the Bible is inerrant because everything in it is true. At the same time, there are certain limits to how far one can come, using the customary methods of historical science, in confirming or refuting the historicity of events that are claimed to be expressions of God's unique interventions, for example, with regard to the resurrection of Jesus (for more on the historicity of the resurrection, see chapter 5.3).

The Inspiration of the Bible

The position that the Bible is inerrant tends to be based on one particular view of the Bible, namely, that it is inspired by the Holy Spirit. And this view in turn is based on texts such as 2 Timothy 3:16: "All scripture is inspired by God and is useful for teaching, for reproof, for correction, and for training in righteousness." In its context, this is an affirmation about the books in the Old Testament, but when the Bible is understood as inspired, these words are readily extended to include the New Testament writings.

This understanding has, however, taken many different forms. The view of the Bible as inerrant tends to assume a so-called *doctrine of verbal inspiration*, where one thinks of the wording of the Bible as infused by God. A theory of this kind was elaborated in Lutheran Orthodoxy in the seventeenth century, but it is also found in somewhat differing forms in many Protestant groups. Once again, the problem with such a theory is that it does not agree with what the texts themselves say about how they came into being. For example, they speak of human initiatives in gathering and systematizing the message that was received (see the introduction to the Gospel of Luke, quoted above). This understanding is also theologically problematic, because it risks making the Spirit's "dictation" of the content of the biblical texts the real revelation, instead of seeing the Bible as testimony to a revelation that has already taken place.

In addition to variants of the doctrine of verbal inspiration, inspiration has also been understood as *personal inspiration* (the Bible is written by authors who were especially full of the Spirit) or as *real inspiration* (it is the substantial content of the Bible that is inspired, not its wording), but such theories too have their problems. It is unproblematic to affirm that the Holy Spirit was involved in the history of revelation, and that the Spirit guided those who wrote the biblical texts. It is likewise a central Christian conviction that the Spirit continues to use the biblical word to create faith in people today. But it is more dubious to employ the inspiration by the Spirit to reduce or eliminate the human factor in the genesis of the Bible; nor is it necessary, in order to affirm the authority of the Bible as testimony to revelation.

To use a theory of inspiration to establish the authority and reliability of the Bible is also a circular argument that convinces only those who are already convinced beforehand. The Bible's authority should rather be anchored in the fact that it bears witness to God's salvific actions and communicates the apostles' message about Jesus Christ. The authority of the Bible is not in the least decided by some theological theory. On the contrary, the Bible becomes an authority for people today when they experience what it has to say about God and about God's action in Jesus Christ, and are convinced by this. In the perspective of faith, this is a result of the Holy Spirit's action in and through the word of the Bible.

2.3 SCRIPTURE AND TRADITION

As I have mentioned, the idea of "Scripture alone" was central for Luther and the other Reformers, and this has often been understood subsequently as a principle that distinguished Protestant from Catholic theology. The alternative in Catholic theology has been to speak of "Scripture and tradition" as the source for theology. It is, however, possible to understand both "Scripture alone" and "Scripture and tradition" in various ways. Although there remain important differences in this area, the ecumenical discussion has shown that the differences are not necessarily as large as was initially supposed.

Historically speaking, there is no sharp distinction between the Bible and tradition. If we understand tradition as the transmission of the Christian message, the New Testament is to be understood as a written record of this transmission in an early phase, as it was practiced in the Christian fellowships. For a few generations, material that went back to Jesus was transmitted without necessarily being written down. Not all the words of Jesus were included in the Gospels, as we see from Acts 20:35, where Paul quotes such a word of Jesus ("It is more blessed to give than to receive").

It is impossible to determine to what extent genuine words of Jesus are transmitted in some of the apocryphal gospels, but what they show is that alternative versions of the tradition gradually came into existence, all claiming to be the correct version. Above all, there were various gnostic groups that challenged the tradition that was dominant in the church. By delimiting the canon, the church accepted only the New Testament writings as valid expressions of the tradition. The employment of the link of these writings to the apostles as a criterion for their canonicity laid down a boundary with regard to what was acceptable as the content of the tradition. The source of the church's message thus lay in the apostolic tradition, as this was found in the New Testament.

The anchoring of the tradition in the apostles was also used as an argument to justify that it was precisely in the *church* that this tradition had been handed on. Around 180 AD, Irenaeus rejected the gnostics' claims that they possessed a secret oral tradition that went back to Jesus himself, by demonstrating that many of the bishops, historically speaking, were successors of apostles, and that none of them was known to have been a gnostic. In later Catholic tradition, this idea of the historical continuity back to the apostles through the episcopal succession has been employed as an argument for according the church's magisterium a special authority with regard to defining the content of the tradition, including the interpretation of the Bible.

In some parts of Catholic theology, the relationship between Scripture and tradition has been understood as a "two sources theory": this means that the tradition from the apostles has been handed on both through the Bible and through an unbroken oral transmission in the church. In recent years, however, the primary tendency has been to see the tradition as having a decisive role in the interpretation of the Bible, not as an autonomous source of dogmatic assertions that cannot find support in biblical texts.

Important for the Catholic understanding is the role of the church and the magisterium as stewards of the tradition, when an authoritative interpretation of the Bible is to be made. The strongest expression of this line of thought is the teaching of the First Vatican Council (1869–70) that the pope is infallible in his doctrinal decisions, even if this is an authority that the popes have used extremely seldom. It also makes decrees by church councils and papal decisions on doctrinal matters centrally important sources for understanding the apostolic teaching today.

The stark antithesis to the Catholic understanding of tradition is the total rejection of any church tradition that we find in some Protestant groups. The most extreme positon is taken by those who understand church history as a long history of decay and who seek to get back to the original Christianity that one finds in the Bible. In this perspective, some have understood their own group as the re-establishing of the true church, which died out in the early church. While other currents have not necessarily rejected the church of earlier times, they too have believed that the path to renewal lay in having recourse to original Christianity. "Back to the early Church" has in some circles been an important slogan.

The problem with such an approach is that the understanding of the original biblical Christianity can vary from group to group. And in practice, a tradition is quickly established within the movement—a tradition that can be just as authoritative for the interpretation of the Bible as other, older traditions.

This kind of radical rejection of every church tradition also contrasts with the Reformers' position. For Luther, the point was not to found the church afresh, but to reform the church on points where an unhealthy theology and ecclesial praxis had developed. Both Luther and the Lutheran confessional texts appealed on many occasions to the tradition (first and foremost, to theologians and councils in the early church) in support of their claim that they were not teaching anything new. At the same time, they were aware that the tradition is not a uniform reality, and that it can contain contradictory points of view. The tradition can also err, and must therefore be tested by means of the Bible. Accordingly, respect for the tradition does not exclude criticism of the tradition.

One important argument for taking account of the tradition, when one wants to take a position on doctrinal questions on the basis of the Bible, is that this is a question of the *church's* doctrine. Christian doctrine is not primarily to be understood as the opinions and standpoints of individual theologians. It deals with what the church, as a fellowship, regards as the expression of its faith. The ecclesial fellowship is not something that only exists here and now; it has existed since the time of the apostles. This means that church teaching today is a continuation of what the church has understood in earlier periods too as the Bible's message.

It is therefore valuable, in judging doctrinal questions, to look for what is "universally Christian," that which can count as far as possible as the expression of "what has been believed everywhere, at all times, and by everyone," to borrow the celebrated words of Vincent of Lérins.[6]

The difference between a Catholic and Protestant understanding of this starting point is, first, that Catholic theology thinks in more restricted terms of who represents the ecclesial fellowship in the past and the present—namely, the Catholic Church's hierarchy, under the leadership of the pope. Secondly, even if Catholic theology thinks that it is possible, within the framework of the tradition, to develop new nuances in the understanding of the biblical message, it is not free to say that the authoritative ecclesial tradition has erred on any point. In practice, however, the fact that the importance of continually interpreting the tradition is underlined, and that one is compelled to distinguish more central parts of the tradition from its less central parts, makes an adjustment on various questions possible.

The tendency to identify the normative ecclesial tradition with one's own tradition is, of course, not unique to the Catholic Church. In Lutheran confessionalism, for example, the Lutheran church was seen as continuing the genuine tradition of church doctrine, in contrast to the doctrinal deviations of other churches.

Although the part of the tradition to which one belongs will always necessarily play a special role, the individual church fellowship also belongs within the broad spectrum of the Christian tradition, both past and present, and one must take this into account when deciding what the Bible's message means today. The breadth in the tradition is important both because it demonstrates a large measure of agreement about what is central, and because it contains a wide spectrum in the elaboration of what is central. When one's point of reference is the breadth of the tradition (and not just one limited, authorized part of it), one must necessarily also have a *critical* relationship to it. The criterion for a critical evaluation will lie in the starting point of the tradition, namely, in the apostles' testimony to Jesus as this finds expression in the New Testament, and in the Old Testament as the basis of the New. The scriptural principle thus

---

6. Latin: *quod ubique, quod semper, quod ab omnibus creditum est*. Vincent, *Commonitorium* 2.5.

means, not that the tradition is irrelevant as a theological source, but that the tradition ultimately must be evaluated on the basis of the Bible.

Although modern scriptural scholarship on its own cannot supply the foundations for a decision about the doctrinal significance of the biblical texts, this research into the historical meaning of the texts has created a shared point of reference that has proved fruitful in doctrinal discussions between the churches.

Bible and Confession

From the very earliest Christian times, we have examples of brief summaries of the central content of the Christian message, and we find some confessional formulas of this kind in the New Testament (for example, the formula "Jesus is Lord" in 1 Cor 12:3, Paul's summary of the tradition about Jesus' death and resurrection in 1 Cor 15:3–5, and the so-called Christ hymn in Phil 2:6–11). There are several examples of more detailed confessional texts from the early church, many of which were confessional formulas linked to baptism. When it was used in that context, the text was meant to summarize the content of the faith into which the catechumen was baptized. We find a further development of these early Christian baptismal formulas in the Apostolic Creed, which is used today both at baptism and in many other liturgical settings in many churches of the Western tradition (that is to say, in the Catholic and many Protestant churches).

When such confessions of faith are used in the liturgy, they also take the character of the congregation's response in praise to the gospel that is read. When the church formulates the central content of the gospel in its common act of worship, it proclaims that it adheres to this content and makes it its own.

At the same time, such confessional texts functioned at an early date as boundary markers vis-à-vis *deviant* understandings of the content of the gospel. The foremost example of this is the Nicene Creed from the council of Nicaea in 325, which acquired its final form in Constantinople in 381. This creed probably builds on an earlier baptismal confession, and it has also been used later in the liturgy. Alongside the Bible, this is probably the text that the greatest number of churches today regard as binding, and that they employ in their worship. (Nevertheless, disagreement about one line in the text is an important aspect of the schism between the church in East and West: see the discussion of the *filioque* in chapter 3.2). In its historical context, the Nicene Creed was formulated as polemic against the Arians, who refused to accept the Son is "of one being with the Father."

As I have said, the Nicene Creed is the most ecumenical of all confessional texts, because it is accepted by churches in East and West. Even churches that in principle do not accept any confessional texts as binding usually accept the understanding of the Bible that finds expression in the Nicene Creed. In the Western church, the Apostolic Creed and the Athanasian Creed were also given the status of confessional texts.

The ecclesial and doctrinal conflicts of the Reformation period produced a large number of confessional texts that served to define the doctrinal standpoints of the various parties. The oldest of these is the Augsburg Confession (*Confessio Augustana*), which was presented at the Imperial Diet in 1530 to document the positions taken by the Protestants. Its intention, according to its preface, was not to be the basis for a new church, but to show how the Protestant positions were in agreement with the Bible and also with the church's tradition, thus making it possible to re-establish ecclesial unity. But since the disagreements led to a lasting church schism, the Augsburg Confession came to be the foremost identifying mark of the Lutheran churches. In Denmark and Norway, the Augsburg Confession, together with Luther's Small Catechism, came to be seen as the confessional basis of the church, in addition to the three confessional texts from the early church. In most other Lutheran churches (including in Sweden and Finland), a number of other texts from the Reformation century were included; these were collected together in the Book of Concord in 1580. The most comprehensive of these texts, the Formula of Concord from 1577, was intended to clear up internal disputes in the Lutheran camp.

The Reformed churches gradually received their own confessional texts too, but none of these acquired the same central significance that the Augsburg Confession enjoyed in Lutheranism. Examples are the Heidelberg Catechism (1563) and the Second Helvetic Confession (1566). The Thirty-Nine Articles (1563/71) played a similar role in the Anglican church. As a kind of response to the confessional texts in the churches of the Reformation, the Catholic Church in turn elaborated a confessional text at the Council of Trent, the Tridentine Creed (1564).

More recent church history has also seen texts that were composed in special situations that demanded a confession of faith. The Barmen Declaration of 1934, composed during the struggle against Nazism, has the status of a confessional text in several German churches and elsewhere. *Kirkens grunn* ("The Foundation of the Church," 1942) had a similar function in Norway, although it did not subsequently receive the status of a confessional text. The Belhar Confession (1986), born of the struggle against apartheid, is a confessional text in churches in South Africa and other countries.

The different ecclesial traditions attach differing weight to such confessional texts. Because of the principle of Scripture alone, some churches (for example, in the Pentecostal tradition) do not accept any official confessional texts. Other churches, such as the Reformed, have operated with a number of different texts of varying official importance. The distinctive feature of the Lutheran tradition is that it operates with a more limited group of texts that are regarded as very important. But while they have a normative function in terms of determining what is Lutheran doctrine, it must be emphasized that their content is derived from the Bible, and that it must be evaluated continuously on the basis of the Bible.

One customary way of expressing this is to say that, while the Bible is the *norma normans* ("the norm that lays down the standard"), the confession is *norma normata* ("the standard that has been laid down"). This is the account Lutheranism gives of the relationship between Scripture and tradition, where the priority of the Bible is clear, but one must take the insights of tradition into account if one is to understand the Bible correctly. Even if a confessional text was formed in a particular context, it can never be content merely to formulate the doctrine in one particular church; it must at the same time be read as an attempt to express the content in the same apostolic tradition that finds written form in the Bible. This is why such texts must always be tested in the encounter with other churches' reading of the same Bible.

Bible, Tradition, Reason, and Experience

While a scriptural principle of the Reformation affirms that Scripture alone is to be the highest norm for theology and church, it is clear that the Bible never *is* alone, since it must be read and interpreted by human beings who are located in one particular situation and share in one particular tradition. In practice, therefore, the argumentation in dogmatics will have to take account of several elements.

The Methodist tradition appealed to its founder, John Wesley, in operating with what is known as the Wesleyan quadrilateral, a fourfold basis for theological reflection: Bible, tradition, reason, and experience.

We have already discussed the relationship between the Bible and tradition. The relationship between the Bible and reason is also a comprehensive theme that can be understood in various ways, depending on what one means by "reason." As the human being's fundamental ability to understand and think, the reason is of course absolutely necessary in order to read and comprehend the Bible. The reason is also necessary, if we are to argue on behalf of various interpretations and their doctrinal significance. But the reason also concerns the human being's ability to see existence in a connected manner and to draw consequences from one sphere or life to another. How the reason's possibilities are seen in this context depends *inter alia* on how one understands the relationship between the general and the special revelation, that is to say, how "rational" the revelation is in relation to what we otherwise know about existence. But the fact that one seeks to understand the Bible in the framework of a Christian interpretation of life that is also able to relate to other knowledge about existence—knowledge that genuinely helps to interpret the content and meaning of the biblical message—does not mean that the Bible loses its role as the decisive norm for the content of the Christian faith.

"Experience" is another wide-ranging concept, and its role in theology is a wide-ranging theme. On the one hand, it refers to Christian experience in a more restricted sense, that is to say, experiences of various Christian practices and various interpretations of the biblical message. Experiences of how far such interpretations have a liberating effect, or a restrictive and binding effect, are a theme that is taken up by various forms of liberation theology and feminist theology. Charismatic theology too draws on experience, in the sense that specific experiences of the Holy Spirit influence the interpretation of the Bible. On the other hand, "experience" also refers to human experience in a broad sense. It refers to the fact that one also interprets the Bible in the light of the experience one has of human life as such. It is important that the ecclesial fellowship gives space for various types of experience in its work in understanding the Bible's message.

It is not difficult to identify examples of how tradition, reason, and experience have been given a position that in reality set aside the fundamental normative significance of the Bible. The tradition supplies resources, but if it is allowed to stand on its own, it is easy to end up in a traditionalism with few possibilities of correction and new orientation. The reason is important, if we are to understand the faith; but if we build on it alone, we end up in a rationalistic theology where the perception of what sounds reasonable becomes the decisive criterion for what we can approve of in the Bible's message, and for how it is to be interpreted. If experience is allowed to stand on its own, one ends up in an experiential theology where one holds, on the basis of one's own experiences, that one knows what God's will is for oneself and for others.

"Scripture alone" thus does not mean that one can read the Bible independently of tradition, reason, or experience. If one is not aware of the role that these realities play, one can end up with an interpretation of the Bible that is both unreflecting and arbitrary. But while all this is necessary, it is equally important to underline that the fundamental source of knowledge of God and of his salvific action lies in the Bible, because, as we have pointed out earlier in the present chapter, the source of such knowledge lies in the revelation in Jesus Christ. Since it transmits both the narrative of God's salvific action in the history of the people of Israel and the apostles' testimony to Jesus, the Bible plays a decisive role in understanding the content of the Christian faith.

3

Who Is God?

3.1 CHRISTIAN BELIEF IN GOD AND OTHER THEISTIC BELIEF

THE QUESTION OF GOD touches the deepest layers in the human understanding of existence. It is a question about meaning and about the anchoring of existence. Why does anything at all exist, and how did it come into existence? Is there a meaning in existence that lies outside our immediate experience of existence? Is there a power behind everything? And is this power itself a part of the world, or is it separate from the world? Is it a personal or an impersonal power, and what else can one say about this power?

These questions are more "theoretical," but the existential questions connected with this matter are just as important: Am I left to my own devices, or does my life have a meaning that is anchored in something outside of myself? Is my life merely an expression of the play of arbitrary chance, or does it have a meaning? Is there someone whom I can thank for the gift of life, and someone whom I can ask to help me when life is difficult? Is there someone who has a will in regard to my life, a will that my way of leading my life ought to take into account? Is there someone who can save me from what threatens life—including death? And is it possible to address this power, or even to have a personal relationship to it?

Many different answers have been given in the course of human history to questions like these, and the various religions and worldviews offer a variety of answers today. Ideas about powers that are above or outside the human world, but that nevertheless can intervene in it, have followed the human race from its very earliest phase, and ideas about one or several gods have developed throughout history.

Christian Belief in God and Belief in God in Other Religions

The Christian belief in God too belongs in this context of the history of religion. Judaism and Christianity have shared presuppositions here, in the development of the image of God that finds expression in the Old Testament. The existence of a number of gods, often linked to specific regions or ethnic groups, was accepted in the environment in which the Old Testament came into being. The people of Israel worshiped only one God; the reason given in the earliest texts is not that other gods were non-existent, but that Yahweh was the only God for the people of Israel. This kind of *monolatry* (the worship of no other gods than the one) gradually developed into a *monotheism* that denied the existence of other gods than the one. We find one expression of this fully developed monotheism in the second part of the Book of Isaiah ("Deutero-Isaiah"), which declares that there is no other god than Yahweh, who is the Creator of heaven and earth (cf. Isa 45:5).

This monotheism is also presupposed in the New Testament, which bears the imprint of the faith that the God who has revealed himself in Israel's history is present in a special way and reveals himself in Jesus of Nazareth. It is precisely this faith in Jesus' special relationship to God, and the doctrine of the Trinity as a consequence of this relationship (see below), that distinguish the Christian belief in God from other forms of monotheism, such as rabbinic Judaism and Islam.

The Old Testament monotheism is also characterized by the idea of a *personal* God who is related to the world (as its Creator), but who nevertheless is not himself a part of the world. This idea is often called the *transcendence* of God. Such ideas are also found in Judaism and Islam, but Eastern religions such as Hinduism are marked by a pantheistic understanding that conceives of the deity and the world as two sides of the same reality, and that understands the deity in more impersonal categories.

Theologians debate the relationship between the God who is confessed in the Christian faith and the theistic belief within the framework of other questions. The answer will be closely linked to how one understands the relationship between the general and the special revelation (see the discussion in chapter 2). One fundamental idea underlying the idea of a general revelation is that God (as Paul puts it) has made himself known through his works in the creation (Rom 1:19–20). This starting point makes it possible to see non-Christian understandings of God in both a positive and a critical light.

In a positive light, we can see other religions' understanding of God and of the divine as expressions of attempts to comprehend the traces of himself that God has left in the creation, and we can say that they contain truth to the extent that they are in harmony with a Christian understanding of God. In a critical light, a non-Christian understanding of God also represents misunderstandings and distortions of who God really is. Whether the positive or the critical evaluation dominates, depends *inter alia* on the parameters of the theological understanding within which one operates.

While some wish to reject all non-Christian theism as an expression of idolatry, others will see it as a valuable but incomplete knowledge of God that is a potential point of contact for the proclamation of the gospel—and perhaps as a reality that even has something to teach Christians.

I believe that every evaluation of non-Christian theism must find an equilibrium between these two perspectives. An unqualified rejection of all non-Christian theism as totally false risks denying that God is the Creator who also created human religiosity. But the view that each and every theism is equally true represents a relativist approach that does not take seriously the Christian conviction that God has revealed himself in a definitive manner in Jesus Christ. For the Christian faith, belief in God is not just one question among many. It is the absolutely fundamental question for the understanding of existence. From a Christian perspective, the question of what truth is necessarily includes the question of God and of God's action in Jesus.

Christian Belief in God and the Philosophical Concept of God

The idea of God is not only a theme in various religions; it has also been a theme for philosophy. While the early church had a consistently critical attitude to pagan religions, which were mostly polytheistic, there was a tendency to see philosophy as more of an ally. One reason for this was the critical attitude taken by philosophy to the polytheistic religions of that period. Another reason was the correspondence between philosophy's desire to discover universally valid truths and the Christian faith's confession of the one God as the Creator and Lord of the world. Many philosophers have argued that it is rational to believe in a God who is the author of the world, and Christian theologians have taken over the philosophers' reasonings in their doctrine of God.

One of those who used philosophy in this way was Thomas Aquinas. We have seen in our discussion of the understanding of revelation how he operates with a "two-storey model" of the relationship between the natural and the supernatural knowledge of God. He thus holds that it is possible, on the basis of the reason, to argue for the existence of God as the highest being. One way in which he does so is through five different versions of the proof of God's existence, where he draws inferences from the way the world is to the God who is its author. According to Thomas, however, this kind of rational knowledge of God has its clear limitations. It is only through the special revelation that we receive true insight into the being of God.

While many theologians, like Thomas, have taken their starting point in a philosophical concept of God, others have rejected the usefulness of such an approach, dismissing an image of God based on philosophy as no better than the ideas of God in other religions. One spokesman for this point of view was Blaise Pascal, who expressed the difference between a philosophical and a theological concept of God as follows: "God of Abraham, God of Isaac, God of Jacob, not of the philosophers and of the learned."[1]

The first part of this quotation from Pascal is an allusion to Exodus 3:6, where God reveals himself to Moses in the burning bush and makes himself known thus: "I am the God of your father, the God of Abraham, the God of Isaac, and the God of Jacob." This points to an essential dimension in a biblical and Christian understanding of God, namely, that God reveals himself in history. In other words, the understanding of God that is expressed by the biblical writings does not build on philosophical speculations or rational conclusions, but on concrete experiences of a God who makes himself known to human beings in historical events. When God reveals himself to Moses, he is told of earlier generations' encounters with God. Who, then is God? The answer is not primarily a definition ("the highest being," or some similar term), but a reference to God's action in history. In the narrative about Moses, God initially refuses to answer Moses' question about God's name: "I am who I am" (Exod 3:14), but the text then employs the allusion to the Hebrew verb for "to be" as the starting point for the divine name "Yahweh" (Exod 3:15; usually rendered in English translations as "the LORD"), which is used widely in the Old Testament as a personal name for God. This name safeguards the identity: it is one and the same God who chose Abraham and who spoke to Moses and led the people of Israel out of Egypt. It was this God who chose David as king and who led them back from exile in Babylon. Gradually, the insight emerged that Yahweh is not merely one god among many, but is in fact the only true God, the Creator of the world.

It is interesting here to note that the divine name Yahweh is not the only one given to God in the Old Testament: some texts employ more general divine names such as El or Elohim. The Greek text of the New Testament adopts the more general concept of *theos* ("God"), which had been used both in Greek religion and in Greek philosophy, as the name for God. In this way, the historically given experiences that lie behind the divine name Yahweh are linked to a more general understanding of the divinity that exists in religion and philosophy. The God who reveals himself in the history of salvation is also the God whom philosophers and other religions seek to grasp, even if the complete and true understanding of who is God is, is accessible only through the biblical revelation. This understanding also finds expression in Paul's speech on the Areopagus in Athens: "What therefore you worship as unknown, this I proclaim to you" (Acts 17:23).

Christian Belief in God and Other Forms of Monotheism

When we speak about the relationship between a Christian understanding of God and the understanding of the divine in other religions, it is important to point out

---

1. Pascal, "Mémorial."

that Judaism is in a fundamentally different situation here. Jews and Christians agree that the Old Testament is sacred scripture, and both religions confess the God who revealed himself in the history of the people of Israel. "The God of Abraham, Isaac, and Jacob" is the God of both Jews and Christians. However, they part company on one decisive point, namely, the question of whether this God has also revealed himself in Jesus. While the mainstream in Judaism has given a negative answer, this is a basic presupposition in the Christian belief in God, which affirms that Jesus is the Messiah who fulfills the promises to Israel. As "the Father of Jesus Christ" (Rom 15:6 and many other passages), God is not only the God of the people of Israel. He summons the members of every people to believe in the gospel.

To say that Judaism has rejected Jesus as Messiah is not the whole picture. The first Christians were initially a movement within Judaism, and down through history there have been individual Jews or groups of Jews who have accepted Jesus as Messiah. "Messianic Jews" is one name used today for a movement of this kind.

The Christian belief in God has also a special relationship to post-biblical religions that relate in various ways to the biblical tradition, or that have adopted parts of this tradition. This applies, for example, both to Islam, where Jesus is regarded as a prophet, and to new religious movements whose understanding of God is influenced by elements drawn from the Bible.

The Challenge from Atheism

The Christian belief in God faces competition today, not only from other forms of theistic belief, but also from atheism, the conviction that there is no god or higher power that lies beyond material reality. A practical atheism, where people live in a way that pays no heed to God, is an ancient phenomenon to which the Bible too bears witness (Ps 14:1, "The fool says in his heart, 'There is no God'"). It is only in the last two centuries that we find a more developed theoretical atheism, first in the intellectual elite, and then spreading gradually to wider sectors of the populace. Modern atheism has largely appealed to arguments from natural science to prove that there is no basis for belief in God, and that God was created by the human being—not the other way round.

Atheism challenges the Christian belief in God both theoretically and practically. The principal challenge for one who wants to defend the Christian faith is to show how faith in God is not an isolated theory devoid of consequences, but is the center of a coherent Christian interpretation of life. (See chapter 1. I return in chapter 4, when I speak about God as Creator, to some of the concrete questions one faces in this context.) In the discussion with atheism, it is necessary to discuss on a scientific and philosophical basis the possibility and probability of faith in God. But it is only in the encounter with God's revelation in Jesus Christ that a decision is taken about whether the Christian understanding of God is credible.

3.2 GOD AS TRIUNE

The understanding of God as triune is absolutely central to the Christian belief in God. Although the doctrine of the Trinity is not directly expressed in the Bible, it builds on the picture of God and of God's actions that we find in the Bible. And in this context, the understanding of who Jesus was plays a central role. It was in the encounter with Jesus that the first disciples became convinced that he was not only a person who bore testimony to God or who had a message about God, like the prophets in earlier times, but that he mediated God in his own person. This conviction was anchored in what he said and did, but also in the way he spoke of himself. Through his resurrection from the dead, this conviction was confirmed and deepened: by raising him from the dead, God himself had confirmed Jesus' special status (cf. Rom 1:4).

At the same time, God's presence was experienced in a special way after Jesus' ascension, through the coming of the Holy Spirit. Both Jesus' words about the Spirit and the experience of the Spirit meant that the Spirit was understood, not as some kind of impersonal force, but as God himself at work in the life of the church and of the individual believer.

The question that then arose was how it was possible to combine an understanding that God was the Father of Jesus and the one who sends the Spirit, and that both Jesus and the Spirit *are* God, with the monotheism that had been taken over from the Old Testament and that Christians shared with their Jewish contemporaries. There was an intense discussion in the early church about how one could both preserve monotheism and hold fast to the conviction that one encounters God in the Father, the Son, and the Spirit. The understanding of the Trinity that Christian churches accept today is in many ways the endpoint in this discussion.

The doctrine of the Trinity is not fully elaborated in the New Testament, but it has its foundation and its justification in the New Testament and in the understanding of God that we find there. This means that the development of Trinitarian doctrine is not to be seen as adding something to the New Testament picture of God or as changing it. It must be understood as a hermeneutical process, a process of interpretation. This also means that Trinitarian doctrine is not immune to criticism: it must be checked against the Bible.

I have insisted (in chapter 1) that when dogmatics works on a formulation of the church's teaching, it cannot be content with an investigation of biblical theology alone, and Trinitarian doctrine exemplifies this principle well. When the theologians of the early church endeavored to understand the biblical message about God, they were compelled after a time to make use of other concepts than those in the Bible—not in order to say something different from what the Bible says, but precisely in order to interpret it appropriately. A driving force in this process was a theological disagreement about how the Bible's affirmations about God, Jesus, and the Spirit should be interpreted. The elaboration of Trinitarian doctrine can thus be understood as a process of clarification in which some interpretations were rejected, while others were confirmed.

The fact that Trinitarian doctrine is the result of a process of interpretation does not, however, mean that this process is finished once and for all. Although the councils of Nicaea (325) and Constantinople (381) were important stages, not least thanks to the elaboration of the Nicene Creed, theological work on Trinitarian doctrine did not stop there, and it still continues. Even with the Nicene Creed as the common starting point, differing presentations of Trinitarian doctrine have been made both in the early church and in later theology, and recent theology is no exception here.

Within the framework of a Trinitarian understanding of God, individual points have been presented and interpreted in various ways, without thereby posing a threat to the fundamental unity in the understanding of God. Disagreement on the doctrine as such has, however, been perceived as grounds for schism or as a question of heresy *versus* orthodoxy. This was how the dispute with the Arians, who rejected the full divinity of Jesus, was seen. At a later date, acceptance of Trinitarian doctrine has often been regarded as a criterion for inclusion in the Christian ecumenical fellowship, as we see (for example) in the Constitution of the World Council of Churches, which understands itself as a fellowship of churches built on faith in the triune God. This is why most churches do not recognize non-Trinitarian groups such as the Unitarians, the Mormons, and the Jehovah's Witnesses as Christian churches.

The Biblical Foundations of the Doctrine of the Trinity

Before we discuss the form that the understanding of God as triune was given when the early church's confessions were taking shape, let us look more closely at the biblical foundations of this doctrine. First of all, we must speak of the understanding of the one God that the first Christians took over from the Old Testament, and that is also confirmed in the New Testament. The idea of the one God is central to belief in God in the Old Testament. This is expressed *inter alia* in the so-called *shema* in Deuteronomy 6:4: "Hear, O Israel: The Lord is our God, the Lord is one." This confession is also confirmed by Jesus in Mark 12:29, and Paul alludes to it in Romans 3:30, "God is one."

Belief in the one God is also expressed in the first of the Ten Commandments: "You shall have no other gods besides me" (Exod 20:3; Deut 5:7). The one God is the only one who is to be adored. There is a reflection of this idea in the New Testament, at Revelation 22:8-9, when John wants to throw himself to the ground at the feet of the angel who has shown him all his visions. The angel refuses this, because he is only a servant, like John himself: "Worship God!"

Despite the idea of God's unicity, some passages in the Old Testament show that qualities or aspects of God take on an autonomous character and act on behalf of God himself. This is true of God's Spirit, which acts in relation to the world and to human beings (Gen 1:2; Ps 104:30; Ezek 11:5), and of God's angel or messenger, who acts on

God's behalf (Gen 16:7–11; Exod 3:2; Judg 6:11–24). It applies also to God's word, which expresses the fact that God speaks, but can also be spoken of as an autonomous reality (Jer 1:12). The most striking example of such an idea is God's wisdom, which is personified in the sapiential literature of the Old Testament and becomes an agent that acts on God's behalf (see, e.g., Proverbs 8). This idea of God's wisdom is further developed in the prologue to the Gospel of John, which speaks of the Word (Greek: *logos*), where the Word that was "in the beginning with God" and that "was God" (John 1:1–2) is identified with Jesus: "And the Word became flesh and lived among us, and we have seen his glory, the glory of the Father's only Son, full of grace and truth" (John 1:14).

In addition to the idea of the Word as divine, yet at the same time distinct from God, the concept of "son" is introduced here in order to describe Jesus' special position in relation to God as his Father. The concept of "father" is used of God in some Old Testament passages, to denote his relationship to the people (Deut 32:6), and the king can be described as God's son (Ps 2:7). In the New Testament too, God can be spoken of as the Father of all believers (e.g., in the Lord's Prayer, Matt 6:9), and the believers are called God's children (John 1:12). At the same time, however, we see that Jesus' relationship to God, as Son, is understood in more exclusive categories. According to John 1:14 and 18, he is the "only Son" (a formulation that made its way into the Apostolic Creed: "I believe . . . in Jesus Christ, his only Son, our Lord."). All the groups of writings in the New Testament use "Son of God" as a designation of Jesus. One important example is the narrative of Jesus' baptism in the Jordan, which is found in the Synoptic Gospels. The Spirit descends on him, while God's voice resounds from heaven: "You are my Son, the Beloved; with you I am well pleased" (Mark 1:11; Matt 3:17; Luke 3:22).

This father-son relationship is something more than other people have to God when they are called God's children. We see this in situations where Jesus plays roles that otherwise belong only to God, for example, when Jesus forgives human sins—something that it was thought only God could do (Mark 2:5–7). According to the Gospel of John, this led to the accusation that Jesus was blaspheming against God: "You, though only a human being, are making yourself God" (John 10:33). In this Gospel, he is spoken of directly as "God" (John 1:1.18; 20:28). Throughout the New Testament he is referred to as "Lord" (Greek: *kyrios*), a noun that translates the divine name "Yahweh" in the Greek translation of the Old Testament (1 Cor 1:2; 8:6). Jesus also plays a role that is reserved to God alone when he becomes the object of worship (Phil 2:10) or one to whom people pray (John 14:14). And this filial relationship was not something that started when his life on earth began: he was the Son of God from all eternity (John 1:1–14), whom God sent to the world to save it (Rom 8:3; Gal 4:4).

Various New Testament texts show how Jesus partly identifies himself with God and partly draws a distinction between himself and God as the Father. Jesus speaks on behalf of God, but he also addresses God in prayer (Matt 11:25–27; 14:23; John 17).

At the same time, he identifies himself so closely with God that he can say that "The Father and I are one" (John 10:30) and that "I am in the Father and the Father is in me" (John 14:10).

In a similar manner, the Holy Spirit is described both as one with God and with Jesus, and also as sent from the Father and from the Son. We read in John 4:24: "God is Spirit." The Spirit is God's Spirit (Rom 8:14), and also the Spirit of the Son of God (Gal 4:6). The Spirit is distinguished from the Father and the Son by being sent to the world by the Father and the Son (John 14:26; 16:7).

Although there is no developed Trinitarian doctrine in the New Testament, many passages have what we could call *triadic formulas* that presuppose both the unity and the distinction between the Father, the Son, and the Spirit. For example, Matt 28:19 speaks of baptizing "in the name of the Father and of the Son and of the Holy Spirit." Similar combinations are found at 1 Cor 12:4–6 and 2 Cor 13:13.

The Development of the Doctrine of the Trinity

The later development of Trinitarian doctrine was a response to the need to clarify the meaning of the New Testament affirmations about the Father, the Son, and the Spirit, and about their reciprocal relationship, while holding fast to the faith in one God. This clarification became necessary not least because of a sequence of conflicting interpretations, all of which claimed to represent a correct understanding of the biblical message. In what gradually became the dominant ecclesial understanding, expressed *inter alia* in the confessions of the early church, various positions that were regarded as heretical were rejected.

Introductions to church history and the history of dogma give a more complete overview of the historical development in this area. Here, I mention only some of the interpretative possibilities that were rejected. These tended in various ways to be premised on the unity of God:

- *The modalists* (from the Latin *modus* = mode, manner) acknowledged both the Son and the Spirit as God, but understood them as modes in which God the Father appeared. The three are thus only different forms in which the one God appears at different stages in salvation history.

- *The adoptionists* sought to safeguard the unity of God by understanding Jesus as a human being who became in a special way a bearer of divine power. He was an ordinary human being who was "adopted" by God.

- *The Arians* (the followers of Arius) accepted that Jesus was more than an ordinary human being, and that he was God's Son even before he was born of Mary. But this pre-existence had a beginning: in other words, the Son is not coeternal with the Father. His existence presupposes an act of creation by God: he is the first of everything that God created. In this way, the Son is not one with God himself; he is an intermediary being between God and human beings.

While various versions of modalism and adoptionism had been rejected earlier on, the primary issue at the council of Nicea in 325 was the dispute with the Arians. The rejection of their understanding of God is expressed here primarily in the statement that the Son is "of one Being [Greek: *homoousios*] with the Father." It is important to note the theological arguments that were put forward in support of the two positions. The discussion concerned, not only how the individual biblical texts were to be understood, but how the totality of the biblical message was to be understood. The Arians insisted on the unity and transcendence of the Godhead. Athanasius and others argued against them that the central point was Jesus' role as savior: if he is to save us, he cannot be only a creature. He must be God himself. He also pointed out that the Arians' position entailed giving something created a position that belonged to God alone: if Jesus is not God, this means that the place he has in the church's worship is in reality idolatry.

After the council of Nicaea, a discussion arose about whether one can predicate of the Spirit what is predicated of the Son, namely, that he is of the same being as the Father. This is why the affirmation about the Spirit in the final version of the Nicene Creed, which was promulgated at the council of Constantinople in 381, is more detailed than in the version of 325. The later version says that the Spirit "proceeds from the Father" and "with the Father and the Son is worshiped and glorified."

The formulation in the Nicene Creed of the relationship between the Father and the Son is also the point of departure for the concepts that were employed in the further elaboration of Trinitarian doctrine. The concept of *being* ("of one Being with the Father") was used to denote that which the Son has *in common* with the Father. The concept of *person* was gradually introduced, to state that the Son (and the Spirit) are *distinct* from the Father. This is set out consistently in the Athanasian Creed (which has nothing to do with Athanasius, but was formulated in the western church, ca. 500), which affirms that although distinctions are drawn between the three persons (Father, Son, and Holy Spirit), the one being of God must not be divided. With this conceptual starting point, the paradoxical coexistence of the three-ness and one-ness of the Trinity is elaborated: "Thus, the Father is God; the Son is God; the Holy Spirit is God—and yet there are not three gods but one God" (Athanasian Creed 15–16). The three divine persons all share in the glory and majesty of the one God (6), and like the one God, they are uncreated, unlimited, eternal, and almighty (8–14). At the same time, the three divine persons are distinct from each other. There are thus not three fathers, three sons, or three holy spirits, but one Father, one Son, and one Holy Spirit (23).

The problem with concepts such as "being" and "person" as designations of the unity and the trinity in God is that these concepts can mean different things in different contexts. When they were first employed, they bore the mark of the meaning they had at that time, including in the philosophy of that period. And this means that the way in which we spontaneously understand these concepts today does not necessarily agree with their original use in Trinitarian doctrine.

Above all, the way the concept of *person* is understood has undergone a fundamental change, partly because of the influence of modern psychology. For us, a "person" is primarily an individual, distinct from other individuals, and this makes it misleading to take such a modern concept of person as the basis for our understanding of Trinitarian doctrine. The original meaning of the Latin concept of *persona* is a "mask." It thus refers, not to an autonomous individual, but to the various ways in which the same being appears (something that should not be interpreted in a modalist sense: see above). The original use of the concept was also complicated by the fact that the church in the East employed Greek, while the church in the West employed Latin, and there were somewhat different nuances in the Greek and Latin concepts that were chosen.

In addition to defining the relationship between the one being and the three persons in God, the Athanasian Creed also describes the specific character of the three persons. The distinction between the persons is understood on the basis of their relationship to each other. Although they are all equally eternal, the Father nevertheless has a logical priority in relation to the other two persons, who are defined on the basis of their relation to the Father: the Son as "begotten" by the Father (21), and the Spirit as "proceeding" from the Father and the Son (22). Naturally, these are not concepts that should be understood literally. When we say that the Son is "begotten" by the Father, this is primarily a way of emphasizing his origin—as Son—in the Father. This is not to be thought of as an event at one particular point in time. It is an "eternal begetting," a relationship that has no beginning, but is anchored in the eternal being of God.

We find the use of these concepts to grasp the relationship between the persons in the Trinity in the Nicene Creed too, which states that the Son is "begotten from the Father before all the ages" and that the Spirit "proceeds from the Father." This was later expanded in the Latin text to say that the Spirit "proceeds from the Father and the Son." The Eastern church has always protested against this. Since "and the Son" is *filioque* in Latin, this disagreement has often been called "the *filioque* controversy" (more on this below).

The Nicene Creed draws distinctions between the three persons not only by saying something about their reciprocal relationships (as does the Athanasian Creed), but also by saying something about their roles vis-à-vis the world. This creed has the same triadic structure as the Apostolic Creed, where God's actions in relation to creation and redemption are ascribed to the Father, the Son, and the Holy Spirit. The Father is characterized here as the Creator of heaven and earth, while the Son is the one who became a human being in Jesus Christ in order to save human beings. The Holy Spirit is the "Life-giver," *inter alia* by communicating revelation and giving people a share in salvation.

These two ways of understanding the relationships between the divine persons have often been called the relationship between the *immanent* and the *economic* Trinity—terms that are not readily comprehensible and that need some explanation. The immanent Trinity refers to God's "inner life," that is to say, the relationship between the three divine persons independently of their relation to the world. The economic Trinity (from Greek *oikonomia* = administration [of salvation]) refers to God in his relation to the world in creation and redemption.

But one should not absolutize the "distribution of roles" in the Godhead that we find in the Nicene and Apostolic Creeds. The Father is not alone in the work of creation, since all that was created came into existence through the Son: "In him all things in heaven and on earth were created" (Col 1:16; cf. John 1:3; 1 Cor 8:6). The Spirit was present at creation (Gen 1:2), and the Spirit continues to create new life: "When you send forth your Spirit, they are created; and you renew the face of the ground" (Ps 104:30). When the Son comes to the world to redeem it, this is because he is sent by the Father: "For God so loved the world that he gave his only Son" (John 3:16). When the Son became a human being in Jesus, this was mediated by the Holy Spirit (Luke 1:35). And it is through the Spirit that people receive a share in salvation, a salvation that is not the Spirit's own salvation, but the salvation that the Father accomplished when he sent the Son. One attempt to express the united action of the divine persons in every aspect of what God does in relation to the world has been attributed to Augustine: "The works of the Trinity *ad extra* are indivisible" (Latin: *opera trinitatis ad extra sunt indivisa*). Another way of expressing this (which goes back to the three Cappadocian fathers: see below) is to say that the divine persons share in each other's works.

Differences between East and West

One central question in various elaborations of Trinitarian doctrine is what constitutes the *unity* in God: What is it that unites the three persons? Theologians in East and West gave different answers to this question, thus contributing to the differences between theology in the Eastern and the Western churches. Simplifying somewhat, we can say that while the East more strongly tended to take its starting point in the three persons, the West took its starting point in the unity of the Godhead.

The formulation of Trinitarian doctrine in the East was influenced especially at the close of the fourth century, in the period after the council of Nicaea (325), by the three Cappadocian fathers, Basil of Caesarea, Gregory of Nyssa, and Gregory of Nazianzus. It was not least due to them that the Nicene understanding of the relationship between the Father and the Son gradually became dominant in the church. Their understanding of the Trinity takes its starting point in the three persons and their reciprocal relationships. They emphasize that these relationships concern not only God's activity vis-à-vis the world (the economic Trinity), but also God himself, independently of his relationship to the world (the immanent Trinity). That which unites the persons is their reciprocal relationship, and especially the Father's role as "the fountainhead of the Trinity," that is to say, as the one by whom the Son is begotten and from whom the Spirit proceeds.

In the West, Augustine played a very important role in the formulation of Trinitarian doctrine. He held that although the Trinity is a mystery that we cannot fully understand, analogies from human life can help us to draw nearer to an understanding of the relationship between one-ness and three-ness. Human love is an important analogy for Augustine. It presupposes one who loves, one who is loved, and their love itself. In this image, the Holy Spirit is compared to the love between the Father and the Son. Augustine finds in the human psyche, which consists of thought, memory, and will, another example of something that can simultaneously be one and three.

In the Western tradition after Augustine, the starting point for understanding the Trinity tends to be the one being of God, which unites the three divine persons. The Athanasian Creed is one text in which traces of this kind of understanding of Trinitarian doctrine can be seen.

Although somewhat different accounts of Trinitarian doctrine were given in the East and the West, these differences were not necessarily perceived as mutually exclusive until they were made acute by the addition of the *filioque* to the Nicene Creed. This Western addition affirmed that the Spirit proceeds from the Father *and* the Son, while the East insisted that the Spirit proceeds from the Father alone. Considerations of space make it impossible to give an exhaustive presentation of this complex question here. This disagreement was one element in the great schism between the Eastern and the Western churches in 1054, because the *filioque* had become a symbolic question, interwoven with power politics. The addition of the *filioque* in the West was motivated primarily by the confrontation with Arianism, which lasted much longer there than in the East: when the Westerners said that the Spirit also proceeds from the Son, the intention was to reject emphatically the Arians' claim that the Son is less God than the Father.

In addition to such factors, we can also see the connecting lines to what we have said above about Trinitarian doctrine in East and West. When one emphasizes as strongly as the Cappadocian fathers that the Father is the "the fountainhead of the Trinity," it is natural to mark this position by saying that the Spirit proceeds from the Father alone. When one understands the Spirit (as Augustine does) as the mutual love between the Father and the Son, it is natural to think of the Spirit as proceeding from them both.

Modern ecumenical conversations involving churches in the East (the Orthodox churches) and in the West (the Catholic Church and various Protestant churches) have concluded that the disagreement about the *filioque* is not of such a character that it must divide the churches. Both Eastern and Western churches have said that the text can be interpreted in a theologically acceptable way, whether with or without the *filioque*. At the same time, it is recognized that there are still some divergent nuances in the understanding of the Trinity. In consequence, the Nicene Creed is often used in an ecumenical context in its original form (without the *filioque*).

Trinitarian Doctrine in Recent Theology

After the disputes about the understanding of God and Trinitarian doctrine in the early church, this point of doctrine did not give rise to any large-scale theological debates for many centuries, not even in the Reformation period (with the exception of a few more extreme groups). For example, the Augsburg Confession simply bases itself on the understanding of the Trinity in the Nicene Creed and the early church (article 1), and the Catholic adversaries found nothing to criticize in this position.

Trinitarian doctrine became the object of a new and serious discussion only in the Enlightenment period in the eighteenth century, when many theologians held that Trinitarian doctrine was simply irrational and could no longer be maintained. They operated instead with a theology of God the Father in which Jesus became not much more than a unique human being. Similarly, there was little room for Trinitarian doctrine in the liberal theology of the nineteenth and early twentieth centuries. Although the churches retained it as their official teaching, and more conservative theologians defended it, it played only a limited role in theological thinking.

The twentieth century witnessed a renaissance in Trinitarian doctrine, not least thanks to the influence of Karl Barth's theology. For Barth, Trinitarian doctrine is not merely one doctrinal point among many: it is the fundamental structure in theological thinking. We see this above all in his understanding of revelation as a Trinitarian event in which the Father is the one who reveals, the Son is the revelation, and the Spirit is the presence of the revelation. In order to avoid the individualizing associations that the concept of "person" has for us today, Barth speaks of the Father, the Son, and the Spirit as three "modes of existence" of the one God.

A number of leading theologians, Orthodox, Catholic, and Protestant, have continued in the footsteps of Barth by asserting the centrality of Trinitarian doctrine. One interesting aspect is that the ecumenical rapprochement has led theologians in the Western (Catholic and Protestant) tradition to adopt elements and concerns from a more Eastern/Orthodox understanding of the Trinity.

One example of this influence is the criticism of the tendency in Western theology to make the divine "being" the starting point for the understanding of God, instead of the three persons, Father, Son, and Spirit. This means that one cannot speak about "God" independently of the understanding of God as triune, nor can one say that the one God lies behind or is antecedent to the three persons. The one God whom Christians confess is none other than the Father, the Son, and the Spirit.

The understanding of the triune God as the fellowship between the Father, the Son, and the Spirit means that God is not only the three persons, or the sum of them. Rather, God is precisely the three persons in their mutual relationship and fellowship. In himself, therefore, God is fellowship and relationship, in the mutual love between the Father, the Son, and the Spirit. It is not the case that God enters into a relationship to something only when God creates the world—God is already in himself fellowship and relationship. A Trinitarian doctrine that underlines this aspect of the understanding of God is often called "social trinitarianism."

Although fellowship and relationship characterize God even independently of the relationship to the world, the same divine love that sets its imprint on the relationship between the divine persons also sets its imprint on God's relationship to the world. Through his action as Creator and Redeemer, God brings human beings and the creation into the fellowship of love that is the life of the Trinity.

The Relationship between God in Himself and God in His Relationship to the World

The question of the relationship between God in himself (the immanent Trinity) and God in his relationship to the world (the economic Trinity) has been a central problem throughout the history of Trinitarian doctrine. Many theologians, motivated by the wish to safeguard God's freedom and otherness in relation to the world, have emphasized the difference between the immanent and the economic Trinity, arguing that one cannot necessarily draw inferences from what God does in regard to the world to how God is in himself. In more recent theology, however, there has been a greater tendency to emphasize the connection between what God does in history and what God is in himself. One expression of this tendency is what is often called "Rahner's rule," which was formulated by the Catholic theologian Karl Rahner: "The economic Trinity is the immanent Trinity, and the immanent Trinity is the economic Trinity."[2]

Rahner's point is not that there is nothing more to say about God than what he does in history, but that it is entirely the same God who is God in himself and who acts in history. This makes it pointless to engage in speculations about God's inner life independently of the world, since we know what we know about God through God's revelation and his actions in regard to the world. This also means that the God whom we encounter in salvation history is the real and true God, and the relationship between the Father, the Son, and the Spirit that comes into play in salvation history is also an expression of this relationship in God's inner life. This does not mean that there is no difference between the economic and the immanent Trinity. Nor does it mean that God is not *more* than revelation allows us to know about God. The point is not that God is not *more*, nor that the reality of the triune God remains a mystery on

---

2. Rahner, *Trinity*, 22.

its deepest level, but that God is none other than as he shows himself to be through salvation history.

The Structural Significance of the Doctrine of the Trinity

If we are to grasp the significance of Trinitarian doctrine for Christian faith and theology, it is important to realize that this is not merely one point of doctrine among many others, but that it gives its form to the structure itself. It is not by chance that classical confessions such as the Apostolic and Nicene Creeds have a triadic structure in which the various aspects of the faith are understood in the light of the Father, the Son, and the Spirit. We may borrow George Lindbeck's comparison of Christian doctrine with the rule that grammar plays in a language (see chapter 1) and say that speaking of God as triune is one of the most important elements in the formulation of the Christian faith.

This Trinitarian "grammar" leaves its imprint not only on theological discourse, but also on the language of liturgy and worship. An examination of the liturgical books in use will show the use of Trinitarian formulas and a Trinitarian structure in the language of prayer, not least in the liturgy of the eucharist.

The ideal that faith and theology should be formed by a Trinitarian pattern is not always realized so fully in practice. In some contexts, we find a rather undifferentiated language about "God" without any particular Trinitarian perspectives, and in other contexts, a one-sided concentration on Jesus or on the Spirit can lead to a one-sidedness in the image of God and in how Christianity is understood. Accordingly, the doctrine of the Trinity can serve as a crucial perspective that helps to achieve a holistic image of God and of God's dealings with the world.

3.3 WHAT IS GOD LIKE?

The answer that the Christian faith gives to the question of who God is is to point to God's self-revelation in salvation history as Father, Son, and Spirit. This revelation is also the source that permits us to say something about what God is *like*. Dogmatics has traditionally discussed this question under the heading of "the attributes of God."

The question of the attributes of God has often been discussed relatively independently of the understanding of God as triune. Instead of beginning with what the Bible says about God, the question of God's attributes has been formulated almost as a general philosophical question about what characterizes "the divine" *per se*—in contradistinction to what is not divine.

A question formulated in this more general manner is not necessarily unjustified, since if there exists a God who has created the world, it is of course perfectly acceptable to ask both what characterizes God in contradistinction to the world and what God might have in common with the world. But this becomes more problematic if general ideas, anchored in philosophy, about what characterizes the divine become determinative of the understanding of God, as has been the case in certain periods of church history. In particular, the image of the deity in ancient philosophy has played a dominant role in theology. According to such a philosophy, the divine is exalted far above the mutability and limitations of the world, and for such a line of thought, it is utterly impossible that God could suffer. Taken to its extreme conclusion, this makes the idea of the incarnation, that God became a human being in Jesus, impossible. Although (naturally enough) the church's theology has not been willing to draw this conclusion, the philosophical image of God has nevertheless been very powerful in various ways. Recent theology has made several criticisms of this inheritance, and especially of the idea that God cannot suffer.

How Is It Possible to Talk about God?

Before we go into details here, we must look more closely at the question of how it is possible *at all* to say anything about God. The problem is that, because we have no direct experience of the reality of God, we are obliged to employ words and concepts drawn from human reality. Such words and concepts are used *analogically* (from "analogy" = correspondence/similarity). In other words, there is a similarity between the human phenomena to which the words originally refers and the reality of God, while we are aware that differences also exist.

For example, when we say that "God is love," we begin with a concept that describes an interpersonal human phenomenon, and transpose it onto God. This means that there is a similarity between human and divine love, while we are fully aware that there are also differences. This becomes even clearer when we speak of God as "Father" and human beings as his "children." We do not mean that God is a father in the same sense that human fathers are the biological origin of their children. We want to affirm that some aspects of a human father/child relationship resemble the relationship God has to us, but that this latter relationship is also different.

When we thus say that God's reality "resembles" human reality, we can also turn this around and say that it is the human reality that resembles God's reality. This is the logic that underlies the affirmation in the creation narrative in Genesis that God created the human being "in his image" (1:27, see 1:26: "according to our likeness"). Words and concepts linked to phenomena in human reality can be used analogically to express something about God because God has left traces of himself both in the creation in general and in the human person in particular. This idea is expressed when Eph 3:14–15 speaks of God as "the Father, from whom every family [literally translated: fatherhood] in heaven and on earth takes its name." Here, it is not in the first place God who resembles human reality, but human reality that reflects something of God's reality.

The fact that we are dependent on the aid of concepts drawn from human reality when we speak of God entails that language about God will necessarily be *anthropomorphic*: something that is not human is described with the aid of human attributes. This is unproblematic, as long we are aware that these are anthropomorphisms, and reflect on what the use of such concepts means when we talk about God.

One example of a much-used concept to describe a Christian understanding of God is *person*. When we say that God is a person, or that we believe in a personal God, the intention is often to draw a boundary line against more impersonal understandings of God such as we find in a popular belief in destiny or in pantheistic religions. The use of the concept of person in this concept is meant to highlight the fact that God is a subject who speaks, who wills, and who acts, separate from other subjects, and that it is possible to enter into an "I–Thou" relationship with God.

At the same time, the concept of person has its limitations. A human person depends on other persons for his or her existence, and relates to other persons as one among many. God, on the other hand, is unique and does not owe his existence to anyone else. Nevertheless, God can enter into relationships with human beings that have similarities to the relationships between human persons. When we employ the concept of person about God, therefore, we must be aware of what we want to express thereby—and of what we are not saying. We must also be aware that the concept is employed rather differently (*a*) when we describe the triune God as a person and (*b*) when we distinguish between the three divine persons in the concept of Trinitarian doctrine (see above in the present chapter).

God and Gender

One question in this connection has been much discussed in recent theology, namely, the use of gender-based words and concepts to designate God. The Bible draws on masculine and feminine images and expressions to speak of God, although the masculine images predominate. God is described in masculine categories as father and king, but he can also be compared to a mother who takes care of her children (e.g., Isa 49:15; 66:13; Hos 13:8; Matt 23:37). The masculine terms are also very prominent in Trinitarian doctrine, thanks to the use of the names "Father" and "Son" for two of the persons in God.

Feminist theologians have sharply criticized this excess of masculine names for God. They have pointed out that an understanding of God as a man creates the impression that men are closer to God, and helps to justify and consolidate women's role in society as oppressed persons. To quote a well-known formulation by the feminist theologian Mary Daly, "If God is male, then the male is God."[3] This impression is strengthened by the fact that, traditionally, the ecclesiastical hierarchy has consisted

---

3. Daly, *Beyond God the Father*, 19.

only of men (as is still the case in many churches). There is, however, no consensus about how to solve this problem. For example, ought we to adjust the imbalance by speaking just as much about God in feminine terms as in masculine terms, or ought we to look for gender-neutral terms? One attempt in the latter direction is the widespread use of formulas as "in the name of the Creator, the Redeemer, and the Life giver" instead of the traditional Trinitarian formula, "the Father, the Son, and the Spirit."

In order to tackle this question appropriately, we must first point out that God in himself is exalted above human gender differences. God "is" neither man nor woman. When we employ anthropomorphic, gender-based concepts about God, we are employing them as *analogies*. God has attributes that make him resemble a father, a king, or a mother, but he is none of these in the way that human beings are fathers, kings, or mothers. The fact that the Bible uses both masculine and feminine terms shows not only that God is exalted above gender differences, but also that both genders have characteristics that can tell us something about God. Man and woman are equally created in God's image, and "resemble" God in equal measure. If we start from this insight, we must also dismiss every tendency to let masculine terms for God serve as a justification for the discrimination or oppression of women, whether in society or in the church.

The Bible also contains gender-neutral terms for God (e.g., "rock" and "shield," 2 Sam 22:3), and the concept of God does not in itself have associations in the direction of one or other gender. If the gender-based terms nevertheless dominate, this is connected with what we have said above about God as person: as persons, we human beings are always either a woman or a man. It would be much harder for the use of gender-neutral concepts about God to include this personal element, and we would easily tend towards an understanding of God as an impersonal force or something similar.

Some believe that one way to adjust the imbalance would be to use the same number of feminine and masculine terms for God, and to coin new terms if the selection in the Bible is insufficient. Why cannot one supplement the biblical divine name of "the Father" by speaking of God as "the Mother"? One argument against this is that a Christian understanding of God is indissolubly linked to one particular history and to particular historical documents. To cut loose from the use of concepts that we find here is to risk detaching the affirmations about God from this historical context. In particular, one must be very cautious about replacing a classic Trinitarian formula like "the Father, the Son, and the Spirit" with other expressions. At the same time, there are good reasons to make active use of more feminine metaphors and to avoid "gender language" about God where this is unnecessary.

We see how difficult it can be to avoid gender language about God, when we wish to speak of God with the help of personal pronouns. English translations of the Bible consistently speak of God as "he," and this practice is followed in the present book, although it is not without its problematic aspects.

Two Types of Affirmation about God

In the theological tradition from the Middle Ages onwards, it has been customary to approach the question of God's attributes in two ways, which are often combined. Both approaches draw inferences from created reality to God's reality:

- *Apophatic* affirmations about God (also known as the *via negationis*, "the path of negation") have their starting point in the limitations in the world and in human beings, and contrast or negate these: God is that which the world is *not*. While the world is finite, God is infinite; while the world is mutable, God is immutable; while the world is tied to time, God is eternal; and so on.

- *Kataphatic* affirmations about God (also known as the *via eminentiae*, "the way of eminence") have their starting point in qualities in human life and in the world that can ascribed to God to an even greater and more perfect degree. While human beings can be good, God is absolutely good; while human beings can have power, God is all-powerful; while human beings have knowledge, God is omniscient; and so on.

This tradition is expressed in article 1 in the Augsburg Confession ("On God") that professes faith in "one divine essence which is called God and is God: eternal, incorporeal, indivisible, of immeasurable power, wisdom, and goodness." When the text says that God is eternal, incorporeal, and indivisible, these are attributes that human beings do not possess. When the text says that God has power, wisdom, and goodness, these are attributes that human beings too can possess, but that God possesses to an infinitely higher degree.

God Revealed in History

As I have mentioned, ideas with their roots in ancient philosophy played an important role both in the selection and in the understanding of the attributes that have been ascribed to God in this way. At the same time, each of these has also a background in biblical descriptions of God. Recent theology has consistently been critical of the role played by philosophical inputs in the understanding of God's attributes, not least where this has led to an image of God as immovable and uninfluenced by the world and its history. Attributes such as God's omnipotence and omniscience have been interpreted as somewhat abstract realities, detached from what God *de facto* does in regard to the world. (See the discussion of the question of God's omnipotence in chapter 4.)

Instead of taking our starting point in philosophical ideas about how the divine reality "must" be, we should rather begin from how God, according to the Bible, has revealed himself in history. When the Bible tells the story of God as Creator and Redeemer, this is not something God does "in addition" to how God is "in himself," independently of his relationship to the world. On the contrary, we know God only through his relationship to the world, and it is through this relationship that his attributes become visible. On this question, therefore, we can argue in the same way as on the question of the relationship between the economic and the immanent Trinity (see above). As God is in his relationship to the world, so is God also in himself.

It is therefore natural for a Christian understanding of God to take its starting point in the image of God that is expressed in the Bible. For the Christian faith, it is the same God whom we encounter in both the Old and the New Testaments. At the same time, there are aspects of the Old Testament image of God that can look problematic from the perspective of the image of God that we find in the New Testament. This is true above all of texts where God is portrayed as petty and vengeful (2 Kgs 2:23–24), or where mass killings and genocide are seen as expressions of God's will (Deut 20:16–18; Josh 6:21). One can approach such texts in various ways. One strategy has recourse to the idea of a progressive revelation of God, that is to say, that God continually reveals more and more of himself through biblical history, until the revelation of God reaches its culmination and its end point with Jesus (cf. Heb 1:1–2). This allows us to envisage that some aspects of the earliest revelation of God will prove incomplete and misleading in the light of the later revelation.

Another way to approach this problem takes its starting point in the fact that the revelation of God is always seen through human eyes, and is therefore marked by the understanding of reality that the biblical authors share with the historical periods in which they live. Where Old Testament texts speak about God in a way that is incompatible with the image of God in the New Testament, one can see this as connected with the limited horizon of the authors. And this means that we can subject these texts to a theological critique.

No matter how we may attempt to tackle this question, it is clear that the image of God that emerges through God's revelation in Jesus is the definitive norm for a Christian image of God. The words of John 1:18 apply here: "No one has ever seen God. It is God the only Son, who is close to the Father's heart, who has made him known." This does *not* mean that the Old Testament can be dismissed as the foundation of a Christian understanding of God, as Marcion claimed in the second century: he found it unthinkable that the Redeemer God should be the same as the Creator God. In the New Testament, however, the God of the Old Testament and the Father of Jesus Christ are one and the same.

God Is Love

Among the many concepts that are employed to understand God's attributes, there is nevertheless one that is more fundamental than others for a Christian understanding of God, namely, the concept of *love*. Love is not just one of many aspects of God: it is the most basic expression of God's being. This is stated directly in the First Letter of John: "God is love" (4:8, 16).

This pointed expression is nothing other than a summary of the picture that the Bible paints of God, both in the Old Testament and in the New. We see this in God's saving deeds in relation to the people of Israel, where it is God's free love that is the reason for their liberation from Egypt (Exod 15:13, "In your steadfast love you led the people whom you redeemed"). And God's love is not reserved exclusively for the people of Israel, as we see (for example) in the promise to Abraham: "In you all the families of the earth shall be blessed" (Gen 12:3).

According to the New Testament, God's salvific action in Jesus is due to the fact that he loves, not only the people of Israel, but the whole world. This finds classic expression in John 3:16: "For God so loved the world that he gave his only Son, so that everyone who believes in him may not perish but may have eternal life."

God is love, not only in relation to the world and to human beings, but also in the relationship between the Father, the Son, and the Spirit. According to the Gospel of John, the Father loves the Son (3:35; 5:20) and the Son loves the Father (14:31). Since God is triune, love characterizes God independently of his relationship to the world. God does not begin to love only when he creates the world, and when he loves the world, he does so with the same love that characterizes the relationship between the Father, the Son, and the Spirit. The understanding of God as love is an important example of how indispensable Trinitarian doctrine is in a Christian understanding of God.

Love is, in its own way, also an anthropomorphic concept, that is to say, a concept that is drawn initially from human reality. Because we know love as a phenomenon in human life, it is meaningful to transpose the concept, in an enlarged and perfected sense, to the understanding of God. (This is thus an example of a kataphatic statement about God.) This also makes it necessary to be aware of the differences between that which is perceived as love between human beings and the divine love. In human relationships, love often contains selfish elements; one loves, not only for the sake of the other person, but also for one's own sake. Love in an erotic sense is linked to physical and emotional needs that loving helps to satisfy. Unlike human love, God's love is an unselfish and self-giving love.

While the New Testament employs a variety of Greek words to describe love and loving in human relationships, only one word is employed for God's love: *agape*. Paul gives classic expression to the content of this *agape* in 1 Corinthians 13:5, when he describes it as a love that "does not insist on its own way."

The fact that God's love is other and more perfect than human love does not, however, mean that there is any contradiction between the two, or that human love has nothing in common with divine love. On the contrary, human love for God and for other human beings is portrayed as an answer to—and an imitation of—God's love for human beings. This is a particularly important theme in the Johannine writings, which see Christian love as a result of the encounter with God's perfect love. We read, for example, in 1 John 4:7, "Love is from God; everyone who loves is born of God and knows God." The idea of analogy is turned on its head here: it is not God's love that is understood on the analogy of human love, but human love that is understood on the analogy of God's love. And this means that love is not primarily an anthropomorphic concept. Rather, true love is *theomorphic*: loving with a true love is to imitate and to be formed by the divine love.

The most fundamental affirmation about God in a Christian understanding of God is thus that God is love. This means that other definitions of God's attributes are not something *additional to* "God as love." Rather, they express various characteristics or dimensions of the loving God. And this also means that other such definitions of God help to define what it actually means to say that God is love.

God's Freedom and Faithfulness

It is particularly important to hold fast to the affirmation that "God is love" when we speak of attributes of God that can appear to be in antithesis or tension to this. One of these is God's *freedom*. That God is fundamentally free and not bound to anything outside of himself is a basic idea in the Bible; but if we take it to its extreme consequences, the idea of God's freedom could contradict God's love: if God is perfectly free, is he not also free *not* to love? One can also argue that to love is a form of binding oneself to the one whom loves, and that love therefore limits freedom.

Such an understanding of freedom is, however, not in accord with an understanding of God's freedom. God is not free to choose whether or not to love; it is precisely when he loves that he is free. Because God in his own being is love, he is himself in freedom when he loves. Accordingly, God's freedom does not entail arbitrariness, nor does it mean that God can do anything at all. What God does, he does in love and as an expression of his love. In the encounter with the world, God thereby shows that he is a merciful and gracious God.

The fact that God's freedom is not arbitrary is expressed when the concept of *faithfulness* is employed to characterize God. God is "a faithful God" (Deut 32:4) who shows "steadfast love" (Exod 20:6). His faithfulness is expressed in the Bible when God makes promises and keeps them. The Old Testament history of salvation is the history of how God makes promises and fulfills them. One fundamental promise here is made to Abraham, when God says that he will bless his descendants and, through them, the entire world (Gen 12:1–3). When he leads the people of Israel out of Egypt and into the promised land, this is understood as a fulfillment of this promise (cf., e.g., Deut 7:8: "It was because the LORD loved you and kept the oath that he swore to your ancestors, that the LORD has brought you out with a mighty hand").

The idea of God who gives promises and fulfills them is a central element, not only in the story of the liberation from Egypt, but throughout the Bible. This is why God's salvific action in Jesus is always perceived as a fulfillment of God's promises in the Old Testament (cf., e.g., Rom 1:2; 2 Cor 1:20). This, however, does not mean that all the promises are already fulfilled. It is only when God creates the world anew that all of his promises will be completely fulfilled (cf. 2 Pet 3:13: "But, in accordance with his promise, we wait for new heavens and a new earth, where righteousness is at home").

God's Wrath and Judgment

But when we say that "God is love," is there nothing more to be said? What place shall we give to the biblical idea of God's wrath, the idea that God judges? Is there not a tension between this idea and the image of God as love? Does this mean that love is only one aspect of God, while judgment and wrath are another aspect?

If we are indeed dealing with two aspects of God, we must at any rate find something that holds them together, for otherwise our image of God will disintegrate into two contradictory images. In classical Reformed theology (for example, in Calvin), the idea of God's glory provided a "hinge" of this kind. Irrespective of whether God shows grace or judges, whether he saves or rejects, this ultimately happens to the glory of God.

The idea of such a duality in the image of God is, however, neither correct nor necessary. God's love is the fundamental attribute of God, not one among many. As I have pointed out above, other attributes of God must be understood on the basis of his love, and the other attributes help to define how we understand this love. God's love, as the Bible portrays it, is neither indifferent nor indulgent; it is actively at work. Love must therefore confront all that is contrary to love, and this is why love reacts with wrath and judgment in the encounter with wickedness and sin. The intention of love's reaction is, however, that love may ultimately reach its goal. This is a fundamental motif in the Old Testament narrative, where God's judgment is never the last word, but is followed by a new beginning.

The term "God's wrath" is used in many biblical passages as a designation of God's reaction to sin and wickedness. One example is Paul's words in Romans 1:18: "For the wrath of God is revealed from heaven against all ungodliness and wickedness of those who by their wickedness suppress the truth." As a concept drawn from human life (and hence also an anthropomorphism), this carries associations that are irrelevant to the understanding of God, such as anger, fury, fickleness, and a lack of self-control. There is nothing unpredictable and fickle about God's wrath. It is a consequence of the injury done to love. It is important to emphasize that the concept of wrath does not designate an *attribute* of God. God "is" not angry, as if this were one of his attributes. The wrath is an expression of God's *reaction* to sin and evil.

Nor is this a reaction that follows "automatically," so to speak, as if God did not have power over his own anger. On the contrary, it is important for many biblical texts to affirm that God is *patient* and that he therefore *refrains* from reacting with wrath, even if he might have good reasons for doing so. He can therefore be described as "slow to anger and abounding in steadfast love" (Num 14:18), and Paul speaks of "the riches of [God's] kindness and forbearance and patience" (Rom 2:4). If he can wait before executing judgment, this is not because he does not take evil seriously, but because he wants to make it possible for people to be saved.

God as Holy

One central concept that the Bible uses to describe God is *holiness*. Unlike many other concepts that are used as designations for God, this is not an anthropomorphic concept taken from human life. It draws on universal religious ideas of the divine as something qualitatively separate from human reality, something that therefore evokes reverence and worship on the part of human beings. In the Bible, the concept of holiness is exclusively linked to God and to what in some way or other has a special relation to God. This is also why God's Spirit is called *the Holy Spirit*. In the Old Testament, in addition to God himself, it was above all the Temple, as the place of God's special presence, that was called holy, but the people of Israel too are called a holy people (Deut 7:6). In the New Testament, the idea of a holy people is transposed to the church (1 Pet 2:9) and to the individual Christian (Rom 1:7). Since God is holy, that which has a special relation to him can also be described as holy.

One special characteristic of the biblical concept of holiness (which is not always present in the history of religions in general) is its *ethical* dimension. This is expressed above all in the antithesis between holiness and sin. One important text here is the description in Isaiah 6 of the prophet's vision in the Temple. The cry of the seraphim calls God holy: "Holy, holy, holy is the LORD of hosts; the whole earth is full of his glory" (Isa 6:3). (The central importance of this text in the Christian tradition is seen for example in the inclusion in the eucharistic liturgy of the hymn of praise "Holy, holy, holy.") The prophet reacts with fear, because he knows that he has "unclean lips," that is to say, he has sinned with his words. The situation is resolved when his lips are cleansed with a live coal from the altar, and Isaiah is told that his sin is forgiven and his guilt is taken away (Isa 6:7).

God's holiness must not be understood as an attribute alongside God's love, but precisely as one aspect of love, or as one way in which love finds expression. Holiness and love are not alternative attributes of God: love is a holy love. If holiness and sin are in conflict with each other, this is precisely because sin counteracts love's good will in relation to the creation and to human life.

If, therefore, God reacts to sin with anger and wrath, this is not something that happens in contradiction of love, but is precisely an expression of God's holy love. In the judgment, God removes evil from the world, so that ultimately he can create anew a world where there is no longer any place for evil. But judgment also has a pedagogical function: by confronting us with our sin, God wants to make it possible to save us.

Law and Gospel

It has been important, particularly in Lutheran theology, to underline that God acts in relation to the world in two ways: for judgment and for salvation. This corresponds to the distinction between law and gospel (see chapter 2).

The law, as it is summed up for example in the double commandment of love (Matt 22:34–40), expresses God's will. Through the law, God demands that the human being shall do what is good, he limits the power of evil, and he accuses and judges when his will is not done.

The gospel, on the other hand, is the message of God's salvific action in Jesus. Through the gospel, God gives human beings a share in salvation and frees them from sin and from judgment.

Lutheran theology has been especially concerned to avoid mingling law and gospel together. If the gospel is mingled with the law, the radicality of the demand is lessened. If the law is mingled with the gospel, we can no longer speak of an unconditional gift on the part of God. At the same time, Lutheran theology is aware that the two acts of God belong together. Law and gospel must therefore be distinguished, but not separated from one another. These are not two juxtaposed aspects of God's activity, because the ultimate intention of what God does is salvation and new creation. This is why the law is the expression of God's "alien work" (*opus alienum*), and the gospel of God's "proper work" (*opus proprium*).[4] In both cases, the fundamental purpose is for God's love to reach its goal.

When We Do Not Understand God

Although we know that everything aims at the accomplishment of love's will, it is in practice far from easy to grasp how everything that God does, does indeed aim at this goal. Often, we simply do not see the victory of love. Many passages in the Bible describe this frustrating experience, for example in the Book of Psalms, many of which complain that God does not intervene in human distress (e.g., in Psalm 22). Another

---

4. Melanchthon in the Apology of the Augsburg Confession. Kolb and Wengert, eds., *Book of Concord*, 583.

example is Job in the Book of Job, who cannot see how the distress that strikes him is compatible with what he thought he knew about God.

One attempt to come to terms with this tension is Luther's distinction in his treatise *De servo arbitrio* ("On the Bondage of the Will") between the "hidden God" (Latin: *deus absconditus*) and the "revealed God" (*deus revelatus*). He discusses the question why some are saved, while others are not, and argues that since the human being has no possibility to do anything that influences his or her salvation in any way, it can seem that God wants some people not to be saved. Luther has no theoretical answer to this question, but he claims that we must hold fast to God as he has revealed himself in Jesus, and make no attempt to know anything about God's hidden will. Instead of speculating about things about which we can know nothing, we must hold fast to the gospel and to the cross of Christ. Although experience does not always confirm this, the believer can cling to the promise, in the belief that God keeps what he promises.

The distinction between the hidden and the revealed God does not mean that there is no connection between the two, or that we are not talking about the same God. The fact that God has revealed himself does not mean that we know everything about God. It is only in the state of fulfillment (in what Luther calls "the light of glory") that we will be able to see the pattern in everything.

For Luther, Jesus' cross is the primary locus of God's revelation. In other words, God lets himself be found in weakness and suffering, not in strength and glory. This is why Luther calls true theology the "theology of the cross" (Latin: *theologia crucis*), in contradistinction to the "theology of glory" (*theologia gloriae*). Of these two, it is only the theology of the cross that communicates the true knowledge of God. Luther thus points to an important motif in Paul, who also insists that God reveals himself through the cross in weakness and foolishness (1 Cor 1:17–31). God reveals himself precisely in the cross because God's being is love, and the cross is the expression of God's most important salvific action. This biblical understanding of God is summarized in 1 John 4:9–10: "God's love was revealed among us in this way: God sent his only Son into the world . . . to be the atoning sacrifice for our sins."

There is an undeniable tension between the idea that God reveals himself in weakness and suffering, and the image of God in Greek philosophy, which has also influenced Christian theology—for according to such a way of thinking, God is exalted far above both mutability and suffering. It can also be difficult to unite the idea of God as all-powerful (as this has often been understood) with the powerlessness that is expressed on the cross. In our own time, as I have mentioned earlier in this chapter, many theologians have attempted to understand God in a way that links God more closely to the world and to history. It is the triune God himself whom we encounter in history. This means that it is not only the human being Jesus, but also the Son, who suffers on the cross. It is precisely in this uttermost act of love that God is revealed in his own being: God is love.

Faith in God as an Existential Question

Like other theological questions, the question of how to understand God can easily be treated as a purely theoretical matter. And indeed, the relatively advanced distinctions that are a characteristic of Trinitarian doctrine and the discussion of God's attributes are an invitation to do so. At the same time, however, it is clear that the question of God both in the Bible and in the Christian tradition is first and foremost an existential question. Ultimately, it involves answering the question of where the source and the meaning of life are to be found, and where one can place one's hope for the future.

Luther summed up this aspect of the understanding of God in his Large Catechism, in his explanation of the first commandment. He begins by asking what it means to have a god, or what a god is, and his answer runs: "A 'god' is the term for that to which we are to look for all good and in which we are to find refuge in all need."[5] The Christian faith professes that the God who has revealed himself in Jesus is the source of all good, and one in whom we can find refuge. This is also why the first commandment is a fundamental principle in the Christian faith in God: "You shall have no other gods besides me" (Exod 20:3), or, in a more positive formulation: "You shall love the LORD your God with all your heart, and with all your soul, and with all your might" (Deut 6:5; cf. Matt 22:37). The God who is love waits to be loved in return, freely and not out of coercion. This is why we cannot speak of God without also speaking of the human being and of the world, just as we cannot speak of the human being and of the world in a theological context without also speaking of God.

---

5. Kolb and Wengert, eds., *Book of Concord*, 386.

4

The World, the Human Being, and Evil

4.1 GOD AND THE CREATION

IN THE PREVIOUS CHAPTER, we looked at a Christian understanding of God. In this chapter, we shall look more closely at the understanding of everything that is *not* God—what theological language calls *the world*. The most important concept that characterizes a Christian understanding of the world is that it is *created*. In other words, it is God's *creation* or *work of creation*.

For a Christian interpretation of life, faith in God as Creator means, on the one hand, that there is a fundamentally important *distinction* between God and the world: God is not the world, and the world is not God. On the other hand, belief in the Creator entails that there is a close *link* between God and the world. The very existence of the world is due to God's creative action. And this means that, for a Christian interpretation of life, how we understand the world—and the human being—is closely connected to faith in God. A Christian interpretation of life in the world means that the world is seen in the light of faith in the triune God. In this chapter, we shall explore more fully what such an understanding entails.

It is in the understanding of the relationship between God and the world that Christian faith differs from other religions and worldviews, although there are some aspects held in common. For example, Judaism and Islam too understand God as the Creator of the world and as separate from the world. Other religions can regard God or the deity as the origin of the world, but without drawing a strong distinction between the two. In pantheistic religions such as Hinduism, God and the world are identical on the deepest level. And in various nature religions, God or the gods are understood as a part of nature. In worldviews with an atheistic orientation, on the other hand, the world is understood without any relationship whatever to anything outside itself.

God, the World, and Hope

Faith in God as the Creator of the world is a central idea that permeates the Bible. This idea is elaborated not least in the Old Testament, which begins precisely with the story of how God created the world and everything that is in it (Gen 1–2). Many other texts have the character of a confession that the God who has shown himself to Israel is also the Creator of the world (see, e.g., Ps 8; 104; 136; 148; Isa 40). The New Testament presupposes the Old Testament belief in the Creator, and builds upon it (see, e.g., Acts 17:24–28). The Old Testament faith is quite simply the basis here, and it forms a background against which Jesus and his work are understood. And this means that Jesus, as the Son, is thought to have had a role also in connection with the act of creation. One example of this conviction is John 1:3, "All things came into being through him, and without him not one thing came into being" (see also Col 1:16).

The idea of the Son's role in creation points to two facts that are important for the Christian faith in the Creator. First, it entails that creation is the work of the triune God. Although creation is often ascribed to the Father, both in biblical and in confessional texts, this does not mean that the other two divine persons have no role here. In addition to the biblical passages that point to the Son's role in connection with creation, we can also read, already in the creation narrative in Genesis 1:2, that the Spirit was active at creation, and the Spirit is spoken of in other passages too as one who creates and gives life (e.g., Job 33:4; Ps 104:30; 2 Cor 3:6). This underlines an important insight in the understanding of God as triune, namely, that the divine persons work together and share in each other's activity. The world is created by the triune God, Father, Son, and Holy Spirit.

The second reality to which the Son's function in connection with creation points is the indissoluble link between creation and redemption. It is the same God who created the world and who also acts to accomplish salvation for the world in Jesus. Nor does redemption mean an abolition of what is created: on the contrary, it confirms the work of creation and brings it to fulfillment. This is why, early on in the church's history, there was a resolute opposition to currents that denied this—such as Marcion's claim that the Creator God of the Old Testament is another God than the savior God of the New Testament. The church insisted that the Creator of the world is also the Father of Jesus Christ, and rejected Marcion's proposal that the Old Testament be eliminated from the church's canon. It is precisely when the New Testament is read in the light of the Old that one holds fast to the link between belief in creation and belief in redemption.

Belief in God as Creator is clearly expressed both in the Apostolic Creed and in the Nicene Creed. This is formulated as follows in the latter text: "We believe in one God, the Father Almighty, maker of heaven and earth, of all things, seen and unseen." Article 1 of the Augsburg Confession affirms faith in the triune God as "the creator and preserver of all things, visible and invisible."

God's Continuing Creation

The formulation "creator and preserver" points to two important aspects in the understanding of the world as created by God. First of all, faith in God as Creator entails a specific understanding of the *origin* of the world. If the world exists, that is because God created it. God's creative action is thus the answer that belief in creation gives to the question of how the world came into existence.

Secondly, the Christian belief in creation also entails that God is the *preserver* of the world, that is to say, that he is responsible for its *continuing existence*. The world continues to exist because God continues to allow it to exist. God has not abandoned his work of creation to its own devices. He continues to be active in the world with his creative power. This is the point at which the Christian belief in creation sharply parts company with *deism's* understanding of God. This understanding of God was especially widespread in the Enlightenment period, when the discovery of the laws of nature easily suggested an understanding of the world as a closed system independent of divine interventions, and (to take one famous example) God could be compared to a watchmaker who had assembled the watch and then left it to tick and run by itself. In contradistinction to a deist understanding of God, the Christian belief in creation presupposes that God continues to be active in relation to the world. This means that the world we experience is not only a result of what God did once, at the beginning of the world: it is also, here and now, an expression of God's creative activity. In the theological tradition, this aspect of God's creative activity has often been called his "continuing creation" (Latin: *creatio continua*), as distinct from the "first creation" (*creatio prima*).

The Bible speaks amply of this aspect of God's creative work too. In the description of God as Creator in Psalm 104, God is not only the one who gives the world its origin, but also the one who cares for his creation every day and who continually renews life on earth. And this is why Psalm 139 understands God as also the origin of the individual human being: "You knit me together in my mother's womb" (v. 13). Jesus presupposes the same perspective when he draws on God's care for the birds of heaven and the grass in the fields to argue that God also cares for human beings (Matt 6:25–34).

We find a classic expression of the Christian belief in creation in Martin Luther's Small Catechism, when he explains the first article of faith:

> I believe that God has created me together with all that exists. God has given me and still preserves my body and soul: eyes, ears, and all limbs and senses; reason and all mental faculties. In addition, God daily and abundantly provides shoes and clothing, food and drink, house and farm, spouse and children, fields, livestock, and all property—along with all the necessities and nourishment for this body and life. God protects me against all danger and shields and preserves me from all evil. And all this is done out of pure, fatherly, and divine goodness and mercy, without any merit or worthiness of mine at

all! for all of this I owe it to God to thank and praise, serve and obey him. This is most certainly true.

The idea of God's continuing creation entails that the Christian belief in creation is not only an explanation of how the world came into existence. It is also a perspective on life here and now. Belief in God as Creator entails a specific interpretation of life: I am not the source of my own life, since this is something that is given to me as a gift. This not primarily an intellectual explanation, but rather a fundamental existential perspective that serves to shed light on existence in general, and on my place in the order of things. According to a Christian interpretation of life, not only the world as such, but also I myself and all other creatures have our origin in God's creative will. In this perspective, the fact that life is given to me as a *gift* means that it also contains a *task* in relation to God, to other people, and to myself.

The Relationship between God and the World

The idea that God not only sat the world in motion, but continues to have a relationship to it, raises the question of how we understand the relationship between God and the world. Although God acts in relation to the world and in the world, he is nevertheless distinct from the world. The world is not a part of God himself (as various versions of pantheism assume), nor is it something that exists independently of God. The concept of "creation out of nothing" (Latin: *creatio ex nihilo*) is often employed to reject the idea that the world has its origin in something other than God. This expression, which comes from 2 Maccabees 7:28, played an important role for theologians of the early church (such as Theophilus of Antioch) in their combat against Greek ideas of a primal matter that God used as raw material for the creation. They countered these ideas by emphasizing that only God has existence in himself and is eternal, whereas the world is not eternal, and does not have existence in itself.

The Bible does not give us an "explanation" of how God created the world. The fact that God *wanted* the world to exist is a sufficient condition for its coming into being (see Rev 4:11). The creation narrative in Genesis 1 expresses this by means of the idea that the world came into being through God's *word*: "Then God said, 'Let there be light'; and there was light" (1:3). Psalm 33:9 expresses the same idea: "For he spoke, and it came to be; he commanded, and it stood firm."

The fact that God creates through his *word* expresses an important aspect of God's relationship to the world, namely, that God *addresses* it. When God creates the world, his intention is to have a *relationship* to it. This is why God's address prompts an answer from that which is created—an answer that the Bible describes as the creation's praise of its Creator. For example, Psalm 148 calls on mountains and hills, fire and hail, snow and frost to join with animals and human beings in praising God. In this perspective, human beings stand in a special position in the work of creation, because they are able—in a manner different from the rest of creation—to understand the content of God's address, and they themselves are able to answer, to turn to God in addressing him and praying. But although human beings, as persons who speak and think, have a special relationship to God, this must not be understood independently of the relationship between God and the rest of creation. It is as a created being, and as a part of that which is created, that the human being has a relationship to the Creator. (I shall return to this in greater detail in the present chapter, below.)

In their work on the understanding of Trinitarian doctrine in our time, some theologians have seen a connection between God's relationship to the world and the relationships that characterize the triune God himself, in the mutual love between the Father, the Son, and the Spirit. It is not only when the world comes into existence that God is in a relationship to something, since he is already relational in his own being. Nor is the case that it is only in his relationship to the world that God expresses who he is. God is relational, and it is *love* that characterizes the relationships in God. Because God is love, his relationship to the world is characterized by love, and his goal in the work of creation is to let the creation participate in the fellowship between the Father, the Son, and the Spirit.

Since God is perfect in himself, he does not "need" the creation. In a Christian perspective, it may be possible to conceive of God without the world, but not of the world without God. God did not create the world out of necessity, but out of his own free love. Since the world is a result of God's free love, it has no other goal or meaning than to exist and to receive God's love and goodness—and thereby to bear witness to its Creator.

God and the Freedom of the World

If the world came into being as a result of God's will, this means that it is continuously willed by God. If God did not maintain the world in existence, it would cease to exist. It is God who gives life and existence to everything and to everyone. In the Nicene Creed, God is spoken of as "Almighty," and this means that all that is created depends on God, and is nothing without God. This does not, however, entail that God determines everything that happens, for that would mean that the world was a machine where everything was controlled from the outside. By making the world something other than his own self, God has also given the world a certain freedom—and since true love presupposes freedom, this freedom is also essential, if the relationship between God and that which is created is to be understood as a relationship of love. However, the world's freedom is not an unlimited freedom, but comes into play within limits that God has set. Accordingly, the *existence* of the world is exclusively a result of God's will, but what *happens* in the world is not exclusively an expression of God's will.

The concept of freedom is much discussed within theology, philosophy, and the natural sciences. One possible position is *determinism*, which claims that everything that happens is determined beforehand, and that the agents' subjective experience of having a choice is merely an illusion. Determinism has tended to find support in a mechanistic understanding of the principle of cause and effect: since everything is an effect of one particular cause, everything is in principle determined beforehand. In a scientific perspective, this has been seen as an expression of the *laws of nature*.

Scientific research in our time has a more nuanced understanding of the laws of nature. Although they represent the framework for everything that happens, not every cause necessarily has the same effect, and this means that *randomness* is a factor in existence. This is a particularly important insight from quantum physics. We can express it in more active terms by saying that *spontaneity* is a factor that means that not everything is predetermined. In theological language, this randomness and spontaneity can be understood as an expression of the freedom that God has bestowed on the creation. This does not mean that everything that happens, happens in complete freedom. It means that it happens within a certain range of possibilities. This means that human beings have the genuine possibility of forming their own lives, even if much is already determined by the history and the context of which they are a part. In a Christian perspective, the fact that human beings' choices are significant both for their own lives and for those of others is an important presupposition, if one is truly to bear *responsibility*. And since freedom is given by God, this responsibility is ultimately a responsibility vis-à-vis God.

The way in which determinism and freedom are understood has also consequences for the way in which one can understand God's possibilities of action with and in the world. According to the biblical narrative, God intervenes in various ways in the development of the world and of the human race. In a closed, mechanistic worldview in which everything is determined by cause and effect, such an idea of God's action in the world becomes problematic. At most, God's role can be understood as that of setting everything in motion: as the "first cause," God establishes the premises for what happens in the ensuing process, but he does not intervene *en route*. (See my remarks about a deistic understanding of God, above.)

In order to "salvage" the idea of God's intervention in history, which is so central in the Bible, appeal has often been made to miracles and to the supernatural as an explanatory model. This means that when God acts, he makes an "exception" to the laws of nature and to the usual link between cause and effect. One variant of such an idea ascribes to God everything that science is unable to explain: that for which there is no natural explanation must be caused by God. This "God of the gaps" strategy has become more and more problematic, as science has gradually learned how to explain larger and larger parts of reality. The advances in medical knowledge of the processes in the human body mean that in many cases, there will be a natural explanation for a healing that was regarded in the past as an expression of God's intervention. And the development of modern meteorology means that it is no longer necessary to make God responsible for good or bad weather.

The space available for the supernatural has become smaller; but this is not the only reason why an understanding of God that makes him a "supernatural" cause alongside the "natural" causes is problematic. There are theological reasons that make it problematic to understand God as one factor among many in the world. As its Creator, God is not a part of the world. As I have already pointed out, his creative working is not limited to giving the world its beginning: he also maintains it in existence. And this in turn is not limited to simply giving the world a continued existence: God's maintenance also means that he works in and through what happens in the world. This is why—without understanding God as a part of nature—Jesus can understand God as the one who ensures that the birds get what they need to live: "Look at the birds of the air; they neither sow nor reap nor gather into barns, and yet your heavenly Father feeds them" (Matt 6:26). In many Old Testament passages, God is understood as the one who stands behind historical events and processes, such as the liberation of the people of Israel from slavery in Egypt, as this is described in the Book of Exodus (cf. also Ps 135 and 136).

The Possibility of Miracles

While God's action in relation to the world mostly happens in and through perfectly ordinary events and processes, these can also take the form of unique events that break with normal expectations. The Gospels relate that Jesus performed many actions of this kind, which are often called "signs" or "wonders." These include healing the sick (for example, Mark 1:40–42; 2:1–12). On a number of occasions, he also raised the dead to life (Mark 5:35–43; Luke 7:11–17; John 11:38–44) and caused other things to happen that do not usually occur, such as turning water into wine (John 2:1–11), walking on the water (Matt 14:22–33), and satisfying the hunger of many thousands of persons with a small quantity of food (Matt 14:13–21). We read in the Acts of the Apostles that the first Christians too performed wonders and signs in the name of Jesus (Acts 2:43).

The point in such narratives is not the miraculous element *per se* in the events, but their character as a *sign*. In other words, they point beyond themselves to the God who is at work in Jesus and in his disciples. They point both to God's power (because he can do things that usually do not occur) and to his good will (because people get their life and health back).

Although the historical basis for some of the miracle stories in the Bible may be uncertain, there is no reason, within the framework of a Christian interpretation of life, to deny either that Jesus performed miracles or that similar things can occur today. Christians can indeed bear witness to experiences of God intervening in a surprising or wonderful manner. But while we maintain the possibility of miracles, it is important not to make the miraculous or the supernatural the most important thing. The essential question is not the extent to which an event has or has not a "natural explanation." Besides this, it is important not to limit God's action in the world to the miraculous. Although nothing is impossible for God, he is active primarily through the ordinary processes in the world.

In traditional Christian vocabulary, God's activity through natural and historical processes is called God's *providence* (Latin: *providentia*). This concept must not be confused with the idea of a fate in which everything is predetermined, because God's providence does not entail an anterior determination of everything that happens. In other words, it does not abolish the fundamental freedom of the creation. Although everything is dependent on God, not everything is determined by him. Rather, God works together with the natural and historical processes; he leads without coercing. Although that which happens is not predetermined, God works in the world in view of one specific goal, namely, salvation and the eternal kingdom of God.

Communication between the Human Person and God: Prayer

In relation to the human person, as a being endowed with consciousness, this means that God also works by means of self-communication. I have spoken of this in chapter 2 as *revelation*, both in the sense of the general revelation in the creation and of the revelation by means of salvation history. In order to attain the goal that he has for the world, God seeks the human person as his collaborator.

The relationship between God and the human person does not only take the form of God's address to the human being. It also takes the form of the human being's address to God. It is probable that the desire to call on something divine that is greater than oneself, and something that in some way or other is behind that which happens, has followed humankind throughout the whole of our history. The Christian faith, makes it clear that the real addressee of such prayers is the Father of Jesus Christ, the Creator of heaven and earth.

In a Christian interpretation of life, prayer is one of the fundamental expressions of the human person's relationship to God. One important aspect of prayer is to praise and thank God for who he is and for what he has done. Praise of what God has done in nature, and of what he does in the course of history, is an important theme not least in the Old Testament; Psalm 136, which combines these two aspects of God's working, is a good example of this. But prayer can also take the form of an address to God that asks for the satisfaction of various needs, or for help in problematic matters, for oneself or for others. For example, the Lord's Prayer contains a request for the satisfaction of fundamental needs: "Give us this day our daily bread" (Matt 6:11). When one prays, one does so in the expectation that the prayer will be heard, and this is why we read, a little further on in the Sermon on the Mount: "Ask, and it will be given you" (Matt 7:7; cf. John 14:14; 15:7).

But prayer can also take the form of a lamentation, when one brings one's distress to God (Ps 6), or of a meditation, when one reflects on what God has done (Ps 1:2; Luke 2:19).

It is difficult to reconcile the idea that it is useful to pray to God for something, with a mechanistic worldview in which everything is determined by the law of cause and effect. If one understands the world in this way, the only place one can find for the answering of prayer is to categorize it as something miraculous and supernatural, as something that breaks with the natural order of things. It is also difficult to find a place for the answering of prayer if one sees God's providence as a fate where everything is determined beforehand.

In the Christian understanding, therefore, the answering of prayer presupposes the idea of the world's freedom. There is a space where things are not predetermined, and where God can realize his will. The answering of prayer also presupposes the idea of *God's* freedom. God is free to act as he himself wills, and prayer, in the Christian understanding, has no guarantee that it will be heard (or at any rate, not as the one who prays envisages this). The one who prays aligns himself or herself with God in the work of realizing God's intention with the world, and this means that prayer has an effect not only on the one to whom it is addressed, but also on the one who prays. When we pray the third petition in the Lord's Prayer, "Your will be done, on earth as it is in heaven" (Matt 6:10), we are also asking that we ourselves may be formed by this will.

The World as Finite

The fact that the world is created by a Creator who himself is not created means that the world, unlike God, is *finite*. In a Christian understanding of the world, this means *inter alia* that the world has a beginning and an end. This is expressed in the biblical creation narrative when the creation is described as something that happened "in the beginning" (Gen 1:1). This beginning is, of course, not God's beginning, but the world's. The fact that the world has a beginning means that it is subordinate to time: that which has already happened remains past, while that which has not yet happened is future, and is inaccessible to us. When all the future has become past, that which the Bible calls "the end of the age" (Matt 13:49) has come. (For more on this subject, see chapter 9 below.) This also means that time, as we know it, is a part of the created order.

In order to describe the difference between a world that is subordinate to time and the world's Creator, who is free from such a bond, the biblical vocabulary applies the word *eternal* to the things of God. It is important to note that "eternity" here does not designate an infinite quantity of time. Nor does it designate a lack of time, a kind of state in which nothing happens. The eternal must be understood as a qualitatively different reality that is not subordinate to the transience that time entails. "Eternal" is thus first and foremost a description of God himself. He is the one who has always been and always will be, the one who works in time but is not bound by time's transience. For him, both past and future are present.

The fact that the world has an end does not mean that it will cease to exist. On the contrary, the end of the world means that it will be created anew, when created things receive a share in God's eternity. And this is why the life that belongs to the world to come is called "eternal life" (Mark 10:30, John 3:15–16, and many other passages).

In the Synoptic Gospels, the future reality that will be created anew is called "the kingdom of God," where God rules and is king. Through Jesus, this reality has drawn near in a special way (cf., for example, Mark 1:15). This does not mean that God becomes king or lord only when the world is created anew. The Bible sees God as already king and ruler of the world, since he is the one who creates it and maintains it in being. Psalm 47:8 says: "God is king over the nations," and this title is confirmed and reinforced by texts such as 1 Timothy 6:15, where God is called "the King of kings and Lord of lords." The fact that God is king does not mean that absolutely everything he wills takes place, but that he continuously seeks to realize his will, without abolishing the freedom of the world. This activity of God has a special goal: the new creation of the world and God's eternal kingdom, when God will be "all in all" (1 Cor 15:28).

The creation of the world anew is the subject of chapter 9, but it must be mentioned here, because it shows that God's work of creation has a *goal*, and this work must be understood in the light of this goal. The new creation can be understood only in the light of the creation, and in exactly the same way, the creation must be understood in the light of the new creation.

Belief in the Creator and the Natural Sciences

In our own time, belief in the Creator has been challenged by scientific knowledge about how the world came into being. This applies not least to the theory of evolution, which was proposed by Charles Darwin in 1859.

The theory of evolution posed a challenge in at least two ways. First of all, it is incompatible with a literal reading of the creation narratives in Genesis, which relate how the earth, with animals, plants, and human beings, was created over a six-day period. The theory of evolution presupposes instead that life on the earth came into being in the course of billions of years, in which the first primordial cell developed into more and more advanced life forms, including the human being, whereas a literal reading of the times given in Genesis entails that the earth with the life on it was created around six thousand years ago. This dating of the beginning of the earth is made impossible, not only by the theory of evolution, but also by modern geology, which assumes that the earth is around 4.5 billion years old.

The question of the age of the earth and of life is problematic first and foremost with regard to the understanding of the Bible; the second problem has a more direct significance for belief in God as Creator. While a literal reading of the creation narrative entails that every species is a result of a direct divine intervention, the origin of species is explained as a natural development from other life forms (cf. the title of Darwin's 1859 book: *On the Origin of Species by Means of Natural Selection*). In other words, the theory of evolution made it possible to explain the state of the world without needing to posit a series of divine interventions. In such a perspective, the only place that might possibly be left for God would be as the one who sets everything in motion. The theory of evolution also meant that it was no longer possible to regard human beings as absolutely unique in relation to the animals, since it was from animals that they developed. (I return to this subject in the next subchapter.)

For some Christian groups, this conflict between a literal reading of the creation narrative and the theory of evolution is so serious that they believe the latter must be mistaken. This position is often called *creationism*, and is especially widespread in the United States. There are several variants of creationism, but most of them attempt to give an alternative account of how the world came into being, arguing that the existence of the various species is due to God's direct intervention. Many also defend the traditional dating of the creation to about six thousand years ago.

The creationists appeal to scientific arguments in support of their position. Although such an argumentation finds little support in established research milieus, a discussion of the content and tenability of the theory of evolution is, of course, fully legitimate. In any case, the concrete elaboration of this theory has changed since Darwin's time, and many elements are still a matter of debate. This discussion, however, lies outside the scope of the present book.

From a theological perspective, it is highly problematic to use belief in God as Creator as an argument for or against particular theories of the natural sciences about how the world and life came into being. First of all, the Christian faith has no reason to lay down boundaries for scientific research or for scientific findings. Since the world is created by God, there ought not to be any fundamental contradiction between scientific research into this world and the Christian faith in God. Secondly, the attempt to justify one particular view of how the world came to be builds on an erroneous reading of the creation narratives, which are certainly not meant as historical accounts. Rather, they are metaphorical narratives that communicate fundamental theological points.

This means that the Christian belief in the Creator does not depend on any particular scientific theory about how the world came into existence. There is no conflict of any kind between the theory of evolution—which understands that life on earth has emerged through a process of development—and belief in God as Creator. As I have pointed out above, God's activity in relation to the world and in the world is not restricted to a miraculous intervention, but takes place through natural processes. Evolution is therefore not an alternative to the belief that God created life in the world, but rather an answer to the question *how* he created it. On the basis of the idea of God's providence, this also means that God has guided the development in one particular direction. Although the development of the human being took place as a result of natural evolutionary processes, it must be understood, in the perspective of belief in creation, as an expression of God's intention for the work of creation.

Although the theory of evolution is not in conflict with the Christian belief in the Creator, this does not mean that every use or interpretation of this theory is equally unproblematic. This is the case when new atheists like Richard Dawkins present evolution as an alternative to belief in the Creator, or when naturalists employ our relatedness to animals as an argument against the special position of human beings. In neither instance is there a contradiction between faith and science; rather, there are different interpretations of life that make an appeal to science. The Christian belief in the Creator cannot resolve this challenge by distancing itself from science. It must instead demonstrate how scientific knowledge can be understood within a Christian interpretation of life, a challenge that includes evolutionary theory.

Heaven and Earth

The natural sciences give us knowledge of God's work of creation, but this does not exclude the possibility that the creation itself can have aspects that are not accessible to empirical science. This topic is relevant not only to a Christian interpretation of life, but to other interpretations too. In our own time, this has found expression in an interest in angels and in other forms of "spiritual" reality. The Christian faith is not unfamiliar with the idea that reality can also have such dimensions, and this is what the Nicene Creed expresses, when it affirms that God is the "maker of heaven and earth, of all things, seen and unseen."

The reference to "heaven" here is to what the Bible envisages as the place of God's throne (for example, in Psalm 11:4, "The LORD's throne is in heaven," or in the introduction to the Lord's Prayer in Matthew 6:9, "Our Father in heaven"). The word "heaven" also refers in the Bible to the vault above the earth (for example, in Genesis 1:8), and people in biblical times no doubt thought that God's throne was localized "up there." But while modern knowledge of the universe naturally makes such a localization meaningless, this does not undermine "heaven" as a theological concept.

Theologically speaking, the concept of heaven is meant to hold fast to the idea of God's transcendence, the idea that God himself is not a part of the world. This is the point in Psalm 115, where faith in a heavenly God is contrasted with faith in idols made by human hands. Unlike the earth, heaven is the place where God's will is always done. This is why the Lord's Prayer asks: "Your will be done, on earth as it is in heaven" (Matt 6:10).

Although heaven is in a special way the place of God's presence, heaven too belongs to created reality. This means that God is not bound or restricted to heaven (cf. 1 Kgs 8:27, "Even heaven and the highest heavens cannot contain you!").

The Angels

The beings that, according to the Bible, are linked to heavenly reality are likewise created. This applies first of all to the *angels* (whom some biblical passages also call cherubim or seraphim). Angels have two basic functions. First, they are continuously active in praising God (see, for example, Isa 6:1–4 and Rev 7:11–12). Secondly, they have the role of God's emissaries to the world, either to carry out a specific task or to deliver a message. In the narrative of Jesus' birth in Luke's Gospel, it is the angel Gabriel who tells Mary that she is to be the mother of Jesus (1:26–38). Later on in the same narrative, an angel proclaims the birth of Jesus to the shepherds, while a heavenly host praises God (Luke 2:9–14).

Throughout the church's history, there have been different ideas about the angels' appearance and about their functions, often with varying measures of support in the Bible itself. The idea that God has heavenly emissaries in his service has also a legitimate place in a Christian interpretation of life today, although one need not adopt all the ideas that have so often been linked to belief in angels. It is also important to draw a distinction between a Christian belief in angels and the image of angels we encounter in many new religious movements.

There are two important points here. First of all, in a Christian context, angels do not act autonomously or with an agenda of their own. They always act on behalf of God and as his emissaries. This also means that the angels are not at the disposal of human beings' wishes or orders.

Secondly, it is important to underline that although angels act on behalf of God, they are God's creatures and must not be confused with God himself. There is a powerful expression of this principle in the book of Revelation, when John falls down at the feet of an angel and wants to adore him. The angel replies: "You must not do that! I am a fellow servant with you and your brothers and sisters who hold the testimony of Jesus. Worship God!" (Rev 19:10*).

As long as the belief in angels helps to strength trust in God and adoration of God, it can play an important role in Christian faith. But a belief in angels in which they themselves become the most important thing, drawing attention away from God, is problematic for a Christian interpretation of life.

4.2 THE HUMAN BEING—CREATED FOR FELLOWSHIP WITH GOD

Most interpretations of life include not only questions about the world and reality as such, but also about the human being's place in it. Are we merely a chance part of life on earth, or have we been given one particular place or task? A purely naturalistic understanding of reality is unwilling to see any fundamental difference between human beings and other animal life, but most religious interpretations of life are willing to ascribe to the human being a special position, in some form or other.

In a Christian interpretation of life, the human being occupies a special position as the crowning point of God's work of creation, as we see clearly in the first creation narrative in Genesis 1:1—2:3, where the work of creation reaches its culmination through the creation of the human being on the sixth day. In this narrative, there are two factors that distinguish the human being from the rest of the creation. First, he or she has a special relationship to God: the text says that God creates the human being "in his image" (Gen 1:27—we shall return below to the meaning of this passage), and God also speaks directly to the human being. Secondly, the content of what God says to the human being shows that he or she occupies a special place in the work of creation: "Be fruitful and multiply, and fill the earth and subdue it; and have dominion over the fish of the sea and over the birds of the air and over every living thing that moves upon the earth" (Gen 1:28). The human being thus has a leading role in the creation.

The second creation narrative (Gen 2:4–25) also emphasizes that the human being belongs to the rest of the creation, but that he or she has a special position. Here we are told how God forms the human being of the dust and breathes the breath into him: "Then the LORD God formed man from the dust of the ground, and breathed into his nostrils the breath of life; and the man became a living being" (Gen 2:7). The original text employs a play on words to underline that the human being belongs to the earth: "earth" in Hebrew is *adamah*, while "human being" is *adam*. In this narrative too, God addresses the human being, whose special position in relation to the animals is expressed in the fact that it is he who gives them names (Gen 2:19–20).

Both creation narratives emphasize that the human being exists in two genders, as man and as woman. This is linked in the first creation narrative primarily to procreation and fruitfulness (Gen 1:27–28), while the emphasis in the second narrative lies on the fellowship between the two: since it was not good for the man to be alone, God created the woman, so that the two might stay together (Gen 2:18, 21–24). In all their simplicity, the creation narratives raise the fundamental questions in a Christian anthropology. We shall look at these in turn.

Made in the Likeness of God

Both the creation narratives and the rest of the Bible presuppose that there is a special relationship between God and the human being. In the Christian tradition, the affirmation in the creation narrative (Gen 1:26–27) that God created the human being "in his image" has played an important role here. Many interpretations of what "God's image" (Latin: *imago dei*) actually entails have been proposed over the course of time. The context in the text indicates that being in the image of God is something that places the human being in a special position vis-à-vis God. But what is this special position?

Many biblical scholars hold that this expression refers primarily to the human being's role as God's representative in relation to the rest of the creation, since it is employed precisely in a context in which God gives the human being the right to rule over the earth and the animals (Gen 1:28). This interpretation is, however, not undisputed. In any case, the meaning of the expression cannot be restricted to an original historical meaning, since it has been filled with theological content both in other passages in the Bible and in the ecclesial and theological history of interpretation. There is therefore no great point in seeking to define it with great precision. The concept functions primarily as a collective concept covering various aspects of the human being's relationship to God and his or her special position in the creation.

One widespread interpretation in the early church and the middle ages understood being in God's image as an expression for the human reason or soul. Luther saw being in God's image as identical with the original righteousness before God, which the human being lost through the fall. In modern theology the being in God's image has often been understood as the human being's special *relationship to God.* Among all created things, it is only the human being that God addresses. It is only to him or her that God speaks, and it is only the human being who addresses God in prayer and adoration.

One question that has been much discussed is the consequences that sin has for the human being as the image of God. One common answer distinguishes various aspects of the image of God, only some of which remain intact. For example, Emil Brunner draws a distinction between the formal image of God, which includes the human being's reason, and the material image of God, which presupposes fellowship with God. Others affirm that the image of God was completely lost through the fall, and that it can be regained only through salvation in Jesus Christ. When, for example, Luther identifies the image of God with the human being's righteousness before God, it is difficult to think that he is speaking of something that is still intact after the fall. Nor would Karl Barth accept that the sinful human being remains the image of God.

The answer one gives to this question depends in part on how one understands the concept of the image of God, and in part on the general theological understanding of the consequences of sin. There is nothing in the use of this concept in the Bible to indicate that it refers, not to those of whom it is speaking in the present day, but exclusively to the human being in some remote primal state. Genesis 9:6 argues that it is wrong to take a human life because humans are made in the image of God. We find a similar idea in the New Testament, in James 3:9: since the human being is the image of God, praise of God is incompatible with cursing human beings.

At the same time, however, the New Testament can regard the human person's image of God as *imperfect.* This is expressed not least when it calls Jesus the "image of God" (2 Cor 4:4; Col 1:15; Heb 1:3) and states that Christians are to be conformed to him (Rom 8:29; Eph 4:24; Col 3:10). Such texts also say something about a subject to which we shall return below, namely the relationship between creation and salvation.

Salvation is not a replacement of what has been lost, but its renewal and perfecting. This allows us to understand salvation as a renewal and realization of the image of God that every human person possesses in virtue of being created.

Human Dignity

One consequence of the fact that we are created in God's image is the unique *dignity* this entails—not only for the human race as such, but also for each individual. According to Genesis 9:1–7, both animals and human beings will be held to account if they take a human life, because "in his own image God made humankind" (9:6). This text emphasizes the difference between humans and animals: one is permitted to kill animals in order to eat them, but it is forbidden to kill a human being.

Since all human beings are created in the image of God, it is not permissible to draw a boundary for human dignity. This does not depend on particular qualities or skills, nor on whether one belongs to one particular social or ethnic group. Human dignity is not based on anything that the human being *does*, but on what the human being *is*. Since the human being is in the image of God, he or she shares in an inviolable dignity simply in virtue of being human. Human dignity also applies to human life at the fetus stage, to infants, to the mentally disabled, and to those in the last stages of life. This is why the Christian tradition has opposed actions such as abortion, infanticide, and euthanasia, and it has provided an impulse to care for those who cannot take care of themselves, in children's homes and in hospitals, or in helping the poor.

Where human dignity has not been acknowledged, this has often been a consequence of regarding those who belong to other groups as of less value than one's own group. This is an important element in all forms of racism, such as that which propelled the Nazis' genocide of the Jews. It is also easy to think that one's ethical obligations reach no further than those who belong to one's own group. Jesus' reply to the question: "Who is my neighbor?" is an important corrective to such a way of thinking. When he was asked how far the double commandment of love—which enjoins one to love's one neighbor as oneself—applied, he told the story of the Good Samaritan to show that this obligation shatters all the boundaries that separate persons. Every other human being has a right to respect and care (Luke 10:25–37). A similar point is made by his injunction that one should love, not only one's friends, but also one's enemies (Matt 5:43–48).

Despite these lofty ideals, the church and Christians have not always respected human dignity in practice; and the Christian faith has sometimes been used as an argument to justify discrimination, exclusion, and treating people differently. For example, the attempt was made to provide a theological justification for the racist apartheid ideology in South Africa. And Christians have regarded those with a different faith (for example, Jews), as inferior. The idea of all human beings' dignity, rooted in the fact that we are all created in God's image, is an important part of the church's message in the world, but it must also be a continuous source of ecclesial self-criticism.

Society and Gender as Constitutive of the Human Being

One fundamental point in a Christian anthropology is that the human being is created to live in fellowship with others. This, of course, is not a specifically Christian insight—the human person is a social being. In purely biological terms, we are dependent on other human beings, if we are to come into the world, and we are dependent on other human beings, if we are to grow up. Even as adults, we are dependent on other persons, for both practical and psychological reasons. This applies both in close relationships and in the larger societal structures in which we live. It is above all the social sciences that seek to describe human persons as social beings in all their complexity.

In this context, the contribution of a Christian anthropology is a resounding affirmation that God's fundamental will is that human life should be a life in fellowship. The human being is created for fellowship, both in close relationships and in society. In addition, the idea of human fellowship as something willed by God is not only a confirmation of the fellowships that exist at every moment in time: it is also a normative starting point.

The idea that the human being is created for fellowship is a corrective to a one-sided *individualism* where one either lives in isolation from others or else uses the fellowship to gain advantages for oneself. Against an individualism of this kind, a Christian anthropology affirms that human life is lived best in fellowship with others, and that we belong to a fellowship not only for our own sake, but also for the sake of others. The individual belongs to the fellowship not only in order to receive, but also in order to give and to contribute.

At the same time, a Christian anthropology opposes a one-sided *collectivism* where the individual's needs are completely subordinated to the needs of the fellowship (whether the family or the state). This kind of collectivism goes against the idea of the unique dignity of each individual human being. This value is not something bestowed only through membership in a fellowship, but something that is given in virtue of being a human being, created in the image of God. The philosopher Immanuel Kant expressed a basic Christian insight when he said that one must never treat a human being as merely a means: a human being is always also an end *per se*.

The human being's need of fellowship is already expressed in the creation narrative in Genesis 2, when God says: "It is not good that the man should be alone; I will make him a helper as his partner" (2:18). He then creates the animals and leads them to the man, but none of them can function as his partner. This is why God creates the woman out of the man's rib and leads her to the man—this time with greater success. The narrative closes with a declaration that the two are to be together and to be "one flesh" (2:24). This must be understood as referring not only to sexual union, but to the close personal fellowship between the two.

In the Christian tradition, statements like this have been understood to mean that marriage between man and woman is established by God. This view also finds support in Matthew 19:4–6, where Jesus quotes the words from Genesis 2 and affirms that it is God who brings together man and woman in marriage. Marriage is important, not only with regard to the fellowship between the two partners, but also with regard to them as parents, and this is why Christian thinking sees the family as a fundamental institution. Its importance is also expressed in the strong moral and legal regulations that have governed marriage and sexuality, as we see in the sixth of the Ten Commandments: "You shall not commit adultery" (Exod 20:14). The fourth Commandment indicates not only that the family presupposes that the parents have obligations to the children, but that the responsibility also applies in the opposite direction: "Honor your father and your mother" (Exod 20:12). Although polygamy was known—and accepted—in the Old Testament, the New Testament assumes that marriage is a relationship between only two persons, and this has been the dominant position in the Christian tradition.

In recent years, a traditional Christian understanding of marriage and the family, and a corresponding negative evaluation of homosexual relations (based *inter alia* on biblical passages such as Romans 1:26–27 and 1 Corinthians 6:9–10), have been challenged by a growing acceptance of partnerships between persons of the same gender, and by changes in the marriage laws in several countries that have made marriage gender-neutral. The question of the position that Christian churches should take on this development has created huge controversies in many churches. It is not possible, within the scope of the present book, to discuss this question in detail, but it is worth pointing out that it raises a number of important problems both with regard to our understanding of the Christian theology of creation and of anthropology, and with regard to the interpretation and application of biblical texts in questions of this kind.

Another controversial question is how Christian theology should understand the relationship between the sexes, when we consider gender roles and equality. In many instances, biblical texts have been employed to legitimate traditional gender roles and a subordinate position for women in the family and in society; this applies not least to the so-called household codes (Eph 5:21—6:9; Col 3:18—4:1; 1 Pet 3:1–7). There can, however, be no doubt that the Bible assumes a basic *equality* between man and woman, not least because both are created in the image of God (Gen 1:27), and because they are equal in the context of salvation (Gal 3:28). This means that we have good reasons to affirm that modern ideals of equality is not in conflict with a Christian anthropology. On the contrary, such ideals can find justification and motivation precisely here.

Marriage has been understood in the Christian tradition as divinely willed, but this does not mean that single persons lead a less whole human life. Jesus himself never married, and Paul even recommends the unmarried life (1 Cor 7:32–35). In varying degrees, the Christian tradition has regarded celibacy both as a possibility and as an ideal.

The human need for fellowship concerns not only the close relationships in the family, but also the larger fellowship in society. Paul's description of the governing powers as "God's servant" (Rom 13:1–7) is one of the starting points for the generally positive view Christian theology has taken of the necessity of political authorities, independently of whether or not the rulers themselves are Christians. At the same time, theologians have envisaged the possibility that the authorities can also behave in ways that violate human dignity and God's good will for his creation.

The idea that all human beings share the same origin in God's creative act, and that all are in the image of God, also excludes every notion that some people—whether individuals or groups—possess a greater dignity than others. The human fellowship is not limited to the immediate or extended family, to one people or nation. Ultimately, it includes the whole of humankind. The Christian message speaks of a God who has created all human beings and who wants to save them all. Accordingly, no one is entitled to treat another person as an irrelevance. We see this in Jesus' parable of the Good Samaritan, where it is the foreigner who treats another person as his "neighbor" (Luke 10:25–36).

Body and Soul

As a bodily being, the human person is a part of material reality, woven into the biological and chemical processes of nature. At the same time, the human person is a living organism who is conscious or his or her own existence. This duality in the human being is well expressed in the description in the creation narrative of how God formed the human being of the dust of the ground and breathed the breath of life into his nostrils, so that he became a living being (Gen 2:7). The Hebrew term that the New Revised Standard Version translates as "living being" is also translated as "soul." In the Bible, the "soul" can designate the internal dimension of the human being, the center of his or her personality, and it often denotes that aspect of the human being that is in relationship to God. The concept of "spirit" can also be used somewhat synonymously to speak of this aspect of the human being (see, e.g., Luke 1:46–47: "My soul magnifies the Lord, and my spirit rejoices in God my Savior").

Although body and soul represent different dimensions of the human being, there is a close link between them in the Bible, so that it is scarcely possible to think of the one without the other. Accordingly, bodily death is the death of the whole human being (cf. Gen 3:19, "You are dust, and to dust you shall return"). This in turn means that hope for new life after death does not signify living on in a bodiless existence, but rather the resurrection of the body (cf., e.g., 1 Cor 15). Since the human being is a unity of body and soul, it is impossible to conceive of a salvation that does not encompass the whole human being (more on this in chapter 9 below).

In this context, Christian anthropology has been strongly influenced by the world of Greek ideas that was dominant in the first Christian centuries. Various versions of Platonic philosophy were particularly influential. The relationship between body and soul was thought of here as a dualistic antithesis in which the soul had the greater value. This led to a negative evaluation of the physical and the bodily, and hope for salvation meant the liberation of the soul from the prison of the body.

Although not every aspect of such an understanding was adopted by the church, it gradually came to leave its mark on theology. This could entail a disparagement of the physical aspect of the human being, and an understanding of salvation primarily as the salvation of the soul. Recent theology has consistently criticized this way of thinking, because it does not do justice to the biblical understanding of the human being as a unity of body and soul.

One question that has been much discussed here is that of the immortality of the soul. Platonic thinking regards the soul (unlike the body) as immortal, with the consequence that the soul existed before it was united to a body, and that it can be thought of as reincarnated in a series of new bodies.

Many theologians, while refusing to accept these consequences, nevertheless thought of the soul as a substance that goes on living after the death of the body and that will be reunited with the body only at the resurrection of the dead. This idea has been much criticized, above all in recent times, by theologians who have pointed out that it undermines the understanding of the human being as a unity of body and soul. The difficult question that then arises is whether this means that the human being completely ceases to exist between the moment of death and the resurrection, or whether some kind of intermediate existence is conceivable (for more detail, see chapter 9.3 below).

In any case, it is important for Christian thinking to maintain that the human being never possesses in himself or herself life or immortality, so that a part of the human being would be able to survive death in virtue of an inherent ability or quality. In a biblical perspective, only God "has immortality" (1 Tim 6:16), and everything that has life and existence receives this from God, who is "the fountain of life" (Ps 36:9).

The Human Being and Nature

In the biblical creation narrative, the human being is brought into a connection with the rest of the created world: he or she is formed from the dust of the ground and must return to the earth (Gen 2:7; 3:19). At the same time, the special position of the human being is emphasized, as the only one said to be created in the image of God, and as the one who is given the task of subduing the earth and ruling over animals and plants (Gen 1:26–29). This task has often been called the responsibility of stewardship of the world: the world continues to be God's world, but the human person is appointed to use and administer it on behalf of God.

The ecological crisis that the world is experiencing today shows that human coexistence with nature is under threat. An exaggerated exploitation of the natural resources threatens both biological variety and the very basis of human existence. It has been claimed that one important source of this development is to be found in Christian theology. It is alleged that Christian thinking has contributed to the ecological crisis through a one-sided emphasis on the idea that the human being has a special position vis-à-vis nature and is entitled to make use of nature for his or her own needs. To the text that this is true, the picture must be complemented by reference to the influence from a mechanistic worldview that understood nature primarily as a machine that the human person was to dominate for his or her own needs. It is also clear that modern technology has made it possible to dominate and exploit nature in a way that was impossible for earlier generations.

In the light of the ecological crisis, many theologians have proposed a Christian ecotheology that more strongly understands the human being as a part of nature. It is not difficult to find a basis for such a theology in the Bible, which understands all living beings as created by God. Although Christian theology must maintain that human beings have a special position in the creation, since they are created in the image of God, they are nonetheless a part of nature, and have a responsibility to take care of it. This also means, in some cases, that they must put the needs of non-human nature before their own needs.

The New Testament affirms that nature is more than a backdrop for human activity. For example, Paul states that the definitive salvation concerns not only the human being, but the whole of creation (Rom 8:18–23).

4.3 SIN AND EVIL

Not everything in life is good—that is a basic human experience. People are affected by accidents, sickness, and death. They also inflict suffering on others—and on their own selves—through what they do or fail to do. Both good and evil exist in human life.

How to cope with this fundamental experience is a central theme in worldviews and religions. One possibility is to deny the basic difference between good and evil, and to hold that it is merely apparent. In a purely naturalistic view of reality, the distinction between good and evil is nothing more than a subjective experience: that which we experience as evil is nothing more than an expression of natural life processes. In religions with a monistic orientation, such as Hinduism and Buddhism, the distinction between good and evil is often perceived as merely apparent, something that ultimately merges in a higher unity. In more dualistic tendencies, such as Manichaeism and other gnostic groups, the opposition between good and evil is thought to go right to the bottom of existence, which is understood as a struggle between a good and an evil power.

Unlike naturalism or religions that think in monistic terms, Christianity regards the antithesis between good and evil as real. But unlike Manichaeism, it believes that there is only one God, and that this God is good.

How is evil to be understood? This can be seen as both a theoretical and a practical problem. As a theoretical problem, it asks how we *explain* evil, not least in relation to the belief that the world was created by a good God. As a practical problem, it asks what we can *do with* evil: How can we fight it, or live with it? In the light of faith in God, this can also be the question of what *God* does with evil. The Christian faith is characterized here by its refusal to give an unambiguous answer to the problem of evil as a theoretical problem; it is primarily concerned with evil as a practical problem, not least because the Christian faith is a *faith in salvation.* It is not for nothing that the petition "Deliver us from evil" has its place in the prayer Jesus taught his disciples to pray (Matt 6:13*).

In what I have said about "evil" up to this point, I have employed it as a somewhat comprehensive concept that covers both the evil that derives from human beings and that which derives from nature. In order to clarify this concept, it has been proposed that we should draw a distinction between "moral evil" and "natural evil." The latter term refers to all the suffering that is not due to human actions, but rather to events and processes in nature, such as sickness, natural death, accidents, and natural catastrophes. "Moral evil" refers to that which is caused by specific human actions and intentions, such as the desire to inflict pain or suffering on other persons.

Although this distinction is useful, the two are, of course, not unconnected. For example, sickness and accidents can be connected in many cases with what human beings do or fail to do. Lung cancer can be caused in many instances by active or passive smoking, and it is highly probable that the climate changes that cause many people suffering today are connected with our emissions of climate gasses.

The Concept of Sin

We shall now look primarily at evil as a human phenomenon, as something that has human beings as its subject. As I have said, it is a universal basic human experience that people inflict pain and suffering on each other and on their own selves. The concept of *sin* is often employed in the Bible and in the Christian tradition to help describe this phenomenon. The important point about this concept is that it not only sees the phenomenon in a moral and interpersonal perspective, but also connects it to the human person's relationship to God.

It is has become difficult to use the concept of sin today, because it evokes associations that unfortunately narrow it down and trivialize it. Not least, the concept evokes associations with the sphere of sexuality, where the question tends to be whether or not certain actions are sinful. It is often used about things that people do not really see as dangerous, but rather as exciting and titillating. There can be no doubt that the Christian use of this concept is responsible for much of the background to such associations; it has sometimes been applied to things that other people found harmless and enriching, such as dancing, fiddle playing, and the cinema.

An absolutely fundamental element in a Christian understanding of the concept of sin is that this is a *theological* concept. In other words, it concerns the human person's relationship to God and God's relationship to the human person. Sin basically means that the human person's trustful relationship to God is broken. The fact that sin also involves our relationship to other persons means that actions vis-à-vis other persons are seen in the light of our relationship to God. And this means both that sin against our fellow human beings can be understood as a consequence of the destruction of the relationship to God, and that sin against our fellow human beings can be understood as sin against God.

Since sin involves our relationship to God, it involves not only the understanding of the human being as a creature, but also—and to the highest degree—the understanding of salvation. Since sin destroys the human being's relationship to God, the human being needs salvation. How we understand sin and its consequence in the human person is therefore significant for how we understand salvation, and for how the human person can receive a share in salvation. This is the starting point for much of the theological debate about the understanding of the human being as a sinner (see the discussion of Augustine and Pelagius, below).

The various dimensions of the concept of sin find classic expression in the narrative of the fall in Genesis 3, where we read about the rebellion of the first human beings against God, and about its consequences. As sin is described here, it primarily concerns the human beings' relationship to God. When they listen to the tempter's question, "Did God say?" (Gen 3:1), they display a lack of trust in God. Eating of the forbidden fruit also means that the human person wanted to be like God (Gen 3:5). At the same time, however, the sin also has consequences for their relationship to their fellow human beings: when God calls them to account for what they have done, they accuse each other and deny any personal responsibility (Gen 3:11–13).

The following chapters describe the influence of sin on human life. Genesis 4 relates how Cain murders his brother Abel, and a later passage says that "the inclination of the human heart is evil from youth" (Gen 8:21; cf. 6:5).

The description of sin in the first chapters of Genesis brings out some important points that we find elsewhere in the Bible too, such as the understanding of sin as anchored in the human "heart," that is to say, in the center of the personality. The concrete actions are manifestations of an orientation that already lies in the human being. In the same way, Jesus identifies the heart as the source of all evil actions: "For out of the heart come evils intentions, murder, adultery, fornication, theft, false witness, slander" (Matt 15:19). Paul employs the Greek concept *sarx* (literally, "the flesh") to designate this orientation to evil that lies within the human being.

While sin is something that is in the human being antecedently to specific actions, it is expressed concretely, in thoughts, words, or actions, all of which go against God's good creative will and harm our relationship to God and to our fellow human beings. God's good creative will is concretized in the Bible by means of various commandments, the most fundamental of which is the "double commandment of love": "You shall love the Lord your God with all your heart, and with all your soul, and with all your strength, and with all your mind; and your neighbor as yourself" (Luke 10:27; cf. Mark 12:30-31; Lev 19:18; Deut 6:5). Sin thus means acting against love. And the Ten Commandments (and other texts) specify what this love entails (Exod 20:1-17; Deut 5:6-21; cf. Matt 19:16-19; Rom 13:8-10). It is significant that the Ten Commandments are introduced by words about the relationship to God: "You shall have no other gods besides me." It is only after this that we hear the commandments regarding one's relationship to other people: prohibitions of murder, adultery, theft, false witness, and desiring the property of others.

Jesus' preaching in the Sermon on the Mount shows that the commandments concern not only actions, but also words and thoughts (Matt 5:21-30). But Jesus radicalizes not only the understanding of sin, but also the demand for love, which must not be restricted to those who are nearest, but must even embrace one's enemies: "Love your enemies" (Matt 5:44). Sin is not only the inflicting of harm on others, but also the failure to act where one could assuage pain. This is expressed in the parable of the Good Samaritan (Luke 10:25-37).

In a theological perspective, sin is never only sin against other people: it is always also sin against God, who is always a "party" in what takes place in the created world. This is why God's *reaction* to sin is an important biblical theme here: he calls the human being to account for his or her actions. And this is why the idea of God's judgment is an important biblical motif (for more on this, see chapter 9 below).

Original Sin

The Christian tradition agrees in general that sinful actions have their starting point in an inclination to evil in the human being himself or herself, but there is considerable debate about how this inclination is to be understood. Is the inclination itself to be regarded as a sin, or is it only a starting point for sin? We must also ask how sin arises in the individual human being: is it based on the individual's choices, or is it something inherited? And does an inherited sin entail *guilt*? Questions of this kind coalesce in the discussion of sin, understood as *original sin*.

Augustine's debate with Pelagius at the beginning of the fifth century had decisive significance for the further development of the understanding of sin. Pelagius was a preacher of repentance whose sermons appealed to the human being's free will.

According to Pelagius, sin is not something that lies in human nature; it is merely an expression of misguided actions. And this means that the human being is capable of choosing the good and avoiding evil. If evil is nevertheless often chosen, this is not because of any indwelling original sin. It is the result of the human choice of evil. Sometimes, this choice is made because of other people's bad example; but the example of Jesus can be a starting point for choosing the good, Pelagius asserted.

Against this position, Augustine claimed that it was only the first human beings who had a free choice between good and evil. Since they chose evil, sin became a determinant of their identity and of all who came after them. After Adam's fall, therefore, no one can avoid doing evil. Augustine holds that sin is transmitted from one generation to the next via procreation; this is why original sin is called "Erbsünde"in German and "arvesynd" in Norwegian (literally, "inherited sin"). Original sin is not only a starting point for committing sin: it is in itself a sin that also incurs guilt vis-à-vis God. Unlike Pelagius, Augustine held that infants are sinners who stand under God's judgment. It is only with the aid of God's unmerited grace that the human being can be set free from sin's guilt and power.

Although it did not go unchallenged, Augustine's teaching on original sin became very important, not only for the theology of the Catholic Church, but also for the Lutheran Reformation, which was largely based on this way of thinking. In one of his best known writings, *De servo arbitrio* ("On the Bondage of the Will"), Luther directs his polemic against the idea of human free will and claims that the will is in bondage to sin. An Augustinian understanding of original sin is also expressed in article 2 of the Augsburg Confession, which says that "since the fall of Adam all human beings who are propagated according to nature are born with sin, that is, without fear of God, without trust in God, and with concupiscence. And they teach that this disease or original fault is truly sin, which even now damns and brings eternal death to those who are not born again through baptism and Holy Spirit."

Lutheran theology has often been criticized for having a very pessimistic anthropology. The formulation in the Augsburg Confession gives the impression that there is not much good to say about the human being and his or her possibilities. If we are to understand this matter correctly, it is important to underline that the perspective here is primarily the relationship to God and salvation. In relation to God, human sin means that we stand under God's judgment and are unable to contribute to our own salvation. If we nevertheless are able to hope for salvation, this is due exclusively to God's grace in Jesus Christ.

This, however, does not mean that it is impossible for the human being to do good on the interpersonal level. There is a fundamental distinction here between what applies in relation to God (Latin: *coram deo*) and what applies in relation to other people (*coram hominibus*). The human being can do a great deal of good on the interpersonal level, even if sin is never far away (see, e.g., article 18 of the Augsburg Confession). It is possible to see the Creator at work in the good works of human beings. When parents look after their children, when marriage partners care for each other, or when the state sees that justice is done in society, these are expressions of how God acts through his creatures. Because of sin, the Creator is concerned not only to promote the good, but also to limit the bad. One means that he uses is the law, which lays down boundaries for human actions; other instruments are people who use power to lay down boundaries for evil. This is how Paul describes the role of the governing authorities in Rom 13:1–7.

The Human Being as Created and as Sinner

It is nevertheless clear that the human being's sinfulness can be understood in a way that in reality conflicts with the belief that the human being is created by God. Some in the Lutheran tradition have occasionally gone too far in this direction. A classic example is Luther's pupil Matthias Flacius, who emphasized the reality of original sin by claiming that after the fall, sin had become the very essence of the human being, who was no longer in God's image, but rather in that of the devil.

Flacius' position was subsequently criticized by the Formula of Concord, because it was a threat to the understanding of the human being as created by God. The Formula declares that even the sinful human being is created by God. Accordingly, sin is not to be understood as the human being's nature, but as something that corrupts and destroys the created nature. God created the human being, but he did not create sin:

> We believe, teach, and confess that there is a difference between original sin and human nature—not only as God originally created it pure, holy, and without sin, but also as we have it now after the fall. Even after the fall this nature still is and remains a creature of God. This difference is as great as the difference between the work of God and the work of the devil.[1]

This does not diminish the seriousness of sin. Since human nature is corrupted by sin, there is no part of human life in which sin does not make its presence felt, and it is only through God's new creation that human nature will once again be without sin.

Various Views of Original Sin and Original Guilt

The understanding of sin has been a topic of discussion, not only within Lutheranism, but also between the confessional traditions. A shared starting point in Augustine's thinking means that the Catholic and the Lutheran understandings of original sin are very similar. One important difference is that Catholic teaching does not understand original sin as a personal guilt, but as the lack of the original righteousness and holiness. According to Catholic doctrine, original sin is removed in baptism, although one retains a disposition to sin. A Lutheran understanding holds that the guilt of original

---

1. Kolb and Wengert, eds., *Book of Concord*, 448.

sin is forgiven in baptism, but the sin itself remains present throughout one's life, alongside the new righteousness in Christ (see the Lutheran formulation: "simultaneously righteous and sinner," Latin: *simul justus et peccator*).

While Augustine's understanding of sin became very important in the Catholic and the Lutheran churches, it was not equally influential in the Orthodox church in the East, where greater emphasis was placed on the human being's freedom in relation to sin. Besides this, the East did not accept the idea that one inherits the guilt of earlier generations.

The question whether the inherited sin also means that the human being bears the burden of the *guilt* of sin from birth onwards is also a matter of dispute between various Protestant churches. The Reformed churches that build on Calvin largely follow the Augustinian line, but others hold that although the human being has a congenital inclination to sin, this does not amount to sin in the true sense of the word—and therefore not to *guilt*—before one is old enough to commit conscious sins. Such a view is particularly common in Baptist theology. This is also part of the explanation of the varying views about infant baptism. While Lutherans and others argue for the necessity of infant baptism by affirming that the human being has a share in the guilt of original sin from birth onwards, and hence needs salvation, Baptists reject this claim.

An understanding of sin as inherited is, of course, problematic for a purely individualistic understanding in which each one has the sole responsibility for what he or she has done. In biblical times, people thought about this matter in a more collectivistic way: to be part of a fellowship also meant sharing in a common guilt. One important text in this connection is Romans 5:12–21, where Adam's fall is understood as the starting point for death and condemnation for all human beings—just as grace in Jesus Christ leads to life and salvation for all who accept it.

Irrespective of how precisely one sees this question, it is certainly not easy to give an account of the relationship between sin and guilt. Even if one affirms that one can incur guilt only for what one has done personally, it is nevertheless the case that all human beings sin as soon as they make conscious choices. One simply cannot choose not to sin, and sin thus looks like a kind of fate from which no one can escape—although it is, of course, possible to affect the role that sin will play in one's life. One cannot appeal to this fact to absolve people from responsibility or guilt in relation to what they do, since although one will always be determined by one's background, one can never escape from responsibility—for that would undermine the dignity of the human person.

Where Does Sin Come From?

If, then, sin is not only something that one of us chooses, but something that lies in the constitution of the human being, we must naturally ask how and why this is so. If it was God who created the human being, why do we have an indwelling tendency to act against God's will? The text from Romans 5, mentioned above, has traditionally played an important role here. Paul derives both sin and death from the fall of the first man: "Sin came into the world through one man, and death came through sin" (Rom 5:12). He alludes here to the narrative of the fall in Genesis 3, which relates how the first two human beings were expelled from the Garden of Eden after defying God's command not to eat from the tree of knowledge.

One frequently discussed question is how far this narrative refers to a concrete historical event, or is to be read more metaphorically. It is problematic to read the story literally, both because of the literary genre of the text and because of the scientific knowledge we have about the development of the human being (see chapter 2.2, above). This has led many theologians to seek to read the account as a parable of what happens with each individual human being when we are confronted by the temptation to choose evil. In this way, Adam and Eve are an image of each one of us; they are not persons who lived in the past.

The weakness of such a purely ahistorical interpretation is that it makes the fall something purely individual, thereby failing to do justice to the fact that the narrative of the fall also says something about humankind as a fellowship, or about the human being as essentially different from all other species with regard to the possibility of doing good or evil. It makes little sense to apply moral criteria to the actions of animals: they act according to their inherited instincts. From the perspective of the history of evolution, therefore, a transition from a behavior governed exclusively by instincts to an incipient moral consciousness must have occurred at some point in time. And precisely this "knowledge of good and evil" (Gen 2:17; cf. 3:5) is one of the thing that characterize human beings as we know them.

Another challenge in the narrative of the fall is intensified by Paul's interpretation of it, which posits a link between sin and death. According to Genesis 3:3, the human beings were to die if they ate of the forbidden fruit, and according to Romans 5:12 and 17, they incurred death because of sin. Some parts of church tradition, including Lutheran orthodoxy, have interpreted this as signifying a "primal state" in which human beings originally possessed immortality.

This, however, is not the immediately obvious interpretation of the texts, which do not say that human beings were immortal before the fall. From the perspective of natural science, it is inconceivable that at some point in their development, human beings were exempt from the generation change that characterizes all biological life on earth. Death is quite simply a presupposition of life as we know it. At the same time, it is a fact that, although death is something "natural," people in every age have experienced it as something evil. One possible perspective, therefore, is that death acquired a new character thanks to the fall: from being a death in trust in God, it became a death in defiance and rebellion against God. Accordingly, Paul can say: "The sting of death is sin" (1 Cor 15:56).

Another possible perspective is to see suffering and death as an expression of the imperfection that was present in the creation even before the human being's fall. This may be indicated by Paul's affirmation in Romans 8:18–23 that the transience of the creation is one of the things that will be overcome by the definitive redemption.

The problems involved in conceiving of a perfect primal state have led many theologians in recent times to envisage more strongly this kind of perfect state as something that belongs to the *future*, as an expression of what mankind is *meant to be*. According to Pannenberg, it is difficult to read the biblical texts as supporting the idea of a primal state, although they are in fact often read thus. When the Bible says that the human being was created in the image of God, this does not mean that he or she was perfect to begin with, but that he or she was destined for perfection. The realization of this destiny is anticipated in Jesus Christ, and it will be bestowed on us in the definitive redemption. In such a perspective, salvation is not primarily a re-establishing of what was lost, but a realization of the *goal* of the work of creation.

Irrespective of the answer we give to the question of when and how sin came into the world, there remains a more fundamental question, namely: How are sin and evil at all possible in a world created by a good God? Since the Bible does not give a clear answer, this question has been the object of both discussion and speculation. Article 19 of the Augsburg Confession, entitled "Concerning the cause of sin," comments on this question that "the cause of sin is the will of those who are evil, that is, of the devil and ungodly."

Two points are important here. The first is the anchoring of sin in the "will," which indicates that it is the *freedom* of the world and of the human being that makes sin and evil possible. Since God created a world with an inherent freedom, it is also possible to act against his will. But it is the one who chooses to do so, who bears the responsibility for this. The second point is the reference to the "devil," which means that sin and evil are not restricted to the human being alone.

Evil as Demonic

There is plentiful evidence in the Bible for this understanding of evil as a power external to human beings. In the account of the fall in Genesis 3, the human being encounters the evil tempter in the form of a serpent, and evil is identified in other passages by means of names such as "the devil" or "Satan." According to 1 John 3:8, "everyone who commits sin is a child of the devil; for the devil has been sinning from the beginning." Human sin is located here in a larger cosmic drama, where the human being has his or her place in the struggle between God and the evil one. In most passages, the devil is spoken of in the singular, but other passages see him as representing a larger demonic reality. According to Paul, "our struggle is not against enemies of blood and flesh, but against the rulers, against the authorities, against the cosmic powers of this present darkness, against the spiritual forces of evil in the heavenly places" (Eph 6:12).

It is difficult to decide how literally we should take what the Bible says about the evil one. It is, at any rate, certain that evil is not only a human phenomenon, but also has suprahuman dimensions. Evil is something that is in us, but also something that can attack us and take control of us—without thereby exonerating us from responsibility for what we ourselves do.

We see above all in the Gospel stories of human beings possessed by demons (see, for example, Mark 1:23–28) that it is possible for evil to take control of human beings. We hear of similar phenomena today in some cultural contexts, such as in Africa. Much of what was explained in New Testament times as possession by evil spirits can be explained today in other ways, *inter alia* through psychiatric diagnoses, although this does not mean that we can dismiss the possibility of diabolical possession today. However, we should be cautious about explaining something as demonic, when in reality it is an expression of human weakness and sin. At the same time, the radicality of wickedness is sometimes so extreme that it points beyond the human dimension to something that is evil in itself. In the New Testament accounts of diabolical possession, the interesting thing is not the possessions *per se*, but the fact that Jesus has the power to drive out the demons, just as he can forgive sins and heal sickness.

To speak of the devil as God's adversary can sound like a form of dualism in which a good power (God) stands over against an evil power (the devil). Ethically speaking, there is indeed a dualism—good against evil—but this is not the case ontologically speaking, since the devil is not an anti-god, but a part of created reality. This does not mean that God created the devil and the demons evil. Rather, they belong to the part of creation that has turned its back on God. A link has often been made between the evil spiritual powers and the reference in 2 Peter 2:4 and Jude 6 to the angels who sinned.

The Problem of Theodicy

How are we to make sense of the fact that a good God has created a world marked by suffering and wickedness? This question is often referred to as the *problem of theodicy*. If God is omnipotent, why does he not abolish evil? This question can be posed both in the encounter with human wickedness ("moral evil") and in the encounter with the suffering that is a consequence of events such as illness and natural catastrophes ("natural evil").

This question has been posed down through ages by philosophers and theologians, and it is the subject of the Book of Job in the Bible. Numerous solutions have been proposed, with varying degrees of compatibility with a Christian perspective.

One type of solution tends to relativize the seriousness of suffering and evil, by understanding this as a kind of imperfection. One example is the claim by the philosopher Gottfried Leibniz that despite everything, ours is the best of all possible worlds. This does not take the wickedness of evil seriously. Another type of solution tends to attribute to God some intention with regard to evil—perhaps as a kind of divine pedagogy. This does not take seriously the radical antithesis between God and evil. Although God can use evil for a good purpose (cf. Rom 8:28), it is false to say that God is the cause of evil.

In accordance with what I have said above, it is more natural to identify the cause of evil in the world's freedom: since God has created the world and the human being as something other than himself, and as something that has freedom, this also includes the possibility of wickedness and suffering. This, of course, does not answer the question why God created the world in such a way, nor why freedom was in fact used to oppose God's will. Indeed, part of the problem of evil is perhaps its inexplicability. One aspect of the wickedness of evil is its irrationality, its meaninglessness. (Compare the description of the devil as a liar devoid of truth, in John 8:44.)

The Christian answer to the problem of evil is not, however, primarily a *theoretical*, but rather a *practical* answer: God *does something* with suffering and evil. The Bible tells not only how he seeks to set boundaries for the dominion of evil, but also how he ultimately will do battle with evil and renew the work of his creation. In the world that is created anew, there will be no place for death, suffering, or wickedness. The path that leads there, and the way in which the sinful human being can have a place in this context, is the subject of that part of the doctrine of faith that deals with God's salvific action in Jesus.

5

Jesus

5.1 JESUS—HOW CAN WE KNOW WHO HE WAS?

JESUS OF NAZARETH is probably the single most important individual in world history. The movement that was founded by his followers has played an important role in historical development, and almost one-third of the world's population today belong to various Christian churches. But the importance of Jesus is not restricted to Christianity. He has played a role in other religions too, such as Islam, where he is included in the series of prophets.

The dominant ecclesial understanding of Jesus faced competition already in the early church, *inter alia* from the alternative portraits of Jesus in gnostic currents. In a similar way, one can find alternative pictures of Jesus today in various new religious movements. But the importance of Jesus is not limited to religious currents; spokespersons for non-religious worldviews have also pointed to Jesus as a model of humanity and of love of neighbor. There is a regular stream of books that offer various (and often contradictory) pictures of Jesus.

There has been no consensus within what we can call the Christian movement about how Jesus is to be understood. The discussion of this question was particularly intense in the first centuries of church history, but divergent views claiming to be Christian have also arisen at a later date. We find modern examples among the Jehovah's Witnesses and Mormons.

The Significance of This Question

For the Christian faith, the question: "Who is Jesus?" is absolutely decisive. It is simply impossible to think of Christian faith without Jesus, because of the central role that Jesus plays in the faith: Christian faith is faith in Jesus. But this is also because of the significance that Jesus has for all the other aspects of a Christian interpretation of reality: it is Jesus who gives the key to understanding who God is and who the human being is. He does this, not only by *telling* us about God, but also because it is in him that we encounter God himself.

Jesus' role is so important for Christian faith, not only because he gives keys to interpret or understand reality, but also because he helps to *change* reality. When Christian faith experiences that the world is not as it ought to be—for, on the contrary, it is marked by evil and suffering, as we saw in the preceding chapter—it sees in Jesus a hope for change, a hope that, ultimately, life and the good will be victorious. The principal concept that is used to designate this hope for change is *salvation*. In a biblical perspective, salvation means being liberated from that which destroys life. The understanding of Jesus precisely as *savior*—and not merely as one savior among many, but as *the* savior—is central to a Christian understanding of Jesus. This perspective is already expressed through the name that is given to him in the infancy narrative of Matthew's Gospel, where Joseph is told that Mary "will bear a son, and you are to name him Jesus, for he will save his people from their sins" (Matt 1:21). This alludes to the meaning of the name "Jesus" in Hebrew: "God saves."

The question: "Who is Jesus?" can be understood as a historical question: What can we say with probability about Jesus as a historical figure? But it is also a fundamentally relevant existential question: What does he mean for people today, for their lives and for their relationship to God?

The latter question goes further than the significance we sometimes attribute to historical personages, when we say that they remain important for posterity. This is because Jesus' resurrection and the hope in his second coming mean that Jesus is understood as a person who is present here and now. However, these two questions cannot be separated from each other. When Christians believe in a living Jesus, this is not some other Jesus than the one who lived as a historical person at the beginning of the Christian era. This is why the question of what we can know about him as a historical person is also important for faith in Jesus today.

Since the existential aspect of the relationship to Jesus plays such an important role, a neutral and objective interpretation of the figure of the historical Jesus is difficult. Both the New Testament texts and the later church tradition present challenging claims about Jesus. If he is truly God's Son and the redeemer of the world, this is something that concerns everyone. Such claims challenge us either to accept them or to reject them, and this is why every portrait of Jesus will be colored by the individual's position with regard to faith. The New Testament texts themselves are not neutral accounts of Jesus' life and words, but an expression of the testimony by believers in Jesus to the one they had come to believe in.

This does not mean that the New Testament writings lose their value as historical sources, but that one is obliged to pay heed to their specific character when one interprets them. Nor does this mean that the question of who Jesus was can be reduced to a question about the position one takes with regard to faith, with no possibility of discussing this in a rational manner. On the contrary, every interpretation of life, whether religious or not, must be able to relate to the figure of Jesus and take a position with regard to him. In the dialogue between differing views, one must also ask which interpretation corresponds best to the historical facts.

In this context, the question of how one evaluates what the New Testament calls the resurrection of Jesus will play a particularly important role. The arguments put forward here can make one or other view probable, but they will never be able to supply the definitive "proof" of who Jesus is. Ultimately, this will be an expression of faith, even if faith will never hang in thin air, but will be based on historical circumstances. For a Christian, knowledge of Jesus as a historical person will never be decisive on its own; the experience of him as a living reality will also play its part. In a Christian perspective, the ultimate "proof" of Jesus' identity as the Son of God and the savior of the world will be present only at his second coming when, according to Paul, "every tongue will confess that Jesus Christ is Lord, to the glory of God the Father!" (Phil 2:11*).

We see already in the New Testament texts that the authors emphasize that what they write is reliable, *inter alia* because it builds on information from eyewitnesses. This can be seen, for example, in the introduction to Luke's Gospel (Luke 1:1–4), in Paul's list of people who had met the risen Jesus (1 Cor 15:5–7), or when the author of 1 John speaks of his role as an eyewitness of the events concerning Jesus (1 John 1:1–3).

The Question of the Historical Jesus

The question of historical reliability took on a completely new meaning from the Enlightenment period onwards, thanks to the emergence of the modern historical consciousness and of historical methods. Until then, the biblical texts had largely been taken for granted as the basis for understanding who Jesus was. There might be disagreements about the interpretation and the application of the texts, but their reliability was assumed. As a critical science, however, the emergent study of history set question marks against both the reliability and the unity in the image of the person of Jesus in the texts. Instead, scholars sought to form their own pictures of "the historical Jesus" in contradistinction to the Jesus whom the church had read out of the biblical texts.

One of the first to attempt to draw such a picture was Hermann Samuel Reimarus, at the end of the eighteenth century. He depicted Jesus as a failed Jewish rebel; after his death, the disciples claimed that he had risen from the dead. Some decades later, David Friedrich Strauss claimed that there is not much we can know about Jesus, once we have peeled away the myths and legends with which the early church embellished the New Testament texts. For Strauss himself, the most important thing was Jesus as an ethical ideal.

These views were later criticized by Albert Schweitzer, who showed how scholars had to a large extent formed the figure of Jesus in accordance with their own ideals. He held that this research had produced only a very limited amount of knowledge of the historical Jesus. He himself regarded Jesus as an apocalyptist who hoped for a kingdom of God that never came, but who nevertheless is able to inspire people to do good in their own days.

Portraits of the allegedly historical Jesus that deviated extensively from the traditional picture were, of course, highly problematical for the church. On the one hand, there were theologians who said that historical knowledge must lead the church to change its view of Jesus; one consequence of this was that the idea of Jesus' divinity became problematic. On the other hand, there were theologians who attempted to defend the church's traditional picture of Jesus. Some did so by presentations of his story that were closer to the picture that the church's teaching presupposed, while others asked whether it was genuinely necessary for the picture of Jesus in historical research and in faith to be identical. One example of the last approach was Martin Kähler, who claimed that historical methods are incapable of capturing the suprahistorical reality that Jesus represents, a reality that is accessible only to faith.

The New Testament scholar Rudolf Bultmann took a radical position that is a further development of Kähler's. For Bultmann, the New Testament texts are highly unreliable sources for the historical Jesus, and must instead be understood as expressions of the earliest church's belief in Jesus. Besides this, it is impossible for modern people to believe in the miracles that are related in the New Testament. It is, however, not a problem for the church that there is so little common ground between the Jesus of faith and the Jesus of history, since the church builds its faith, not on historical events, but on the *message*, which represents a challenge to adopt a new form of existence. It is not even necessary for the church to hold fast to the resurrection of Jesus as a historical event, according to Bultmann. The decisive point is that faith in Jesus lives on.

Bultmann's theology was very controversial when it was first put forward in the 1940s, and many, even including some of those who had studied under him, held that he went too far in writing off the theological significance of the historical Jesus. Many biblical scholars also disagree strongly with his negative evaluation of the historical credibility of the New Testament sources. There are many systematic theologians who reach the opposite conclusion to Bultmann, and who wish to anchor faith in Jesus much more strongly in history.

One of those who have gone furthest in this direction is Wolfhart Pannenberg. According to Pannenberg, God reveals himself in history (see the discussion in chapter 2, above), and this means that God's revelation in Jesus is linked to Jesus as a historical person and to events that actually happened in his life. What is involved here is not some kind of metahistory, but the history of which we all are a part, and that can be investigated by the methods of historical science. Pannenberg criticizes earlier research into Jesus for being based on criteria that do not bring out the uniqueness in the Jesus-event. This happens when historical research is based on a principle of analogy, that is, the assumption that historical events are always similar in character. Such an approach does not take into consideration the elements in the story of Jesus that are unique and have no analogy. This applies not least to the resurrection of Jesus, which is an eschatological event, an anticipation of what is to happen at the close of history. Pannenberg believes that one can make a case for the probability that the resurrection is a historical event, although this does not preclude taking a critical view of the historical accuracy of many details in the New Testament texts. But even if they are inaccurate, this does not affect the role of these texts as the basis of the church's faith in Jesus today.

This identification of the Jesus of history with the Jesus of faith is significant, not only for the question of the historical credibility of the New Testament picture of Jesus, but also for the theological importance of the story of Jesus. Pannenberg and other theologians have criticized traditional theology for being one-sidedly oriented to the idea of God sending the Son. He argues that, in addition to this "Christology from above," we need a "Christology from below" that takes its starting point in Jesus' life and history.

The tension between a Christology from below and a Christology from above is already present in the Gospels. Mark's Gospel gives a very sober account of Jesus' activities and of the disciples who only gradually acquire some understanding of who Jesus really is; John's Gospel, on the other hand, begins by affirming Jesus' eternal origin as the Word from God. In the New Testament, therefore, these perspectives are not mutually exclusive.

5.2 TRUE GOD AND TRUE HUMAN BEING

Although the Gospels are written in a retrospective perspective and bear the imprint of the faith of the earliest church, they nevertheless communicate the confusion that those around Jesus felt about who he really was. It seems that Jesus himself was not always very explicit about his self-understanding, and we read that he forbade people to tell about what he had done (Mark 1:44; 7:36). According to the Gospels, Jesus often called himself "the Son of Man." Scriptural scholars disagree about what this term meant, but there is much to indicate that it refers to a figure spoken of in the Book of Daniel, where God himself gives "one like a son of man" dominion over peoples and nations (Dan 7:13–14). In this way, Jesus locates himself and his activity in an eschatological perspective: that which is now taking place is nothing less than God's saving intervention in the world in the last days.

Two other points are important here. The first is Jesus' relationship to John the Baptist, who is depicted as a prophet preaching repentance in the last days (Matt 3:1–12; Mark 1:2–8; Luke 3:1–20; John 1:6–8, 15, 19–28). The start of Jesus' public ministry seems to have been his baptism by John in the river Jordan, an event related in all four Gospels (Matt 3:13–17; Mark 1:9–11; Luke 3:21–22; John 1:32–34).

The second point is the content in Jesus' preaching. According to the evangelists, he preached that the kingdom of God (Matthew mostly employs the term "the kingdom of heaven") had come near. For example, his preaching is summed up as follows at the beginning of Mark's Gospel: "The time is fulfilled, and the kingdom of God has come near; repent, and believe in the gospel" (Mark 1:15). Many of Jesus' parables deal with how the kingdom of God is to be understood, and this concept also says something about an eschatological perspective, namely, that God is doing something new in the world, and that Jesus himself plays a central role here.

The kingdom of God has "come near." This means that through Jesus, it is present in the world *already now*, but that it is *not yet* fully realized. As we shall see later on (especially in chapter 6), this "already now, but not yet" is a structure that supplies an important key to understanding the salvation Jesus brings.

In addition to preaching, Jesus' activity included healings, exorcisms, and even raising the dead. In the Gospels, the point is not the miraculous quality of these events, but their function as signs of what is taking place through Jesus. This is exemplified in Jesus' answer to John the Baptist, who was in prison and had begun to doubt whether Jesus was really the one they had been waiting for: "Go and tell John what you have seen and heard: the blind receive their sight, the lame walk, the lepers are cleansed, the deaf hear, the dead are raised, the poor have good news brought to them" (Luke 7:22; cf. Matt 11:4–5).

Another aspect of Jesus' encounter with other people is that he forgives them their sins. One example is the story of a lame man whom Jesus heals (Mark 2:1–12; cf. Matt 9:1–8; Luke 5:17–26). We read that Jesus' words to the lame man—"Son, your sins are forgiven" (Mark 2:5)—provoke reactions in some scribes, who see this as blasphemy, because Jesus is attributing to himself a role that belongs exclusively to God: "Who can forgive sins but God alone?" (Mark 2:7). When Jesus then heals the man, so that he is now able to walk, this demonstrates Jesus' power (or authority), which is able both to forgive sins and to heal. The theological point in the narrative is placed here on the lips of the critics: namely, that Jesus takes on the role of God and shows in this way that he represents God in a special manner. This is an example of what the New Testament scholar Sverre Aalen has called a "Yahwistic analogy," where Jesus takes on roles that the Old Testament ascribes to God (Yahweh) alone.

God, the World, and Hope

The Confession of Jesus as Christ

In the Gospels, the disciples come to understand who Jesus really is, although it appears that this understanding is not fully developed until they can also see his life in the light of his death and resurrection (cf. John 2:22; 12:16). This understanding finds expression not least in the text about Peter's confession (Matt 16:13–20; cf. Mark 8:27–30; Luke 9:18–21). The passage begins with Jesus' question: "Who do people say that the Son of Man is?" The disciples relate the various answers that are in circulation: "Some say John the Baptist, but others Elijah, and still others Jeremiah or one of the prophets" (Matt 16:13–14). When he asks what the disciples themselves think—"But who do you say that I am?"—Peter speaks on behalf of them all: "You are the Messiah, the Son of the living God" (Matt 16:15–16). Jesus replies that Peter's answer is perfectly accurate: "Flesh and blood has not revealed this to you, but my Father in heaven" (Matt 16:17). Peter's answer is thus an anticipation of the later church's confession of who Jesus is.

His words contain two terms that are central both in the New Testament and in the church's faith in Jesus. The first is the address as "Messiah," a Hebrew title that means "the anointed one." The Greek translation of the Hebrew *meshiach* is *christos*—Christ. In the Old Testament, anointment with oil expresses a special consecration, especially of the kings in Israel from Saul and David onwards (1 Sam 10:1; 16:13). In the course of time, after the monarchy was abolished, people began to hope that God would send a new king descended from David. This hope is expressed, for example, in Isaiah 9:7:

> His authority shall grow continually, and there shall be endless peace for the
> throne of David and his kingdom. He will establish and uphold it with justice
> and with righteousness from this time onward and forevermore.

As this passage shows, much more was expected of this figure than of an ordinary king. The expectation of a Messiah was alive in Judaism at the time of Jesus, and it continues to play a role in Judaism today.

When Jesus is called Messiah (or Christ) in Peter's confession and in other New Testament passages, this thus expresses one particular claim about who he is. It is easy to forget this, when we speak about "Jesus Christ" as if the title was a part of his name. In reality, it expresses a claim: Jesus *is* the Christ—the Messiah (cf. 1 John 5:1).

This claim expresses above all the link between who Jesus is and what he does, on the one hand, and God's promises of salvation to the people of Israel, as these are attested in the Old Testament, on the other hand. In many ways, the Old Testament has an "open ending," in which promises of a new salvific deed and a new savior figure are not yet fulfilled. It was here that the first Christians perceived Jesus as the fulfillment of this promise, and according to the Gospels, this was in keeping with his own self-understanding too.

One important perspective in the New Testament is therefore to show that Jesus is the fulfillment of the Old Testament promises. This is especially true of Matthew's Gospel, which seeks to demonstrate by means of specific references how Jesus is the fulfillment of the Old Testament prophecies (the first such passage is Matt 1:22–23). At the same time, many texts indicate the problems involved in being associated with messianic expectations, since many people at the time of Jesus envisaged the Messiah as a political leader and liberator (see, e.g., John 6:15). Immediately after Peter confesses his faith in Jesus as Messiah, Jesus begins to speak to them about his coming suffering and death, and Peter reacts violently against this idea. It is clear that Jesus, as Messiah, is a different kind of Messiah.

The perspective of fulfillment is important because it anchors the understanding of Jesus in the Old Testament. Although Jesus brings something new, and in many ways bursts through the parameters of the Old Testament, it will always be an absolutely necessary interpretative key to understanding Jesus and his significance (cf. Rom 1:2; 1 Pet 1:10–11). This connection also locates Jesus as a link in a longer salvation history: it is the same God who in the past acted to save Israel, and who spoke through the prophets, who has now made himself known in Jesus (cf. Heb 1:1–2). In the controversy with Marcion in the second century, the church distanced itself from all attempts to understand Jesus independently of the Old Testament revelation of God.

The idea of Jesus as Messiah has another aspect that is often overlooked, namely, his anchoring in the Jewish people and the Jewish tradition. Jesus was a Jew, and he saw himself as sent primarily to the Jews (Matt 15:24). Since the majority in the church gradually came to consist of non-Jews, and rabbinic Judaism rejected Jesus as Messiah, Jesus' Jewish identity often moved into the background in church history. In our own days, the recognition of the church's share in responsibility for the continual attacks on Jews in our civilization has led in many instances to a new consciousness of Christianity's Jewish roots and of Jesus the Jew. For the church, this means that the relationship to the Jewish people will always have a special importance. In order to understand who Jesus really was, the church's testimony to Jesus as the Messiah must always be in dialogue with the synagogue's claim that the Messiah has not yet come.

Jesus as the Son of God

Peter's confession speaks of Jesus not only as the Messiah, but also as "the Son of the living God" (Matt 16:16). The idea of Jesus as the Son of God is very important for the understanding of Jesus both in the New Testament and in the development of Christology in the early church. In an Old Testament context, being called "the son of God" does not necessarily express a divine status; rather, it means that one has a special relationship to God. This is why the people of Israel can be called God's "son"

(Hos 11:1; Jer 31:9), and the same is said of the king descended from David (2 Sam 7:14; Ps 2:7).

The Gospels express Jesus' special relationship to God in many passages by speaking of him as the Son of God. One central text here is the account of Jesus' baptism. All three Synoptic Gospels speak of God's voice from heaven, which declared: "This is my Son, the Beloved, with whom I am well pleased" (Matt 3:17; cf. Mark 1:11; Luke 3:22). It is a striking feature of the Synoptic Gospels that it is often the devil and the evil spirits who address Jesus as God's Son—as if they possess knowledge of something that is not generally known (cf., e.g., Matt 4:3, 6; Mark 3:11; Luke 4:41). Another point is that the recognition of Jesus as the Son of God occurs in the encounter with what he does (Matt 14:33; 27:54).

Taken in isolation, the concept of "Son of God" can be seen as something that Jesus has *become*. In other words, he is a human being whom God has chosen to stand in a completely special relationship to himself, for example, on the occasion of the baptism in the Jordan. Such an understanding is often called adoptionism (that is to say, Jesus is "adopted" as God's Son), but it is ruled out by many texts that see Jesus' filial relationship to God as something that already exists *antecedently to* his birth. This perspective is particularly dominant in the Johannine writings, where Jesus is seen as sent to the world by God. Here, the story of Jesus does not begin with his conception and birth, but with God before time began. The prologue to John's Gospel states that the Word (Greek: *logos*)—which the text later identifies with Jesus—was "in the beginning," that he "was with God," and that he "was God" (John 1:1). Here, therefore, the text is not content only to speak of a divine *origin* ("was with God"): it also speaks of a divine *identity* ("was God"). The affirmation that the Word both was with God and was God points to a unity between God and the Word, but also to a distinction, and it is precisely this combination of identity and distinction that is the starting point for the later formulation of Trinitarian doctrine (see chapter 3, above).

The term *preexistence* is often used to express the idea that the Word was antecedent to Jesus' conception and birth. This was an existence before the world came into being; but he also—as the Word—shared in the work of creation itself: "All things came into being through him, and without him not one thing came into being" (John 1:3). In this perspective, his conception and birth are seen, not as the beginning of his existence (as is the case with every other human being), but as a transition: "And the Word became flesh and lived among us" (John 1:14). The term *incarnation* (from the Latin *caro* = flesh) is often employed to affirm that the preexistent Word becomes a human being.

The prologue to John's Gospel also speaks of the Word as God's Son, and God is correspondingly spoken of as Father. In order to mark his unique position, Jesus is called "the only Son" (literally: "the only-begotten Son"; John 1:14, 18; cf. 3:16, 18; 1 John 4:9). He is simply called "the Son" elsewhere in John's Gospel and in the rest of the New Testament. There is no doubt that "the Son" is identical with Jesus; but the use of this concept sees him in one particular perspective, as one who belongs in a special way to God.

The fact that Jesus is the Son of God, his Father, also says something about a close and intimate relationship between them, as we read, for example, in Matthew's Gospel: "No one knows the Son except the Father, and no one knows the Father except the Son and anyone to whom the Son chooses to reveal him" (Matt 11:27), or in John's Gospel: "Believe me that I am in the Father and the Father is in me" (John 14:11). In other New Testament writings too, the designation of Jesus as the Son of God is important, if we are to understand who he is. In Galatians 4:4, for example, Paul expresses as follows the connection between Jesus' identity as a human being in history and his origin in God's sending of him: "When the fullness of time had come, God sent his Son, born of a woman, born under the law."

When Jesus is spoken of as "Son" in the singular and with a definite article, this means that his relationship to God differs from that of other people, although they too can be spoken of as God's "children" (e.g., in Matt 5:9; John 1:12; Rom 8:14-17; Gal 3:26) and God can be called their "Father" (Matt 6:8-9; 1 Cor 1:3; 8:6; Eph 4:6). Although there is a difference between the ways in which Jesus is God's Son and other people are God's children, there is also a close connection. According to John's Gospel, those who receive the Son are given "power to become children of God" (John 1:12), and Paul writes in a similar manner that God sent his Son so that human beings "might receive adoption as children" (Gal 4:4-5). This is why Jesus can also be spoken of as "the firstborn among many brothers and sisters" (Rom 8:29*).

In addition to the concepts linked to the idea of Jesus as God's Son, the New Testament also in other ways links him closely to God, as the one who acts on God's behalf, or even acts as if he himself were God, for example, when he forgives people their sins (see above) or takes on other roles that belonged to God in Jewish and Old Testament thinking. This is why he is accused of blasphemy: "You, though only a human being, are making yourself God" (John 10:33). In other passages, he is spoken of directly as "God" (John 1:1; 20:28) or as "Lord" (Greek: *kyrios*), a term that was used in the Greek translation of the New Testament to render the divine name Yahweh (John 20:28; 1 Cor 1:2; 8:6; 12:3; Phil 2:11).

Jesus also takes on a role that was restricted to God alone when he is made the object of worship (Phil 2:10), or is one to whom one prays (John 14:14). The Revelation of John gives us an impression of how unthinkable it was in a Jewish context to adore anyone other than God himself, when John's attempt to worship an angel is sharply rejected with the words: "Worship God!" (Rev 19:10; 22:8-9). But the same book also relates how Jesus—in the form of a lamb—is worshiped in heaven (Rev 5:8-14).

While Jesus identifies himself with God, he also makes a distinction between God, as Father, and himself. This becomes most obvious when Jesus turns to God in prayer (Matt 11:25-27; 14:23; John 17). In the account of Jesus in Gethsemane, he asks to be allowed to avoid suffering, but he nevertheless accepts the Father's will (Matt 26:39, 42).

The Development of Christology in the Early Church

How are we to understand the relationship between Jesus, as God's Son, and God himself as Father? This gradually emerged as one of the central topics in the early church. This led in the dominant ecclesial tradition to a clarification both in the understanding of God (Trinitarian doctrine) and in Christology, which found its expression in confessional texts. I have already given an account of central elements in this development in chapter 3.2, above. One important phase here was the conflict with Arius and his adherents. They too thought of Jesus as the incarnation of the preexistent Son of God, and they too could call him divine; but the Son was not divine in the same way as God the Father. This meant that he belonged to the created order, and the Arians therefore claimed that there was a time when Son did not exist, and God was alone.

It is worth looking at the arguments that Athanasius and others employed against the Arians' position. First of all, they accused the Arians of opening the door to the adoration of something created, since the Arians continued the customary ecclesial praxis of adoring Jesus. Secondly, they accused the Arians of tearing down the foundations of salvation, since if the one who brings salvation is not himself God, he cannot bring human beings into the right relationship to God.

In modern times, the Jehovah's Witnesses have a similar Christology. They too understand Jesus as the incarnation of a heavenly spiritual being and as the first one created by God. Unlike the Arians, however, they do not believe that it is right to pray to Jesus.

The controversy with the Arians is reflected in the Nicene Creed, above all when Jesus, as the Son, is said to be "of one Being (Greek: *homoousios*, 'consubstantial' or 'of one substance') with the Father." This concept is employed to reject the idea that the divinity of the son is on a "lower level" than that of the Father, or that he is some kind of divine heavenly being. It also rejects an alternative that attempted to go some way to meet the Arians, namely, the affirmation that the Son was *homoiousios*, "of a similar substance" with the Father.

In keeping with a Trinitarian understanding of God, the son is understood as one God with the Father and the Spirit, but as distinct from the Father and the Spirit. The Nicene Creed expresses this by saying that he is "begotten from the Father before all the ages." This does not mean that the Son has a beginning, nor that this "begetting" took place at some specific point in time. It expresses an eternal relationship between the Father and the Son—and precisely *qua* Father and Son. Unlike what the Arians believed, God the Father was never alone. From all eternity, he was always in fellowship with the Son and the Spirit.

Thanks to the Nicene Creed, one dimension of the Christological problem finds its solution: namely, how we are to understand Jesus' relationship to God. This, however, does not automatically resolve the other aspect of the problem: namely, how Jesus is not only true God, but also a true human being. The Nicene Creed therefore became the starting point for a discussion of how Jesus' full divinity was to be understood in relation to his humanity.

The Doctrine of Two Natures

A clarification that was subsequently accepted by large sections of the church took place at the Council of Chalcedon in 451. The use of "substance" in the Nicene Creed is taken further here, so that it applies not only to Jesus' divinity, but also to his humanity: "consubstantial with the Father according to the divinity, and consubstantial with us according to the humanity, in every respect like us apart from sin."[1] Chalcedon also employed the concept of "nature" to speak of this double consubstantiality: it speaks of Jesus' "two natures," the divine and the human. This is why this articulation of Christology is often called *the doctrine of two natures.*

This doctrine was formulated after wide-reaching Christological disputes in which two tendencies dominated. The first tendency, which we find in Nestorius and the later Nestorians, emphasized Jesus' full humanity in such a way that the relationship to his divinity became unclear. Here too, faith in his full divinity was maintained, but it was more problematic to keep the two natures together, since each nature almost acted on its own.

The second tendency emphasized Jesus' divinity in such a way that it became problematic to affirm his full humanity. At the close of the fourth century, Apollinaris asserted that the divine Logos had taken the place of the human soul in Jesus, and that the nature of his body too was divine. Later versions of such a "doctrine of one nature," which is often called "monophysitism," did not go as far as this, and attempted more strongly to hold fast to Jesus' full humanity; their concern was to preserve the unity in the person of Jesus, which they believed lay in his divine nature.

The decision at Chalcedon thus sought to hold fast to Jesus' full humanity by speaking of two perfect natures, the divine and the human. At the same time, it attempted to do justice to the Monophysites' concerns by underlining the unity between the natures in the one person Jesus Christ. However, the question that Chalcedon did *not* answer was how this unity between the natures in the one person comes into being.

The solution that gradually predominated, and that was confirmed by a council at Constantinople in 553, was to understand the divine Logos as the element that formed the person (or "hypostasis") in the union of the two natures. This understanding does

---

1. Translated from the Greek text in Denzinger and Schönmetzer, eds., *Enchiridion Symbolorum,* 108.

not, however, do away with Chalcedon's understanding of Jesus' humanity as a perfect humanity, with a human body and soul.

This understanding of the doctrine of two natures also finds expression in the Athanasian Creed, which emphasizes that Jesus is both true God, of one substance with the Father, and also a true human being, of one substance with his mother. The one person is also emphasized, when the Creed affirms that "although he is God and a human being, nevertheless he is not two but one Christ." When the text describes the incarnation as "the taking up of the humanity in God," it presupposes that it is the divine that comes first.

The doctrine of two natures has been the expression of official Christology since Chalcedon in the Orthodox churches, the Catholic Church, and Protestant churches. Article 3 of the Augsburg Confession confirms the idea of the two natures in the one person. This consensus does not exclude disagreement about how this is to be understood, nor about the consequences it entails. One important aspect of the disagreement between Lutherans and Reformed in the Reformation period concerned precisely how the relationship between Jesus' human and divine natures was to be understood with regard to his presence in the eucharistic elements (for more on this, see chapter 7.3, below).

Although the doctrine of two natures has predominated, there have been churches, going back to the fifth century, that have not accepted the decision of the council of Chalcedon. Some churches went in a Nestorian direction, and the Assyrian church in Iran, Iraq, and Syria stands in this tradition today. Other churches went in a Monophysite direction. These are the so-called Oriental Orthodox churches, which include the Coptic (Egyptian), Ethiopian, Syriac, and Armenian churches. They do not call themselves "Monophysite," since this concept also includes currents (for example, the theology of Apollinaris) from which they keep a strict distance.

Churches that recognize Chalcedon and churches that do not do so have drawn closer to each other in recent years. Doctrinal conversations have clarified the content and the significance of doctrinal differences in Christology. This applies particularly to the Oriental Orthodox churches: numerous documents of the ecumenical dialogue have affirmed that there is no fundamental disagreement in how Jesus is understood. Instead, the traditional disagreement is understood as primarily terminological: when the Oriental Orthodox speak of the one nature of the incarnate Christ, they believe that they are expressing what Chalcedon expresses by employing the concept of person. All agree on the understanding of Jesus as true God and true human being. A similar clarification and recognition has also taken place in meetings with the Assyrian church.

The traditional doctrine of two natures has been criticized in recent theology, not least with reference to the use of the concept of "nature" to say something about both that which is divine and that which is human. When it is used of human beings, this concept speaks of something that is common to all of them, but God is not one among many gods, but the only God—and this makes it rather meaningless to speak of God's nature as if this were something he shared with others of the same "species." When the concept of nature is used of God, it also has a somewhat static quality, as if one were expressing what a god or the divine is in general terms, independently of what the only God *de facto* is. Affirmations about God ought thus to be formulated, not as general characteristics of the divine, but as affirmations about how the God whom we encounter in Jesus Christ *de facto* is. Ideas about the characteristics of the divine were not indeed unknown in Greek thought in antiquity, and these ideas also played an important role in Christian theology. These included the idea that God is exalted above change and suffering (see also chapter 3, above). One consequence of this was the attempt to distribute various characteristics and functions between the natures. For example, one could say that Jesus suffered in his human nature, but not in his divine nature, since the ability to suffer is not a divine characteristic. As long as the two natures were held together in the one person, this did not necessarily have great consequences, since when the person Jesus suffers, it is the one who is both God and human being that suffers.

If, however, we lay aside some of the ideas about the divine that have their origin in Greek thought, the picture looks somewhat different. If we envisage, not a God who is immutable and immune to influence from outside, but a God who suffers with his creatures, there is less need to distribute roles and characteristics between the natures. The problem about speaking of the divine and the human as two different natures is also that they are perceived as mutually antithetical. For Greek thinking, an antithesis of this kind was completely natural, but not necessarily for a Christian theology of creation. Although it is necessary to distinguish the Creator from the created, a biblical perspective holds that God has nevertheless located something of himself in what is created. We see this not least in the idea that the human being is created in the image of God, and in the idea in the prologue to John's Gospel that the divine Logos (the Word) played a role at creation (John 1:3). When the Word became a human being, therefore, he did not enter into a reality that was alien to him. On the contrary, "he came to what was his own" (John 1:11). When Jesus is called "the image of God" in the New Testament (2 Cor 4:4; cf. Col 1:15; Heb 1:3), this entails not only that he is the perfect human being, but also that he represents God's presence in the created order.

Although there may be good reasons to question the use of the concept of nature, it is nevertheless important to hold fast to what the doctrine of two natures seeks to express, namely, faith in Jesus as true God and true human being. Every elaboration of Christology that makes Jesus less God than God himself, less a human being than us, or a kind of demigod between the two, fails to do justice to the understanding of who Jesus is that has characterized the principal current in the Christian tradition, and that has a good biblical basis. At the same time, neither faith nor theology gets to the bottom of how a human being can at the same time also be God, and of what this entails for us. This, however, does not dispense theology from attempting to understand—as far as our thoughts can take us. But the foundation of such an understanding can never be general principles about how one thinks God ought to be, or what he ought to do: the only foundation can be what God has in fact done, as this is attested in the biblical history. The same applies to Christology. With our starting point in Jesus' life and preaching, we attempt to understand God and what he does in relation to the world.

5.3 THE SIGNIFICANCE OF JESUS' LIFE, DEATH, AND RESURRECTION

Up to this point, we have been primarily concerned about the question: "Who is Jesus?" This, however, cannot be detached from what he did, and from what this signifies. This is why the story of Jesus' life is central to the Christian understanding of Jesus, as we see already in the New Testament, where the four Gospels are precisely narratives of this kind. The discourses in the Acts of the Apostles show that the story of Jesus' life, death, and resurrection was an important ingredient in early Christian proclamation (Acts 2:22–36; 10:34–43). The story starts here with Jesus' baptism in the Jordan and closes with his resurrection and ascension. In Mark's Gospel too, the story of Jesus begins with John the Baptist. Matthew and Luke also relate the prehistory about Jesus' conception and birth, and Luke includes a story from Jesus' childhood (Luke 2:41–52). Apart from this incident, we hear nothing about the time up to his baptism by John and the beginning of his public ministry, presumably when he was around thirty years old. John's Gospel has likewise no historical details about what happened in the first part of Jesus' life, but it draws a trajectory back to the Son's preexistence with God; Jesus' earthly history is seen as a result of the Word becoming flesh (John 1:14). There are also examples in the New Testament epistles of brief summaries of the story of Jesus from incarnation to exaltation (see Phil 2:6–11; 1 Tim 3:16). There is much to indicate that such texts reproduce confessional formulae that were in use in the first Christian communities.

There is a similar brief narrative in several confessional texts. The story is told as follows in the Apostolic Creed:

> I believe . . . in Jesus Christ . . . who was conceived by the Holy Spirit, born of the Virgin Mary, suffered under Pontius Pilate, was crucified, died, and was buried. He descended to hell. On the third day he rose again from the dead. He ascended into the heavens. He is seated at the right hand of God, the Father Almighty. From there he will come to judge the living and the dead.

The Nicene and Athanasian Creeds have similar accounts. One striking characteristic of these texts is that they hop directly from birth to death, apparently putting brackets around what takes up the largest amount of space in the Gospels, namely, Jesus' public ministry from his baptism to his arrest. This is probably because theological interest gradually came to concentrate on the incarnation and on Jesus' death and resurrection. From such a perspective, one could easily regard Jesus' life between birth and death as merely a necessary intermediary stage devoid of any independent theological significance. In our own times, many theologians have criticized this one-sided focus and advocated a greater appreciation of the significance of Jesus' life. At the same time, a traditional use of the concept of incarnation has been criticized for being excessively focused on his conception and birth. For example, Pannenberg points out that the incarnation, whereby the Son of God became a human being, embraces the *totality* of Jesus' life and its theological significance.

Conception and Birth

Matthew and Luke are the only Gospels that tell us something about Jesus' conception and birth. The two accounts are different, but they also have strong similarities. While Matthew traces Jesus' genealogy back to Abraham (Matt 1:1–17) in order to demonstrate that he belongs to the people of Israel, Luke locates Jesus in the human race by tracing his genealogy back to Adam (Luke 3:23–38). Both Gospels relate that Jesus' mother was engaged to Joseph, but that they had not had sexual intercourse before it became clear that she was pregnant (Matt 1:18; Luke 1:34).

This is linked in both Gospels to the activity of the Holy Spirit. According to Matt 1:20, "the child conceived in her is from the Holy Spirit." Luke too explains the conception as the Spirit's intervention, when the angel tells Mary: "The Holy Spirit will come upon you, and the power of the Most High will overshadow you; therefore the child to be born will be holy; he will be called Son of God" (Luke 1:35). The Apostolic Creed declares in the following words that Jesus was conceived by a virgin through the working of the Spirit: "conceived by the Holy Spirit, born of the Virgin Mary."

Apart from Matthew and Luke, no other passages in the New Testament mention the virginal conception or other circumstances of the birth of Jesus. John's Gospel sees everything from the perspective of preexistence ("The Word became flesh," John 1:14), without saying anything about how this happened. Paul mentions only that Jesus was "born of a woman" (Gal 4:4), but neither he nor the other New Testament writers say anything about the circumstances of his conception or birth.

These circumstances were to attract greater attention in later church tradition, as we see for example in the mention of the virginal conception in the confessional texts of the early church. One reason for this was that the virginal conception became an important element in the understanding of Jesus as true God and true human being: just as he has his human nature from his mother, so he has his divine nature from his Father: "He is God, begotten from the substance of the Father before all ages, and a human being, born from the substance of his mother in this age" (Athanasian Creed, 29).

Another factor is the enormous attention that gradually came to be paid to Mary. In church tradition, the story of Mary was elaborated in a manner that goes far beyond the information found in the New Testament writings; Mary as a virgin becomes almost equal in importance to the virginal conception itself. Some of these traditions are also enshrined in the official teaching of the Catholic Church, such as the idea that Mary remained a virgin both during the birth and after the birth. When the New Testament speaks of brothers and sisters of Jesus (Matt 13:55–56; Mark 6:3; Gal 1:19), this is interpreted as a reference to close relatives, not to younger children of Mary and Joseph. (Protestants usually understand this as referring to Mary's and Joseph's children born after they got married.) There can be no doubt that virginity became so important in this connection because of the link between sexuality and original sin that we find in Augustine. The affirmation that Jesus' conception did not involve sexual intercourse thus helped to safeguard the idea of his sinlessness.

The virginal conception has been a disputed doctrine in recent Protestant theology, and many theologians have rejected it for both historical and theological reasons. With regard to history, it has often been argued that the relevant texts in Matthew and Luke have a clearly legendary character; these legends were created at a later stage in order to explain how it was possible for the human being Jesus to be the Son of God, and they drew on other accounts of virginal conceptions that were well known in classical antiquity. With regard to theology, it has been claimed that the idea of Jesus' full humanity makes the virginal conception problematic, for if he is indeed a true human being, this ought to mean that his life began in the same way as that of other human beings. The idea that he had no human father risks making him a demigod instead of true God and true human being.

The assertion that the texts are legendary is certainly not universally accepted. The fact that Matthew and Luke basically tell the same story, although in different ways, may indicate that they are building on two independent traditions, and this would strengthen the historical reliability. One can also argue that the story of Jesus' conception without a legitimate father was so detrimental to his reputation that it would never have been told unless people believed it to be true.

The theological argument that Jesus' full humanity also presupposes that he had an earthly father deserves to be taken seriously, but one should be cautious about moving from a theological point of this kind to a claim about what actually happened. A similar reservation is also necessary with regard to the opposite standpoint, namely, that it was necessary for Jesus to be conceived without an earthly father, in order for him to be the Son of God. To have a view about how the incarnation "had to" take place demands an insight that is utterly outside the scope of a human theology.

This does not mean that theology ought not to attempt to make the content of the faith comprehensible—including faith in the incarnation. But in this work of reflection, theology must take its starting point in what God *de facto* did, not in what we think should or could have taken place. Whether God could have done it differently, is a question that cannot be answered; nor is it necessary to ask it. If we trust the claim in the Bible and the confession of faith that the Son of God was "conceived by the Holy Spirit, born of the Virgin Mary" (the Apostolic Creed), this must be the starting point for theological reflection. In such a perspective, Mary is the link between Jesus and the rest of humankind, while the working of the Spirit ensures the connection and identity between Jesus and God's Son from eternity. The fact that Jesus is conceived without a human father also underlines the new beginning that is expressed by his birth. This has often been seen in connection with Paul's description of Jesus as the second Adam (Rom 5:12–21; 1 Cor 15:45). Like the first human being, Jesus had no human father, and is thus like Adam "son of God" (Luke 3:38).

It is, however, necessary to take a critical attitude to many of the ideas that have tended to cluster around the doctrine of the virginal conception, not least a negative position on sexuality in general, and on women's sexuality in particular. Consequences of this kind, as well as a general Protestant protest against the Marian piety and Marian theology that are also connected to the doctrine of the virginal conception, have certainly played a role in the criticism of this doctrine. But it ought surely to be possible to criticize such consequences without thereby rejecting the doctrine of the virginal conception itself.

Kenosis and Sinlessness

When the Son becomes a human being, what are the consequences for his divinity? Does the incarnation entail any limitation or abridgement of the divinity? One important text in this context has been the so-called "Christ hymn" in Phil 2:6–11, which describes how Jesus debased himself when he became a human being. The first part of this text runs as follows:

> Though he was in the form of God, [he] did not regard equality with God as something to be exploited, but emptied himself, taking the form of a slave, being born in human likeness. And being found in human form, he humbled himself and became obedient to the point of death—even death on a cross. (Phil 2:6–8)

In Greek, "he emptied himself" is *heauton ekenosen*. From this verb derives the term *kenosis*. There has been considerable discussion of how the kenosis is to be understood. Does "he emptied himself" refer to the incarnation itself, to his becoming a human being? Or does it refer to what Jesus endures *as* a human being, that is to say, his assuming "the form of a slave" and entering into suffering and death?

Various versions of so-called kenotic theology, especially in the sixteenth and nineteenth centuries, found it hard to envisage that Jesus, as a human being, retained all his divine qualities, or that his human consciousness could contain a divine self-awareness. In Norway, Ole Hallesby was a representative of this kind of theology.

Their solution was that the Son at the incarnation laid aside all or some of his divine qualities, or else that he at any rate renounced the *use* of them. A related idea can be found in some forms of charismatic theology, where Jesus is perceived first and foremost as a human being filled with the Holy Spirit: thus, it is claimed that when Jesus healed and performed miracles, this was not primarily because of his divinity, but was something he did in the power of the Spirit.

The problem with the various versions of kenotic theology is that while they hold fast in principle to the understanding of Jesus as true God and true human being, they depict the earthly Jesus—as his contemporaries encountered him, and as we encounter him through the Gospel texts—only as a human being. But one important concern of the doctrine of Jesus as true God and as true human being is that we not only encounter God "behind" the human being Jesus, but that we encounter God precisely *in* Jesus. This is expressed, for example, in Jesus' words in John 14:9, "Whoever has seen me has seen the Father." This is not affected by the fact that the earthly Jesus does not seem to put into practice qualities that one might expect of one who is also God (such as omniscience and omnipresence), and that he can even say that he does not know everything (Mark 13:32)—unless, of course, one has a solidly defined picture of how God and the divine must be. In a biblical perspective, God is understood, not on the basis of abstract qualities, but on the basis of how he *de facto* reveals himself. In Jesus Christ, he has shown that to become a human being, with the limitations this involves, and to enter into suffering and death, are certainly not antithetical to being God. It is precisely in what is apparently his antithesis that God becomes visible.

The fact that Jesus was full of the Spirit, and that the Spirit was active in Jesus' life (Mark 1:10, 12; Luke 4:1; 10:21; Acts 1:2; Rom 1:4), is not something that replaces his divinity, but rather an expression of the fact that the Father, the Son, and the Spirit always work together.

As a human being, Jesus shared the conditions of life with other people, with the exception of sin. The classical expression of this is Hebrews 4:15, where Jesus is described as "one who in every respect has been tested as we are, yet without sin" (see also 2 Cor 5:21; Heb 7:26–27; 9:14, 1 Pet 2:22; 1 John 3:5). The fundamental distinction between the human being's created status and the human being's sinfulness is given a concrete expression here in the human being Jesus. He is thus a true human being, not only by being like us, but also by being different from us. In him, it is not only God that is revealed, but also God's will for the human being.

This true humanity does not mean being exalted over temptations to do evil, but rather being tempted and nevertheless choosing to do God's will, as we see, for example, in the narratives of Jesus' temptations by the devil at the beginning of his ministry (Matt 4:1–11; Mark 1:12–13; Luke 4:1–13). When he meets the temptation to avoid suffering, he chooses to let the Father's will be done (Matt 26:39, 42; Mark 14:36; Luke 22:42).

Jesus
Life and Work

I have pointed out, earlier in the present chapter, that the incarnation must not be understood only as the event in which the Son *became* a human being through conception and birth; it also means that he *is* a human being. Jesus' life from birth to death is not merely a necessary stage that brings him from the one point to the other. It is an important aspect of the way in which God encounters human beings through Jesus. Jesus' public ministry, from his baptism in the Jordan by John to his suffering and death, has a special position here, and the longest sections of the Gospels cover precisely this period.

The Gospel accounts show us three important components in Jesus' activity: his preaching, his working of miracles and his healings, and his relationships to other people. Each of these is connected in its own specific way to the central theme of his activity, namely, that the kingdom of God was coming. The kingdom of God was a central theme in his preaching; his working of miracles and his healings were signs that the kingdom was coming; and his fellowship with other people was a foretaste of the fellowship in God's kingdom. In all this, Jesus is not merely one who gives information about what is taking place. He himself represents what is taking place. Through his presence, the kingdom of God is also present. This is why his own person plays an important role in his ministry.

There is no space in the present book to give a complete account of Jesus' *preaching*, but two principal perspectives must be mentioned. The first is his ethical preaching, where his starting point is the law in the Old Testament, which however he both radicalizes and relativizes. He radicalizes it by interpreting God's will as making demands, not only of external actions, but also of words, thoughts, and attitudes (Matt 5:17-42); by interpreting the precept of love of one's neighbor as including even one's enemies (Matt 5:43-48); and when he puts concern for a human being's good above ritual commandments (Matt 12:1-14).

The second perspective is his proclamation of the possibility of salvation and new life that is represented by the kingdom of God. While he intensifies the moral demands, he also mediates forgiveness and grace to those who do not live up to them (John 8:1-11). But he is sharply critical of those who think that they are up to standard (Matt 23:1-36). The customary standards of the world are turned upside-down in the reality of the kingdom of God: the poor, the mourners, and the persecuted are declared "blessed" (Matt 5:1-12). This different perspective is based on the belief that something new is happening in the world, because the kingdom of God is close at hand, through Jesus. The coming salvation is linked even more explicitly to Jesus himself in the Gospel of John (e.g., in John 5:24).

Jesus' *miracles and healings* have often been regarded as a kind of illustration of his preaching, or as a demonstration of who he was; but this understanding does not go far enough. Here, a text like Luke 7:18-23, where Jesus' works are understood as signs that the promised salvation is on its way, offer us a key to what is involved. When Jesus heals, this is not in order to illustrate a point; the healing is an anticipation and foretaste of what is now becoming reality. This meaning of Jesus' works can also be expressed through the concept of *sign* (cf. John 2:11). A "sign" can be understood here as something that points beyond itself, but that also shares in the reality to which it points, as an anticipation or foretaste. When Jesus heals people, this is an anticipation of a reality in which sickness, grief, and pain will no longer be found (cf. Rev 21:4). When Jesus raises the dead (Mark 5:35–43; Luke 7:11–17; John 11:38–44), this is a sign of a reality where death is vanquished. When Jesus drives out the evil spirits, this is a sign that ultimately, all the demonic powers will be conquered.

In his *relationship to other people*, Jesus showed that the fellowship in the kingdom of God is different from what is often the case in this world. He characteristically spent time with those who were not respectable members of society, and people noticed this, as the Pharisees' question to Jesus' disciples shows: "Why does he eat with tax collectors and sinners?" (Mark 2:16). To eat with someone in the culture of that time was a particularly strong sign of fellowship and acceptance. Jesus' fellowship with people at meals was thus a sign of the fellowship in the perfection of God's kingdom (Matt 8:11; 26:29).

Jesus' relationship to other people also finds expression when he gathers around himself a crowd of followers, both women and men, twelve of whom are given a special calling to be his disciples. In this way, Jesus lays the foundation for the fellowship—the church—that is to carry on the message of the kingdom of God after his death and resurrection (see chapter 8, below).

Suffering and Death

The narrative of Jesus' suffering and death plays an important role in all the four Gospels. The passion narrative covers several chapters, and earlier chapters too contain indications of what will happen to Jesus. In Luke's Gospel, Jesus' fate is already hinted at in the infancy narrative (Luke 2:34–35). In the Synoptic Gospels, after Peter, on behalf of the disciples, has confessed faith in Jesus as the Son of God and Messiah, Jesus predicts his suffering, death, and resurrection in Jerusalem (Matt 16:21–23; Mark 8:31–33; Luke 9:22), and he repeats this on two subsequent occasions (Matt 17:22–23; 20:17–19; Mark 9:30–32; 10:32–34; Luke 9:44–45; 18:31–34).

One striking element in these texts is that the disciples either failed to grasp what he was talking about, or else protested, as Peter did (Matt 16:22). The narratives of Jesus' suffering and death also show that the disciples found it hard to perceive the meaning of what took place: what was happening to Jesus seemed to them to form a stark contrast to the confession of Jesus as Messiah and Son of God. It was only in the light of the resurrection, and in the encounter with the risen Lord, that they were able to make a meaningful interpretation of what had happened.

One important element here seems to be their use of the Old Testament in the attempt to find a meaning in what had taken place. According to Jesus' words in Luke 18:31, what was to happen to Jesus was a fulfillment of the words of the prophets. This is also what the risen Jesus tells the disciples on the way to Emmaus: "Oh, how foolish you are, and how slow of heart to believe all that the prophets have declared! Was it not necessary that the Messiah should suffer these things and then enter into his glory?" (Luke 24:25–26).

Jesus' death and resurrection were the very heart of the early Christian preaching, as the key to understanding both who Jesus was and what salvation was. This is expressed with particular clarity by Paul, who summarizes the whole of the Christian message as "the message about the cross" (1 Cor 1:18; cf. Gal 6:14). Here, what happened to Jesus in Jerusalem is no longer a confusing episode, but the very kernel in the message that is communicated. This means that the significance Jesus took on after his death is not due only to the tradition about what he said and about the impact he made on other people; it is due primarily to the circumstances surrounding his death and to what happened afterwards. It is, of course, true that the tradition about his words and deeds also contributes to the interpretation of his death and resurrection—and that his words and deeds are understood in the light of what happened later.

The Christian proclamation and theology that emerged after the events of Easter does not only tell the story of what happened (that Jesus suffered, died, and rose again). It also seeks to interpret these events on the basis of faith in God and in God's salvific action. The attempt to understand the meaning of Jesus' death and resurrection has been a vital project for later Christian theology too, down to our own days.

The Gospels are our most important sources for the sequence of the historical events (Matt 26–28; Mark 14–16; Luke 22–24; John 18–21). Although they diverge to some extent from each other and have different details, they agree on the main elements in the sequence. Jesus is arrested by the Jewish authorities, who put him on trial. He is then handed over to the Roman authorities, represented by the procurator, Pontius Pilate, who condemns Jesus to death. This sentence is carried out by Roman soldiers, who crucify him. A few days after his death and burial, it was reported that the corpse had disappeared, and it was claimed that Jesus had shown himself to several of his disciples.

The Theological Significance of Jesus' Suffering and Death

There are many questions of a historical nature in connection with the accounts of Jesus' death and resurrection, but we cannot examine them here. We shall instead concentrate on the theological significance of the events. In other words: What does what happens to Jesus mean for God's action in relation to the world?

This question is important because the Christian interpretation of Jesus' death soon perceived that it happened in some way in accordance with God's will. In the external sequence of events, it is always human beings who are active. Everything is set in motion by Jesus' Jewish opponents, and it is brought to a close by the Romans. Jesus himself takes a relatively passive role throughout: he offers no resistance, nor does he attempt to extricate himself from the situation.

From a theological perspective, however, it appears that those who put Jesus to death are unwittingly carrying out a divine plan. We see this when Jesus' death is understood as the fulfillment of Old Testament prophecies. This does not mean that those who act against Jesus in his trial are understood as mere instruments with no will of their own and with no responsibility for what happens. This is expressed in an interesting way in Peter's discourse in Acts 3, where he accuses his fellow countrymen of killing Jesus ("You killed the Author of life," v. 15) and asks them to repent and turn to God (v. 19). At the same time, he states that "In this way God fulfilled what he had foretold through the prophets, that his Messiah would suffer" (v. 18).

In other passages, God can be made the subject of what happened. 1 John 4:10 affirms that God has shown his love when he "sent his Son to be the atoning sacrifice for our sins." Paul too can say that God "did not withhold his own son, but gave him up for all of us" (Rom 8:32; cf. 3:25). Jesus himself is not seen here as a victim with no will of his own. On the contrary, he can be depicted as the one who is active, the one "who gave himself for our sins" (Gal 1:4; cf. Eph 5:2; 1 Tim 2:6; Titus 2:14). In John 10:18, Jesus says about his life: "No one takes it from me, but I lay it down of my own accord." He then states that this happens in accordance with the command he has received from his Father (cf. Matt 20:28; Mark 10:45). According to the Christ hymn in Philippians 2:8, "he humbled himself and became obedient to the point of death—even death on a cross."

This act of self-sacrifice took place against a specific background and with a specific intention. Its starting point was love for the world, and its intention was the salvation of the world (see, for example, John 3:16). And this means that it had consequences for the relationship between human beings and God. Paul writes: "in Christ God was reconciling the world to himself" (2 Cor 5:19). The death of Christ thus leads to reconciliation and a restored relationship between humans and God.

How does the Christian doctrinal tradition understand what happens through the suffering and death of Jesus? As in other theological questions, later theology could not be content simply to repeat the New Testament formulas: it was necessary to give them a coherent interpretation for the age in which one lived, and what happened with the doctrine of reconciliation was the same as happened with doctrines such as the Trinity and the two natures. The difference is that the doctrine of reconciliation was never at any time the object of the same precise doctrinal definition as these other two doctrines. This means that there is a much broader theological spectrum on this point, linked in various ways to motifs in the New Testament texts. Before we look more closely at the various models in the history of the doctrine of reconciliation, we must say something more about motifs that are linked to the understanding of Jesus' suffering and death in the New Testament.

Jesus' Death as a Sacrifice

One very central motif in the New Testament interpretation of what happens on the cross is the understanding of Jesus' death as a sacrifice. Although various types of sacrificial actions were known from other cultures and religions at that time, the primary background here is the sacrificial cult that was prescribed in the Old Testament, especially in the Pentateuch, and that was practiced in Jesus' lifetime in connection with the Temple in Jerusalem. To sacrifice meant giving something of one's own to God, either from crops or from livestock. When an animal was sacrificed, it was slaughtered and then either eaten or burnt. Sacrifice could have many different functions, such as expressing thanks to God (Lev 7:12–15). Another central category was expiatory sacrifice, where an ox, a goat, or another animal was presented in expiation for sins, either for those of an individual person or group (Num 15:22–29) or for those of the whole people, as on the Day of Atonement (Lev 16). The animal's *blood* seems to have had a special significance for the effectiveness of the sacrifice, because the blood contains in a special way the life that was given in sacrifice: "For the life of the flesh is in the blood. . . . for, as life, it is the blood that makes atonement" (Lev 17:11). A cleansing function can also be ascribed to the blood (Lev 16:19).

The function of the expiatory sacrifice was thus to atone for human sins. This is necessary because sin creates an impurity that makes it impossible—and dangerous—to draw near to the holy. Sin is thus a hindrance to human beings' relationship to God, and causes wrath and judgment on the part of God. Through the expiation, the human being's sin is taken away, and his or her relationship to God is re-established.

A widespread misunderstanding of the Old Testament sacrifices holds that their intention was to placate God or make him more kindly disposed towards the human being. Such ideas are indeed known from the history of religion, where sacrifices can be seen as something one does for the sake of the deity, and because the deity needs them. In the Old Testament sacrificial prescriptions, sacrifice is something one does for the human being's sake, in order to remove the sin that separates him or her from God.

Another important sacrifice, in addition to those just mentioned, was the Passover lamb that was slaughtered and eaten each Passover in remembrance of the liberation from Egypt (Exod 12). The lamb was to be eaten, but the blood was smeared on the doorposts in remembrance of the angel of death who passed by the Israelites' houses. Here, the blood is not described as a means of expiation, but as a means of protection against evil.

Through the sacrifice, the animal acquires a vicarious function: since the animal dies, the human being need not die. This idea finds a powerful expression in the idea of the scapegoat that was to bear all the sins of the Israelites out into the wilderness (Lev 16:20–22). Another Old Testament text that played an important role in the understanding of Jesus' suffering and death concerns the Suffering Servant of the Lord, who suffered for the sin of others (Isa 53).

It is clear in many New Testament passages that Jesus' death is interpreted in sacrificial categories, not least through the significance that is ascribed to Jesus' *blood* when the authors speak of his death. For Paul, Jesus' death means that "God put [him] forward as a sacrifice of atonement by his blood" (Rom 3:25), and that he "gave himself up for us, a fragrant offering and sacrifice to God" (Eph 5:2). According to the First Letter of John, Jesus is "the atoning sacrifice for our sins, and not for ours only but also for the sins of the whole world" (1 John 2:2; cf. 4:10). The understanding of Jesus' death as a sacrificial death is the great theme of the Letter to the Hebrews. He is the high priest who sacrifices himself, not over and over again, but once and for all: "this he did once for all when he offered himself" (Heb 7:27; see the entire section 4:14—10:18). The sacrificial perspective is also obvious in Jesus' institution of the eucharist, when he speaks of the bread as "my body, which is given for you" and of the wine as the expression of "the new covenant in my blood" (Luke 22:19–20; cf. Matt 26:26–28; Mark 14:22–24; 1 Cor 11:23–25).

The motif of the Passover lamb is also employed to understand Jesus' fate. Paul writes that Jesus is "our paschal lamb" who "has been sacrificed" (1 Cor 5:7), and John's Gospel calls him "the Lamb of God who takes away the sin of the world" (John 1:29). And in the visions in the Revelation of John, he is presented in the form of a lamb, "the Lamb that was slaughtered" (Rev 5:12).

Other Perspectives on Jesus' Death

There are also other concepts than those that refer to the sacrificial cult, for example, the idea of Jesus' death as a ransom: "For the Son of Man came not to be served but to serve, and to give his life a ransom for many" (Mark 10:45; cf. Matt 20:28; 1 Tim 2:6). This concept is not *per se* a religious concept; it can designate the sum of money that buys a slave's freedom. It thus includes a vicarious element: Jesus gives his life so that others may go free. The fact that Jesus died for others is also expressed by the statements that he "died for us" (Rom 5:8; 1 Thess 5:10; cf. Titus 2:14; 1 John 3:16) or that "one has died for all" (2 Cor 5:14).

The vicarious element is also expressed in the idea that Christ takes the human being's sin upon himself: God "made him to be sin who knew no sin, so that in him we might become the righteousness of God" (2 Cor 5:21). There may also be an allusion here to the passage about the Suffering Servant of the Lord in Isaiah 53, which we also find in 1 Peter 2:24: "He himself bore our sins in his body on the cross, so that, free from sins, we might live for righteousness; by his wounds you have been healed."

But Jesus' fate can also be seen in a perspective of battle and victory, where Jesus, by dying, conquers death and the powers of evil. This, of course, becomes particularly clear when the resurrection is included; but it can also be employed as a perspective on the cross, as we find in Colossians 2:15: "He disarmed the rulers and authorities and made a public example of them, triumphing over them in it." There is thus a trajectory from Jesus' fight against Satan and the demons during his public ministry to what happens on the cross. This motif of battle and victory is also linked to another principal motif in the understanding of Jesus' death, namely, the removal of sin: in the preceding verse, we read that "the record that stood against us with its legal demands" was removed when "he set this aside, nailing it to the cross" (Col 2:14).

Theories of Atonement

It is not enough for Christian preaching and theology simply to repeat the New Testament formulations. One must also attempt to interpret and understand the significance of Jesus' death in terms accessible to our own age. The history of theology contains many such attempts, and it is necessary to know them and to bear them in mind when we attempt to understand the significance of Jesus' death for our own age.

Various attempts to explain how Jesus' death could lead to reconciliation with God are often referred to as "theories of atonement." A much used typology of such theories is the tripartite typology of an "objective," a "classic," and a "subjective" theory of atonement, a typology which goes back to the book *Christus Victor* from 1931 by the Swedish theologian Gustaf Aulén.

When Aulén wrote, the debate centered on the relation between an objective and a subjective understanding of atonement. The question was whether atonement and reconciliation is only something that happens in the human being himself or herself (subjective), or whether it also entails a change in God's relationship to the human being (objective). Aulén held that these alternatives failed to include what he saw as an important tradition throughout the history of theology, namely, what he calls the *classic* understanding of atonement. Although Aulén writes here primarily as an historian, there is no doubt that it is this understanding that he himself prefers, and that he wants to give it a prominent place (as is also indicated when he calls it "classic").

Aulén does, however, emphasize that the classic theory of atonement too holds that something objective happens to the relationship between God and human beings. He gives the name *Latin* to what had hitherto been called the "objective" theory of atonement, because it is so widespread in Western Christianity. To a large extent, he identifies the elaboration of this form of an objective theory of atonement with the interpretation of the significance of Jesus' death that we find in Anselm of Canterbury in the High Middle Ages.

In his work *Cur Deus homo* ("Why God became a human being"), Anselm seeks to give a logical explanation of why God had to become a human being and Christ had to die. His starting point is the fall of the human being, which threatens God's plan for the world—and thereby threatens God's honor. In order to re-establish God's plan, either the human being must be punished for his or her sin, or else compensation must be paid (in Latin: *satisfactio*). If God were to punish human beings, they would perish, and this would make it impossible for God to realize his plan. This leaves compensation as the only possibility—but it is impossible for human beings themselves to pay it. Even if one lived in complete obedience to God, this is in any case something that human beings are already obliged to do, and it is therefore impossible for the human being to pay anything over and above this. Since an infinite compensation is demanded, it is only God who can bring this about. At the same time, however, it is the human being who has sinned and who must therefore pay the compensation. The only solution is for God to become a human being; in other words, the incarnation is a logical necessity. Jesus pays the compensation, not through his sinless life—which he in any case was obliged to lead in relation to God—but by dying—which he was not obliged to do. The result of Jesus' death is an infinite merit that is ascribed to human beings, reconciles them to God, and re-establishes God's plan.

In his attempt to interpret the significance of Jesus' death for the people of his own age, Anselm employs an almost juridical line of thought, drawn from the law of compensation. This was probably familiar to his contemporaries, but it is far removed from the conceptual world of the New Testament, and it seems alien to us today. As Aulén also points out, Anselm's model contains several problematic elements, not least the fact that the resurrection has no real significance for atonement. It is also problematic that he takes his starting point in God's honor, rather than in his love.

One problematic aspect of Aulén's use of Anselm is that he so directly identifies an objective theory of atonement with Anselm's version of it. It is not hard to find other versions of the doctrine of reconciliation that are similar to Anselm's but are closer to a biblical line of thought, and do not have the same theological weaknesses.

Various versions of a subjective theory of atonement have often been chosen as an alternative to an objective understanding. Such a perspective is often ascribed to Abelard, a contemporary of Anselm. He saw the problem, not in God's wrath at sin or in the offense to his divine majesty, but rather in the human being's lack of trust in God—and it is this lack that is overcome through Jesus' life and death, which manifest God's love. Here, therefore, it is not God who needs reconciliation, but only the human being. A similar understanding of atonement has been central not least in liberal theology from the nineteenth century onwards. Here, God is seen as boundless love; the problem lies in the human being's inability to open up to this love. This, however, becomes possible when people encounter the demonstration of God's love through Jesus.

The alternative that Aulén prefers to these two models is what he calls the "classic" theory of atonement, a term he uses because believes that it has been central in important periods of church history, not least in the patristic period and in Luther.

In this model (in contradistinction to the other two), atonement is not seen only as a matter between the human being and God. Rather, it involves other powers and forces. The chief problem of the human being is that he or she is in thrall to the forces of corruption, which are represented by sin, death, and the devil. Here too, sin is understood as the human being's fundamental problem, but it is perceived more as a power than as guilt. The resurrection plays a completely different role than in Anselm. It is central, because the battle that takes place on the cross is fully won through the victory over death. In this perspective, the idea that Jesus gives his death as a ransom (cf. Mark 10:45) can be understood as something that is paid to the devil so that he will loosen his grip on human beings; but it is through the resurrection that the devil is ultimately defeated, since not even death could hold Jesus fast.

Some versions of the classic theory of atonement focus more strongly on the human being's relationship to God. These versions include not only sin, death, and the devil among the forces of corruption, but also the law and God's wrath. Aulén points out that this is the case in Luther, where the consequence of human sin is not only that one ends up in the power of death and the devil, but also that one is condemned by the law and is struck by God's wrath. Jesus' death as a sacrifice plays an important role in overcoming this wrath: the wrath strikes Jesus, and thereby the human being is set free. Since the human being is no longer subject to the demands of the law, and no longer subject to God's wrath, death and the devil likewise lose their "rights" to the human being. In this way, this model comes close to fundamental points in an objective understanding of atonement.

In the aftermath of Aulén's book, the perspective on atonement that he calls "classic" has been very influential in theology, where it has been interpreted and used in somewhat different directions. This perspective has been particularly important in liberation theology, where the forces of corruption are identified, not primarily as metaphysical entities (as in Aulén), but as oppressive structures and regimes. The message about Jesus' death and resurrection becomes an impulse to take up the struggle to set people free from what oppresses them. This way of thinking can replace the idea of reconciliation as peace with God, but it can also function as a consequence or a deepening of this idea.

One problem with Aulén's typology is that it presents as mutually exclusive alternative ways of thinking that can equally well be perceived as complementary views. In historical terms, it is not hard to demonstrate that perspectives focusing on Jesus' death as the expiation for sin often stand alongside perspectives focusing on Jesus' death as the victory over the forces of corruption. In the Augsburg Confession, the perspective is on Jesus' death as the sacrifice that reconciles human beings to God by making amends for sin. Article 3 states that Jesus "truly 'suffered, was crucified, died, and was buried' that he might reconcile the Father to us and be a sacrifice not only for original guilt but also for all actual sins of human beings," and article 4 states that he "by his death made satisfaction for our sins." In Luther's Small Catechism, on the other hand, it is the motif of battle and victory that is dominant. The explanation of the second article of the Creed states that Jesus "has purchased and freed me from all sins, from death, and from the power of the devil, not with gold or silver but with his holy, precious blood and with his innocent suffering and death." Luther's Large Catechism includes both perspectives in one and the same text, thereby showing that this cannot simply be reduced to a difference between Luther and Philipp Melanchthon (the author of the Augsburg Confession). It states that Jesus has "brought us back from the devil to God, from death to life, from sin to righteousness, and keeps us there," and that "he suffered, died, and was buried so that he might make satisfaction for me and pay what I owed, not with silver and gold but with his own precious blood."[2]

Since the reformation, Protestant theology has often made use of the juridical metaphor of punishment in a certain version of an objective theory of atonement. According to this line of thought (often called "penal substitutionary atonement theory"), the sin of humanity had to be punished in order to be forgiven, and this punishment was suffered vicariously by Jesus on the cross. The interpretation of Jesus' death as punishment has sparse biblical basis (the sole explicit use of the concept is in Isaiah 53:5), and might be theologically problematic if understood as a divine vengeance that was needed, in order for God to forgive. If punishment means, instead, that Jesus carries the consequences of sin in the world (cf. Romans 6:23: "For the wages of sin is death"), it is easier to see the cross as an expression of divine love.

A conclusion that might be drawn from the preceding is that if we want a holistic interpretation of the theological significance of Jesus' death, it is necessary to include different perspectives. The various "theories of atonement" need not necessarily be mutually exclusive. The problem arises if they are presented as mutually excluding alternatives, or if perspectives central to the New Testament is denied or neglected, for example the understanding of Jesus' death as a sacrifice for the sin of the world.

The theological interpretation of Jesus' death is often expressed in liturgical texts, not least in the eucharist. To take one example: the 2011 liturgy of the Norwegian Lutheran church expresses this in the interpretation of the significance of Jesus' death that lies in the words used after the communion: "The crucified and risen Jesus Christ has given us his holy body and blood which he gave as atonement for all our sins." The following formulation, in one of the alternative prayers of thanksgiving after communion, shows that this perspective is not in conflict with the motif of battle and victory: "We thank you, gracious God, who through this bread and wine have allowed us to share in Jesus Christ's victorious death and resurrection." We also find the subjective perspective, in the wish that the encounter with the crucified Jesus may lead to love and faith, for example in the following prayer: "Teach us to love one another as you have loved us."[3]

---

2. Kolb and Wengert, eds., *Book of Concord*, 434–35.
3. Church of Norway, *Order of the Principal Service*, 14, 15, 34.

Jesus' Death as Answer to the World's Injustice

When we seek to formulate the significance of Jesus' death, this naturally depends to a large extent on what we perceive as the "problem" that this death is meant to solve. For Anselm and his contemporaries, this was first and foremost God's honor, which had been offended and demanded compensation. For Abelard and later liberal theologians, it was the human being's lack of trust and faith in God. For many of the theologians to whom Aulén refers, it was the human being's slavery under the forces of corruption.

There can, of course, be a variety of questions that challenge people today, but it is worth mentioning the role played in our time by questions about guilt and justice. In the past, such issues were often seen from the viewpoint of the rulers, but in our days, greater attention is paid to the perspective of the victim. This means that one is concerned, not only to punish the assailant, but also to ensure that the victim receives redress and justice. In many cases, such a redress is impossible—especially where the victim has been killed. Immense crimes against humanity, like the Nazi holocaust, have raised existential questions that are far from easily answered: one must either conclude that injustice has the last word in our lives, or else one must have recourse to the idea of a divine justice. In the face of cruelty of that kind, the idea of a God who forgives in all circumstances is also problematic. That he should forgive on his own behalf may be acceptable; but the idea that he can simply forgive the attacks on the many victims throughout history can all too easily look like a new assault. In this perspective, modern theologians (among them Jürgen Moltmann) have sought to understand Jesus' death as an action of divine solidarity with the victims, where God himself, through the death of Jesus, becomes a victim of the world's injustice. When God can forgive the sinner, he does so as the one who himself has suffered. Instead of punishing the sinner, he lets the punishment fall upon himself, so that the sinner can go free. Thanks to Jesus' resurrection, this is not merely a theoretical redress, but something that happens in reality, since they are raised up to new life just as Jesus was raised up to new life.

Feminist theologians are among those who have criticized the whole idea that God is behind the death of Jesus as the expression of a violent image of God. Is it possible to believe that a loving God inflicts pain and suffering on his Son? Is this not a form of divine child abuse? Two points must be made in reply to these questions. First, it is not correct to see God as the one who actively inflicts pain on Jesus on the cross: the crucifixion exposes Jesus to the violence that is characteristic of this world. His life ends on the cross because he represents truth and justice in an evil world. But God allows this to happen, and God also uses what happens to bring about salvation for the world. Secondly, it is important to see what happens on the cross in a Trinitarian perspective. It is the Son of God who hangs on the cross, and this means that God the Father also shares in what takes place. God does not offer Jesus as another in sacrifice.

Rather, the death of Jesus must be understood as God's offering himself in sacrifice out of love for the world.

Although these arguments can offer some help towards understanding the significance of Jesus' death, they can never completely explain the way God acts. Here, faith and theology must accept the basic reality that God has *de facto* given his Son, and seek to reflect on what has in fact happened, rather than constructing other ways in which this "could have" happened.

He Was Buried and Descended into the Realm of the Dead

According to the Gospels, after it was recognized that Jesus was dead, he was taken down from the cross and laid in a grave (Matt 27:57–59; Mark 15:42–47; Luke 23:50–56; John 19:38–42); this is also affirmed in the Apostolic and the Nicene Creeds. These words confirm that Jesus truly was dead, and this is theologically significant. It means that he was a genuine human being capable of dying, and this in turn means that he took the path of suffering to its very end. As early as the second century, there were gnostics like Basilides who denied that Jesus had died on the cross, and this view was further developed in Islam. Muslims believe that Jesus did not die, but was taken up bodily into heaven. According to the Ahmadiyya Muslims, Jesus survived the crucifixion and later went to India, where he died in his old age.

There is no historical basis for such ideas, and they are, of course, problematic for a Christian faith that sees Jesus' death and resurrection as fundamental events in God's work of salvation for the world. This is why the reference to his burial is an important clause in the creeds.

While the Nicene Creed goes directly on to the resurrection, the Apostolic Creed has a clause between the burial and the resurrection: "He descended to hell." "Hell" is here not used as a designation for the place of eternal damnation, but rather as the place where the dead rest before the final judgement. The biblical basis for this clause has been found in 1 Peter 3:18–20, which says that Jesus "was put to death in the flesh, but made alive in the Spirit, in which also he went and made a proclamation to the spirits in prison." 1 Peter 4:6 says that "the gospel was proclaimed even to the dead," although it is not clear whether this refers to the same event.

The idea of Jesus' descent to the realm of the dead can make several theological points, although we should be cautious about building too much on such a slender foundation. First of all, it helps to underline the point about the reference to Jesus' burial: namely, that he did in fact die. And this means that he came to where all the other dead persons come—to the realm of the dead.

Secondly, while the Apostolic Creed is content to say that he descended to the realm of the dead, without saying what he did there, the text in 1 Peter says that he took the occasion to preach to those who were there. The point may thus be that the visit to the realm of the dead is understood as an expression of the victory that had been won on the cross and that would soon be manifested in the resurrection from the dead.

Thirdly, this may be an expression of the universal significance of what Jesus does. The gospel he preached concerned not only those who were alive in his own time, but also those who had lived in earlier times.

This idea has often led to the conclusion that death is not the last boundary for receiving the gospel: there may be a chance after death for those who did not hear the gospel while they lived, and perhaps even a new chance for those who heard it but did not accept it. But while we cannot set any limits to God's possibilities of saving human being, it is inadvisable to construct a doctrine on such a slender basis. (For more on this subject, see chapter 9 below.)

The Resurrection

If the cross and the grave had been the last word in the story of Jesus, it is highly unlikely that the narratives about him would have been preserved for posterity. At any rate, they would not have become the basis for a worldwide movement. However, something that happened shortly after the crucifixion put what had happened into a new perspective for his disciples. What had looked like a defeat now turned into a victory that gradually formed the foundations of the Christian preaching and mission. The event usually referred to as "Jesus' resurrection" turned everything upside-down.

Belief in the resurrection of Jesus is widely attested in the New Testament, both in the Gospels and in other writings. The oldest source for belief in the resurrection is probably Paul's First Letter to the Corinthians, where he emphasizes that the resurrection is something that actually happened and that it is fundamentally significant for the Christian faith. He repeats here what he himself has received: "that Christ died for our sins in accordance with the scriptures, and that he was buried, and that he was raised on the third day in accordance with the scriptures, and that he appeared to Cephas, then to the twelve" (1 Cor 15:3–5). There were other apparitions too: "Then he appeared to more than five hundred brothers and sisters at one time, most of whom are still alive, though some have died. Then he appeared to James, then to all the apostles" (1 Cor 15:6–7).

In Paul, the foundation of belief in the resurrection is the encounter with the risen Jesus. The Gospels add one further element, namely, the empty grave. Although the narratives diverge to some extent in their details, they all speak of the disciples' surprise when they found Jesus' grave empty on Easter morning. But they Gospels too relate encounters with the risen Jesus that became the key to understanding why the grave was empty (Matt 28; Mark 16; Luke 24; John 20–21; Acts 1:1–5).

A Disputed Event

The question whether the resurrection is an event that actually took place has always been a matter of dispute. Matthew relates that some people claimed that the grave was empty because the disciples had stolen the corpse; he explains that this was a rumor spread by the Jewish leaders (Matt 28:11–15). This is why the New Testament writers argue for the factual nature of the resurrection by pointing to those to whom Jesus had appeared. (See, for example, Paul in 1 Corinthians 15, and Acts 1:3: "After his suffering he presented himself alive to them by many convincing proofs, appearing to them during forty days and speaking about the kingdom of God.")

With regard to the historical credibility of the resurrection, we should note some unusual details. For example, we read that women were the first witnesses to the resurrection, although this carried less weight, according to the criteria of that period, than testimony by men. We can also ask how fearful and despairing disciples could have been changed in such a short time into courageous witnesses, unless they had had an experience that convinced them that Jesus was alive. But although the historicity of the resurrection can be made probable, one cannot produce any definitive proof. One of the difficulties in evaluating the resurrection as a historical fact is its uniqueness: it differs from every other event in world history, and this means that accepting the resurrection also involves faith that God has acted in a unique manner in Jesus.

The Resurrection as Transformation

The resurrection of Jesus is presented in the New Testament as different from other raisings of the dead that are related there (or elsewhere, for that matter). Those whom Jesus raised from the dead returned to the human life they had led before, and they later died again. But Jesus underwent a transformation in the resurrection. We see this in the Gospels when Jesus appears to the disciples, even through doors that are closed (John 20:19), but then disappears (Luke 24:31). At the same time, the Gospels emphasize that he is still a human being of flesh and blood, whom one can touch physically (Luke 24:37–40; John 20:27). We see this also when he eats (Luke 24:41–43).

Paul's presentation of the resurrection in 1 Corinthians 15 gives us a key to understanding both the continuity and the discontinuity between Jesus' physical existence before and after the ressurection. Paul presents what happened to Jesus as a foretaste of what will one day happen to all human beings: Jesus is "the first fruits of those who have died" (v. 20). In other words, Jesus' resurrection is an eschatological event, that is to say, an anticipation of what is to happen at the close of history. In order to explain how the body that dies is related to the body that rises from the dead, Paul employs the metaphor of seed and plant: it is the seed that becomes the plant, but the difference is nevertheless great (vv. 36–38). Although it is the body that rises from the dead, it has become a "spiritual body" with other qualities than it had before: "What is sown is perishable, what is raised is imperishable. It is sown in dishonor, it is raised in glory. It is sown in weakness, it is raised in power. It is sown a physical body, it is raised a spiritual body" (vv. 42–44). When the body is called "spiritual," this is not an antithesis to the physical. It denotes a body with new qualities, a body that will perish no more.

The Resurrection as a Historical Event

When the resurrection of Jesus can be perceived as an eschatological event, this raises the question of how it can simultaneously be perceived as a historical event. This has led some to affirm that Jesus' resurrection is not a historical, but a metahistorical event. For the nineteenth-century liberal theologians, the story of Jesus' resurrection was a way of expressing his great significance for posterity; it was not to be taken literally. In Bultmann's existentialist theology, the message about the resurrection is not an affirmation about a historical miracle, but a faith in God's grace and love in Jesus.

To understand the resurrection in this way may appear to resolve all the potential conflicts between faith and historical research—we may exaggerate and say that, even if Jesus' dead body was found, that would not shake faith in the resurrection. The problem, however, is that such an understanding transposes God's action outside of the physical world that we experience. God will renew the world at the close of history, but it is *this* world he will renew. If, then, this renewal is anticipated through the resurrection of Jesus (understood as an eschatological event), it is something that takes place in this world and in its history, even if it bursts all the normal frameworks for events in history. But this does not make the resurrection of Jesus something *less than* historical. Rather, it makes it something *more than* an ordinary historical event.

Another problem about saying that the resurrection did not take place in physical and historical reality is that this is completely contrary to the point Paul makes in 1 Corinthians 15, when he claims that the Christian faith stands or falls on the question whether the resurrection actually occurred: "If Christ has not been raised, your faith is futile and you are still in your sins" (v. 17).

Jesus' Death and Resurrection Belong Together

Jesus' resurrection is a decisively important event, not only in a historical perspective, but also for the content of the Christian faith. The encounter with the risen Jesus led to a new perspective on earlier events. In the light of the resurrection, the cross no longer appears as a defeat, but as an expression of God's saving action. And in the light of the resurrection, every doubt about Jesus' filial relationship to God vanishes. Paul affirms that the resurrection is the decisive key to understanding Jesus' true identity: he "was declared to be Son of God with power according to the Spirit of holiness by resurrection from the dead" (Rom 1:4).

It is important to see Jesus' death and resurrection as connected with each other. There has been an unfortunate tendency in the history of theology to see them detached from each other. One example is Anselm's understanding of atonement, where it is Jesus' death that is important; for him, the resurrection tells us that death cannot hold the divine fast, but otherwise it has no genuine reconciliatory significance.

In the New Testament, on the other hand, Jesus' death and resurrection can be mentioned in the same breath as expressions of one and the same divine salvific action, where the one has no particular meaning without the other. This is the case, for example, when Paul says that Jesus "was handed over to death for our trespasses and was raised for our justification" (Rom 4:25). When Jesus speaks in John's Gospel of the crucifixion as his being "lifted up" (John 3:14; 8:28; 12:32), it is clear that crucifixion and resurrection are seen as two parts of one and the same event.

The indissoluble link between the crucifixion and the resurrection sheds light on both of them. The Jesus who submits to suffering and death is the same Jesus who has the power to conquer death. The Jesus who rises from the dead is the same Jesus who entered fully into human suffering, death, and debasement. This means that God's power and greatness manifest themselves precisely in that which is their opposite. It also means that suffering and death will not have the last word—in complete contradiction of normal human experience.

Resurrection as Anticipation

As I have mentioned, one important perspective on Jesus' resurrection is its proleptic character: all human beings will share one day in what happens to Jesus (1 Cor 15:20–24). When he is the first to be "raised from the dead" (v. 20), this is a signal of "the resurrection of the dead" (v. 21). But this general raising of the dead belongs to the close of history, when Jesus returns and all the evil powers are destroyed (vv. 23–24; more on this in chapter 9, below).

This also means that Jesus' resurrection can be understood as an anticipation of the close of history and of the coming of the kingdom of God. It is here that the truth of Jesus' own words that "the kingdom of God has come near" (Mark 1:15) find their clearest expression. This also tells us what God's kingdom means—namely, a new creation and the victory of life over death. In the light of the resurrection, the Christian faith lives out of a hope that is no mere airy speculation: it is "a living hope through the resurrection of Jesus Christ from the dead" (1 Pet 1:3).

If the resurrection is an anticipation of the coming of God's kingdom, this also means that it is a demonstration of the truth of faith in Jesus as the Son of God and the redeemer of the world. According to Paul, the resurrection was precisely a confirmation of Jesus' identity as the Son of God (Rom 1:4; cf. Acts 17:31). This does not mean that the resurrection supplies a proof that compels belief, since it can in fact also be denied. This means that faith itself contains an element of anticipation: when we confess Jesus as the Son of God, we are anticipating what will happen one day, when everyone must acknowledge him (cf. Phil 2:10–11). At present, it is an object of faith. This, however, does not mean that it lacks a basis in experience. On the contrary, it builds on all the signs of God's coming in history—and in the first place, on the resurrection of Jesus.

It is easy, when one discusses the theological significance of the resurrection, to forget its most immediate consequence, namely, that Jesus is alive. For the disciples and the first Christians, the belief that their Lord not only belonged to the past, but was still present with them, was decisively important. When Jesus sends the disciples out into the world to spread the message, he does so with a promise of his own personal presence: "And remember, I am with you always, to the end of the age" (Matt 28:20).

It is decisively important for the church today too that Jesus genuinely lives. When Christians come together for worship, it is not in remembrance of a man who lived long ago, but to meet their living redeemer, in the belief that he is present among them (cf. Matt 18:20).

Ascension and Exaltation: He Sits at the Right Hand of the Father

According to the Gospels, Jesus was physically present among the disciples (albeit in a transformed form) after the resurrection. According to the Acts of the Apostles, these encounters with Jesus lasted for forty days, until he was taken away from them "into heaven" (Acts 1:1–11; cf. Luke 24:50–52; Mark 16:19), an event which is said to have taken place on the Mount of Olives outside Jerusalem.

The event itself is spoken of only in the Gospel of Luke, the Acts of the Apostles, and the secondary conclusion to the Gospel of Mark (the version that is not found in the oldest manuscripts), but there are allusions to it in other passages. In John's Gospel, Jesus says "I am ascending to my Father" (John 20:17); he also asks: "What if you were to see the Son of Man ascending to where he was before?" (John 6:62; cf. 3:13; 20:17). An early Christian hymn quoted in 1 Timothy 3:16 says that he was "taken up in glory" (see also Eph 4:10; 1 Pet 3:22). The ascension was later included as a clause in the Nicene and Apostolic Creeds.

The description of this event as "ascending into heaven" seems to refer first of all to how the disciples experienced the event in very concrete terms. But it also has a clearly theological meaning: in the biblical vocabulary, heaven is the place where God's throne is. The ascension, together with the resurrection, must therefore be seen as an expression of the *exaltation* that forms a counterpart to the *debasement* that Jesus experienced when he entered the world. This connection between debasement and exaltation is described above all in the Christ hymn in Philippians 2. After speaking of the debasement and the death on the cross, the hymn proclaims: "Therefore God also highly exalted him and gave him the name that is above every name" (v. 9).

The exaltation thus represents a kind of reversal of the debasement. He now receives back what he had had to give up. This, however, does not mean that the clocks are turned back, and that the Son returns to his starting point as if nothing had happened. According to the hymn in Philippians 2, it is because of his debasement that Jesus receives "the name that is above every name." It is also important to emphasize that the exaltation does not mean a reversal of the incarnation: it is not as if Jesus lays aside his human nature when he is taken up to heaven. On the contrary, the Jesus who sits at God's right hand in heaven remains true God and true human being. When the Word through whom the world was created (John 1:10) becomes flesh (John 1:14), this was not a passing episode, but something that for all time to come binds God together with the world and with the human race. This means something for the world; but it also means something for God. The incarnation of the Son is not a passing episode, but something that profoundly affects the relationship between the Father, the Son, and the Spirit.

A number of New Testament texts affirm that his exaltation to heaven means that the Son has taken his place at the "right hand" of the Father (Luke 22:69; Acts 2:33; 5:31; 7:56; Rom 8:34; 1 Pet 3:22; Heb 1:3). This formulation is also used in the Nicene and Apostolic Creeds. The background to the theme of sitting at God's right hand is in ideas linked to the kings in the Old Testament. Many New Testament passages allude to, or quote from, Psalm 110:1, "The Lord says to my lord, 'Sit at my right hand until I make your enemies your footstool'" (e.g., 1 Cor 15:25–27; Heb 1:13). The Psalm speaks of the enthronement of the Davidic kings, who are depicted as reigning at the right hand of God. When we read that Jesus takes his place at the Father's right hand, this means that he takes on the role of a king, the one who rules and has power. A similar perspective of power is expressed, for example, in Ephesians 1:20–21, where we read that God "seated him at his right hand in the heavenly places, far above all rule and authority and power and dominion, and above every name that is named, not only in this age but also in the age to come." The same point is made when Jesus sends his disciples out into the world with the words: "All authority in heaven and on earth has been given to me" (Matt 28:18).

Jesus is at the right hand of the Father not only as the Lord of the world, but also as human beings' representative before God, as we see not least in the idea that Jesus intercedes for us. For example, Paul writes that it is Jesus "who is at the right hand of God, who indeed intercedes for us" (Rom 8:34; cf. Heb 7:25; 9:24; 1 John 2:1).

When the New Testament texts locate the exalted Jesus at the right hand of the Father "in heaven," this naturally accords with the worldview of that time, where it was thought that God's throne was somewhere up in the skies. Given our knowledge of the universe, such an idea is meaningless for us. But this does not mean that "heaven" as a theological concept has lost its meaning (see chapter 4.1, above). On this point, Luther was relatively modern when he understood Jesus' place at God's right hand not as a localization in the skies, but rather as meaning that he is now everywhere that God is. In other words, the exalted Christ shares in God's omnipresence.

The affirmation that Jesus sits at God's right hand means that his significance is not limited only to the church or to those who believe in him. Rather, he is the Lord of the whole universe. The reconciliation he won through his death and resurrection thus has cosmic dimensions, as we see not least in Colossians 1:20: "through him God was pleased to reconcile to himself all things, whether on earth or in heaven, by making peace through the blood of his cross."

After the ascension, Jesus is no longer present in the world in the same way as before. This means, not that he is absent, but that his presence is mediated in a new way, through the Holy Spirit. The Acts of the Apostles relate that he promised before the ascension to send the Holy Spirit (Acts 1:4–5), and this promise was fulfilled a few days later, at Pentecost, when the disciples were filled with the Holy Spirit (Acts 2). The promise of the Spirit is also a central theme in the farewell discourse in John's Gospel, where Jesus promises that the Spirit ("the Advocate") will come to the disciples when Jesus departs from them (John 14:26; 15:26; 16:7). The Spirit's task is not to replace Jesus and his significance, but on the contrary, to mediate Jesus and what he has done: "He will glorify me, because he will take what is mine and declare it to you" (John 16:14). From Pentecost onwards, Jesus' continuing presence is mediated by the Holy Spirit, and this is why the confession of Jesus as the Son of God and Lord is an expression of the Spirit's working (1 Cor 12:3). One important instrument of Jesus' continuing presence through the Spirit is the church (for more on this, see chapter 8, below).

He Will Return in Glory

Although Jesus sits at the right hand of the Father and has received "all authority in heaven and on earth" (Matt 28:18), this does not mean that his will is always done on earth. That Jesus is Lord and savior is something about which one must be convinced in faith, by hearing the gospel. At the same time, a central New Testament perspective is that Jesus will return visibly to earth one day. This is already expressed in the narrative of the ascension, when two angels tell the disciples: "This Jesus, who has been taken up from you into heaven, will come in the same way as you saw him go into heaven" (Acts 1:11). According to the Gospels, the second coming was already a topic in Jesus' own preaching (Matt 24:30; Mark 13:26; Luke 21:27), and it is also presupposed in other New Testament writings (1 Cor 15:23; 1 Thess 4:15–17; 2 Pet 1:16; Rev 1:7). Several modern languages have borrowed the Greek noun *parousia*, which is used in several New Testament passages in this sense, to designate the second coming. When he returns, Jesus will be the savior who brings the definitive victory of the kingdom of God, but also the judge who confronts the wickedness and sin of the world. The early church creeds conclude their affirmations about Jesus by saying that he will come again and will set up his kingdom. This is stated in the greatest detail in the Nicene creed: "He is coming again in glory to judge the living and the dead. There will be no end to his kingdom." (For more on this subject, see chapter 9, below.)

Through the belief in the second coming, the entire history of the world and of the creation is embraced by Jesus Christ. In the beginning, he was the creative Word through which the world came into being (John 1:3), and at his return, it is he who has the last word. The Revelation of John expresses this by means of the first and last letters of the Greek alphabet: "I am the Alpha and the Omega, the first and the last, the beginning and the end" (Rev 22:13). This says something about the centrality of faith in Jesus for the Christian faith and interpretation of life. Fundamentally speaking, Christian faith is a faith in Jesus where the world, human life, and God are understood in the light of Jesus.

6

Receiving Salvation—the Work of the Holy Spirit

6.1 WHAT IS SALVATION?

IDEAS ABOUT SALVATION PLAY an important role in most religious traditions. The experience that not everything in the world is as it should be generates the notion that changes for the better are possible—whether for individuals, or a group of persons, or the whole world. This can be perceived as a possibility within the framework of this life, or as something that happens after death, or in a future world that will take the place of the present world.

In purely linguistic terms, the concept of salvation designates both being set free from something and a particular state where life unfolds to the full. The Norwegian noun *frelse* (which comes from *fri hals*, "free throat," that is to say, liberation from servitude) points in the former direction, while the English noun *salvation* and the German *Heil*, which are related linguistically to concepts such as "wholeness" and "health (Latin: *salus*)," point more in the latter direction. Ideas about salvation thus presuppose a problematic state from which salvation frees one, a state that is replaced by something better. This problematic state can lie in the present day, but it can also be understood as something in the future from which one is to be saved (for example, a future judgment). Salvation can be something that is to occur through the intervention of divine powers, or something one should be able to attain without external aid. Although salvation is usually a religious concept, one can find similar ideas in political ideologies. The Marxist notion of the classless society that will come about after the revolution can be understood as a secularized version of biblical ideas about salvation.

Creation and Salvation

Salvation is one of the most central concepts in the Christian faith. Viewed with the eyes of a historian of religion, Christianity is indubitably a religion of salvation. This means that a one-sided perspective based on the theology of creation is inadequate for a Christian interpretation of life. In the Christian faith, belief in God as the Creator of the world is intimately linked to belief in God as the Savior of the world. Accordingly, one cannot understand the world as created by God, if one does not understand the world in the light of what it is destined to become. Nor can human life be understood correctly, if it is not seen in the light of what God destined the human being to become—and salvation is a realization of precisely this.

This makes the understanding of the relationship between creation and salvation an important theological theme, if we are to understand both creation and salvation. It is in this context that we must see the significance of human sin, understood as a rupture with the will of God the Creator and as the fundamental reason why salvation is necessary.

There is an important treatment of this problem in the second century, in Irenaeus. His theology is directed against the gnostics, who saw salvation as being liberated from the material world with its limitations. Irenaeus counters this by affirming the connection between salvation and the created order: salvation is not something that is to replace the created order, but on the contrary, the realization of the Creator's will for the created order. According to Irenaeus, the goal of creation is the same as the goal of salvation: namely, that the human being will be like God. Thanks to sin, the human being was no longer the image of God, but his image is restored in the human being through salvation. In other words, the human being needs to be set free, not from the status of a created being, but from the power that sin and the devil have over the created order. Salvation means that the creation is reestablished, and its destiny is realized. This happens through the reconciliatory work of Jesus, who conquers the evil powers. That which was not realized through the first Adam, because of his disobedience, is realized by Christ as the second Adam.

Irenaeus thus understands Jesus' salvific work as "recapitulation" or "restoration" (Greek: *anakephalaiosis*), a concept borrowed from Ephesians 1:10, which speaks of God's "plan for the fullness of time, to gather up all things in him [Christ], things in heaven and things on earth." But this recapitulation is not merely the restoration of state of things at creation: this concept also contains an idea of the perfection or perfecting of created things. Salvation is a restoration of created things, but it is at the same time something *more* than what existed through the act of creation. It is the perfection of the created order.

Irenaeus' understanding of the relationship between creation and salvation lays down non-negotiable points in a Christian soteriology. This is especially true of the insight that he formulates in his controversy with the gnostics, namely, that salvation comes, not as a replacement of the created order, but as a renewal of the created order and as a realization of God's will for his creation. In the course of church history, the emphasis in the understanding of the relationship between creation and salvation has varied. On the one hand, we find such a strong emphasis on the wretchedness of the world that salvation has been understood as a flight from this world. On the other hand, we find such a positive evaluation of the world and its condition that salvation virtually becomes an ennobling of that which already lies within our grasp. Against one-sided approaches of this kind, we must maintain both that it is *the created order* that is to be saved, and that the created order must be *saved*. In other words, something must take place that lies outside the inherent possibilities of the human being and of the world.

Various Dimensions of Salvation

In the Bible and in the Christian tradition, "salvation" is a concept with a relatively wide spectrum of meanings. Given that salvation involves precisely the realization of God's will for the creation, it is perfectly natural that it is impossible to define "salvation" by means of a simple formula. The differences and contradictions between Christian traditions in this area are often a sign that they emphasize differing dimensions of salvation. From a more holistic perspective, there need be no conflict between such emphases; but problems can arise if the concept is narrowed down too much, and "being saved" is identified with very specific phenomena or experiences.

In the Old Testament, salvation tends to have a rather concrete meaning: it is about being set free from difficult situations in the life of the individual or of the people. In the perspective of faith, salvation is something one awaits from God, and this is why thanksgiving for the salvation one has already experienced, and the prayer that God may intervene and bring salvation anew, are important motifs in the Old Testament texts. This applies both to the prayer that God may save the individual from his enemies (Ps 7:1; 59:1–2) and to the prayer that he may act to bring salvation to the people of Israel (Ps 28:9; 69:35–36). The divine salvific act *par excellence* in the Old Testament is the liberation of the people of Israel from Egypt (Exod 1–15; Ps 105 and 106). The memory of this event also inspires the hope that God will save once more from new crises and from exile (Isa 43:1–7).

Although the threats often come from other peoples, one can also see the finger of God in the evils that occur—which are understood as a punishment for the people's sin. When the people have recognized their sin, God intervenes anew to bring salvation. God judges the people, but because of his love for the people and the promises he has given in the past, he brings salvation anew, provided that the people are willing to repent. This interpretation of the ups and downs in Israel's history is a particularly prominent characteristic in the Deuteronomist historiography (see, e.g., Deut 4:25–31).

The fact God brings salvation is very important for the image of God in the Old Testament. Salvation is not merely one of many things that God does: it defines who he is, as Psalm 68:20 puts it: "Our God is a God of salvation." This means that the one who longs for salvation should go to God: "Deliverance belongs to the LORD!" (Jonah 2:9).

Initially, salvation was understood as help in personal or political crises, but it gradually acquired other dimensions that went beyond this framework, as we see above all in texts in the prophetical books that do not limit God's salvation exclusively to the people of Israel. Now, salvation is something in which the whole world is to share: "Turn to me and be saved, all the ends of the earth! For I am God, and there is no other" (Isa 45:22; cf. 49:6). The prophet's vision speaks of this future state of salvation as "new heavens and a new earth," that is to say, a situation that goes beyond all previous experiences of salvation (Isa 65:17–25; cf. 2:2–4).

In the New Testament, the idea that God is a God who saves is the key to understanding what God does in Jesus. Already in the angel's message about his birth, we hear that "He will save his people from their sins" (Matt 1:21), and this is linked to the name that he receives ("Jesus" = "The Lord saves"). The idea that Jesus is the Savior is fundamental both in the New Testament and in the later Christian tradition. Salvation is something people receive through the encounter with Jesus, as in the case of Zacchaeus: "Today salvation has come to this house" (Luke 19:9). Jesus' death and resurrection have a special significance for salvation, so that Paul can say that we are saved "by his blood" (Rom 5:9). For Paul, this also means that the message about Jesus' death and resurrection has saving power: "For I am not ashamed of the gospel; it is the power of God for salvation to everyone who has faith" (Rom 1:16). Salvation is something one receives here and now through the encounter with Jesus, but also something that will be brought to perfection in the future through his second coming (Phil 3:20).

In a New Testament perspective, salvation is not something meant only for some persons: it is for the whole world, and this is why Jesus is called "the Savior of the world" (John 4:42; 1 John 4:14). There is a close link here between belief in creation and belief in salvation: it is one and the same God who created the world and who now acts through the Son for the salvation of the world. Since there is only one God, there is only one Savior: when God acts to bring salvation, he does so through Jesus. The belief that he is the only path to salvation is expressed, for example, in Peter's words in the Acts of the Apostles: "There is salvation in no one else; for there is no other name under heaven given among mortals by which we must be saved" (4:12). A similar claim to exclusivity is affirmed in Jesus' words in the Gospel of John: "I am the way, and the truth, and the life. No one comes to the Father except through me" (14:6).

The New Testament employs a variety of ideas or groups of motifs to tell us what salvation specifically entails. We can identify at least five different ways of thinking about salvation. The fact that they are different does not mean that they are contradictory, but that they shed light on one and the same reality from differing angles.

Receiving Salvation—the Work of the Holy Spirit

The first group of motifs is linked to guilt and making amends. Here, the problem is identified as human sin and the guilt that this entails vis-à-vis God. The solution lies in repentance and forgiveness. One example of such an understanding of salvation is Jesus' declaration that human sins are forgiven (Mark 2:5). The understanding of salvation as the forgiveness of sin is closely connected to the understanding of Jesus' death as the expiation of sin (see the previous chapter). This is expressed in Jesus' words at the institution of the eucharist, when he speaks of his blood as "poured out for many for the forgiveness of sins" (Matt 26:28). Salvation as the forgiveness of sin is often linked to the idea of repentance: one turns from one's sins and repents of them, and making amends and forgiveness permit one to lead a new life. The Gospels present John's baptism as a baptism of repentance (Mark 1:4–5). Jesus picks up this idea when he preaches: "Repent, and believe in the good news" (Mark 1:15), and when he says that has come to call sinners to repentance (Luke 5:32). Luke 24:47 sums up the message of salvation from this perspective when Jesus says "that repentance and forgiveness of sins is to be proclaimed in his name to all nations" (cf. Acts 3:19).

The second group of motifs involves slavery and liberation. The idea here is that the human being is bound and that salvation means being set free. This is the perspective when Jesus in the synagogue at Nazareth interprets his own activity on the basis of the prophecy that captives will receive their freedom and the oppressed be set free (Luke 4:16–21). The liberation that Jesus brings can find very concrete expressions in being freed from illness (Luke 13:10–17); it can also signify more generally that Jesus wants "to set us free from the present evil age" (Gal 1:4) or "from the power of darkness" (Col 1:13). The freedom he brings surpasses every other freedom: "If the Son makes you free, you will be free indeed" (John 8:36). This group of motifs is linked especially to what I have described in the previous chapter as the motif of battle and victory in the understanding of Jesus' death.

The third group of motifs involves life and death. Death here means both physical death and death in a more spiritual sense. The latter meaning encompasses people who are spiritually dead until they are given a share in new life through salvation in Jesus Christ. The Letter to the Ephesians affirms: "You were dead through the trespasses and sins in which you once lived," but this condition is immediately contrasted with what God has done to save us: "But God, who is rich in mercy, out of the great love with which he loved us even when we were dead through our trespasses, made us alive together with Christ—by grace you have been saved" (2:1–2, 4–5). Salvation, as a new life, can also be described as a birth (John 3:5; Tit 3:5; 1 Pet 1:3, 23). This corresponds to the image of Jesus as the giver of life (John 5:21), and indeed, as the one who is life itself (John 1:4; 11:25; 14:6). While salvation as new life is given already here and now, salvation as new life also means that ultimately, life will conquer physical death through the resurrection of the dead (1 Cor 15:20–23). A concept that unites the present and the future elements is "eternal life," which can be used both of life in the coming world (Luke 18:30) and of the life that believers already possess in Jesus: "Whoever believes in the Son has eternal life" (John 3:36).

The fourth group of motifs involves falsehood and truth. Salvation is understood here as turning away from falsehood and coming to know the truth. In this perspective, human beings' need of salvation is perceived as a consequence of their "exchanging the truth about God for a lie" (Rom 1:25). Accordingly, salvation entails coming "to the knowledge of the truth" (1 Tim 2:4). Learning to know the truth is, however, more than gaining insight into some particular content of knowledge: it also means entering into a relationship with the one who in his person *is* the truth: "I am the way, the truth, and the life" (John 14:6).

The fifth group of motifs speaks of the relationship between human beings and God, a relationship that is broken through sin, but is renewed through faith in Jesus. Through his death, those who once were God's enemies are reconciled to him (Rom 5:10). Salvation therefore means having fellowship with God. "Everyone who confesses the Son has the Father also," we read in the First Letter of John (2:23), and this is equated with "abiding in the Son and in the Father" (1 John 2:24*). In Paul, being "in Christ" is a central theme that describes the situation of the believer, as we read, for example, in 2 Corinthians 5:17: "If anyone is in Christ, there is a new creation." The renewed fellowship with God also means a renewal of human fellowship. In the Christian fellowship, those who have fellowship with God receive fellowship with one another (see further, on the understanding of the church, in chapter 8).

The existence of different groups of motifs linked to the understanding of salvation in the New Testament does not mean that they are mutually exclusive. On the contrary, they can often be linked and complement each other. Besides this, the fact that salvation is presented as a many-faceted phenomenon tells us that salvation concerns *the totality*. Just as there is no part of human life that is not influenced by sin and evil, so too there is nothing that will not be embraced by the reality of salvation, a salvation that means that "God may be all in all" (1 Cor 15:28).

The Relationship between Biblical and Dogmatic Concepts

While the New Testament texts employ many different concepts, which are often metaphorical (for example, when they speak of a new birth), the church's theology has tended rather to look for unambiguous concepts for the various aspects of salvation. Such attempts to specify and interpret the New Testament message with the aid of defined concepts are both necessary and useful in the understanding of salvation (as in the understanding of other questions, such as Trinitarian doctrine and Christology). This also means that the way in which words and concepts are employed in the New Testament texts is not necessarily identical with the concepts that are employed in dogmatics. In the New Testament texts, words can often be used in a variety of ways, or different words can be used to designate the same reality. In dogmatics, on the other hand, one attempts to work with more unambiguous concepts. (See what was said in chapter 1 about the relationship between biblical theology and dogmatics.) This does not dispense us from the obligation to give an account of the way in which the formation of the dogmatic concepts builds upon and interprets the New Testament message.

It is, however, necessary to be aware of a number of risks that accompany such a conceptualization. One risk is that one draws such a strong distinction between the various elements in salvation that they appear to be separate events or stages. In some cases, the attempt has also been made to describe one particular sequence of the various elements in salvation, an "order of salvation" (Latin: *ordo salutis*). In Lutheran theology, such attempts to describe an *ordo salutis* had particularly practical consequences in Pietism, where it was seen as a pattern that the individual believer was expected to realize. It is highly problematic to give normative status to one particular pattern of experience, not least because people can experience salvation in very different manners. Such a schema also risks detaching from one another elements that belong together, or that are two sides of the same coin.

Another problem with a conceptualization of this kind is that it tended to be done differently in the various Christian traditions and confessions. It is above all in the understanding of salvation that doctrinal formulations were elaborated that were regarded as conflicting with each other, and soteriological differences of this kind have indubitably been an important element in the divisions between the various churches—not least in the schism between the Catholic Church and the Protestant churches after the Reformation. While some of these differences are certainly real, others can be explained by differing understandings of theological concepts and somewhat different emphases on the individual aspects of salvation. An important rapprochement has occurred in recent years between various churches in this field, not least because they have worked together in going behind the formulations in the various traditions to see how each one had sought to do justice to particular motifs in the New Testament. This has generated an understanding that the various confessional accounts of salvation need not be mutually exclusive, but can also be complementary. Taken together, they express something of the breadth in the understanding of salvation that is already found in the New Testament. (On the understanding of the doctrine of justification, see below.)

Salvation as Already Now, but Not Yet

One important problem in the understanding of salvation is whether it is something that happens here and now or in the future, and whether it is a single event or a process. We can find a key to this question in what we have said in the previous chapter about the understanding of the kingdom of God. I pointed out there that the kingdom of God is both something that already is near, something in which people receive a share, *and* something that has not yet come fully. This reality is anticipated through the life, death, and resurrection of Jesus, but at the same time, it is not fully realized until Jesus returns at the end of the world. The kingdom of God is present *already now*, but it is *not yet* fully realized. This "already now, but not yet" structure can also apply to the understanding of salvation. In the encounter with Jesus through the gospel, people receive a share in salvation already here and now, but at the same time, this salvation is not fully realized: it is an anticipation of the salvation that one day will come in fullness. This makes it necessary to see salvation in an eschatological process, as something in which people already receive a share here and now, but that is to be realized fully only at the end of the world.

This perspective also means that salvation cannot be understood as something purely individual, as something that concerns only the individual. In the New Testament, salvation has not only a collective, but also a cosmic dimension. According to Paul, "the creation itself will be set free from its bondage to decay and will obtain the freedom of the glory of the children of God" (Rom 8:21). Accordingly, salvation means, not a flight from the world, but a faith that God will renew the world and create "new heavens and a new earth, where righteousness is at home" (2 Pet 3:13).

The theme of the present chapter is closely connected to the discussion of Christology in the previous chapter. What salvation is, is naturally linked closely to who the Savior is, and to what he has done. There is a close connection between the abundance of motifs we observed in the understanding of Jesus' death and the corresponding abundance of motifs in the understanding of salvation. But while the discussion of the doctrine of reconciliation concerns the foundation of salvation, which was laid through Jesus' death and resurrection, soteriology is about how the individual is to receive a share in salvation. In other words, it is about what is often called *the appropriation of salvation*.

6.2 THE HOLY SPIRIT: GIVER OF LIFE

The Holy Spirit has a central role in the doctrine of the appropriation of salvation. While the objective foundation for salvation is laid through the life, death, and resurrection of Jesus, people receive salvation through the work of the Holy Spirit. In his farewell discourse in John's Gospel, Jesus promises that he will send the Spirit to continue Jesus' work when he himself has left them; similarly, the Acts of the Apostles relate that before Jesus was taken up into heaven, he promised that the Holy Spirit would come upon them (1:8). The rest of the Acts of the Apostles is really nothing other than a narrative of how this promise was fulfilled: first, how the Spirit came upon the disciples on the day of Pentecost, and then how the Spirit led them out into the world to proclaim the gospel so that more and more people could receive salvation and the Spirit. Peter's words to those who felt that the message about Jesus had touched them on the day of Pentecost affirm that the Spirit and salvation belong together: "Repent, and be baptized every one of you in the name of Jesus Christ so that your sins may be forgiven, and you will receive the gift of the Holy Spirit" (Acts 2:38).

The Role of the Spirit

The Spirit's role in salvation is also expressed in the Apostolic Creed. The section that begins with a confession of faith in the Holy Spirit ("I believe in the Holy Spirit") also contains affirmations about matters such as the church, the forgiveness of sins, and eternal life. When we speak of themes that belong to the "third article of faith," what we have in mind is precisely the work of the Spirit in mediating salvation in the church and in believers.

Although the New Testament too speaks of the Holy Spirit primarily in such contexts, the Spirit's work is not restricted only to the appropriation of salvation, as we see not least in the Old Testament, which states that the Spirit shared in the creation of the world (Gen 1:2). In other passages, the Spirit is spoken of as an expression of God's creative and saving work, for example, in Psalm 104:30: "When you send forth your Spirit, they are created, and you renew the face of the ground" (cf. Job 33:4; Ezek 37:14).

In other passages in the Old Testament, the Spirit is linked above all to chosen persons who have a special task in the history of the people of Israel, such as the leaders described in the Book of Judges (3:10; 6:34), and the kings Saul and David (1 Sam 10:10; 16:13)—to say nothing of the future savior king (Isa 11:2). The prophets form a group who are particularly prominent as instruments of the Spirit (Num 24:2; Isa 61:1; Mic 3:8).

The prophets' role as instruments and spokesmen for the Spirit also finds expression in the Nicene Creed, which confesses faith in the Spirit "who has spoken through the prophets." This understanding of the prophets as persons filled with the Spirit is found in the New Testament, when it is said about John the Baptist: "even before his birth he will be filled with the Holy Spirit" (Luk 1:15; cf. 1 Pet 1:10–11).

The possession of the Spirit is linked in the Old Testament primarily to some chosen persons, but the prophet Joel paints a picture of the eschatological age in which God's Spirit is to come over everyone: "Then afterward I will pour out my Spirit on all flesh; your sons and your daughters shall prophesy, your old men shall dream dreams, and your young men shall see visions. Even on the male and female slaves, in those days, I will pour out my Spirit" (Joel 2:28–29). Peter's sermon on the day of Pentecost interprets what has just happened as a fulfillment of precisely this prophecy (Acts 2:16–21). In other words, the new age has come through Jesus: now, the gift of the Spirit is bestowed on all who repent and receive baptism (Acts 2:38).

In the New Testament, the Spirit plays a key role in the understanding of Jesus and of the salvation he brings. The angel's message declares that Jesus' conception was the result of the Holy Spirit coming over Mary (Luk 1:35; Matt 1:20). The Spirit came over Jesus at his baptism (Matt 3:16), and the Spirit then led him out into the wilderness (Matt 4:1). When he casts out the evil spirits, he does so by the Spirit of God—a sign that the kingdom of God has come (Matt 12:28). "God anointed Jesus of Nazareth with the Holy Spirit and with power" (Acts 10:38), and his resurrection took place through the Holy Spirit (Rom 1:4).

John the Baptist says that Jesus would baptize, not with water as he himself had done, but "with the Holy Spirit and fire" (Matt 3:11). Jesus says in the Gospel of John that one must be born anew through the Spirit, in order to receive a share in the kingdom of God (3:3–8). In Paul, receiving a share in salvation is almost synonymous with receiving a share in the Spirit. For example, he writes in the Letter to the Romans: "You have received the Spirit of adoption" (8:15*). It is the Spirit who creates the confession of faith in Jesus (1 Cor 12:3), and being a Christian means "living by the Spirit" (Gal 5:16*) and being "a dwelling place for God in the Spirit" (Eph 2:22*; cf. 1 Cor 3:16). The Spirit also gives the church various gifts that it needs (1 Cor 12:1; 14:1). (For more on this subject, see chapter 8.)

The Spirit as the Power of God

In purely linguistic terms, the noun "spirit" is connected in most languages to natural phenomena such as "breath" and "wind." The basic observation that it is the breath that distinguishes a living human being from a dead one (Gen 2:7; Job 27:3) makes it natural to see God's life-giving power precisely in the "spirit." This does not mean that life *per se* is divine, but that all life has God as its source. If God withdraws his Spirit, the basis of life also disappears. The Nicene Creed has good biblical foundations for calling the Spirit the "Life-giver" (*zoopoion*) (see, for example, Ps 104:30; John 6:63; 2 Cor 3:6).

The analogy between the Spirit and the wind also implies that the Spirit is outside human control. As the Spirit of God, the Spirit is free like God himself. This perspective finds expression in Jesus' words in John 3:8: "The wind blows where it chooses, and you hear the sound of it, but you do not know where it comes from or where it goes. So it is with everyone who is born of the Spirit."

Another aspect linked to the Spirit is the idea of the Spirit as an expression of God's *power*. "Spirit and power" are often mentioned together, almost as synonyms (Luk 1:17, 35; Acts 10:38; 1 Cor 2:4), or else we read that the Spirit *gives* power (Acts 1:8; Eph 3:16; 2 Tim 1:7). The Spirit's power equips people and enables them to serve. But we also see how the experience of the Spirit helps to convince people of the truth in the message, as when Paul says that he proclaimed his message "with a demonstration of the Spirit and of power" (1 Cor 2:4).

Receiving Salvation—the Work of the Holy Spirit

The Spirit as a Person in the Trinity

In the Bible and elsewhere, the Spirit is often called *the Holy Spirit*, in order to affirm that we are speaking of the Spirit of *God*, in contradistinction to all other spirits or spiritual powers. The adjective "holy" refers here to that which belongs exclusively to God and is, of course, completely different from demonic spiritual powers. According to Paul, there is a difference between "the spirit of the world" and "the Spirit that is from God" (1 Cor 2:12), but this distinction also applies in relation to the spirit, or the spiritual, as an aspect of human reality. The fact that we encounter God as Spirit does not mean that the spiritual aspect of the human being is divine.

We have seen in chapter 3 how the relationship between the Father, the Son, and the Spirit is understood in the framework of Trinitarian doctrine. With a basis in the New Testament understanding of the Spirit, it has been affirmed that the Spirit is not only a power that God employs as his instrument: the Spirit also *is* God. The Spirit can be described as one with God and with Jesus, and at the same time as sent out from the Father and from the Son. "God is spirit," according to John 4:24. The Spirit is "the Spirit of God" (Rom 8:14) and "the Spirit of his Son" (Gal 4:6). At the same time, the Spirit is distinguished from the Father and the Son by the fact that the Spirit is sent to the world by the Father and the Son (John 14:26; 16:7). The Nicene Creed affirms the full divinity of the Spirit as "the Lord and Life-giver, who proceeds from the Father [and the Son], who with the Father and the Son is worshiped and glorified."

The fact that the Spirit is sent to the world means that the Spirit represents in a particular way God's life-giving and recreating *presence* in the world. When the triune God draws near to human beings and human experience, he does so as the Spirit. When God makes his dwelling in human beings and transforms their lives, he does so as the Spirit. When God creates faith in Jesus in human beings and gives them salvation, he does so as the Spirit. When God builds his church, equips people, and sends them out in service, he does so as the Spirit.

The fact that the Spirit is God, present in the world, means that through the Spirit, we also encounter the Father and the Son. The New Testament describes the working of the Spirit as pointing, not to the Spirit himself, but to the Son whom the Father has sent. Jesus expresses this in the farewell discourse as follows: "He will glorify me, because he will take what is mine and declare it to you. All that the Father has is mine" (John 16:14–15; cf. 14:26). The Spirit is thus the one who reveals God and his will (1 Cor 2:10–11). It is he who imparts conviction about the truth in the message (John 16:8). Because the Spirit brings conviction about the truth and guidance in the truth, he is called "the Spirit of truth" (John 16:13).

Although the New Testament describes a very broad spectrum of activity by the Spirit, some parts of the theological tradition have often tended to see this much more restrictively. This is the case not least in Western theology, both in its Catholic and its Protestant versions. Here, the focus on Jesus and on salvation in him has frequently been so strong that it has not always been equally clear that it is the Spirit who brings Jesus near. This applies *inter alia* to the understanding of the eucharist (see chapter 7 below). Pneumatology (the doctrine of the Holy Spirit) has played its primary role in the doctrine of the appropriation of salvation and in ecclesiology (the doctrine of the church).

In Eastern Orthodox theology, greater emphasis has traditionally been laid on the importance of the Spirit and on various aspects of the Spirit's working. This applies *inter alia* to the understanding of the work of the Spirit in the creation. Ecumenical rapprochement in our own days has led to a greater awareness in Western theology too of the importance of the Spirit.

In ecumenical terms, however, it is the growth of the Pentecostal movement and the charismatic movement in the twentieth century that has been the most significant factor in the development of pneumatology. This is because these movements took up afresh elements in the New Testament understanding of the Spirit's work that had not been prominent in the church's tradition. This applied, first, to the work of the Spirit as something that could be experienced, with reference to the accounts in the Acts of the Apostles; and secondly, to the charisms as gifts of the Spirit, and to the role they play in the church's life. Here too, appeal was made to New Testament texts about phenomena such as speaking in tongues and prophetic speaking. Pentecostal and charismatic experiences and positions gradually acquired importance in the traditional churches too, while on the other hand, Pentecostal and charismatic theology has often been moderated somewhat in the encounter with traditional theology. But pneumatology remains an area where further clarification is both necessary and important.

The Appropriation of Salvation as the Work of the Spirit

When the Apostolic Creed includes salvation in the article about the Holy Spirit, this is an affirmation that not only the basis of salvation, but also its appropriation, is God's work. To receive salvation means, not that the human being reaches out towards a heavenly reality, but that God in the Spirit draws near to human beings. A classic expression of the fact that the appropriation of salvation is not a result of human striving, but an expression of the work of the Spirit, is found in the explanation of the third article of faith in Luther's Small Catechism:

> I believe that by my own understanding or strength I cannot believe in Jesus Christ my LORD or come to him, but instead the Holy Spirit has called me through the gospel, enlightened me with his gifts, made me holy and kept me in the true faith, just as he calls, gathers, enlightens, and makes holy the whole Christian church on earth and keeps it with Jesus Christ in the one common, true faith. Daily in this Christian church the Holy Spirit abundantly forgives all sins—mine and those of all believers. On the Last Day the Holy Spirit will

raise me and all the dead and will give to me and all believers in Christ eternal life. This is most certainly true.

In addition to speaking of the human dependence on the Spirit in the appropriation of salvation, Luther here expresses the breadth in soteriology that I have pointed out earlier in the present chapter. This applies both to the various dimensions of salvation (enlightenment, sanctification, the forgiveness of sins, living in the fellowship of salvation, etc.) and to the various phases of salvation: the Spirit gives salvation, preserves in salvation, and leads the individual believer and the whole church forward to eternal life in the kingdom of God.

6.3 JUSTIFIED BY FAITH

In Western theology, the appropriation of salvation has largely been understood from the perspective of *justification*. This became particularly important in mediaeval theology, and the understanding of justification was central in the doctrinal disputes in the Reformation period. In the aftermath of the Reformation, divergent positions on justification have been regarded as one of the most important differences between Catholic and Lutheran (and other forms of Protestant) theology. Nevertheless, the doctrine of justification was the subject of one of the most remarkable breakthroughs in our own days, namely the Catholic and Lutheran rapprochement in the *Joint Declaration on the Doctrine of Justification* (1999).

The Concept of Justification

The concept itself has its origin largely in the Letters of Paul, especially Romans and Galatians, and the theological discussion of justification has therefore been largely a discussion of how these and other texts in the New Testament are to be interpreted.

The English adjective "just" has a somewhat narrower meaning than the biblical concept. When we say that something is just, we tend to mean that people are being treated in a way that they deserve, or that is reasonable; when something or someone is unjust, this tends to designate a failure to match such norms or expectations.

"Just" and "justice" have a more comprehensive meaning in the biblical and theological vocabulary. In the Old Testament, a just (or "righteous") person is one who follows God's will and lives in accordance with his will. In Psalm 1, the righteous person is the one who delights in God's law—unlike the sinners. Righteousness thus becomes almost synonymous with goodness, while unrighteousness is equated with wickedness and sin. Another example is Ezekiel 18:5–9, where the righteous man is described *inter alia* as one who does not worship idols, defile his neighbor's wife, or commit robbery. Instead, he gives bread to the hungry and clothing to the naked. The righteous person is thus the one who keeps to the various aspects of God's law, as this law is expressed in texts like the Ten Commandments.

The reference to God's law entails that the concept has a certain juridical, legal note, since people are also condemned on the basis of the law. This perspective is expressed above all when God is spoken of as just, often as "a righteous judge" (Ps 7:11), as one who "judges the world with righteousness, judges the peoples with equity" (Ps 9:8). When a human being can be spoken of as righteous, this means that he or she can remain standing before the judgment seat of God, whereas the unrighteous person is condemned (1 Kgs 8:32; Ps 7:8–9). But the fact that God is a righteous judge also means that he establishes justice for those who have been harmed by injustice, not least the poor and the helpless (cf., for example, Isaiah 11:4: "with righteousness he shall judge the poor, and decide with equity for the meek of the earth"). This is why justice can be used in some passages almost synonymously with "salvation" (Isa 61:10).

Although we find an assurance that the righteous person will remain standing in the judgment (Ps 68:3), we also find several passages that are uncertain about whether any human being can really meet the standards of God's righteousness. For example, Psalm 143:2 says: "No one living is righteous before you" (cf. Job 25:4). And this is why God's righteousness is juxtaposed with his grace and mercy (Ps 116:5). Even for the unrighteous person, it is possible to repent and receive God's mercy and forgiveness (Isa 55:7).

In the Synoptic Gospels, the concept of righteousness is used in a way that corresponds to the Old Testament usage. In the parable of judgment in Matthew 25, those who have done good are called righteous and receive eternal life (Matt 25:34–40; cf. also 12:37; 13:41–43). We also find a harsh criticism of those who regard themselves as righteous, although this is a merely external righteousness that veils hypocrisy and injustice (Matt 23:28). This also means that much more is demanded, if one is to be accounted as righteous: "For I tell you, unless your righteousness exceeds that of the scribes and Pharisees, you will never enter the kingdom of heaven" (Matt 5:20). The gospels also indicate that righteousness is not something one attains by one's own moral endeavor, but something given by God's grace, and something that is linked to the coming of the kingdom of God. Jesus says that the tax collector who asked God to be merciful to him "went down to his home justified" (Luk 18:14), and Jesus tells the disciples to "strive for the kingdom of God and his righteousness" (Matt 6:33).

It is above all Paul who uses the concept of righteousness most extensively to elaborate his understanding of salvation. This occurs primarily in the Letters to the Galatians and the Romans. In Paul too, the concept is connected to the law, which offers the initial definition of what righteousness is. However, he rejects the idea that it is possible for a person to become righteous by following the law (Gal 2:21), because although the human being knows the law of God, he or she does not follow it. He observes: "There is no distinction, since all have sinned and fall short of the glory of God" (Rom 3:22–23). This means that the function of the law is to unmask sin and demonstrate human guilt vis-à-vis God: "We know that whatever the law says, it speaks to those who are under the law, so that every mouth may be silenced, and the whole world may be held accountable to God" (Rom 3:19). Accordingly, every notion that one can become righteous before God by following the law is erroneous: "For 'no human being will be justified in his sight' by deeds prescribed by the law, for through the law comes the knowledge of sin" (Rom 3:20).

The good news in this situation is that God's righteousness is revealed as a *saving* righteousness, independently of the demands of the law. This is a righteousness that is linked to Jesus' death as expiation for human sins, and it is given as a gift to all who believe in Jesus: "But now, apart from the law, the righteousness of God has been disclosed, and it is attested by the law and the prophets, the righteousness of God through faith in Jesus Christ for all who believe" (Rom 3:21–22). Righteousness is not won through works of the law, but is given through faith in Jesus: "We hold that a person is justified by faith apart from works prescribed by the law" (Rom 3:28). But faith is not a new "achievement." Justification occurs "by his grace as a gift" (Rom 3:24). It is not based on human merit, as we see not least in the fact God is a God who "justifies the ungodly" (Rom 4:5).

In the Letter to the Galatians, Paul's theme is those aspects of the law that separate the Jews from other peoples, especially the precept of male circumcision. Against those who demanded that Gentile Christians must be circumcised, Paul affirmed that this in reality was an attempt to become righteous by works of the law. If one makes circumcision a precondition for salvation, one is obliged to keep all the other parts of the law. And that means setting aside the righteousness that is given through faith in Jesus: "I testify to every man who lets himself be circumcised that he is obliged to obey the entire law. You who want to be justified by the law have cut yourselves off from Christ; you have fallen away from grace" Gal 5:3–4). Here, as in the Letter to the Romans, faith in Jesus is the only path to become righteous: "We know that a person is justified not by works of the law but through faith in Jesus Christ" (Gal 2:16).

Luther's Doctrine of Justification

Paul's understanding of justification has been immensely important, not least thanks to Martin Luther and what he himself saw as a rediscovery of Paul's understanding of the gospel. For Luther, unlike Paul in the Letter to the Galatians, the problem was not the relationship to the Jewish law, but the understanding of salvation that was prevalent in the theology of his time. This theology too emphasized that salvation was a result of God's grace, but it tended to claim that it was necessary for the human being to collaborate with grace, and that grace bore fruit in the individual's life in order for the human being to be righteous before God. For Luther, this meant that he could not be certain of his own salvation, for if something—even something that was very small—depends on the human being oneself, one can never be certain of being saved. Luther found the solution when he grasped that "the righteousness of God" in the Letter to the Romans does not mean a demanding and judging righteousness (or justice) on the part of God, but rather the righteousness that he bestows on the human being out of grace, through faith in Jesus. The fact that the human being is justified by faith means, for Luther, that one is justified, not by faith in combination with works, but by *faith alone* (Latin: *sola fide*). Works have their place in the Christian life, but as a *consequence* of salvation—not as its precondition.

Luther's understanding of justification came in many ways to be a distinguishing mark of the Reformation, and not only on the Lutheran side. When Melanchthon formulated the Protestant faith in the Augsburg Confession, he made the doctrine of justification the central point. Article 4 puts it as follows:

> Likewise, they teach that human beings cannot be justified before God by their own powers, merits, or works. But they are justified as a gift on account of Christ through faith when they believe that they are received into grace and that their sins are forgiven on account of Christ, who by his death made satisfaction for our sins. God reckons this faith as righteousness (Rom 3 and 4).

Justification thus involves something that happens in the relationship to God ("justification before God"). One aspect of putting this relationship in order is the forgiveness of the human being's sin, which takes place on the basis of Jesus' death for human sins. But justification means, not only that sin is forgiven, but also that through faith, the human being is positively accounted righteous. This takes place free of charge and by grace, through faith, for Christ's sake. At the same time, the text guards against any position that sees what the human being does as any kind of contribution to making him or her righteous.

We should note that the Lutheran understanding of the concept of *grace* differs from the way in which the concept was used in mediaeval and in later Catholic theology. In the tradition that goes back to Augustine, grace was understood as a healing power from God that renews the sinful human being. Since the renewal is a result of grace, it also provides a basis for calling the human being righteous. According to Augustine, the works wrought by grace can be regarded as meritorious because they are wrought by God: "When God crowns our merits, he is crowning nothing other than his own gifts."[1]

Where Augustine understood grace as a gift (Latin: *donum*) that renews the human being, Luther thinks of grace as an expression of God's good favor (Latin: *favor*) towards the human being. Justification thus takes place, not on the basis of the work of grace *in* the human being, but on the basis of God's grace *towards* him or her. Luther also rejects any idea of meritorious works, irrespective of whether these are wrought by grace or by the human being oneself.

---

1. Augustine, *Epistulae* 194.19.

A key concept for comprehending the Lutheran understanding of justification is *imputation* (see article 4 of the Augsburg Confession: "God reckons [Latin: *imputat*] this faith as righteousness"). This *imputation* is a declaration on the part of God that the human being is righteous in his eyes, independently of whether this person is *de facto* a sinner. The righteousness that is given through faith is not the human being's own righteousness, but an "alien righteousness," that is to say, the righteousness of *Christ*. While Christ takes upon himself the human being's sin, the righteousness of Christ is imputed to the sinful human being in what Luther calls the "blessed exchange." This also means that justification is not, as in the Augustinian and Catholic understanding, a process whereby the human being is justified more and more, but something that occurs fully when a human being believes the gospel.

Luther's view of *faith* also differs from the Augustinian and the later Catholic view, which emphasized the connection between faith and love, and claimed that the faith that justifies is the faith that is "formed by love" (Latin: *fides caritate formata*), that is to say, the faith that manifests itself in good works. In Luther's eyes, such an understanding confuses faith and works. He argues that it is not the quality of one's faith that justifies, but the fact that faith takes hold of Christ and trusts in him. It is thus not faith, as a quality, that justifies, but rather the Christ in whom faith believes. To believe means more here than simply having knowledge, or believing that something is true. The faith that saves is the faith that has trust (Latin: *fiducia*) in Christ and that believes that what he did, he did *for me* (Latin: *pro me*).

Although it is the human being who believes, faith is not to be understood as a human achievement, as article 5 of the Augsburg Confession makes clear when it states that faith is brought about by the Holy Spirit, and that the Spirit is given to human beings through the Word and the sacrament as means. Faith is thus something that comes to the human being from the outside, not something that is among the human being's inherent possibilities. We shall discuss in chapter 7 the role played by the Word and the sacraments in the appropriation of salvation.

The fact that justification takes place by faith alone, and not on the basis of changes in the human being, does not, however, mean that salvation does not *also* entail a change in the individual's life. In a Lutheran context, this aspect of salvation has often been called *regeneration*—taking up the idea of the new birth in John 3:5–8. Salvation thus means that the Spirit takes his dwelling in the human being and creates him or her anew. This new creation is, however, not a presupposition of justification, but one of its consequences.

The Augsburg Confession expresses this in article 6, under the heading "Concerning the New Obedience" where we read: "Likewise, they teach that this faith is bound to yield good fruits and that it ought to do good works commanded by God on account of God's will and not so that we may trust in these works to merit justification before God." Faith in Christ must therefore lead to good works as the fruits of faith, but it is not on the basis of these fruits that one is justified. This also alters the motivation for doing good works. The Christian does not need to do good works in order to be justified before God, but rather, because it is *per se* good to do the will of God, and because other people need one's good works. The doctrine of justification by faith alone is thus not a point of departure for moral indifference. On the contrary, it liberates the human being to do good without the idea of acquiring merit vis-à-vis God. This was an important insight in Luther's vocation ethics, where the Christian calling means serving one's neighbor in everyday living.

The understanding of the relationship between faith and works became a controversial topic among the Lutheran theologians after Luther's death. In order to protect the doctrine of justification by faith alone, some went so far as to claim that "good works are harmful to salvation." This consequence is rejected in the Formula of Concord, which points to the organic connection between faith and works.[2] If faith is true, it will manifest itself in good works, like the fruit of a good tree. It is thus faith, not works, that justifies, while at the same time, the works are a sign that the Holy Spirit dwells in the believer.

It was so important to maintain firmly that justification occurs by faith alone because this was connected to the possibility of attaining the *assurance of salvation*. If salvation depends on something that I myself must achieve—even if that is something very small—I can never be certain of salvation. But if salvation depends on something outside myself, namely, on God's promise of salvation for Jesus' sake, I can be certain that I am saved. This does not mean that believers are exempt from doubt and inner qualms. But it means that the path to the assurance of salvation does not mean looking at oneself, but rather believing in the gospel.

The Forensic or the Effective Understanding?

One question that has been much discussed in the Lutheran tradition is the relationship between righteousness as something that is imputed to the human being (cf. article 4 of the Augsburg Confession) and righteousness as something the human being *de facto* receives. In Melanchthon and much of the later Lutheran tradition, the understanding of justification centered primarily on the first dimension, while the second dimension was seen as a consequence of justification, not as an expression of justification itself. This kind of understanding of justification is often called *forensic* (from Latin *forum* = judgment seat). This means that justification is something that happens before God's heavenly judgment seat, where the human being is declared righteous on the basis of God's grace in Jesus, not of anything in the human being oneself.

A forensic understanding of justification has often been seen as an alternative to an *effective* (from the Latin *effectus* = effect) understanding that focuses on the

---

2. Kolb and Wengert, eds., *Book of Concord*, 497–500, 574–81.

change that takes place in the human being oneself (as in a Catholic understanding). The problem with a purely forensic understanding of justification is that it cannot give a satisfactory explanation of the connection between the justification that takes place in heaven and what happens to the human being on earth. The biblical perspective presents this as one saving act on the part of God, but here it disintegrates into separate acts. Such an understanding also finds it problematic to make sense of the human being's *faith*. If justification takes place completely outside the human being, yet nevertheless takes place by faith, how can one avoid understanding faith as a human work?

A renewed reading of Luther in our own days has shown that a purely forensic understanding of justification does not do full justice to his position. In particular, Finnish Luther scholarship has played an important role here; one of its central insights is the significance that the relationship between Christ and the believer has for Luther's understanding of justification. When Christ's righteousness is imputed to the human being through faith, this involves, not righteousness in an abstract or general sense, but receiving Christ himself through faith. When he points to the believer's union with Christ, Luther also picks up a central theme in Paul, for whom it is important that the believer is "in Christ" (Rom 8:1; 2 Cor 5:17) and that Christ lives in the believer (Gal 2:20).

Christ himself as the righteousness of the believer is a key to understanding both the forensic and the effective aspects of justification. When God declares the believer to be righteous (the forensic aspect), this is because Christ dwells in that person. When justification entails renewal and a new creation of the human being (the effective aspect), this too is because Christ dwells in that person. Although righteousness dwells in the human being, therefore, it is still the righteousness of *Christ* that we are talking about, and hence a "foreign" righteousness. And this excludes the idea that this righteousness entails any kind of merit on the part of the human being. This approach does not have the same weaknesses as a purely forensic approach. First of all, it is able to hold together the various aspects of salvation (both the forensic and the effective) in one act on the part of God. Secondly, faith does not become a purely human work, since it is an expression of Christ's dwelling in the human being. The Christ who is present is the content of faith.

For Luther, the Holy Spirit too plays a decisive role here, because it is the Spirit who makes Christ present and thereby creates faith. The new creation of the human being, which justification entails, is thus an expression of the Spirit's creative and life-giving activity in the world.

The Lutheran and the Catholic Understanding

At the Council of Trent (1545–63), the Catholic Church formulated its doctrine as a response to the Reformers' theology, while at the same time defining Catholic doctrine more precisely and narrowly in relation to the many theological currents of the late Middle Ages. One of the themes it discussed was the understanding of justification, which was formulated partly in a polemic against the Protestant understanding.

In its understanding of justification, the Council of Trent takes its place in the Augustinian tradition: in other words, grace is seen as a renewing power, and justification as a process. Although the Council maintained that God is the one who justifies, it emphasized more strongly than the Reformers the collaboration of the human being in this process. The Lutheran understanding of faith as trust was also rejected. The Council affirmed that faith does not save unless it is united to love and hope. When people collaborate with grace and do good works, righteousness too grows.

The Council also rejects completely the idea that the one who is justified is not obliged to do good works or to keep God's law. Although what is criticized here is not in fact the Lutheran position, it nevertheless expresses something that Catholics have tended to see as a weak point in the Protestant understanding of justification.

The great differences between the Augsburg Confession and the Council of Trent in the understanding of justification subsequently remained one of the most prominent expressions of the difference between Lutheran and Catholic theology. In their understanding of justification, other Protestant churches largely followed the Lutheran position, with the result that the doctrine of justification became one of the most important Protestant objections to Catholic theology. And just as Catholics have often caricatured the Protestant view by claiming that good works played no role at all, Protestants have caricatured the Catholic view by claiming that one was justified by one's own works.

The differences between Lutheran and Catholic theology have appeared in a new light thanks to the *Joint Declaration on the Doctrine of Justification* between the Catholic Church and the Lutheran World Federation (1999), a document that was the fruit of lengthy conversations in which the attempt was made to discern whether condemnations in the past were still valid, and how far it was possible to go in the direction of a common understanding. The World Methodist Council and the World Communion of Reformed Churches later endorsed the Joint Declaration.

As I have shown in chapter 1, the methodological rapprochement in the Joint Declaration is an attempt to reach a *differentiated consensus*. This means that the signatories believe they can demonstrate a consensus on fundamental truths in the doctrine of justification, while at the same time noting that differences and disagreement remain. However, the latter concern primarily vocabulary and differing emphases. It is also decisively important to go back to the biblical texts and investigate how the theology of the two traditions has endeavored to preserve what these texts express.

The two parties to the Joint Declaration agree in underlining that justification is God's work, that it can only be received in faith as a gift, and that we can never in any way deserve it (par. 15–17, 19). This means that when Catholics say that the human being cooperates in justification by consenting to it, this is to be understood as a result of grace, not of his or her own powers (par. 20); and when Lutherans have rejected the idea of a human cooperation, this does not mean that the believer is uninvolved in faith (par. 21). Both parties thus understand salvation as something that is wrought by God *and* as something in which the human being is involved (although only Catholics wish to call this "cooperating").

One special problem in the relationship between the Catholic and the Lutheran understandings of justification has been how to understand the relationship between the forensic and the effective elements in justification. In the Joint Declaration, both parties affirm that two aspects of salvation must not be separated: namely, that God does not impute to human beings their sin, and that he creates an active love in them through the Holy Spirit (par. 22). Although Lutherans have emphasized an understanding of grace as forgiving love (grace as *favor*), they do not thereby deny the power of grace to renew life; their intention is to ensure that justification does not depend on this power to renew life (par. 23). And when Catholics underline that, by receiving grace, the believer also receives a renewal of one's inner life, they want to affirm that God's forgiving grace always leads to new life, and that the gift of grace does not depend on human cooperation (par. 24).

One important factor behind the rapprochement in the Joint Declaration is the recognition that salvation in the New Testament is a reality with many dimensions, and that the various theological traditions have employed different concepts to describe these dimensions. Lutheran theology has reserved the concept of justification for what happens in the appropriation of salvation itself, while the process that happens after the appropriation of salvation has been designated primarily by means of the concept of *sanctification*. Catholic theology, on the other hand, has employed the concept of justification in a more comprehensive sense that includes both receiving salvation and the subsequent process.

One key to this rapprochement on the Lutheran side has certainly been supplied by scholars who have pointed out the significance that the idea of "Christ in us" has for Luther's understanding of justification (see above). This is expressed above all in the statement that "Justification and renewal are joined in Christ, who is present in faith" (par. 26).

6.4 THE DIVINE AND THE HUMAN ROLES IN SALVATION

When a person is saved, this is a result of God's salvific act in Jesus Christ. Salvation is not a reward merited by something one has done: it is due to God's love and grace. The unmerited dimension of salvation is emphasized very strongly in Paul's Letters, for example, in Ephesians 2:8: "For by grace you have been saved through faith, and this is not your own doing; it is the gift of God."

This salvific act by God does not concern only some few persons. It is addressed to the whole world. Paul writes that "in Christ God was reconciling the world to himself" (2 Cor 5:19). This does not mean that salvation has been bestowed automatically on all human beings; and this is why Christians are "ambassadors for Christ" who appeal on his behalf: "Be reconciled to God!" (2 Cor 5:20). This duality between God's universal love and saving will, and the individual reception of salvation, is also expressed in John 3:16: "For God so loved the world that he gave his only Son, so that everyone who believes in him may not perish but may have eternal life." The text goes on to state that although God wanted the world to be saved through him, "those who do not believe are condemned already, because they have not believed in the name of the only Son of God" (John 3:17–18). When Jesus sent the disciples out into the world after his resurrection, so that they might bear witness to him (Matt 28:18–20; Acts 1:8), this was because it was through hearing the message about Jesus that people were to come to faith and receive salvation.

The question here is why some come to faith and receive salvation, while others do not. A first answer is that one must have heard the message, in order to be able to believe and thereby be saved. "But how are they to believe in one of whom they have never heard?" asks Paul rhetorically (Rom 10:14). But it is not in fact the case that all those who hear the message also come to faith—and this was the experience already in the New Testament period. The Acts of the Apostles speak both of "those who welcomed his message" (2:41) and of "the unbelieving" persons (14:2). Acts 28:24 sums up the result of Paul's preaching in Rome as follows: "Some were convinced by what he had said, while others refused to believe." People respond in different ways to the message, and this also has consequences for their relationship to God and to salvation. As we read in John's Gospel, "But to all who received him, who believed in his name, he gave power to become children of God" (1:12).

If, however, the human response to the message is an important factor in whether or not one receives salvation, what does this mean for the idea that God is the one who brings about salvation, and that one is saved by grace alone? If the human being must receive the message, does not this mean that one makes a contribution to one's own salvation (even if only a very little contribution)?

This problem is also connected to the question of human free will, on which we have touched in chapter 4 above. If one must decide to receive salvation, does this mean that one takes this decision of one's own free will—or that the decision is in fact determined by other factors? And to what extent does God actually contribute to whether or not the human being receives salvation?

Election and Predestination

The idea that the reason why a person receives salvation, or does not receive it, ultimately lies with God seems to find some support in New Testament texts that speak of God's *election*. The notion of election goes back to the Old Testament, which affirms that God chooses the people of Israel (Deut 14:2) and that he chooses individuals for specific tasks (1 Sam 10:24). Just as God chooses, he can also reject, and this rejection can perfectly well affect the one who was chosen, if he fails to live in accordance with his election (1 Sam 16:1; 2 Kgs 17:20). The idea of election is employed in a similar manner in the New Testament. In Romans 9–11, Paul discusses how the election of the people of Israel is to be understood in relation to God's salvific act in Jesus. Individual persons can also be spoken of as chosen for particular tasks, such as Paul himself (Rom 1:1).

The New Testament also speaks of Christians—as a group and as individuals—as chosen. "You did not choose me but I chose you," says Jesus to the disciples in John's Gospel (15:16). The Christians in Colossae are "God's chosen ones, holy and beloved" (Col 3:12).

Does the idea of election mean that ultimately, the reason why the individual believes lies with God? The idea that the salvation of the individual is based on a decision taken by God seems to find support in Paul, in Rom 8:29–30:

> For those whom he foreknew he also predestined to be conformed to the image of his Son, in order that he might be the firstborn within a large family. And those whom he predestined he also called; and those whom he called he also justified; and those whom he justified he also glorified.

The introduction to the Letter to the Ephesians affirms that such an election has genuinely been made "in advance": God "chose us in Christ before the foundation of the world" (1:4).

The idea that God has destined people beforehand for salvation is often referred to as the concept of God's *predestination* (from the Latin *praedestinatio* = determination beforehand). This leads to the question whether God is the cause, not only when some believe, but when others *do not* believe. That would entail a *double* election by God, of some for faith and salvation, and of others for unbelief and damnation.

Although this is not stated in a text like Romans 8, some have drawn this inference from Paul's understanding of the election of the people of Israel, when he affirms that some persons in Old Testament history were chosen and others rejected, and that it is possible to see God behind all this: "So then he has mercy on whomever he chooses, and he hardens the heart of whomever he chooses" (Rom 9:18). However, since this passage deals, not with the salvation of the individual, but with the election of the people of Israel, it is a matter of dispute whether it is relevant in this context.

In Western theology, the discussion of election, predestination, free will, and the human being's cooperation in the appropriation of salvation has been an important but controversial theme since Augustine's debate with Pelagius (see also the discussion of this debate in chapter 4). Pelagius held that the human being could personally contribute to his or her salvation by choosing to do what is good, and that the work of Jesus was necessary for the forgiveness of sin and as an inspiration to do good. Against this, Augustine affirmed that salvation is due exclusively to God's grace. Thanks to original sin, the human being has no free will, nor any possibility to cooperate in his or her own salvation, which is fully a result of the grace of God that forgives sin and renews the human being. It is only through the power of grace that the human will is renewed and becomes able to begin to do good. In Augustine, the affirmation that the human being cannot cooperate in any way in his or her own salvation is anchored in the idea of God's predestination to salvation. With his starting point in Romans 8:30, he claimed that when someone comes to faith, this is a realization in time of what God has already determined from all eternity. Since the cause of the individual's salvation lies exclusively in the will of God, the one who is chosen for salvation will necessarily be saved in reality. Augustine assumes that God's grace is irresistible, and that the chosen cannot fall away. The idea of predestination also entails that if some people are not saved, this is because God has not chosen them for salvation. This conclusion appears to conflict with biblical statements that God "desires everyone to be saved and to come to the knowledge of the truth" (1 Tim 2:4), but Augustine interprets this passage to mean that God wants *all kinds* of people to saved—not each single individual.

The so-called *Semipelagianism* accepted Augustine's doctrine of original sin, but rejected the idea that salvation is due to grace alone. Despite sin, the human being bears in oneself the seed of good, which is awakened into life by grace. In the encounter with grace, the human being has the free will to accept or reject grace. In repentance, grace and the free will collaborate; and this means that the rejection of grace is due to the human being, not to God.

The Synod of Orange in 527 condemned both Pelagianism and Semipelagianism, and confirmed Augustine's teaching on original sin. When someone believes and receives salvation, this is not on the basis of anything good that dwells in one, but because God is working in one. However, the synod did not accept Augustine's teaching on predestination, but condemned the very notion that some people are predestined to evil.

The question of the human being's ability to accept salvation became a controversial topic in the Reformation period too. Erasmus of Rotterdam claimed that the human being has free will either to receive what leads to salvation or to refrain from doing so. In response, Luther formulated his teaching about the "bondage of the will": the human being does not have the freedom *per se* to cooperate in his or her own salvation. When someone is saved, it is because the God who works all things in all people has chosen that person for salvation. When someone receives the gospel, it is because God has already reshaped that person's will and bestowed faith. Why does God not save everyone? That is one of the questions that cannot be answered, since it belongs to the hidden God, not to the revealed God.

One fundamental concern behind Luther's theology on this point was to maintain that salvation is exclusively a result of God's action and does not depend in any way on the human being. This emphasis that salvation depends on God alone is connected to the view that, because of sin, the human being has neither the ability nor the will to receive salvation. Such a view is often called *monergistic* (God works alone) in contradistinction to *synergistic* views (the human being in some way collaborates with God).

From a Lutheran perspective, the Catholic understanding has often been perceived as an expression of synergism, because of the emphasis on the necessity for the human being to cooperate with grace in receiving salvation. The question of predestination has not played any central role in Catholic theology in this context.

Luther's understanding of predestination and of the human being's inability to receive grace had no monopoly in the Reformers' theology. Melanchthon initially followed Luther's position, but later distanced himself from such an understanding of predestination and maintained instead that when the Word and the Spirit influence a human being, he or she receives the possibility either to receive grace or to refrain from doing so. Here, it is the individual's response that is decisive for whether or not one is saved—not God's predestination. The seventeenth-century Lutheran orthodoxy interpreted God's predestination in the light of his foreknowledge and claimed that predestination meant that God had chosen those who he knew in advance would receive salvation and hold fast to it.

In Reformed theology, Calvin took the opposite direction and elaborated a doctrine of double predestination. According to Calvin, the human being's salvation and damnation depend exclusively on God's omnipotent will. This means that some are predetermined for eternal life, while others are predetermined for eternal damnation. In both cases, everything takes place for the glory of God. Like Augustine, Calvin taught that grace was irresistible for those who were chosen, and that the elect could not fall away.

Jacobus Arminius strongly objected to Calvin's understanding of this point, and the Reformed tradition even today is marked by the controversy between Calvinism and Arminianism. The Arminians reject the idea of double predestination, maintain God's universal will for salvation, and affirm that it is possible to resist grace and to fall away. They tend to understand election as a *conditional* election, that is to say, that God has determined from eternity to save all who believe in Jesus, but he has not predetermined which persons will come to do so. The Arminians too maintain the doctrine of the total corruption of the human being by sin, and believe that this makes it impossible for the human being himself or herself to choose grace. When someone comes to faith, this is because God's grace has already worked on that person and called him or her to faith (this has often been called *prevenient grace*). This grace, however, is not irresistible, and this means that ultimately, one is personally responsible for whether or not one receives salvation. Another reason for the importance of the Arminian view is that was adopted by John Wesley, the founder of Methodism, and subsequently became the dominant position in that tradition.

While Augustine, Luther, and Calvin envisage election as something that concerns the individual, others have held that election concerns the believers as a *group*.

One can appeal in support of this view to the idea of election in the Old Testament, where it applies to the people of Israel as a collective.

We find one modern variant of this thinking in Karl Barth, who offers a Christological interpretation of Calvin's doctrine of double predestination: the one who is chosen and rejected is Christ, and because he was rejected, all human beings are chosen to receive salvation. The doctrine of predestination has been employed elsewhere to explain why some are saved and others not, but in Barth it is turned in a universalistic direction to explain why all are saved (for more on this problem, see chapter 9). Barth's thesis that all are saved at last is, however, an eschatological perspective—in other words, all will be saved *at last*. Not even Barth can deny the fact that some people here and now believe in the Christian message, while others do not.

The questions we have discussed in this section may appear highly theoretical and speculative, and one may wonder whether there is any point in ruminating on such questions. It is, however, inescapably true that different positions can have consequences in practice, for example, when one preaches to call people to faith. If one holds that the human being's own choice plays a great role, it will be natural, when one preaches about conversion, to appeal to the person's own decision, as in various forms of revivalist preaching. But if one sees faith as a result of God's activity alone, one will perhaps be content to preach the content of the gospel and leave the rest to the Spirit.

Differing views can also have consequences for the question of the assurance of salvation. If the appropriation of salvation depends on my decision, how then can I be sure of being saved? But if salvation depends only on God's prior determination, and he also determines people in advance for damnation, how then can I be sure of being one of the elect?

We find an interesting approach to this question in the Formula of Concord. Instead of attempting to find a logical solution to the question, the idea of election is presented as a starting point for consoling those who doubt their own salvation:

> Thus, it gives the most reliable comfort to troubled, tempted people, that they may know that their salvation does not rest in their own hands.... Instead, their salvation rests in the gracious election of God, which he has revealed to us in Christ, out of whose hand no one can snatch us.[3]

When someone is saved, therefore, this is because of God's choice, with no cause in our own self. But since God wants everyone to be saved, this text does *not* draw the opposite conclusion, namely, that God has chosen some people for damnation. If some do not believe, despite having heard the Word, this is entirely their own responsibility.

The many different attempts—within Lutheranism and elsewhere—to give a satisfactory account of the idea of election and predestination show that this is a very difficult doctrinal topic, where there is no consensus. It must therefore be possible to approach this question in various ways, although there are good reasons for rejecting

---

3. Kolb and Wengert, eds., *Book of Concord*, 655.

certain versions of the idea of predestination that are in conflict with clear biblical insights. This applies to a doctrine of double predestination that denies God's universal will for salvation and claims that God's will is that some are not to be saved. Such an idea is also problematic because it relieves the human being of all responsibility, by claiming that grace is irresistible and that the chosen cannot fall away. This makes biblical exhortations not to resist God's call (Heb 3:7–8) or to endure in faith (Matt 24:13) purely fictitious. This line of thought turns what happens in the world into a pure reflection of what is already determined from all eternity, and thereby fails to recognize the *freedom* that God has given his creation (on this, see chapter 4). Although God has laid down certain parameters for the world's freedom, and he leads the world towards the close of history, not everything that happens in the world is determined in advance—not even who will, or will not, come to faith in Jesus.

The fact that the world has a basic freedom does not, however, mean that what happens in the world happens independently of God. God also works in and through the events in the world and through human actions, although it is impossible to grasp completely the relationship between the human and the divine. Something that is completely a human act can at the same time also be perceived as the expression of something that God does. When a person comes to faith, this can be understood from an empirical and psychological perspective as a completely human process; and it can at the same time also be understood as the expression of the Spirit's working in that person's life.

This is why it is also necessary to reject an understanding of the appropriation of salvation that makes it the result of the human being's own choices or effort, independently of the recreating power of the Spirit. When someone comes to faith, this is because the Spirit has already created faith—not as an irresistible coercion, but as an expression of the liberation of the human being's bound will, so that it can receive the gift of God in faith and trust.

The difficult question here is why people *do not* come to faith: why does the recreating power of the Spirit not create faith in everyone? To say (like the Formula of Concord) that this is exclusively the responsibility of the human being is to attach too much weight to the individual's decision, for there are many who never heard the message, or at any rate, not in a way that was comprehensible and appropriate, while others heard the message but did not find it convincing. When people are not convinced by the Christian message, this should not be taken as an expression of personal wickedness or bad will. It is an expression of the fact that Jesus in this world took "the form of a slave" (Phil 2:7) and that it is possible to misunderstand, contradict, and deny the message about him. From a Christian perspective, it is difficult to understand how the one through whom the world came into being was not believed when he came to the world. The Gospel of John formulates this paradoxical fact as follows: "He came to what was his own, and those who were his did not accept him" (1:11*). At the same time, the text goes on to state that this rejection was not universal: the gospel was also welcomed: "But to all who received him, who believed in his name, he gave power to become children of God, who were born, not of blood or of the will of the flesh or of the will of man, but of God" (John 1:12–13).

This text also affirms that the human participation and the divine act belong together and presuppose each other in the appropriation of salvation. From the human side, salvation means "receiving him." From the perspective of faith in God, this is not an expression of "natural" processes, but of God's intervention and the recreating power of the Spirit.

6.5 LIFE IN THE SPIRIT

As I have pointed out earlier in this chapter, salvation is an eschatological reality, in the sense that it is fully realized only in the kingdom of God at the close of history. The Christian has already here and now received a share in something that is not yet fully present, and this means that one is still *en route*. This path leads through one's own death to the resurrection from the dead and a life in the coming world. The goal of this path will be the theme in chapter 9; this section in the present chapter will deal with the Christian's life in this world, or with what is often called *sanctification*. Important questions here are how we are to understand the relationship between this new life and ordinary human life, including the relationship to sin. Another question is whether sanctification entails a development or growth in holiness, and whether one can become *completely* sanctified in this life.

Sanctification

It seems clear that the New Testament assumes that salvation entails a real and radical transformation when people receive it, as we see above all when expressions such as "being born anew" or "a new creation" are employed to designate what happens. As Paul puts it: "If anyone is in Christ, there is a new creation; everything old has passed away; see, everything has become new!" (2 Cor 5:17).

The central element here is a transformation in the human being's relationship to God, as we see not least when Christians are called "holy." In the Old Testament, the concept of holiness is closely linked to God himself. God is holy, and that which belongs to God in a special way is also holy. This is why the people of Israel can be called holy, since they are chosen by God: "You shall be holy, for I the LORD your God am holy" (Lev 19:2).

In the New Testament too, the "holy" is linked to that which belongs to God, as we see when the Christians are spoken of simply as "saints" (literally: "the holy ones," Rom 1:7; 16:15; Eph 1:1). But while it is said that the Christians *are* holy, they are also exhorted to *become* holy (for example, in 1 Pet 1:15: "as he who called you is holy, be holy yourselves in all your conduct"; cf. Rom 6:19). The Christian life can thus be seen as "making holiness perfect" (2 Cor 7:1). New Testament texts employ other concepts too to speak of growth and development in the Christian life, for example, when the hope is expressed that "your faith increases" (2 Cor 10:15), or the Christians are told: "Grow in the grace and knowledge of our Lord and Savior Jesus Christ" (2 Pet 3:18).

It may at first sight appear a contradiction to say that one both *is* holy and *becomes* holy, but this is easier to grasp in the light of the idea of salvation as something that we have received "already now," but that is "not yet" fully realized. Accordingly, a Christian is fully holy thanks to the new relationship to God, while at the same time, not every aspect of life bears as yet the mark of this holiness. Although the perfect realization of holiness belongs to the definitive salvation, the New Testament nevertheless envisages the holiness that a Christian possesses not only as a holiness "in principle," but also as a holiness that is to find concrete expression in life. To employ the terminology we have introduced in connection with the doctrine of justification, it involves not only a holiness of a "forensic" character, but a holiness with "effective" characteristics. The New Testament also envisages that holiness can make itself more or less felt in life; it is this idea that lies behind the exhortation to become holy. It is, however, important to underline the direction here: it is not the case that one must lead a holy life in order to become holy. Rather, the one who has already become holy is summoned to let holiness have practical consequences.

It is also important to stress that holiness is not primarily an ethical or moral matter. It means being brought into a new relationship to God. It is, however, clear that holiness *also* has an ethical aspect. Since salvation is salvation from sin and from its consequences, sanctification means turning away from sin to a life in accordance with God's will. We find one example of this understanding in Paul's description of life in the Spirit in Galatians 5:22–23, where he indicates the fruits of the Spirit: "love, joy, peace, patience, kindness, generosity, faithfulness, gentleness, and self-control."

He contrasts these virtues with what he calls "the works of the flesh": "fornication, impurity, licentiousness, idolatry, sorcery, enmities, strife, jealousy, anger, quarrels, dissensions, factions, envy, drunkenness, carousing, and things like these" (Gal 5:19–21). The term "flesh" (Greek: *sarx*) refers to that which characterizes human life antecedently to salvation, that which he elsewhere calls the "old self" in contradistinction to the "new self" (Eph 4:22–24). For a Christian, the "flesh" and the "old self" are not only something that belongs to the past, but also something one brings into the Christian life. This is why a central motif in the New Testament letters is the exhortation to let one's life be marked by the new life of the Spirit, instead of letting it be marked by the inclination to sin that still exists. Thus, Paul can urge the Galatians: "Live by the Spirit, I say, and do not gratify the desires of the flesh. For what the flesh desires is opposed to the Spirit, and what the Spirit desires is opposed to the flesh" (Gal 5:16–17); and in another passage, he writes: "You were taught to put away your former way of life, your old self, corrupt and defiled by its lusts, and to be renewed in the spirit of your minds, and to clothe yourselves with the new self, created according to the likeness of God in true righteousness and holiness" (Eph 4:22–24).

The Christian's Relationship to Sin

In this way, the structure of "already, but not yet," which applies to the definitive realization of salvation, seems to apply also to the liberation from the influence of sin. Although a Christian is free from sin in the light of the gospel promise, this freedom is not yet fully realized, since sin always lurks as a possibility and a reality in the Christian's life. The Christian life, *en route* to the definitive realization, thus takes the form of a continuous struggle *for* the good and *against* sin in one's own life. Since the Christian already belongs to the new reality and has the Spirit of God dwelling in him or her, one must allow this new reality to set its stamp upon one's life. Accordingly, Paul exhorts:

> No longer present your members to sin as instruments of wickedness, but present yourselves to God as those who have been brought from death to life, and present your members to God as instruments of righteousness. For sin will have no dominion over you, since you are not under law but under grace (Rom 6:13–14).

Being under grace does not make how one lives irrelevant. Paul goes on, in the continuation of the passage just quoted, to attack this misunderstanding. Since salvation is liberation from the power of sin, one is set free for a new life in the service of the good: "You, having been set free from sin, have become slaves of righteousness" (Rom 6:18). And this means that surrendering to the powers of sin is incompatible with a life under grace: "if you live according to the flesh, you will die; but if by the Spirit you put to death the deeds of the body, you will live" (Rom 8:13).

The First Letter of John has a similar understanding. Sin is incompatible with the new life, and the author states categorically that "those who have been born of God do not sin" (3:9). If we take such statements literally, they conflict with what the Letter says earlier, namely, that no one is free of sin, and that the Christian life is characterized by the willingness to confess one's sin and by the promise of forgiveness: "If we say that we have no sin, we deceive ourselves, and the truth is not in us. If we confess our sins, he who is faithful and just will forgive us our sins and cleanse us from all unrighteousness" (1 John 1:8–9).

A plausible interpretation of this apparent contradiction is that, while the statements in chapter 1 are about "falling into sin," that is to say, yielding to temptations of which one later repents and on which one turns one's back, the statements in chapter 3 are about "living in sin," that is to say, not repenting or changing one's life, but holding fast to sin. The new life means not only turning one's back on sin, but also doing good, and above all, showing love: "All who do not do what is right are not from God, nor are those who do not love their brothers and sisters" (1 John 3:10).

The need to confess one's sins and have them forgiven also shows that sin continues to play a role in a Christian's life. This is why one of the petitions in the Lord's Prayer asks: "And forgive us our trespasses, as we forgive those who trespass against us" (Matt 6:12*). The Christian fellowship should be characterized by the readiness to confess our sins to each other and to forgive each other (Eph 4:32; Col 3:13; Jas 5:16).

The question of the role of sin in a Christian's life has been a disputed theological topic. In comparison with other traditions, Lutheran theology has tended to take a rather pessimistic view of the human person's ability to escape from the power of sin; this is connected not least with the understanding of sin as original sin (see chapter 4). In the Lutheran view, the Christian has the forgiveness of the guilt of original sin, but is not finished with original guilt as such. "The old self" and the "new self" live side by side in the Christian and are locked in a struggle. This means that a Christian is "simultaneously righteous and a sinner" (Latin: *simul justus et peccator*). The old self disappears only at bodily death, and it is the new self that rises to life on the last day.

The formula *simul justus et peccator* is not current in Catholic theology, where it is held that God takes away not only the guilt of original sin in baptism, but also original sin itself. What remains is an inclination to sin that means that the Christian can in fact commit sin. But although this inclination leads to sin, it is not in itself sin. Catholic theology too assumes that the Christian must continuously fight again sin in his or her life and pray every day for forgiveness of the sins committed.

Paragraphs 28–30 of the *Joint Declaration on the Doctrine of Justification* make it clear that a Lutheran and a Catholic perspective on sin in the Christian's life are not completely incompatible. Here, the Catholics take a step towards the Lutherans by noting that although the inclination to sin is not in itself sin, it is "objectively in contradiction of God and remains one's enemy in lifelong struggle" (par. 30). The Lutherans take a step towards the Catholics by means of an important clarification of the understanding of the Christian who commits sin: although sin continues to be present, it does not have dominion over the believer, because sin is subject to God's power. And this means that the Christian here on earth can at any rate partially live as a righteous person, while he or she must always fight against the sin that dwells within (par. 29).

Many Protestant traditions have taken a different view of the Christian's relationship to sin than that in the Lutheran tradition, and the disagreements on this point have often found expression in two different ways of reading Paul's statements in Romans 7, where he describes his powerlessness vis-à-vis sin, which means that "I do not do the good I want, but the evil I do not want is what I do" (v.19). But the subject of the evil is not Paul himself, but sin in him: "Now if I do what I do not want, it is no longer I that do it, but sin that dwells within me" (v. 20). At the same time, there is something in him that wants the good: "For I delight in the law of God in my inmost self" (v. 22). His situation is thus marked by a struggle between God's will and sin: "So then, with my mind I am a slave to the law of God, but with my flesh I am a slave to the law of sin" (v. 25). The decisive question is whether Paul is here describing his life as a Christian, or his existence as a pious Jew devoted to the law before he came to faith in Jesus. Many have believed that what Paul says here is in contrast to what he otherwise says—namely, that the Christian is led by the Spirit—and that this passage must therefore be read as Paul looking back to his former life. However, a traditional Lutheran understanding has understood this text as a description of the Christian's situation, and thus as evidence for the understanding of the Christian as *simul justus et peccator*.

Exegetes disagree about how this text is to be interpreted, and their disagreement cuts across confessional boundaries. But although one single text cannot resolve the theological question of the role that sin plays in the Christian's life, the interpretation of Romans 7 is extremely important for this question.

How Far Is It Possible to Come in Sanctification?

Sanctification thus entails a struggle against the evil and for the good, both in oneself and outside oneself. The question is whether this is a trench warfare in which no progress is ever made, or whether one can envisage a development in which a growth takes place in the direction of greater holiness and less sin. Is it therefore possible to envisage coming to a point where one is wholly sanctified and no longer commits sin?

We find one example of this idea in Wesley, who saw sanctification as a process that can lead to "entire sanctification." This experience means that the Christian is liberated from the power of sin and enabled to love God and one's neighbor wholeheartedly. One starting point for this idea was Paul's prayer that God might sanctify the believers "entirely" (1 Thess 5:23). This does not mean that one is exempt from every possibility of sinning, nor that one becomes faultless. And a total sanctification of this kind is not the result of the human being's own efforts, but of the work of grace in him or her. Coming to share in a total sanctification of this kind has often been called "the second blessing," that is to say, God's second great act of grace after the appropriation of salvation itself.

Although not all Methodists would go as far as Wesley in envisaging a situation where the Christian no longer commits conscious sins, Methodism is marked by a fundamentally optimistic view of the possibilities of grace in a Christian's life. This means that a Christian should be able to experience the transformative power of grace in life, so that sin has less space, and one's thoughts and actions conform more strongly to God's will.

The Lutheran tradition has been marked more strongly by a pessimistic view of the possibility of experiencing growth in holiness. Article 12 of the Augsburg Confession explicitly rejects the idea of a total sanctification: "They condemn . . . those who contend that some may attain such perfection in this life that they cannot sin." The understanding of the Christian life in the Lutheran tradition has tended to underline the idea of *daily conversion*, which means that confessing one's sin and turning away from it is not only something one does when one comes to faith, but something a Christian must do every day. (This is closely linked to the theology of baptism, to which I return in the next chapter.)

Luther said: "To advance is always a matter of beginning anew."[4] Some have interpreted these words as a rejection of any notion of development in the Christian life, but Luther himself does not draw this inference. On the contrary, Luther sees growth in holiness and "the practice of faith" as an important aspect of being a Christian. He does not, however, think of this as a harmonious process of growth in which the human being becomes more and more perfect, but rather as a struggle between the old self and the new, where the old self is killed more and more and the new self takes more and more space. Here, as in every war, the line of battle can move back and forward, and the struggle is fought on different sections of the frontline at different times.

One important concern in a Lutheran context is that good works and the fight against sin occur not for one's own sake, but on behalf of one's neighbor. Being more concerned with one's own holiness than with one's neighbor's welfare is definitely not an expression of genuine holiness. Experience shows that holiness can also be an external skin, rather than an internal reality, when Christians of whom one would least expect it do the most cruel things. The correct response may not be pessimism, but it is at any rate important to retain a healthy *realism* in the perception of one's own holiness and that of others.

The Christian and the Law

As we have seen earlier in this chapter, justification implies for Paul that the human being "is justified by faith apart from works prescribed by the law" (Rom 3:28). Since these words apply primarily to *receiving* salvation, we must ask what relationship the Christian has to the law in his or her life as a Christian. One complicating factor in reading Paul here is that it is not always clear whether "law" means the commandments that apply specifically to the Jews (such as the precept of circumcision), or whether he has in mind God's will in a more general ethical sense, as this is expressed, for example, in the Ten Commandments and the double commandment of love.

With regard to the first alternative, it is clear that Christians who are not Jews are not obliged to keep the specifically Jewish commandments. With regard to the more universal ethical content in the law, the picture is not equally clear. Although a Christian is not "under law" (Rom 6:14), but is "discharged from the law" (Rom 7:6), Paul can nevertheless say that "the one who loves another has fulfilled the law"

---

4. Luther, *Lecture on Romans*, 478.

(Rom 13:8). He can also say that "the just requirement of the law" is "fulfilled in us, who walk not according to the flesh but according to the Spirit" (Rom 8:4). The line of thought seems to be that although God's will is expressed in the law, the human being is not capable of fulfilling the requirements of the law on his or her own—with the result that the law leads to judgment and despair. Through the recreating act of the Spirit, however, one is made able to live in accordance with God's will, without being coerced by the law into doing so. The result is that God's will is fulfilled—but not because the law demands it.

Although it is through the action of the Spirit that God's will is fulfilled, this does not prevent the New Testament writings from formulating ethical ideals that are assumed to accord with God's will. One example is the list of the fruits of the Spirit in Galatians 5:22–23, which concludes with the observation that "There is no law against such things." In other words, what the law requires is fulfilled independently of the law. In some passages, the concept of the law can also be employed to speak of the ideals that are to guide Christians, as when Paul speaks of "the law of Christ" (Gal 6:2), or James of "the law of liberty" (Jas 1:25; 2:12).

Luther's understanding of the Christian's relationship to the law begins from the distinction between law and gospel. As I have pointed out in the discussion of this subject in chapter 2, the Lutheran tradition draws a distinction between the role of the law in regulating life in society (the first use of the law) and its role in accusing and condemning the human being for sin (the second use of the law). As a citizen, the Christian is naturally not exempt from the first use of the law; and since the Christian still bears the old self within, one does not escape from the second use of the law. When the law unmasks and condemns the sin that dwells in one, this is the starting point for the daily conversion.

This means that the new life is generated, not by the law, but by the gospel. In living the new life that is given through faith in Christ, the Christian can turn to the law in order to learn what a life in accordance with God's will entails. Unlike the situation for the one who lives "under the law," this is not accompanied by coercion and threats of punishment; it takes place on the basis of Christian freedom. The use Luther makes of the Ten Commandments in his Small Catechism shows that a Christian needs to be guided by the law in this way. Here, the Ten Commandments are part of the basic knowledge that every Christian must have, and are thus a guide to how Christians are to lead their lives. Luther sharply rejected the so-called *antinomianism* that held that one should preach only the gospel—not the law—to Christians.

The Lutheran tradition has spoken of the role of the law as a guide to the Christian as the "third use of the law." We find this concept in article 6 of the Formula of Concord. This has, however, been a disputed point both in Lutheran theology and in other traditions. Some have preferred to speak instead of the ethical guidance for Christians as a function of the gospel ("the practical meaning of the gospel") rather than as an expression of the law. Irrespective of the concept one employs, it is important to maintain that the Christian's freedom from the law entails, not a freedom to commit sin, but on the contrary, a freedom to lead a life in accordance with God's good will.

Christ Dwells in the Believer

In our discussion of the doctrine of justification, we saw that a key to understanding the relationship between the "forensic" and the "effective" aspects of the appropriation of salvation lay in the idea that Christ dwells in the believer. This means that Christ's righteousness is an "alien righteousness" (since it is *Christ's* righteousness), while at the same time it is imputed to the believer and is effective in his or her life. The idea that Christ dwells in the believer is also important for the understanding of sanctification, which means, in this perspective, that Christ takes an ever greater space and is ever more active in the Christian's life. To use Paul's expression, this means that Christ "is formed" in the believers (Gal 4:19) or that God makes the Christians "conformed to the image of his Son" (Rom 8:29). The idea that the Christian is to be formed in accordance with Christ also finds expression in the idea of "following" Jesus, a motif that is found, for example, in Jesus' words in Matthew 16:24, "If any want to become my followers, let them deny themselves and take up their cross and follow me." Following Jesus is not primarily a matter of moral and personal development. It also involves the readiness to suffer and to fight, as we see when Paul understands baptism as being brought into fellowship with Christ in his death and resurrection (Rom 6:1–11). Imitating Christ (Latin: *imitatio Christi*) has been an important spiritual motif in some parts of the Christian tradition.

The Fruit of the Spirit and the Gifts of the Spirit

In a Trinitarian perspective, the idea that Christ dwells in the believer means that the triune God is present. After the ascension and Pentecost, this presence is mediated by the Spirit: when Jesus dwells in the believer, this is thanks to the presence and the mediation of the Spirit. This means that the divine presence in the believer is a presence of the Spirit. Sharing in salvation is also sharing in the Spirit. However, the Spirit's work is not limited to the appropriation of salvation: it is also meant to set its imprint on the entirety of the Christian's life. According to Paul, it is precisely this that characterizes the Christian: "All who are led by the Spirit of God are children of God" (Rom 8:14). It is the Spirit who undergirds the confession of faith in Jesus: "no one can say 'Jesus is Lord' except by the Holy Spirit" (1 Cor 12:3). When the Christian's life is formed by that which is in accordance with God's will, this is "the fruit of the Spirit" (Gal 5:22), and this is why the Christians' bodies are "a temple of the Holy Spirit" (1 Cor 6:19).

Although the Christian has received a share in the Spirit through salvation, the believers are exhorted to let their lives be marked more and more by the Spirit. Paul writes: "Live by the Spirit" (Gal 5:16). Instead of being filled with intoxicants, one should be "filled with the Spirit" (Eph 5:18). There are several examples in the Acts of the Apostles of people who had already received the Spirit when they came to faith, and are then "filled with the Holy Spirit" in situations where they are used by God in a special way (4:8, 31; 7:55; 13:9).

One special role attributed to the Holy Spirit is the bestowal of spiritual *gifts* (charisms) that are needed in order to build up the community. Paul writes that the Spirit gives various gifts to different Christians, so that the community as a whole will have what it needs (Rom 12:3–8; 1 Cor 12–14; cf. 1 Pet 4:10). (For more on this subject, see chapter 8.)

One of the charisms Paul mentions is speaking in tongues (1 Cor 12:10). This is presented in some passages in the Acts of the Apostles as demonstrating that people have received the Holy Spirit (10:45–46; 19:6), and this led in the Pentecostal movement to the idea that speaking in tongues is a special sign of the fullness of the Spirit, a sign that all Christians ought to seek. In this context, a theology of "baptism in the Spirit" was developed. This is an experience that one could have at a later point in time than when one came to faith and was baptized in water, and speaking in tongues is the sign of baptism in the Spirit. Historically speaking, this doctrine of baptism in the Spirit builds on the Methodist idea of a "second blessing," except that this is not primarily an experience of sanctification, but of being baptized in the Spirit. The starting point was the experience of the Spirit within the movement. Biblical support was found for a distinction between the appropriation of salvation and baptism with water, on the one hand, and baptism in the Spirit, on the other hand, in texts in the Acts of the Apostles—above all, in Acts 19:1–7, which speaks of some disciples who had not received the Holy Spirit.

The problematic element here is that it draws too great a distinction between being a Christian and having the Spirit. Paul says: "Anyone who does not have the Spirit of Christ does not belong to him" (Rom 8:9). The point in Acts 19:1–7 is that the disciples in question had not received the Spirit, because they had not been baptized in the name of Jesus, but only with the baptism of John. There is no support in the New Testament for the assertion that people receive a share in the charisms only through a special experience after they have come to faith.

It is, however, clear that the historical churches have often had an excessively static understanding of what it means to have the Spirit. By emphasizing that the Spirit is something one "has" through baptism, they have often risked downplaying the dynamic element in the reality of the Spirit, who like the wind "blows where it chooses" (John 3:8). An important corrective is offered by the eschatological perspective on salvation that characterizes the New Testament: salvation is something which we have already received, but that is not yet fully realized. This perspective must also apply to the gift of the Spirit.

Receiving Salvation—the Work of the Holy Spirit

This gift is indeed something which every Christian has received through faith and baptism, but the work of the Spirit in the believer is fully accomplished only in the recreated world. This means that the Christian lives in a tension between "quenching the Spirit" (1 Thess 5:19) and being "filled with the Spirit" (Eph 5:18). Just like sanctification, being filled with the spirit is not a harmonious process. It can involve experiences of the Spirit's absence, just as much as of the Spirit's presence. The Pentecostal movement, like the later charismatic movement, has played a decisive role in a renewed awareness that the Spirit can manifest himself through concrete experiences in a Christian's life, including life-changing experiences that alter the direction of one's life. However, the Spirit's presence in a Christian's life can take a variety of forms, and one should be cautious about prescribing one particular pattern of experience.

One important aspect of life in the Spirit is that it is a life in *prayer*. "Pray without ceasing," writes Paul (1 Thess 5:17), while he also insists that prayer is a result of the Spirit's working (Rom 8:15–16). The Spirit not only moves the human being to pray; he himself also intercedes for the believers (Rom 8:26–27). The centrality of prayer in the life of the church and of the individual Christian indicates that salvation means a renewed relationship to God, a relationship that is expressed in prayer. (On various forms of prayer, see chapter 4.)

7

The Means of Grace

7.1 WORD AND SACRAMENT

THE THEME OF THE last chapter was the understanding of salvation. In the present chapter, we shall look at the question of how salvation is *mediated*. The distinction between creation and salvation means that no one is saved simply in virtue of being created. Rather, one must *receive salvation*. As Christianity understands it, salvation is not something that comes to the human being from within, as if all that were necessary were to discover something one already bears within oneself. Instead, salvation is something that comes *from outside*, something that must be given or mediated to the individual. Dogmatics often uses the concept of the *means of grace* to designate the instruments (or means) that God employs to give the human being his grace. What these means are, and how one is to understand them, is one of the most widely discussed questions in dogmatics and in the relations between the churches. A starting point that is widely shared is that the message about what God has done in Jesus (the Word) is a means for salvation, and thus a means of grace. In addition to the Word, most Christians also perform specific actions to which a role is ascribed in relation to salvation, first and foremost baptism and the eucharist. From Augustine onwards, it has been customary to call these actions *sacraments*, although not all churches use this concept.

When the concept of the means of grace is understood in this way, it therefore includes both the Word and the sacraments. This is an important conceptual pair, not least within Lutheranism, where the idea that God employs particular means to communicate salvation has found a classic expression in article 5 of the Augsburg Confession:

> For through the Word and the sacraments as through instruments [Latin: *instrumenta*] the Holy Spirit is given, who effects faith where and when it pleases God in those who hear the gospel, that is to say, in those who hear that God, not on account of our own merits but on account of Christ, justifies those who believe that they are received into grace on account of Christ.

This text makes another important point, namely, that the salvation that is bestowed in the means of salvation must be received in faith. At the same time, faith itself is created by the Spirit who is given in the Word and in the sacraments.

When the Augsburg Confession so strongly emphasizes the importance of the Word and the sacrament that God employs to give people his grace, this is also connected with the debate with theological currents that envisaged a more direct working of the Spirit in the believer, without any mediating instances. And this is why article 5 concludes with a negative demarcation against those "who think that the Holy Spirit comes to human beings without the external Word through their own preparations and works."

The Word as a Means of Grace

"The external Word" in this passage means that God does not speak directly to human beings through an "internal word." He communicates himself through the Word, as this is attested in Scripture and mediated in preaching. This emphasis on the external Word is based on the faith that God has acted to bring salvation through Jesus' life, death, and resurrection, and that the individual thus receives salvation by encountering the gospel of what God has done in Jesus. This is a message that is mediated to us through the testimony of the apostles, as this is written down in the New Testament and expounded in the church's preaching.

The idea of the efficacy of God's Word is found in many scriptural passages. According to the creation narrative, the world came into being because God spoke (Gen 1:3). The Word is understood in the prophets as a powerful instrument in God's hand (Isa 55:10–11). In Jesus' parable about the sower, the Word is like a seed that bears fruit (Mark 4:1–20). And according to the Letter to the Hebrews, "the word of God is living and active, sharper than any two-edged sword" (4:12; cf. Eph 6:17).

Other New Testament passages affirm that it is as the gospel about Jesus that the Word of God has its effect. For Paul, the gospel is "the power of God for salvation" (Rom 1:16), and he notes that "faith comes from what is heard, and what is heard comes through the word of Christ" (Rom 10:17). In the account of the expansion of the church in the Acts of the Apostles, it is likewise the preaching of the message about Jesus that brings people to be filled with the Spirit and to come to faith (Acts 2:41; 8:12; 10:44).

This means that God does not speak immediately to the inner dimension of the human being. Instead, the message is mediated by means of external physical realities such as writing, speech, soundwaves, and the sense of hearing. It is only once God has reached the human being through the external Word that this can have consequences in the inner dimension, when the Spirit creates faith. In the theological tradition, this has often been spoken of as the "inner witness of the Holy Spirit" (Latin: *testimonium spiritus sancti internum*), which the Spirit adds to the Word, so that it brings about faith. The fact that the Spirit creates faith also means that the message does not automatically lead to faith. Article 5 of the Augsburg Confession, quoted above, expresses this when it says that the Spirit is given "where and when it pleases God."

It is important to underline here that the Word that mediates salvation is something more than mere information about a state of affairs. This Word brings Jesus himself near. John 1, where Jesus is spoken of as "the Word," shows that there is a close connection between Jesus and the Word about Jesus. Karl Barth's distinction between the three forms of the Word and of revelation can help us here. He distinguishes Jesus himself as the incarnate Word, the testimony to the Word in Scripture, and the communication of the Word in preaching. Jesus himself is the revelation, and the Bible bears witness to this. But the revelation does not become life and salvation until it reaches the human heart, and it is here that God makes use of the "living word" of the oral proclamation.

The idea that God works through the word that is preached was a central concern for Luther and the other Reformers, and one consequence of this was the role the sermon took on in the Lutheran and other Protestant churches. For Luther, this is also connected with the distinction between law and gospel (on this, see chapter 2). Although both the law and the gospel must be preached, it is only the gospel that can create faith and new life. The word of the gospel is a word of promise that bears its fulfillment in itself.

When they emphasized the necessity of the sermon, the Reformers were reacting against a praxis in which the sacraments had almost suppressed the preached Word as a means of grace. This did not imply for Luther a dismissal of the importance of the sacraments, and according to article 5 of the Augsburg Confession, it is precisely "through the Word and the sacraments as through instruments" that God gives the Spirit and creates faith. In a Lutheran context, the conceptual pair "Word and sacrament" has tended to play an important role in the description of the means of grace. Before we look more closely at the relationship between the Word and the sacraments as means of grace, we shall first discuss what a sacrament is.

The Concept of Sacrament

The understanding in Western theology of what a sacrament is, is indebted to Augustine, who saw the sacraments as visible signs that point to the invisible grace and grant a share in it. Augustine calls the visible signs "elements" (water in baptism, bread and wine in the eucharist). But it is the Word that makes the elements a sacrament, as Augustine says: "The Word is added to the element, and it becomes a sacrament."[1] This can be expressed in other terms: the sacrament is a "visible word" (Latin: *verbum visibile*).

Augustine's work on the understanding of the sacraments is marked above all by his controversy with the Donatists, who held that baptisms by heretics and apostates were invalid. Here, Augustine affirmed that the validity of the sacrament depends, not on the holiness of the minister, but on its being administered with the correct elements, as well as on the proclamation of the word of the gospel. He introduced an important distinction: although the sacrament does not have a salvific effect when it is administered by heretics, it is nevertheless *valid*. In the case of baptism, this means that it should never be repeated. It works for salvation when it is received in the fellowship of the true church.

The churches disagree about whether other actions than baptism and the eucharist can be counted as sacraments. In the course of the Middle Ages, it became customary to reckon with seven sacraments: baptism, the eucharist, confirmation, confession, the anointing of the sick, ordination, and marriage. These still have the status of sacraments today in the Catholic Church and the Orthodox churches. There is, however, no clear boundary between those holy actions that are counted as sacraments and those that are not. The Catholic Church gives the term "sacramentals" to various blessings and consecrations. Independently of what is or is not counted as a sacrament, there is a large measure of consensus that baptism and the eucharist are the fundamental sacraments.

Luther rejected the idea of seven sacraments because he held that a sacrament must have been instituted by Jesus himself, and he found evidence only for three of the seven, namely, baptism, the eucharist, and confession. This is why the Apology of the Augsburg Confession writes: "Therefore, the sacraments are actually baptism, the Lord's Supper, and absolution (the sacrament of repentance)." Melanchthon is, however, willing to accept priestly ordination as a sacrament, provided that it is understood as a consecration to the service of the Word. He also maintained that "no intelligent person will argue much about the number or the terminology."[2]

With regard to the understanding of confession as a sacrament, reference is often made to Jesus' words in John 20:23, "If you forgive the sins of any, they are forgiven them; if you retain the sins of any, they are retained." Luther held that confession consists of two parts: first, that one confesses one's sins to a priest or another Christian, and secondly, that this person declares on behalf of God that the sins are forgiven. This assurance of the forgiveness of sins (also known as absolution) is in reality nothing

---

1. Latin: *accedit verbum ad elementum, et fit sacramentum*. Augustine, *Iohannis evangelium tractatus* 80.3.

2. Kolb and Wengert, eds., *Book of Concord*, 219-21.

other than the word of the gospel, but applied to the individual on the basis of the authority that Jesus gave the disciples. Although Luther encouraged frequent recourse to confession, he also thought that it should be voluntary. In practice, however, the removal of the obligation to confess meant that confession lost much of its significance in the Lutheran church. Since confession, unlike baptism and the eucharist, lacked a physical element, later generations of Lutherans did not count it as a sacrament. In recent decades, many have promoted a renewed use of confession in Lutheranism.

Just as the Word must be received in faith, so too the sacraments must be received in faith, if they are to be means of salvation. Luther emphasized this in his criticism of every view that the sacrament's efficacy was independent of whether it was received in faith—in other words, that the efficacy was almost automatic, provided that the action was correctly performed and that one did not directly oppose the effect of the sacrament (Latin: *ex opere operato* = by the performance of the act). Accordingly, article 13 of the Augsburg Confession, with the title "Concerning the use of the Sacraments," says that "sacraments are to be used so that faith, which believes the promises offered and displayed through the sacraments, may increase."

The sacraments must therefore be received in faith, if they are to have their effect in the individual. But this does not mean that it is faith that constitutes the sacrament, so that a sacrament exists only if it is received in faith. What makes the sacrament a sacrament is not the human being's faith, but God's promise, on which the sacrament rests. This also means that the sacrament is an expression of God's action even where it is not received in faith, just as the gospel is the Word of God even when it is not believed. For Luther, it was important to emphasize both the Word and the sacraments as "external," objective realities that do not exist in virtue of the strength in the individual's faith. It is only in this way that they can be the basis of the assurance of salvation.

In order to understand *both* how the sacraments can be an objective divine act *and* how they lead to salvation only when they are received in faith, we must go back to Augustine's distinction between the validity of a sacrament and its effect. Even if it is not received in faith, the sacrament contains God's promise, with no loss of validity. This means, for example, that if someone is baptized without receiving the gift of baptism in faith, that person need not be baptized if he or she later comes to faith. In the case of the eucharist, it means that Jesus' body and blood are given in the bread and wine irrespective of whether or not the one who eats believes. But the gift brings salvation only where it is received in faith.

The special mark of a sacrament, in contradistinction to the Word, is that it contains physical elements that cooperate with the Word. The important point about the elements is not, however, their physical constitution or effect *per se*, but that they point beyond themselves. In this way, we can say that a sacrament is a *sign*. The term sign here means much more than an illustration. It means something that points to a reality by itself sharing in the reality to which it points. In other words, the sacrament is a sign of God's salvation, and it contains and allows us to share in this salvation. Here too, it is necessary to see the salvation we receive in this world in a perspective of "already but not yet" (on this, see chapter 6): we receive salvation already now, but it is not yet fully realized. Another way to put this is to say that salvation must be understood in an eschatological perspective. The definitive salvation will take place only in the new world, but it is already anticipated here and now through faith in Jesus.

The elements become sacramental signs by being joined to the promise in the Word, and the fact that they are physical matter from created reality itself says something about the connection between creation and salvation. They are daily things and products that are taken out of their natural context. As sacramental signs, they become bearers of God's saving act: water that we use for washing becomes a sign of cleansing from sin and of being buried and rising again with Jesus. Foodstuffs like bread and wine become signs of sharing in Jesus' body and blood and of the fellowship in the kingdom of God.

The Relationship between the Word and the Sacraments

How is the relationship between the Word, as a means of grace, and the sacraments to be understood? The various churches hold differing views on this point. There is a broad spectrum here, from churches where the sacraments have a very central significance to churches where they play little or no role. One example of the former is the Catholic Church and the Orthodox churches, where the sacraments play a large role in theology, worship, and spirituality. The Word as a means of grace has not always had the same autonomous role as in Protestantism, although the Catholic Church has paid much greater attention to the significance of preaching, etc. in the aftermath of the Second Vatican Council (1962–65).

It is not difficult to find examples of Protestant churches in which the sacraments play little or no role. The Salvation Army and the Quakers have neither baptism nor eucharist. Other churches have both, but without necessarily understanding them as sacraments in the same way as churches with a more sacramental orientation. Many of them would not in fact use the concept of sacrament at all; many Protestants would prefer to speak of baptism and the eucharist as "ordinances" rather than "sacraments." They underline the character of these actions as human actions in obedience to Jesus' commandment to perform them, and as an expression of the personal confession of faith in what the actions symbolize.

Lutheranism has tended to emphasize the role of both the Word and the sacraments as means of grace (as in the expression "Word and sacrament"). Historically speaking, however, there has been a variation in the role the sacraments played in practice, from a more "low church" Lutheranism influenced by Pietism with the focus on the Word, to a more "high church" Lutheranism with the focus on the sacramental.

An Ecumenical Topic

The concept of sacrament is not biblical, but was formed in the theological tradition. It is a dogmatic concept that attempts to describe important aspects of the New Testament message about God's salvific act in Jesus and that seeks to understand particular acts that the Bible prescribes and that the church has performed. The development of the concept of sacrament thus displays similarities to the development of the concept of Trinity in the doctrine about God. Unlike Trinitarian doctrine, sacramental doctrine has not been marked by ecumenical consensus, but on the contrary by strong antagonisms. Many of the themes that have divided, and continue to divide, churches and confessional traditions lie precisely in the field of sacramental doctrine, and this is why many of the doctrinal conversations that have led to a rapprochement between the churches have dealt with topics from sacramental doctrine. These conversations have paid little attention to the concept of sacrament itself. It is not so important to reach unity on how this concept is to be used, or to which acts it applies, provided that a rapprochement is possible in the understanding of the concrete actions involved here—first and foremost, baptism and the eucharist.

A text that has played a very important role in this context is the so-called BEM document ("Baptism, Eucharist and Ministry") which was agreed at a meeting of the Faith and Order Commission of the World Council of Churches at Lima in 1982. Representatives of most Christian confessions had worked on this text. Although it recognizes that disagreement still exists on many questions, it also points to fundamental shared theological elements and affirms that the churches have come closer to one another in many fields (this is often called "convergence"). This applies particularly to the understanding of baptism and the eucharist.

One key to this rapprochement lies in the understanding of the sacraments as *signs* of a salvation in which we already share, but which is not yet fully realized. For churches that have traditionally emphasized that the sacraments *mediate* salvation by being performed, this has led to a recognition that this mediation has the character of a sign, since it is to be understood as a foretaste of the definitive salvation. For churches that have traditionally understood acts such as baptism and the eucharist are purely symbolic acts, this has led to a recognition that, precisely as symbols in the sense of *signs*, they also share in, and allow us to share in, what they symbolize.

7.2 BAPTISM

Baptism is a basic Christian rite that is used by almost all Christian churches and that is anchored solidly in the New Testament. In terms of religious history, Christian baptism has parallels in many forms of purificatory rituals in which water plays a role; this was also the case in Judaism in the New Testament period. Some purifications with water were already prescribed in the Old Testament (e.g., in Leviticus 15). Unlike

Christian baptism, such rites of purification were not unique occurrences, but could be repeated where necessary.

The Baptism of John and Christian Baptism

The immediate model of Christian baptism is, however, the activity of John the Baptist just before Jesus began his public ministry, as this is described in the Gospels (Matt 3:1–12; Mark 1:2–8; Luk 3:1–18; John 1:19–34). John was a preacher of repentance who rebuked the people for their sins and exhorted them to change their ways. He baptized those who came to him with "a baptism of repentance for the forgiveness of sins" (Luk 3:3). Unlike the usual Jewish rites of purification, where one purified oneself, it seems that it was John who baptized the one who accepted baptism, and this has continued in Christian baptism, where one does not baptize oneself, but is baptized by someone else. John contrasted himself and his own baptism in water with Jesus, who would baptize "with the Holy Spirit and fire" (Luk 3:16). Jesus surprised John by asking to be baptized by him. This event functioned as the start of Jesus' public ministry (Matt 3:13–17).

According to John's Gospel, Jesus' disciples too carried out for a time a baptismal activity like that of the Baptist, but this was not something that characterized Jesus' ministry (John 3:22; 4:1–2). But when Jesus sent the disciples out in the world before his ascension, he instructed them to baptize: "Go therefore and make disciples of all nations, baptizing them in the name of the Father and of the Son and of the Holy Spirit, and teaching them to obey everything that I have commanded you" (Matt 28:19–20). Accordingly, when those who heard Peter's sermon on Pentecost day asked what they ought to do, they were told to accept baptism: "Repent, and be baptized every one of you in the name of Jesus Christ so that your sins may be forgiven; and you will receive the gift of the Holy Spirit" (Acts 2:38). It is interesting to see that the baptism in the Holy Spirit, with which John said Jesus would baptize, is combined here with baptism in water. The context shows that baptism was perceived as an expression of entering the community: "So those who welcomed his message were baptized, and that day about three thousand persons were added" (Acts 2:41).

Although the baptism of John must have been an important background to Christian baptism, they are not identical, as is clearly demonstrated by the account of Paul's encounter with some disciples who had not received the Holy Spirit (Acts 19:1–7). In order to identify the problem, Paul asks: "Into what then were you baptized?" They reply: "Into John's baptism." When they then are baptized in Jesus' name, and Paul lays his hands on them, the Spirit immediately comes over them.

Baptism and Salvation

As these texts from the Acts of the Apostles show, baptism is not only a human act that is meant to express adherence or commitment. It is also seen as an expression of what God does in relation to the one who is baptized. Two motifs are particularly prominent, namely, that baptism gives the forgiveness of sins and that it gives the gift of the Spirit. The forgiveness of sins that baptism imparts corresponds well to our ordinary use of water to wash away physical dirt. Water, as a physical means of cleansing, thus becomes a sign that God cleanses the human being from sin. To be baptized is "to have [one's] sins washed away" (Acts 22:16).

Other New Testament writings likewise speak of baptism as an action with decisive significance for receiving salvation. In the Gospel of John (3:5), Jesus says that "no one can enter the kingdom of God without being born of water and Spirit." The Letter to Titus (3:5) says that God "saved us ... through the water of rebirth and renewal by the Holy Spirit" (cf. also Mark 16:16; 1 Pet 3:21).

Both here and in the texts in Acts, we see a close link between baptism in water and receiving the Spirit. In a Trinitarian perspective, when people receive the Spirit, this means that they also receive fellowship with the Father and the Son. Fellowship with Christ is an important theme in Paul's understanding of baptism, as the following affirmation shows: "As many of you as were baptized in Christ have clothed yourselves with Christ" (Gal 3:27). This subject is set out in particular detail in Romans 6:1–11, where Paul understands baptism as baptism into Jesus' death and resurrection (cf. also Col 2:12). Baptism thus unites the believer to Christ in such a way that one also receives a share in what happened to him. Paul is probably referring to the act of baptism, which was practiced by immersion, when he says: "we have been buried with him by baptism into death" (Rom 6:4). He then employs the Christian's unity with Christ in his death and resurrection to say that a Christian must see oneself as dead to sin and allow oneself be marked by the life of the resurrection. Paul's employment of the way in which baptism was practiced also expresses baptism's character as a sign: through its external form, it points to a larger reality, while at the same time allowing us to share in the reality of which it is a sign.

Baptism means being "baptized into Christ Jesus" (Rom 6:3), and this finds expression in the Acts of the Apostles when it is spoken of as baptism in or into the name of Jesus. When Peter exhorts his hearers on Pentecost day to receive baptism, this is an exhortation to "be baptized in the name of Jesus Christ" (Acts 2:38), and similar formulae are found in other passages (Acts 8:16; 19:5). When Jesus speaks of baptism in Matthew 28, he tells the disciples to baptize "in the name of the Father and of the Son and of the Holy Spirit" (v. 19), but in a Trinitarian perspective, there is no difference between this formula and that in Acts, because Jesus, as the Son, must always be thought of together with the Father and the Spirit.

This, however, is not only a theological question, but also a liturgical question: How is baptism to be performed? The meaning intended by the use of water is clarified by an accompanying declaration of the name in which baptism is administered. Most Christian churches take their starting point in Matthew 28 and desire to make it clear that they have a Trinitarian understanding of God. This is why they employ a baptismal formula such as: "I baptize you in the name of the Father and of the Son and the Holy Spirit."

Baptism and Faith

The texts that speak of baptism assume a close connection between baptism and faith. Galatians 3:26–27 draws a parallel between being "in Christ Jesus children of God through faith" and being "baptized into Christ." This connection is expressed very explicitly in the story of the evangelist Philip, who baptizes the Ethiopian eunuch (Acts 8:26–39). The eunuch is convinced by Philip's proclamation of the gospel and then asks to be baptized. In 8:37 (a verse that is probably a later addition), the connection is stated very explicitly: "And Philip said, 'If you believe with all your heart, you may.' And he replied, 'I believe that Jesus Christ is the Son of God.'" The connection between baptism and faith is also made explicit in the secondary conclusion to the Gospel of Mark, where Jesus says: "The one who believes and is baptized will be saved; but the one who does not believe will be condemned" (16:16). This verse also states that while baptism is a precondition for salvation, it is insufficient, unless one also believes.

As I have mentioned earlier in the present chapter, it was important for Luther to underline the importance of faith in connection with the sacraments, and this includes baptism. We see this in his treatment of baptism in the Small Catechism, where he asks: "How can water do such great things?," and gives the following answer: "Clearly the water does not do it, but the Word of God, which is with and alongside the water, and faith, which trusts this Word of God in the water." Behind this lies the Augustinian understanding of sacraments, where the sacrament consists of the element and the word that is added to it: "What is baptism? Answer: Baptism is not simply plain water. Instead it is water enclosed in God's command and connected with God's Word."

The Significance of Baptism for the Christian Life

In his understanding of baptism, Luther's primary concern is to underline its abiding significance in the Christian life. Although he largely shares the understanding of baptism in the Catholic Church at that time, he criticizes a tendency to value baptism only as that which leads a person into the Christian life, while other sacraments subsequently become more important. This was true not least in regard to confession. The idea was that after all sins have been forgiven in baptism, one must go to confession in order to receive forgiveness for post-baptismal sins. In his Large Catechism, Luther refers to the widespread idea of penance or confession as "the second plank of rescue" that one could use after the ship (baptism) had capsized. Luther objects that the ship does *not* capsize, since it is God's ordinance. What can happen is that we fall overboard, but the solution is to get back up into the ship and sail on. Luther wanted to say here that baptism is not just the entry door to the Christian existence; it encompasses everything in the Christian's life. If one falls away and then turns back, one should not be baptized again. One should return to baptism.[3]

Luther links his own understanding of baptism to Paul's understanding in Romans 6. In his explanation of baptism in the Small Catechism, his last question is about the "significance of such a baptism with water." He replies: "It signifies that the old creatures in us with all sins and evil desires is to be drowned and die through daily contrition and repentance, and on the other hand that daily a new person is to come forth and rise up to live before God in righteousness and purity forever." Death to the old, and life for the new of which baptism is a sign, are to be realized in the Christian's daily life. There is thus a close connection not only between baptism and justification, but also between baptism and sanctification.

This way of understanding baptism has not always been equally clear in Lutheranism. This applies particularly to the idea in Pietism and the revival movements that conversion was necessary for adults. While the idea of salvation and rebirth in baptism was retained for infants who were baptized, it was held that one must be reborn again through the Word as a means of grace, if one fell away after baptism and then experienced conversion as an adult. In reality, this meant that baptism was a means of grace primarily for children; it lost its significance for adults.

Such an understanding is, however, problematic in the light of the idea in Paul and in Luther that baptism is significant for the whole of one's life. Luther's criticism of the tendency to let the role of baptism be replaced, later in life, by the sacrament of confession is also relevant in this context. The fact that baptism applies to the whole of one's life does not exclude the need to be converted if one has departed from faith, but such a conversion later in life must be understood as a return to baptism and to the promise that was given in baptism. Since it is a sign of the definitive salvation, baptism contains all that God has to give the human person. Accordingly, the Christian life does not mean receiving something else or something more than what was given in baptism. It means receiving this and living it every day. There is a place in this perspective for the idea of conversion, both for the momentous experience of returning to faith and for the daily conversion in which one turns from sin and embraces the new life. There is also a place for the idea of growth in the Christian life: growth in knowledge, maturity, or dedication. The point is that all this is not something that replaces baptism or is additional to it. On the contrary, it entails a life in the gift of baptism.

---

3. Kolb and Wengert, eds., *Book of Concord*, 466.

The connection between baptism and faith also has consequences for the question: Who can be baptized, and when should baptism take place? In the Acts of the Apostles, baptism is administered more or less immediately after people have come to faith and ask to be baptized (2:41; 8:36-38; 9:18). As the gospel gradually came to be preached also to persons who did not have the same insight into the Jewish faith, it became necessary to have a longer period of preparation before baptism, in which the catechumens were instructed in the faith. This was a natural consequence of the fact that faith also presupposes knowledge both of what one believes in and of how the faith is to be lived in practice. It also carries out Jesus' commission to make people disciples: "Make disciples of all nations, baptizing them in the name of the Father and of the Son and of the Holy Spirit, *teaching them to obey* everything I have commanded you" (Matt 28:19-20). There is considerable variation from one church to another in how catechumens are prepared for baptism, but there is an ecumenical consensus that baptism and instruction in the faith belong together. When infants are baptized, the instruction must necessarily take place later than the baptism itself.

The connection between baptism and the content of the faith can also be seen in the use of the creeds at baptism, whether the whole congregation confess their faith or the catechumen professes his or her adherence to the creed. In the Western church, the Apostolic Creed has traditionally played an important role in this context.

Infant Baptism

The greatest disagreement with regard to the theology and praxis of baptism is indubitably linked to the question of infant baptism. In the Catholic Church, the Orthodox church, the Lutheran churches, and many Protestant churches, it is customary to baptize infants, older children, and adults. In historical periods when most people belonged to a church, it was customary for almost everyone to be baptized as an infant. This naturally influenced the theological thinking about baptism, which largely became a theology of infant baptism. In a period marked more strongly by secularization and religious pluralism, adult baptism has become more and more customary even in churches that baptize infants.

There are, however, many churches that reject the theological justification of infant baptism. In the Reformation period, such groups were often called Anabaptists (a term that literally means "re-baptizers"). The Lutheran Reformation followed the customary practice in the church and maintained that it was right to baptize children. Article 9 of the Augsburg Confession says about baptism:

> Concerning baptism they teach that it is necessary for salvation, that the grace of God is offered through baptism, and that children should be baptized. They are received into the grace of God when they are offered to God through baptism. They condemn the Anabaptists who disapprove of the baptism of children and assert that children are saved without baptism.

In modern times, the rejection of infant baptism has been represented above all by the Baptists, but other traditions too, such as the Pentecostal movement, have a Baptist understanding of baptism today. These traditions practice the so-called "believer's baptism," where a conscious and personal profession of faith in Jesus Christ is a precondition for baptism. Since it is impossible for small children to make such a profession of faith, only adults or children who are sufficiently mature are baptized. This has often meant that baptism has been understood primarily as an act of profession and obedience, not as an action that *per se* bestows salvation. A more sacramental understanding of baptism has recently gained ground among Baptists too, who understand baptism more clearly as a sign that allows us to share in that to which it points. This development has not, however, had any consequences for the evaluation of the justification of infant baptism.

It is difficult to find direct biblical support for infant baptism, although we do read of persons who were baptized together with their entire household (Acts 16:15, "she and her household were baptized"; 16:33, "he and his entire family were baptized without delay"; cf. 18:8; 1 Cor 1:16). We do not know for certain whether there were children in these households, nor whether they too were baptized. But the comparison of baptism to circumcision (Col 2:11–12) and the fact that children are addressed as a part of the community (Eph 6:1; Col 3:20) suggest that children were baptized.

The fact that the New Testament otherwise speaks explicitly only of adult baptism is not a decisive argument that disqualifies infant baptism, since the praxis of adult baptism will be normal in the situation of a first-generation mission. We do not, however, have certain evidence of infant baptism being practiced in the church before the second century. The silence of our sources on this praxis is not a decisive argument for or against infant baptism, which must be evaluated on the basis of a more holistic theological argumentation.

One decisive argument for believer's baptism and against infant baptism has been the close link between baptism and faith that is presupposed in the New Testament. The idea here is that since faith entails a conscious adherence to the Christian message, it is necessary to put off baptism until one reaches a stage of development at which a personal adherence of this kind is possible. If, on the other hand, faith is understood more as a relational concept—in other words, that faith entails having a relationship to Jesus Christ—faith is not necessarily something reserved only to persons at one specific stage of development. In that case, small children would not be excluded; neither would persons with mental handicaps or dementia.

One can also emphasize the collective aspect of the concept of faith, which is something one does not only on one's own, but also in a believing fellowship. The faith of the fellowship can also sustain those of its members who do not themselves have the mental presuppositions for expressing their faith. Openness to the idea that faith can take such forms must, of course, not signify that an unconscious or collective faith can take the place of the individual and conscious faith in persons who are capable of expressing faith in such a form. The point is simply that faith must take a form that corresponds to the mental stage at which a person is in his or her life.

It is impossible to give a certain answer to the question how faith is to be envisaged in persons who themselves are unable to express it. On this point, one must make use of theological auxiliary concepts. Many have envisaged the faith on which infant baptism is based as a vicarious faith that is present either in the parents and godparents or in the church community. Faith is understood here as the trust in God's promise that makes people bring the child to baptism, just as Jesus healed a paralyzed man when he saw the faith of those who carried him to Jesus (Mark 2:5). Luther held that the child too received its own faith as a gift in baptism. He puts it as follows in the Large Catechism: "We bring the child with the intent and hope that it may believe, and we pray God to grant it faith." This, however, is a theological auxiliary concept that does not decide the question of infant baptism once and for all, as the next words make clear: "But we do not baptize on this basis, but solely on the command of God."[4]

Irrespective of how one envisages the infant's faith in baptism, it must be maintained that baptism is a baptism *for* faith. In other words, as the baptized child grows up, it must be instructed in the faith and learn to practice it in a believing fellowship. This is presupposed (to take one example) by the baptismal liturgy of the Church of Norway, where the parents and godparents are made responsible to "teach her (or him or them) to pray and help her (or him or them) to use the word of God and receive the sacrament of the Eucharist so that she (or he or they) may live and grow in the Christian faith."[5] The connection between baptism and faith is also expressed by the fact that the Apostolic Creed is always read in the context of baptism. It is introduced by these words: "Together, let us renounce the devil and all evil works, and confess the faith in which we baptise our children."[6] The Evangelical Lutheran Church in Denmark requires parents and godparents to confirm, on behalf of the child, their adherence to the articles of faith.

A decisive question for the evaluation of infant baptism is how one understands the child's relationship to salvation. In a Lutheran perspective, the doctrine of original sin means that the child is born with sin and guilt, and that it therefore needs salvation in the same way as adults. Since baptism is "necessary for salvation" (article 9 of the Augsburg Confession), it is desired that infants too may receive salvation, and this happens when they are brought to baptism.

If one rejects this understanding of original sin and holds that the child does not have any personal guilt before it commits conscious sins, it has no need of salvation in the same way as adults. And this means that it has no need of baptism. Some also claim that if children are covered by Adam's sin, they are also covered by Jesus' work of atonement, as long as they have not committed any conscious sin. It is held that

---

4. Kolb and Wengert, eds., *Book of Concord*, 464.
5. Church of Norway, *Order of Baptism*, 7.
6. Church of Norway, *Order of Baptism*, 4.

biblical support for this position can be find in texts such as Mark 10:13–16, where Jesus says of children: "It is to such as these that the kingdom of God belongs," or Matthew 18:1–5, where Jesus says that one must become like a child in order to enter the kingdom of heaven. From a Lutheran perspective, such texts are not taken to mean that children already have received salvation simply in virtue of being children, but that they have a special right to receive it. The consequence of this is that children are brought to baptism, which is the place where God gives a share in his kingdom. This is why Mark 10:13–16 is read in the liturgy for infant baptism in many churches. Although the kingdom of God belongs to children in a special way, this means, not that they have special qualities that adults lack, but rather that they have nothing that they can show. In this perspective, infant baptism becomes a sign of God's unconditional grace.

It must also be said here that the idea that a child is God's child from birth onwards need not necessarily lead to a rejection of infant baptism. If children already belong to God, baptism can be understood as confirming their relationship to God. This has been the dominant perspective in Methodism. Here too, there has been a development in recent years towards a greater understanding of baptism as an entrance into the new life Christ, also for infants.

One perspective on baptism that has dominated in Methodism and the Reformed churches is the understanding of baptism as the sign of a *covenant* between God and human beings. God entered into a covenant with the people of Israel and gave them circumcision as a sign (Gen 17:10–14), and the salvation that Jesus brings can be understood as a "new covenant" (Luk 22:20; 2 Cor 3:6; Heb 9:15). In this perspective, the fact that circumcision was performed on newborn boys is an argument that baptism, as the sign of the new covenant, should also be administered to small children. Although Lutherans too can speak of "the baptismal covenant," the use of the idea of covenant in connection with baptism has been criticized as overshadowing the fact that baptism is first and foremost the sovereign act of God's grace in relation to the human being.

Rebaptism as an Ecumenical Problem

As I have said, practicing infant baptism does not mean that one does not also baptize adolescents and adults. In an ecumenical perspective, it is not *per se* an insuperable problem that different churches have a differing praxis in this area. In some churches, it has been accepted that members and pastors can have a varied praxis here. The real ecumenical problem arises when churches that do not acknowledge infant baptism administer baptism anew to adults who had been baptized as infants. The churches that baptize infants see this praxis as *rebaptism*. Those who practice "believer's baptism" do not see it in this way, since they do not recognize infant baptism as baptism in the biblical sense.

Rebaptism is so problematic because baptism both in the New Testament and in the Christian tradition is an action that is performed only once, at the entrance to life as a Christian. As the beginning of the Christian life, baptism means that one becomes a member of the Christian fellowship, the church, which can thus be seen as a fellowship of baptized persons. This is why the idea of the one baptism and the idea of the church's fundamental unity belong together, as we see with particular clarity in Eph 4:4–6, in a list of everything that unites Christians: "There is one body and one Spirit, just as you were called to the one hope of your calling, one Lord, one faith, one baptism, one God and Father of all, who is above all and through all and in all." Here, the one God and the one faith are put on the same level as the one church and the one baptism. The Nicene Creed likewise confesses "one baptism for the forgiveness of sins." To refuse to acknowledge the baptism of other churches or other Christians by baptizing them anew is therefore equivalent to saying that they have "another" baptism.

In ecumenical discussions about baptism, therefore, the question of the recognition of each other's baptism has been an important topic. The BEM document, which is the work of representatives of various church traditions, states categorically: "Baptism is an unrepeatable act. Any practice which might be interpreted as 'rebaptism' must be avoided." The churches are therefore urged to "refrain from any practice which might call into question the sacramental integrity of other churches or which might diminish the unrepeatability of the sacrament of baptism."[7]

This document, however, ascribes responsibility in this regard not only to those who have a Baptist position, but also to those who practice infant baptism: the latter are put under an obligation to make manifest the connection between baptism and faith. Churches that baptize infants must therefore "guard themselves against the practice of apparently indiscriminate baptism and take more seriously their responsibility for the nurture of baptized children to mature commitment to Christ."[8]

Thanks to a greater rapprochement in this area, there is an increasing tendency today for churches and communities with a Baptist position not to demand that those who were baptized as children and now want to join them must be baptized anew. The criticism of the baptismal praxis in the majority churches that baptize infants has also led to a self-critical reflection there and to renewed efforts in the teaching of the faith for baptized children.

Rebaptism is not only a problem in relation to churches with a Baptist understanding of baptism. It involves a more general problem: How does one relate to persons who were baptized in another church than one's own? The Western church has generally followed Augustine's view that the validity of baptism depends, not on who is the minister, but on whether it is performed in the correct manner. The praxis in the Eastern Orthodox churches, however, has tended more strongly to baptize new

---

7. *Baptism, Eucharist and Ministry*, Baptism, par. 13.
8. *Baptism, Eucharist and Ministry*, Baptism, par. 16.

persons who had previously been baptized in non-Orthodox churches. In several ecumenical agreements, representatives of the Orthodox churches have expressed their recognition of the baptism of other churches, although this does not always correspond to local praxis.

But even when one acknowledges the baptism of other churches, the question arises: What can be understood as a Christian baptism? Other religions too have ceremonies that resemble baptism, and baptism is practiced by groups that themselves claim to be Christian, but are not recognized by other Christian groups, such as the Mormons or the Jehovah's Witnesses. It is customary here to draw the boundary line at churches that see a Trinitarian understanding of God as the basis of baptism. Accordingly, most churches will not recognize the baptism in non-Trinitarian groups. Since this baptism is not performed "in the name of the Father and of the Son and of the Holy Spirit," it is not a valid Christian baptism.

The Form of Baptism

Since it is a sacrament, baptism is an action that makes use of a physical element, namely water. But the way in which the water is used can vary. On the basis of what the New Testament writes about baptisms (Matt 3:16; Acts 8:39), it is likely that baptism was performed by full immersion, a form that also corresponds best to Paul's understanding of baptism as dying and being raised with Christ (Rom 6:3–4). It was not, however, always easy to find enough water everywhere, and baptism thus also came gradually to be performed by pouring water over the catechumen's head ("affusion"). We find an early witness to this praxis in the Didache ("The Teaching of the Twelve Apostles"), which was probably written at the close of the first century:

> Concerning baptism, baptise thus: Having first rehearsed all these things, "baptise in the name of the Father and of the Son and of the Holy Spirit," in running water; but if thou hast no running water, baptize in other water, and if thou canst not in cold, then in warm. But if thou hast neither, pour water three times on the head "in the name of the Father, Son and Holy Spirit."[9]

Today, baptism by full immersion is most common in the Orthodox churches and in churches with a Baptist position. Although some claim that this is the only valid form of baptism, most even of those who practice only baptism by full immersion would also accept baptism by affusion. There is also a tendency today for baptism by full immersion to become more common even in churches that usually baptize by affusion—not because it is thought that this form of baptism is more valid, but because it more clearly expresses baptism's character as a sign that one is buried and rises again with Christ. This does not mean that baptism loses its character as a sign when it is

---

9. *Didache* 7.1–3.

administered by affusion, since this too points in its own way to the Spirit who is "poured out" over human beings (Acts 2:33;10:45; Tit 3:5–6).

Baptism as an Event and as One Stage in a Process

Lutheran theology has tended to emphasize that baptism is the point in time at which God bestows all his gifts. Other traditions have tended to think of baptism as one stage in a process that includes other elements. In the Catholic Church, confirmation is a separate sacrament that completes what happens in baptism. One who is baptized as an infant receives confirmation at the beginning of adulthood: after prayer and the laying on of hands, he or she is anointed with oil. In the Orthodox churches, confirmation is integrated into baptism itself: after the candidate is baptized with water, he or she is anointed with oil (this practice applies also to infants). In these traditions, confirmation is linked particularly to the bestowal of the gift of the Holy Spirit. There is a related idea in the Pentecostal movement, which traditionally thinks of baptism in the Spirit as something that is chronologically subsequent to baptism with water.

Texts such as Acts 8:14–17 and 19:5–6 offer a biblical model for the link between the bestowal of the Spirit and the laying on of hands subsequent to baptism. Other passages link the gift of the Spirit more directly to baptism (Acts 2:38), or else relate that the Spirit is given before baptism, as a result of hearing the message (Acts 10:44-48). In the latter case, Peter's reaction confirms precisely the connection between the Spirit and baptism: now that the Gentiles have received the Spirit, they must also be baptized.

Luther rejected the idea of confirmation as a sacrament that bestowed more of God's grace than had already been given in baptism. When confirmation was reintroduced at a later date into Lutheran churches, this was in order to give adolescents who had been baptized as children an opportunity to be instructed and affirmed in what they had received in baptism. The need for instruction, as well as Luther's insistence that baptism must be lived out every day, shows that although everything is indeed given in baptism, God acts in relation to human beings at other points in time than the moment of baptism. That which is given in baptism must unfold itself and be lived out.

In the document *One Baptism*, issued by the Faith and Order Commission of the World Council of Churches, baptism is understood as one stage in a longer process called Christian initiation, which begins when one first hears the message and then passes through the following stages, in a sequence that can vary: baptism, the confession of faith, instruction in the faith, and participation in the eucharist. Confirmation (interpreted in various ways) can also be included in this process. At the same time, the document affirms that baptism "is the central event of this process, in which a believer is incorporated into the body of Christ."[10]

Methodism is one of the traditions that have also paid attention to what God does *antecedently to* baptism. The idea of *prevenient grace* (Latin: *gratia praeveniens*) is often used to affirm that God's gracious action for salvation cannot be restricted to baptism. Nevertheless, Methodists also affirm that baptism is the decisive transformation in the human being's relationship to God.

A tension is visible here between the idea that everything is given in baptism and that God also works with his grace before and after baptism. To some extent, this tension can be resolved with the help of the idea of baptism as a sign. As such, it bestows that which it signifies, while at the same time pointing out beyond itself. In baptism, one receives Christ and in his salvation, a salvation that is actualized and realized at various points in time over the course of a lifetime, until it is finally to be realized totally in the kingdom of God. In this perspective, nothing prevents God from anticipating something of what is given in baptism even before the baptism occurs. This is what the idea of prevenient grace expresses.

What About the Unbaptized?

Article 9 of the Augsburg Confession states that baptism is "necessary for salvation." This means that salvation is bestowed in baptism. There is no exemption for children, and those asserting "that children are saved without baptism" are condemned. Such affirmations have often been taken to mean that Lutheranism held that unbaptized children were automatically damned. Luther himself did not draw this inference, and the statements in the Augsburg Confession cannot be read in this sense. According to Luther, God has obligated us to use the sacrament, but he has not bound himself in the same way. If there are external reasons why a child is not been baptized (for example, if it dies in the mother's womb), this does not prevent God from bestowing salvation on it.

Luther is not alone in holding that salvation is given in baptism, while God is free to bestow salvation also independently of baptism. It was (for example) assumed in the early church that if catechumens died before receiving baptism, the *desire for baptism* would have the same effect as baptism itself. And if one died a martyr's death, the martyrdom itself, understood as a "baptism of blood," took the place of baptism.

It is natural to see this too in the light of baptism's character as a sign through which God acts, but which also points to what God does to bring salvation, both before and after the act of baptism itself.

---

10. *One Baptism*, par. 3; cf. par. 10, 54–55.

The Means of Grace

7.3 THE EUCHARIST

Alongside baptism, the eucharist is the action that is most widespread in Christian churches. Like baptism, it is an action that can be traced back to the earliest Christian times. But while the eucharist is something that Christians have in common, it is also a very powerful sign of the division among Christians. Different theological understandings of what happens in the eucharist have been a factor in schisms between churches, including between Lutheran and Reformed churches. The eucharist is also the context in which the division manifests itself most clearly, when churches are unable to celebrate it together, do not share in each other's eucharist, or do not permit members of other churches to receive the sacrament. This is why the understanding of the eucharist has been an important theme in ecumenical dialogues in recent years.

The sacrament of the eucharist has traditionally been referred to by various terms. Since Jesus' last meal with his disciples took place in the evening, it has often been called "the Lord's supper." It has also been referred to as "the sacrament of the alter" or as "holy communion." The term "eucharist" comes from Greek *eucharistia* (thanksgiving) and has become more customary in recent years.

The Eucharist in the New Testament

We find the New Testament basis of the eucharist first and foremost in the accounts in the Synoptic Gospels of Jesus' last meal with his disciples before his death (Matt 26:26–29; Mark 14:22–25; Luk 22:14–20). Paul shows the importance of this narrative in the earliest Christian church when he presents it in 1 Corinthians 11:23–25. It is not found in John's Gospel, but an obvious interpretation of Jesus' words in John 6:52–58 about eating his flesh and drinking his blood is that these allude to the eucharist.

According to the Synoptic evangelists, Jesus' last meal with his disciples was a Passover meal in the Jewish tradition, as prescribed in Exodus 12–13. Other passages in the Old Testament speak of eating together as a special expression of fellowship among human beings and between human beings and God. The account of the making of the covenant at Mount Sinai relates that the leaders of the people of Israel ate and drank in God's presence (Exod 24:11). Eating together can also be seen in an eschatological perspective, as in Isaiah 25:6, which says that God will prepare a feast for all peoples in the last days. We also find this idea in Jesus' own preaching, for example, in Matthew 8:11, where he speaks of sitting at table in the kingdom of God. The importance of meals is also expressed in his own praxis. He ate not only with his disciples, but also with the outcasts (Matt 9:10–13).

In his last meal with the disciples, Jesus selects bread and wine from among the food on the table and gives them a special meaning by identifying them with himself: "This is my body," he says of the bread, and "This is my blood" of the wine (Matt 26:26, 28; Mark 14:22, 24). At the same time, the bread and the wine retain their function as elements in a meal, since Jesus asks the disciples to eat the bread and drink the wine. But to eat the bread and drink the wine was not something they were to do only there and then; in the version in Luke's Gospel, they are told: "Do this in remembrance of me" (22:19). This presupposes a repetition at a time when Jesus is no longer physically present among the disciples. This is expressed very explicitly in Paul's rendering: "Do this, as often as you drink it, in remembrance of me" (1 Cor 11:25).

1 Corinthians 11 shows that the eucharist was a regular event in the earliest Christian communities. Paul criticizes the Corinthians in this passage for holding a meal in common at which they did not share with each other, and made no distinction between the eucharist and other food (1 Cor 11:20–34). When Acts 2:42 says that the first Christians in Jerusalem devoted themselves to "the breaking of bread," this too is probably a reference to the eucharist (cf. Acts 20:7).

The repeated celebration of the eucharist points back to the first eucharist ("Do this in remembrance of me"), but it also points ahead to the final fulfillment. Jesus sees his last meal with the disciples in the light of the fellowship they are to have with him in the kingdom of God: "I tell you, I will never again drink of this fruit of the vine until that day when I drink it new with you in my Father's kingdom" (Matt 26:29; cf. Mark 14:25; Luk 22:18). In theological terms, therefore, the eucharist must be understood in an eschatological perspective. Paul puts this as follows: "For as often as you eat this bread and drink the cup, you proclaim the Lord's death until he comes" (1 Cor 11:26).

The Real Presence

Much of the theological discussion of the eucharist has concerned, in various ways, the question of how Jesus can be said to be present in the eucharist. This includes the question of the relationship of the eucharist to the earthly Jesus with his life, death, and resurrection, and the relationship of the eucharist to the risen Jesus at the right hand of the Father in heaven.

There is a wide spectrum of theological positions on this question. On the one side are those who understand Jesus' presence in the eucharist in a relatively concrete and literal manner; and on the other side are those who interpret it in a purely symbolic manner. A variety of intermediary positions lie between these extremes.

Both a Catholic and a Lutheran understanding of Jesus' presence in the eucharist are marked by what is often called the *real presence*, that is to say, an emphasis on Jesus' genuine presence in the bread and wine. For Luther, the formulation in the words of institution played an important role: when Jesus distributes the bread and wine, he says: "This *is* my body" and "This *is* my blood." But how is this identity to be understood, given that the bread continues to look and taste like bread, and the wine like wine?

The doctrine of transubstantiation, which is still the official Catholic teaching, was developed in the High Middle Ages. This doctrine, which was confirmed at the

Fourth Lateran Council in 1215, means that the bread and wine are changed from bread and wine into the body and blood of Jesus. Thomas Aquinas explains this with the aid of the distinction between the substance of a thing and its accidents, a distinction he drew from Aristotle's philosophy. While the substance represents the essence of a thing, the accidents are qualities that have no necessary connection with the essence of the thing. In the case of the eucharist, this means that the substance of the bread and wine are changed into the substance of Jesus' body and blood, while the accidents (appearance, smell, and taste) remain unchanged.

Luther retained the idea that Christ's body and Jesus' blood are present in the bread and wine of the eucharist, but he rejected the attempt at a philosophical explanation by means of the doctrine of transubstantiation as an unfounded speculation. Instead, he maintained that the bread and wine remain bread and wine, while at the same time they become the body and blood of Jesus. In the Small Catechism, Luther answers the question of what the eucharist is as follows: "It is the true body and blood of our Lord Jesus Christ under the bread and wine, instituted by Christ himself for us Christians to eat and to drink." In Lutheranism, the use of prepositions has often been extended here, to say that Jesus' body and blood are given to us "in, with, and under" the bread and wine. Luther makes no attempt to give a philosophical explanation of how this can happen, but he does refer to parallels from physical reality, such as the iron that becomes red-hot in the forge: it has not ceased to be iron and become fire, but is simultaneously iron and fire. In the same way, the bread and wine are Jesus' body and blood, without having ceased to be bread and wine.

Another important concern for Luther was to insist that the eucharist has the character of a meal (cf. the passage from the Small Catechism, quoted above: "instituted by Christ himself for us Christians to eat and to drink."). The doctrine of transubstantiation led to the belief that the consecrated bread and wine continue to be Jesus' body and blood even after the end of the eucharistic celebration. The consequence in Catholic piety was that the bread that was left over was kept ("reserved") in a special way and was made the object of adoration, for example, by carrying it around in a procession on the feast of Corpus Christi. Lutheranism rejected practices of this kind and affirmed that it is as elements in the eucharistic *meal* that the bread and wine are to be understood as Jesus' body and blood.

The idea of the inherent holiness of the elements led in the Middle Ages to a praxis where the priest received both bread and wine, but the laity received only the bread. The Council of Constance in 1415 confirmed the correctness of this praxis of communion "under one kind." Against this praxis, Luther pointed first and foremost to Jesus' words of institution, where he explicitly says of the cup with wine: "Drink from it, all of you" (Matt 26:27). As the eucharist is celebrated because Jesus instituted it; accordingly, it must also be celebrated in accord with its institution. This is why, in the Lutheran and other Protestant churches, all who take part in the eucharist receive both bread and wine. The Second Vatican Council made it possible for the laity to receive the wine in the Catholic Church too, although the old praxis also continues in many places.

The fact that there are two elements of the eucharist—bread and wine—also raises the question of what each of the elements gives. Does the bread give only a part of Jesus (the body of Jesus), while the wine gives another part of him (the blood of Jesus)? This question too was discussed in the Middle Ages, and it was concluded that Jesus' body is never without Jesus' blood. This means that one always receives the entire Christ, both in the bread and in the wine. Luther too maintained this understanding, although he rejected the inference that it would be sufficient to distribute the bread alone. Independently of how the sacrament is distributed, this clarification says something important about what the idea of the real presence implies. The fact that Jesus is present in the eucharist with his body and his blood does not mean that only one particular part of him is present, but that Jesus himself, the entire Jesus, is present.

The Dispute between Lutherans and Reformed

The understanding of Jesus' presence in the eucharistic bread and wine has caused disagreement not only between Lutherans and Catholics, but also between Lutherans and Reformed. Despite his rejection of the doctrine of transubstantiation, Luther held fast to Jesus' genuine presence in the eucharist (the real presence), but this was not so clearly the case among the Reformed. The one who went furthest in the opposite direction was Huldreich Zwingli, who understood Jesus' presence in the eucharist in a purely symbolic manner. For him, the eucharist became purely a commemorative meal in which the essential point was the fellowship of faith with the heavenly Christ. A similarly symbolic understanding of the eucharist can also be found today in many Protestant churches.

In the family of Reformed churches, it was Calvin's position that was most widely accepted. Unlike Zwingli, he emphasized that the eucharist genuinely gives a share in Jesus' body and blood. But unlike Luther, he held that this share is not mediated by eating the bread and drinking the wine: it is the Spirit that gives a share in Christ. There was a very specific Christological reason for this: Calvin held that it was impossible for Jesus' body and blood to be present in the eucharistic elements, since Jesus, after his ascension, sits at the right hand of God in heaven.

This, in turn, is based, first of all, on an understanding of heaven as a specific localization. Secondly, it presupposes one specific understanding of the relationship between the divine and the human natures of Jesus (see chapter 5). While Jesus is omnipresent in his divine nature, this does not apply to his human nature, since the limited human nature cannot contain the qualities of the divine nature. This position has often been summed up in Latin as *finitum non capax infiniti*, "the finite cannot contain the infinite." This means that Jesus' body and blood cannot simultaneously be present in two different places, both in the eucharist and at God's right hand in heaven. Instead, it is the Spirit who unites the believer with Christ in heaven.

Unlike Calvin, Luther did not regard heaven as one specific place, but as an expression of God's presence, so that heaven is everywhere that God is. He also took a different position on the relationship between Jesus' two natures: although they are unlike, they nevertheless share in each other's qualities (Latin: *communicatio idiomatum*). This means that Jesus in his human nature too—and that means, his body and blood—can be present both in the eucharist and in every other place.

The question that most clearly brings out the difference between the Lutheran the Reformed positions is what unbelievers receive when they take part in the eucharist. The Reformed answer was that they receive only bread and wine, since it is by faith that the Spirit mediates the fellowship with Jesus in heaven. The Lutheran position is that what both believers and unbelievers receive is exactly the same, since Jesus' body and blood are united to the bread and the wine. The difference lies in the consequences of this reception: while believers receive the sacrament for salvation, unbelievers receive it for judgment. In 1 Corinthians 11:29, Paul says: "For all who eat and drink without discerning the body, eat and drink judgment against themselves." These words were seen as biblical support for the idea that the bread and wine are objectively the body and blood of Jesus, independently of the individual's attitude.

Article 10 of the Augsburg Confession, on the eucharist, counters the Reformed position by affirming: "Concerning the Lord's Supper they teach that the body and blood of Christ are truly present and are distributed to those who eat the Lord's Supper." It is not by chance that this text states that Jesus' body and blood are given to "to those who eat"—not only to believers.

Ecumenical Developments

Various attempts have been made in the post-Reformation period to overcome the disagreement between Lutherans and Reformed with regard to the eucharist. The most important attempt up to now is the Leuenberg Agreement of 1973, an agreement about ecclesial fellowship between a number of Reformed, Lutheran, and United churches in Europe. The Agreement formulates an understanding of Jesus' presence in the eucharist that is close to the Augsburg Confession, when it states that Jesus in the eucharist "gives himself unreservedly to all who receive the bread and wine; faith receives the Lord's Supper for salvation, unfaith for judgment."[11] It also underlines a position that united Lutherans and Reformed already in the Reformation period, namely, that the significance of the eucharist lies in eating and drinking, with the consequence that speculations about how Christ is present in the eucharist risk making the meaning of the eucharist unclear if they abstract from this act. This can be read

---

11. *Agreement between Reformation Churches in Europe*, par. 18 and 19.

as an acknowledgment that the theological controversies about eucharistic theology have sometimes been too hairsplitting and elaborate, in a way that is perhaps not justified by the biblical material.

It is certain that a renewed understanding of sacraments as signs (as we have seen in the understanding of baptism) has also been important for the rapprochement in eucharistic theology. A sacrament is seen here as a sign that points out beyond itself, but that also gives a share in that to which it points. The BEM document speaks of the bread and wine as "the sacramental signs of Christ's body and blood."[12] This understanding has led churches that traditionally had a more symbolic eucharistic theology (in the Zwinglian or Calvinist tradition) to be more open to seeing that the eucharist, precisely as a symbol or sign, not only points to something else, but is also the bearer of that to which it points. This has led to a more sacramental understanding of Christ's presence. At the same time, churches that have attached greater weight to Christ's real presence in the eucharist recognize that this is not Jesus' ultimate presence in the world, but rather an anticipation of his coming in glory. The sign character of the eucharist thus means that it is understood in an eschatological perspective, and this in turn means that, as a sign, it points, not to another "place" (Christ in heaven, as Calvin thought), but to the future, to the perfect kingdom of God. This also corresponds to the eschatological framework in which Jesus himself places the eucharist when he says: "I will never again drink of this fruit of the vine until that day when I drink it new with you in my Father's kingdom" (Matt 26:29), or, as Luke's Gospel puts it: "I tell you that from now on I will not eat it until it is fulfilled in the kingdom of God" (22:16). This means that the eucharist must be understood as an anticipation of the fellowship between God and human beings in the kingdom of God, a fellowship that is often portrayed as a meal (Matt 8:11; Luk13:29; Rev 19:9).

However, the eucharist points not only forward to the perfection, but also back to Jesus' last meal with the disciples, and to everything else that he was and that he did in the course of his life on earth. This link is expressed when Jesus asks the disciples to eat the bread and drink the wine "in remembrance" of him (Luk 22:19; 1 Cor 11:24–25). The Greek original uses the noun *anamnesis* ("remembrance"), which is also employed in English as a theological concept. In the Bible, the concept of anamnesis must be understood in the light of the role played by historical events in the Jewish tradition. When one remembered what God had done in the past, this action was made effective in the present. One example is the celebration of the Passover, where God's liberation of the Jews from Egypt was made present through the yearly celebration. When the eucharist is understood as an anamnesis, this means that we remember Jesus' life, death, and resurrection as historical events, but it also means that these events become present today and acquire significance for us here and now. At the same time, we look ahead to Jesus' coming in glory, and the eucharist is also a foretaste of the future kingdom of God. In the eucharist, past, present, and future

---

12. *Baptism, Eucharist and Ministry*, Eucharist, par. 15.

become one in the encounter between the community and the crucified and risen Christ.

This understanding of the eucharist as anamnesis has played an important role in the ecumenical rapprochement in eucharistic theology, not least in the understanding of Jesus' presence in the sacrament. It has also helped to shed light on another controversial question in eucharistic theology, namely, the understanding of the eucharist as a sacrifice, which has been much more controversial in the relations between Catholics and Lutherans than the disagreement about the doctrine of transubstantiation.

The Eucharist as a Sacrifice?

We find the background to this question in the texts about Jesus' institution of the eucharist, where this is linked closely to Jesus' death, understood as a sacrifice. For example, Jesus says: "This cup that is poured out for you is the new covenant in my blood" (Luk 22:20). When he ate his last meal with the disciples, he would soon afterward become the sacrificial Lamb of God who died for the sins of the world. This is a sacrificial act that, unlike the sacrifices that were offered in the Temple, does not need to be repeated, since it happened once and for all, as the Letter to the Hebrews emphatically states: "he did this once for all when he offered himself" (7:27).

Since the eucharist was linked in a special way to Jesus' sacrificial death, it gradually came to be understood in the church as a sacrificial action. This also had consequences for how priests were understood: they were seen as sacrificial priests on the analogy of the priests who served in the Jewish Temple. It was possible to think of the priest as offering Christ in sacrifice in the eucharist in an unbloody manner to the benefit of the living and the dead, and the act of celebrating the Mass could be seen as particularly meritorious.

The Reformers rejected such a view, since they insisted that Jesus' sacrifice took place once and for all, and neither could nor should be repeated. Jesus' sacrifice is not something that the church offers to God, but something that God does for our sake. Melanchthon does indeed grant in the Apology that the eucharist can be understood as a *sacrifice of praise*, but this does not mean a sacrifice that entails any merit in the sight of God. It means that the community offers its praise for the salvation that God has already brought about through Jesus' sacrifice. He refers here to the exhortation in Hebrews 13:15 to "continually offer a sacrifice of praise to God, that is, the fruit of lips that confess his name."[13]

The idea of the eucharist as a sacrifice has been central in Catholic theology, and Lutherans have generally regarded this as a hindrance to unity in the understanding of the eucharist. In ecumenical discussions of the sacrament, however, it has been clarified that Catholics do not in any way believe that Jesus is offered in sacrifice anew

---

13. Kolb and Wengert, eds., *Book of Concord*, 262–63.

in the eucharist. In other words, they share the fundamental understanding that there is only one sacrifice, namely, Jesus' death on the cross. What happens in the eucharist is that this sacrifice becomes *present.* In the light of what I have said above about the eucharist as anamnesis, it is not difficult for Lutherans to agree to this position. However, Catholic theology has taken one step further by asserting that the believers have a share in Christ's sacrifice, so that the eucharist is also the church's sacrifice that is offered to the Father. It is difficult to accommodate such an idea in Lutheran theology, not least because it has no support in Scripture.

What Does the Eucharist Give?

Questions in connection with the eucharist have been theologically very important because it is a means of grace, that is to say, an external means that God uses in order to give human beings his salvation. In the church's tradition, participation in the eucharist is particularly linked to the forgiveness of sins, on the basis of texts such as the words of institution in Matthew's Gospel, when Jesu says that his blood is poured out "for the forgiveness of sins" (26:28). As we have seen in the chapter on salvation, the forgiveness of sins is one of several dimensions of salvation. Since the eucharist mediates God's grace and salvation, the various aspects of salvation are also involved here. In a text that probably alludes to the eucharist, sharing in Jesus' body and blood is linked to another important aspect of salvation, namely, the victory of life over death: "Those who eat my flesh and drink my blood have eternal life, and I will raise them up on the last day" (John 6:54).

Although salvation is bestowed through the other means of grace too, the eucharist has a special character of its own. While baptism is an unrepeatable action at the beginning of the Christian life, the eucharist is something one takes part in again and again. The characteristic of the eucharist *qua* sacrament is that one eats and drinks bread and wine in a meal together with other believers. When the bread and wine are identified as Jesus' body and blood, this means that one shares in a special way in Jesus and in the fruits of his life, death, and resurrection. The difference from simply hearing the Word is that this mediation takes place concretely and physically, by eating and drinking.

Receiving a share in Jesus through eating and drinking also means that the eucharist in a special way mediates fellowship with Christ. Jesus expresses this as follows, according to John 6:56: "Those who eat my flesh and drink my blood abide in me, and I in them." The fellowship with God that salvation entails, in virtue of the fact that the believer abides in Christ and Christ in him or her, finds a special expression in the eucharist.

The dimension of fellowship in the eucharist is not only a fellowship between the individual and God, but also a fellowship among human beings. This is expressed not least by the character of the eucharist as a meal eaten in common, even if the character of a meal has been strongly stylized in many cases. This is why the eucharist is at the very center of what it means to be church. When people share in Christ's body together, they themselves also become a part of Christ's body in the sense of the church (see further on ecclesiology in the next chapter). In Paul's words, "Because there is one bread, we who are many are one body, for we all partake of the one bread" (1 Cor 10:17).

But the eucharist not only gives fellowship with those with whom one celebrates it on any particular occasion. What I said above—that past, present, and future become one in the eucharist—applies also to the fellowship with other believers. One has fellowship with those who have gone before us and with those will come after us. And this means that the eucharist is an anticipation of the table fellowship in the kingdom of God, where people from all ages will be gathered together with each other and with their Savior (Matt 8:11; Luk13:29; Rev 19:9).

Just as with baptism and the Word, so too the gifts that God bestows in the eucharist must be received in faith, if they are to be for salvation. Luther expresses as follows the connection between the sign, the word of promise, and faith in the Small Catechism:

> How can bodily eating and drinking do such a great thing? Answer: Eating and drinking certainly do not do it, but rather the words that are recorded: "given for you" and "shed for you for the forgiveness of sins." These words, when accompanied by the physical eating and drinking, are the essential thing in the sacrament, and whoever believes these very words has what they declare and state, namely, "forgiveness of sins."

Faith is not to be understood here as a human achievement or quality that would be a precondition for taking part in the eucharist. It is Jesus who acts in the eucharist and who gives himself to those who eat and drink. In this context, to believe is nothing other than to receive that which is given and to trust that this suffices for salvation.

Who Can Take Part in the Eucharist?

It is also important to see the eucharist in connection with baptism. One who is baptized has already received fellowship with Christ, and it is this fellowship that is confirmed and strengthened in the eucharist. In most churches since the earliest centuries, the link between baptism and eucharist has been emphasized by the praxis that only baptized persons can take part in the eucharist. In other words, the fellowship that shares bread and wine in the eucharist is the fellowship of the baptized. This does not mean that the salvation given by the eucharist is not meant for all human beings; it simply means that the path into the fellowship of the eucharist goes via baptism. In recent years, some have argued that one ought also to be able to give the eucharist to unbaptized persons, but this is a breach with a long ecclesial tradition. It is also problematic, in view of baptism's role as the door of entry into the Christian fellowship.

In some contexts it has sometimes been thought that in addition to being baptized, one must be especially "worthy" in order to receive the eucharist. In a Norwegian context, this idea was generated by criticism of a eucharistic praxis in which receiving communion was an obligation for everyone who lived in one particular place, whether or not this was an expression of a personal confession of faith. This prompted the idea that an especially certain faith or moral behavior was required before receiving the eucharist, and this meant that many churchgoers kept away from the eucharist. In reality, such an understanding is completely alien to the gospel of God's unconditional grace.

This idea can indeed appeal to 1 Corinthians 11, where Paul warns against eating the bread or drinking from the cup "in an unworthy manner" (11:27). This passage, however, is not speaking about the personal piety of the participants. The problem was that the eucharist had become part of an ordinary meal in which the rich did not share with those who had no food. An unworthy celebration of the eucharist is one that conflicts with that of which the eucharist is a sign, for example, when certain persons are refused admittance to communion because of ethnic characteristics (as happened in the churches that practiced apartheid in South Africa). This praxis is not in accord with the fundamental New Testament idea that all the believers are one in Jesus, whether "Jew or Greek . . . slave or free . . . male or female" (Gal 3:28); or, as James writes, "My brothers and sisters, do you with your acts of favoritism really believe in our glorious Lord Jesus Christ?" (2:1).

The Eucharist and the Trinity

One important result of the ecumenical rapprochement in the understanding of the eucharist has been a stronger Trinitarian perspective. This has to some extent corrected the one-sided Christological approach to the eucharist that has often marked Western theology. It is, of course, not unexpected that one would be especially concerned with Jesus in the understanding of the eucharist, since this sacrament involves receiving his body and blood. But Jesus, as the Son, can never be understood independently of the Father and the Spirit.

As the one who sends the Son to bring salvation to the world, the Father is the real subject in the eucharist, and hence it is right that the community's thanksgiving and praise should be addressed to him. This is expressed in the liturgical tradition when the eucharistic prayer is addressed primarily to the Father, not to the Son or the Spirit. In the eucharist, the community thanks the Father for all that he has done and will continue to do both in creation and in redemption, both in the world and in the church.

When the church addresses the Father in the eucharistic celebration, this also means that the created world belongs within the horizon of the eucharist. The fact that the eucharistic elements are the product of human work on the fruits of the earth, corn and grapes, is a clear creation-theological motif. The relationship to the creation can also be seen in the idea that the eucharist is something the church does on behalf of the whole of creation. In the eucharist, the church prays for all human beings and for all that is created, and there is an anticipation of the fellowship between God and his work of creation in the perfected kingdom of God.

Ecumenical impulses have also led to a stronger emphasis on the role of the Spirit in the eucharist. The influence here comes especially from Orthodox theology, where the invocation of the Spirit is taken for granted as part of the eucharistic liturgy. This is often called the *epiclesis* (Greek *epiklesis* = invocation), a prayer that the Spirit may come over the eucharistic elements and over those who share in the eucharist. This brings out a central New Testament insight, namely, that after the ascension, it is the Spirit who brings Jesus near. This does not contradict the idea of the real presence, the idea that Jesus is genuinely present in the bread and the wine. If Jesus is genuinely present, it is because the Spirit has made this mystery a reality. The Spirit is also the bond who unites the believers to one another and to God.

In keeping with the Augustinian understanding of the sacraments, where it is the Word that makes the elements a sacrament (see earlier in the present chapter), Western theology has tended to see the reading of the words of institution as that which makes the eucharist the eucharist. There are, however, examples in the Eastern churches of liturgies that do not contain the words of institution, but have only an epiclesis. But although the words of institution are not read, they resound in the background, since the entire action is a response to the institution by Jesus. Nevertheless, the variations in liturgical praxis say something about the connection between the different components and the need to think of the eucharistic action as a totality in which the words of institution, the invocation of the Spirit, and the eating of the bread and the drinking of the wine by human beings all make the eucharist the means of grace that Jesus instituted for his church.

Eucharistic Theology and Eucharistic Praxis

There is a clear trajectory from eucharistic theology not only to the eucharistic liturgy, but also to other aspects of the way in which the eucharist is celebrated. This applies not least to its frequency. It is unthinkable in the Catholic and the Orthodox churches to hold Sunday worship without the celebration of the eucharist, but in many Protestant churches this occurs much less frequently, and in some cases, only once a year. This prioritization usually says something about the understanding both of the eucharist and of the relationship between the eucharist and the Word as means of grace. An infrequent celebration will often mean that the Word is the real means of grace, and that one attaches little independent value to the eucharist beyond what the Word can do. But it is also possible that respect for the holiness and the seriousness in the eucharist have led to its being reserved to special occasions; this has been one reason for the infrequent eucharist in Lutheranism. A renewed consciousness of the significance of the eucharist and a renewal in the manner of its celebration have led many churches in recent years to celebrate the eucharist much more frequently than in the past. In this way, the sacramental dimension in the life of the church and of the individual believer is strengthened.

This development towards giving the eucharist a greater importance in Protestantism makes it particularly problematic that many churches refuse to welcome Christians from other churches to their eucharist, or to allow their own believers to take part in the eucharist in other churches. It is a huge paradox that the eucharist, which is so strongly a sign of the unity of all Christian in the one body of Christ, is at the same time the clearest sign of the church's divided state. The solution to this division does not lie primarily in eucharistic theology. It is a matter of ecclesiology, of how the church is understood. This is the theme of the next chapter.

8

The Church—the Fellowship of Salvation

8.1 THE CHURCH AND THE HUMAN RACE

HUMANS ARE FUNDAMENTALLY SOCIAL beings. We live together in families, and we form larger or smaller groups that together constitute the whole of society. We depend on other people to get by, both physically and materially, and in order to ensure our mental health. Many human projects and dreams lie precisely in our relationship to other people, whether to our marriage partner and children or in other relationships. And many projects and dreams are of such a nature that they cannot be realized by one person alone. They are collective projects, and may even be projects of society as a whole.

Although human fellowship is essential and positive, it also has negative and destructive traits. Fellowship is something in which one is included, but also something from which one is excluded. Human relationships are marked to a large extent by division, conflict, and violence between individuals, groups, and societies.

In a Christian perspective, these two aspects of human fellowship can be understood as expressing the fact that the human being is both created by God and marked by sin. Human fellowship is good *per se*, and is willed by God; but at the same time, it is a structure where people exploit, oppress, and harm each other. This makes it necessary to see human fellowship in the light of salvation. When God re-establishes and perfects his work of creation, human fellowship is also involved. At the heart of the vision of the new heaven and the new earth in Revelation 21 is a human society, the new Jerusalem in which people have fellowship with God and with one another.

The One Human Race and the People of God

A fundamental idea in the biblical narrative is that all human beings belong together in one human race. The primal history in Genesis traces everyone back to the first two human beings, who are the ancestors of them all, and the last pages of the Bible show us once more the vision of a united human race. The idea of one human race has also existed in a more secular version since the Enlightenment period, *inter alia* in the idea of universal human rights.

The idea that we all belong to one human race has certainly not been taken for granted throughout history. Instead, one's own clan or people has often been understood as the boundary of the fellowship to which one belongs. This has led to the disparagement of other groups and to conflicts between groups. Such ideas about the superiority and special position of one's group have led, in their extreme consequence, to military invasions, wars, and genocide. Religion too has often played a central role in such conflicts, for example, through the idea that different peoples have different gods, or that some groups are chosen while others are not. But although religions have contributed to new divisions between people on the basis of faith, religions with a more universal outlook have helped to bind people together across ethnic and cultural borders.

Genesis begins with the idea that all human beings are created by God, and are related to each other through their common ancestors. Chapter 12 then relates how God calls Abraham and promises that he will become the ancestor of a great people. The Old Testament tells the story of how Abraham's descendants became the people of Israel, and presents the history of this people and their relationship to God. A fundamental idea is that the people of Israel was chosen by God, as Moses says in Deuteronomy 14:2: "it is you the Lord has chosen out of all the people on earth to be his people, his treasured possession." This is why the people of Israel can also be called "the people of God" (e.g., in Deut 27:9). However, the idea of election does not break the connection to other peoples. Although many other gods were understood in that period as clan deities, this is not how the Old Testament perceives Yahweh: it is he who created the world and who also cares for other peoples (Isa 42:5–6; 61:11).

This means that the election of the people of Israel took place not only for their own sake, but because they were to be a blessing for the world. This perspective is expressed already when God calls Abraham and promises him: "in you all the families of the earth shall be blessed" (Gen 12:3). This perspective becomes particularly clear in the later prophetic texts, which say that a figure who is called "the Servant of the Lord" will not only rescue the people of Israel. God will also make him "a light to the nations, that my salvation may reach to the end of the earth" (Isa 49:6; cf. 42:6). A vision of what will happen in the last days depicts Jerusalem as a place where the peoples of the earth seek God's will, and as the central point of a world in which people no longer wage war, but live in peace with each other (Isa 2:2–4).

The understanding of the church in the New Testament is in continuity with the Old Testament idea of the people of God, but it also reshapes this idea radically. The Gospels relate that Jesus gathered a group of persons around himself, and that they became the starting point, after his ascension, of the first Christian community in Jerusalem. This community gradually grew, as more people came to faith in Jesus, and communities were founded in other places too. The New Testament texts show that the very existence of the church was understood as an expression of God's will and as an element in his salvific action. The account of Peter's confession of faith in Matthew 16 states explicitly that it is Jesus himself who will build his church (Matt 16:18). The parallel to God's election of the people of Israel becomes obvious when the church too can be spoken of as a people, as in 1 Peter 2:9–10, where the Christians are called "a holy nation, God's own people." Unlike the Old Testament people of God, one does not become a member of this people by birth, but by being integrated into it through baptism (Acts 2:41). Nor is it limited to one particular ethnic group. It recruits from different peoples and groups, and those who belong to the church continue to lead their lives in various places and as part of various peoples and nations. This motif is especially prominent in the First Letter of Peter, where the believers are described as "the exiles of the Dispersion in Pontus, Galatia, Cappadocia, Asia, and Bithynia" (1:1).

A Church of Jews and Gentiles

It did not go without saying in the earliest Christian period that the church would consist of persons with various ethnic backgrounds. As the Gospels present it, Jesus apparently saw the people of Israel as the target group of his activity (Matt 15:24: "I was sent only to the lost sheep of the house of Israel; cf. 10:5–6), although he could also help non-Jews in exceptional cases (Matt 8:5–13; John 4:1–26). After the coming of the Spirit at Pentecost, however, the Christians soon experienced that Gentiles (i.e., non-Jews) also came to faith. According to the account in Acts 10, Peter was moved to accept that Gentiles too could be baptized and become members of the church, when he experienced the Spirit coming over a Roman officer and those who were gathered in his house. This was also accepted by the community in Jerusalem, who saw what had happened as an expression of a direct intervention by God: "Then God has given even to the Gentiles the repentance that leads to life" (Acts 11:18).

This, however, did not resolve the theological problems that were linked to the Gentiles' place in the church. The question was whether Gentiles who came to faith in Jesus must accept circumcision and observe the Jewish law. Paul was one of those who held that the Gentiles should not accept circumcision and observe the Jewish law: on the contrary, they had their place in the church as non-Jews. He clearly expresses his position in this dispute in the Letter to the Galatians. According to Acts 15, Paul won acceptance for his view at the meeting with the apostles in Jerusalem, which agreed that it was not necessary for Gentiles to be circumcised. These events seem to have been the decisive factor that led to the acceptance of an understanding of the church as a multiethnic fellowship. This is also the theme in Ephesians 2:11–22, where Paul describes how the division between Jews and Gentiles was overcome through Jesus' death on the cross, whereby he united the two in one single body.

Initially, it was the Gentiles' place in the church that was a matter of dispute, but gradually it was the Jews' relationship to the church that became a theological problem. As the number of non-Jews in the church increased strongly, the Jews who believed in Jesus became a minority both in the church and among the Jews, and this led to the widespread idea among both Jews and Christians that being a Christian and being a Jew were incompatible. When a Jew was baptized, this was understood to mean bidding farewell to his or her Jewish identity. In our own days, we have witnessed a renewed emphasis in theology on Christianity's Jewish roots, and this has increasingly meant that Jews who have come to faith in Jesus as Messiah have not abandoned their Jewish identity, but instead understand themselves as Jewish Christians or as Messianic Jews.

One disputed question in this context is the relationship between the people of Israel, as God's people, and the church, as God's people. From the earliest centuries down to our own times, the church has been strongly influenced by supersessionism (or replacement theology), which held that God rejected the Jews because they did not accept Jesus as Messiah. In their place, he chose the church as his people, which thereby took over all the promises that God had given in the past to the people of Israel. Today, it has been seen more clearly that such an understanding does not agree with the New Testament, where (for example) Paul explicitly dismisses the idea that God has rejected his people (Rom 11:1).

This has led in many contexts to the emergence of various versions of a two-covenant theology that sees both the people of Israel and the church as God's people and holds that there are two paths to salvation: for the Jews, by keeping the law, and for the Gentiles, by believing in Jesus. This idea too is difficult to harmonize with the New Testament, which emphasizes precisely that Jesus is the only path to salvation (Acts 4:12) and that the gospel is for salvation both for Jews and for Gentiles (Rom 1:16). It is also difficult to find any support for the idea that there are two peoples of God. If the church can be called the people of God, this is not because it has supplanted the people of Israel, but because, through Jesus, the Gentiles have been permitted to become a part of the people of Israel. This is the point in Ephesians 2, where salvation for the Gentiles means that they have become fellow "citizens with the saints" (2:19): they have received a share in what the Jews already had a share in. In his detailed discussion of the fate of the people of Israel in Romans 9–11, Paul compares the people of Israel to an olive tree into which the Gentiles have been grafted (11:16–24). Although a large part of the people of Israel have rejected the gospel, this does not abolish God's love, nor the promises he gave to the people's ancestors (11:28–29). Paul is therefore convinced that the people of Israel will one day welcome salvation in Jesus, and that this will bring great blessings on the world (11:12, 15, 26).

Unlike the people of Israel, the church exists, not only for one particular ethnic group, but for people of all kinds of backgrounds and origins. In his vision of the great crowd in white garments in heaven, John sees persons "from every nation, from all tribes and peoples and languages" (Rev 7:9). The multiethnic perspective also finds expression in Jesus' so-called Great Commission in Matthew 28, where the disciples are told to go out "and make disciples of all nations" (28:19). The command to make all nations disciples has sometimes been understood in the course of church history to mean that it is the nations as a whole that are to be Christianized, and this idea generated the notion of Christian peoples or Christian nations. Such ideas have played an important role not least in Europe.

Today, such ideas appear untenable, for several reasons. Unitary Christian societies that existed in the past have disintegrated and been replaced by an increasing pluralism in religions and worldviews. This process has been accompanied by the realization that a unitary Christian society is problematic in relation to religious freedom, which is a basic human right. But there are also two specifically theological reasons that make such ideas problematic. First, because the idea of a Christian people risks understanding the church as an ethnic fellowship, rather than as a fellowship that cuts across all ethnic boundaries, and secondly, because it presupposes that a universal acceptance of the gospel is possible in this world. In a New Testament perspective, the former will be the case only on the last day, when "every tongue will confess that Jesus Christ is Lord" (Phil 2:10*). In the present world, the gospel is indeed received in faith, but it is also rejected. This is why the church cannot be identical with humankind as a whole, nor with one particular people. And the fact that the church can be spoken of as the people of God does not mean that those who belong to the church have abandoned the ethnic and cultural context in which they are at home. It means, rather, that they also belong to a fellowship that cuts across all ethnic, cultural, and social boundary lines.

The Church, the World, and the Kingdom of God

Another way to put this is to speak of the church's relationship to the world. The "world" here means all of the created reality, as God made it, and with the imprint of sin that it bears (see chapter 4). It is not difficult to find a wide spectrum of approaches in the past and the present to the understanding of the relationship between the church and the world. On the one hand, some underline the difference and the antagonism between the church and the world. This attitude often leads to a life in isolation from, and hostility to, surrounding society. On the other hand, some strongly underline the continuity and the conformity between the church and the world. This attitude has often been typical of churches with a large membership in one country or one people (sometimes called "national churches"). But such an attitude can also be found in smaller churches, which go very far in assimilating and confirming the culture of which they are a part.

There are different perspectives in the New Testament too on this question. On the one hand, the world can be perceived as an expression of all that is opposed to God, something against which Christians must be on their guard. The First Letter of John admonishes: "Do not love the world or the things in the world" (2:15). However, we are also told that God loved the world (John 3:16), and that God in Christ reconciled the world to himself (2 Cor 5:19). What God did in Jesus, therefore, he did for the sake of the world—not only for the sake of the church. The church is indeed called to be distinct from a world that rejects God's summons to salvation, but the church is nevertheless in the world, because it is sent to the world (John 17:18), where it is to bear witness to the gospel and to the salvation that one day will embrace the whole of creation (Rom 8:19–22). The church is thus in the world, not for its own sake, but for the sake of the world.

The question of the relationship between the church and the world is closely connected to the question of the relationship between the church and the kingdom of God. I have pointed out in chapters 5 and 6 that "the kingdom of God" in the New Testament designates God's saving action in the world. Through Jesus' coming, the kingdom of God has broken into the world, but it is not yet fully realized. The church's task in this context is to bear witness to God's kingdom and to pray that it may continuously be realized in our world, as the Lord's Prayer says: "Your kingdom come" (Matt 6:10). God's kingdom is the goal of God's saving action, and the church is an instrument for God's work. At the same time, God's presence in the world is linked to the church, since it is here that the gospel is proclaimed and people share in God's saving work. Nevertheless, it is not the church that ensures that God's kingdom will come: it is God who does this.

This understanding of the relationship between the kingdom of God and the church is widespread in contemporary theology, and finds expression in many ecumenical documents. A text on ecclesiology, published in 2013 by the Faith and Order Commission of the World Council of Churches, states:

> The Church is an eschatological reality, already anticipating the kingdom, but not yet its full realization. The Holy Spirit is the principal agent in establishing the kingdom and in guiding the Church so that it can be a servant of God's work in this process.... The kingdom of God, which Jesus preached by revealing the Word of God in parables and inaugurated by his mighty deeds, especially by the paschal mystery of his death and resurrection, is the final destiny of the whole universe. The Church was intended by God, not for its own sake, but to serve the divine plan for the transformation of the world.[1]

---

1. *Church towards a Common Vision*, par. 33 and 58.

Although the church is not the goal of God's plan of salvation, it is nevertheless an important instrument for this plan. This means that the church is willed by God, and that God works in and through the church. In a theological perspective, therefore, the church is much more than the organizational framework for the individual Christian's relationship to God. The church is the fellowship of salvation, not only in the sense that it is the fellowship of those who are saved, but also in the sense that it is the fellowship in which salvation is received and lived. The classic expression of this close connection between salvation and the church goes back to Cyprian in the third century: "outside the church there is no salvation."[2]

8.2 THE CHURCH AS GOD'S CHURCH

One way in which the New Testament expresses God's special relationship to the church is the idea of the church as Christ's body, which we find in the Letters of Paul. In Romans 12 and 1 Corinthians 12, he compares the fellowship of the believers to a body that has many different members. This body belongs to Christ: "Now you are the body of Christ and individually members of it" (1 Cor 12:27; cf. Rom 12:4–5). The church is spoken of several times as the body of Christ in the Letters to the Ephesians and the Colossians too (Eph 1:23; 3:6; 4:4, 12; 5:23, 30; Col 1:18, 24; 2:19; 3:15). In both these Letters, Jesus is also identified as the head of the body (Eph 5:23; Col 1:18). The image of the church as the body of Christ affirms strongly that Jesus identifies with the church, is present in the church, and employs the church as his instrument. It likewise says that the individual believer's relationship to Jesus involves the church: to share in Jesus means being a part of the church that is his body.

Another metaphor that shows the close relationship between God and the church is the image of the church as a temple (1 Cor 3:16; 2 Cor 6:16; Eph 2:20–22). In several of these passages, God's presence is linked to the work of the Spirit, as, for example, when we read that the believers are to be "a dwelling place for God in the Spirit" (Eph 2:20*). God's relationship to the church must thus be understood in a Trinitarian perspective—as a relationship to the Father, the Son, and the Spirit.

The Church as a Theme for Faith

The church is not only a social and organizational framework for the Christian faith: it is also itself a theme for faith, as the confessional texts of the early church show when they speak of the church. Both the Apostolic Creed and the Nicene Creed mention the church among the objects of faith. The third article of the Apostolic Creed states: "I believe in . . . the holy catholic Church, the communion of saints." The Nicene Creed

---

2. Latin: *Salus extra ecclesiam non est* (often cited as *extra ecclesiam nulla salus*). Cyprian, *Epistulae* 73.21.

gives a more detailed list of the characteristics or attributes of the church: "We believe ... in one holy, catholic, and apostolic church."

Such formulations prompt the question: What does it really mean to "believe in" the church? How can we genuinely "believe in" a church that consists of people who make mistakes, who have often abused their positions, and have not always lived up to their own ideals? Different ecclesial traditions have approached this question in various ways. The Catholic Church has tended to draw a distinction between the church as an institution and those who represent the church at any particular point in time. While the churches' representatives both sin and commit mistakes, this is not true of the church as such. Within Protestantism, there has not been the same belief in the infallibility of the ecclesial institution. Instead, there has often been the idea of "the invisible church," which must be distinguished from the visible church as we can experience it. In such a perspective, it is the visible church that is the direct object of faith; this is true of the visible church only to the extent that it reflects or expresses the invisible church.

One problem with such a perspective is that there is not a trace of it to be found in the New Testament, where the church is quite simply the human beings who together make up the communities in the various places. Nothing in what is written about these communities suggests that either they, or those who belonged to them, were perceived as perfect or sinless. And yet, as we have seen, they are spoken of as the body of Jesus and the temple of the Spirit. Such affirmations ought therefore to be read primarily as statements about what God has done and intends to do. If the church is something special, this is not because the persons who belong to it are so special, but because God is present there in a special way. God's working in the church must also be understood in the perspective of "already now, but not yet" that is characteristic of his salvific working in the world. God's salvific working is present in the church already now, but salvation is not yet fully realized. In this perspective, the church can be understood as a sign and an anticipation of the reality of salvation—but not as its full realization.

When the creeds speak of the church as "holy," this is not a description of the moral quality of the church or of its members, but an affirmation that the church belongs to the God who is holy, and that God, through the Spirit, performs his work in and with the church. Because it belongs to God, the church is already holy; at the same time, it is continually being made holy.

The Church's Unity

Such a perspective should also be applied to the understanding of the church as one. If there is anything that characterizes the church as we know it *de facto* both from history and from the present day, it is the fact that it is divided. To say that the church is "one" is therefore to make a theological statement: since there is only one God, there is also only one church. This church is *de facto* divided, but that does not alter this fundamental fact. Like the affirmation about the church as "holy," this too is a statement not only about the present, but also about the future. Even if the church is divided here and now, it is *en route* to a common goal in God's kingdom. Paul has the classic expression of how the church's unity is anchored in God and in his salvific action: "There is one body and one Spirit, just as you were called to the one hope of your calling, one Lord, one faith, one baptism, one God and Father of all, who is above all and through all and in all" (Eph 4:4–6).

But while the church's unity is something that is given, it is also something that the church is called to realize. Even if the unity of the church is given, Paul admonishes the Ephesians to make "every effort to maintain the unity of the Spirit in the bond of peace" (Eph 4:3). One text that has played an important role in the question of the church's unity is Jesus' prayer to the Father in John 17. Here, he anchors the church's unity in the unity between the Father and the Son, while at the same time understanding this as something that must continuously be realized, praying "that they may all be one. As you, Father, are in me and I in you, may they also be in us, so that the world may believe that you have sent me" (John 17:21).

Great changes have occurred in recent years with regard to the understanding of what the church's unity entails in practice. The fact that many alternative churches exist, while at the same time the church (theologically speaking) is one, has often led people to identify the church to which they themselves belong as the true church, while other churches either were not accepted as churches at all, or else were regarded at any rate as inferior to one's own. There is a greater tendency today to acknowledge other churches as expressions of the true church, although one must recognize that there remain good reasons why the churches are still separate.

The readiness to acknowledge others does not mean that there is *no* boundary for which groups can be acknowledged as true Christian churches. The boundary has often been set here at churches that have a Trinitarian understanding of God and belief in Jesus as true God and true man. This is the basis of membership in the World Council of Churches, which, according to its Constitution, is "a fellowship of churches which confess the Lord Jesus Christ as God and Saviour according to the scriptures and therefore seek to fulfill together their common calling to the glory of the one God, Father, Son, and Holy Spirit."[3]

The Catholic Church still has a more exclusive self-understanding, since the church that Jesus founded and that is spoken of in the creeds is very largely identified with the Catholic Church and its organization. In keeping with this self-understanding, it is not a member of the World Council of Churches, although it takes part in other forms of ecumenical cooperation. At an earlier period, this could mean a refusal to acknowledge other Christians as Christians, but the Second Vatican Council brought a significant reorientation in this field too. The conciliar texts acknowledge

---

3. *Constitution and Rules of the WCC*, Constitution 1, Basis.

non-Catholic Christians as Christians through whom the Holy Spirit works. While holding fast to the claim that the church founded by Jesus "subsists" in the Catholic Church, it is acknowledged that holiness and truth are found even outside the Catholic Church's organization. Since the Council acknowledges that the Spirit works for salvation even outside the Catholic Church's organization, it strongly emphasizes the obligation to get involved in working for Christian unity.[4]

There are various approaches to the question of how one is to envisage the goal for the work for Christian unity. The Catholic Church has tended to underline that unity must be expressed organizationally, especially as regards a common structure of ministry under the leadership of the pope. Many Protestant churches have been more content with a mutual recognition that does not necessarily lead to a corporate union. As I have explained in chapter 1, the Lutheran tradition has tended to emphasize doctrinal unity, but has not regarded differences and plurality in other questions as a hindrance to church unity. One complicating element in the work for Christian unity is, of course, the fact that the various churches do not straightforwardly agree about what constitutes the unity of the church.

The Church as Catholic

The question of what is implied by saying that the church is one, is also closely linked to the third of the attributes that the Nicene Creed postulates of the church, namely, that it is *catholic*. Although this is a concept that the Catholic Church uses in its name, being catholic is a part of other churches' self-understanding too.

"Catholic" is not a biblical concept, although it contains clearly biblical motifs. The underlying Greek term is *katholikos*, which means that which concerns the totality, the general, or the universal. The church spoken of by the creed is not a "special church" for one particular group or for a few chosen persons. It is the church that is open for everyone, and that is found wherever the gospel is preached and received. Since there is only one church of Jesus Christ, it is also the same church that is present wherever people confess their faith in Jesus.

The idea that the church is catholic does not, however, primarily concern the internal situation of the church. The church's catholicity is not an inherent possession of the church, but something that is bestowed in its relationship to Jesus Christ and to the future kingdom of God. Because Jesus is the Lord of the world, and the kingdom of God is also the future of the world, the church's catholicity also involves its relationship to the world. Since it is catholic, the church must not be shut up in itself: it must be open to the world. Since it is catholic, the church is sent to the world—and indeed, to the whole world. Since it is catholic, the church cannot settle down in one particular

---

4. Second Vatican Council, *Dogmatic Constitution on the Church*, par. 8 and 15.

culture or one particular context: it is continually summoned to cross new borders, because it is sent to everyone and to everything, "to the ends of the earth" (Acts 1:8).

The Church as Apostolic

The fourth attribute that the Nicene Creed ascribes to the church is that it is apostolic. This concept alludes to Jesus' apostles, to whom he gave the task of being his witnesses. According to the Letter to the Ephesians, the church is "built upon the foundation of the apostles and prophets, with Christ Jesus himself as the cornerstone" (2:20). To say that the church is apostolic is to say something about its anchoring in history: namely, that it has its beginning in Jesus' choice of the apostles and in the first communities that were led by the apostles. Since the apostles' testimony to Jesus is transmitted to posterity in the New Testament writings, the church's apostolicity means that it builds upon the Bible and is definitively bound to the Bible.

While most churches today would agree in what I have just said about the church's apostolicity, some would also claim that apostolicity also finds expression in the fact that the church is led by bishops who are the successors of the apostles. The church is assured of standing within the apostolic tradition by means of an unbroken chain of ordinations, in which bishops have been ordained by other bishops all the way back to the apostles (this chain is often called the "apostolic succession"). This understanding of the role of the episcopal ministry is found in the Orthodox churches, the Catholic Church, and Anglican churches. Although most Lutheran churches have bishops, they do not regard the existence of bishops, or an apostolic succession of bishops, as necessary for the church's apostolicity. In the Porvoo Common Statement between Anglican and Lutheran churches, the Anglicans acknowledge the apostolicity of churches that have not preserved the apostolic succession, while the Lutherans acknowledge the apostolic succession as a valuable *sign* of the church's apostolicity, but not as a necessary presupposition.[5]

The Church as Local Congregation

One can speak of the "church" on various levels, from the local to the regional and the national, and up to the worldwide church. The English language does not differentiate between the universal church, of which the creeds speak, and the church in the narrower organizational sense (for example, the Church of England or the United Methodist Church). The term is used in this last sense in the name of the World Council of Churches. The term might also refer to a local Christian community, sometimes referred to as "local church"—together with terms like *congregation* or *parish*. On the local level, the word "church" is also often used as a reference to a *building*.

---

5. *Porvoo Common Statement*, par. 50–54.

The question of how the various levels in the church are related to one another is not simply a question of vocabulary: it is also a central theological question. Most ecclesial traditions attach a very special significance to the local congregation, because it is here that people come together to worship God. From the very earliest Christian period onward, a basic element in the church's life has been the assembly for worship. This was the place for instruction, prayer, and praise, and it was here that the eucharist was celebrated. This is why we read about the first community in Jerusalem: "They devoted themselves to the apostles' teaching and fellowship, to the breaking of bread and the prayers" (Acts 2:42). Worship in common is central to what it means to be "church," because it is held that God is especially present in this context. The Spirit acts through the reading and the expounding of the Word. Jesus is present in a special way in bread and wine in the eucharist. The belief in the divine presence in the community's fellowship has often appealed for support to Jesus' promise in Matthew 18:20: "For where two or three are gathered together in my name, I am there among them."

Lutheran theology expresses this understanding of the role of worship and the local congregation in article 7 of the Augsburg Confession: "The church is the assembly of saints in which the gospel is taught purely and the sacraments are administered rightly." Even if the church may have other aspects as well—organization, buildings, workers, and so on—it is nevertheless the fellowship of people around the means of grace that makes the church a church in the theological sense of the term.

There are two traditions of interpretation within Lutheranism of this "definition of the church" in the Augsburg Confession. One the one hand, there is an emphasis on the personal elements in the definition: the church is a fellowship of people who come together, and the stress lies on these persons' faith and on the motivation that brings them together. On the other hand, there is an emphasis on the institutional element in the definition: the stress lies on the ministry of the Word and the sacraments as the center around which people gather. Such an ecclesiology will often underline the stable and the institutional, as well as the minister who is responsible for the administration. Taken to its uttermost consequence, the first emphasis risks making the church a voluntary association, while the second emphasis risks making the church an institution in which the human fellowship is less important. In practice, most interpreters attempt to include both aspects in their ecclesiology, although the relationship between them can vary. Similar variations between more "low church" ecclesiologies with an orientation to fellowship, and more "high church" ecclesiologies with an orientation to the institution and the ministry, are not uncommon in the general ecumenical landscape.

The Relationship between the Local and the Universal Church

The individual local community is the fellowship and the place where the triune God is present and acts in his Word, in baptism, and in the eucharist. It is therefore church in the full sense. However, it cannot be church *on its own*, since there are other local communities that are also church. Since the church is not only local, but also universal and worldwide, no community can be church on its own, but only in fellowship with other communities.

There are many views of the specific form that the fellowship between local churches ought to take. On the one hand, we find ecclesial traditions that go far in underlining the autonomy and independence of the individual community. For example, Baptist and Pentecostal churches usually belong to this category. Such traditions are often called *congregationalist* (from Latin *congregatio* = assembly). Although the communities cannot intervene in one another's affairs, such traditions usually have structures for deliberations in common and for cooperation. On the other hand, other traditions have emphasized more strongly that local churches are part of a larger structure, and that this structure can also impose obligations on the individual communities.

In an *episcopal* tradition, it is the bishop who has the principal oversight of this structure; the word "bishop" comes from the Greek *episkopos*, "overseer." A bishop has the oversight of the local communities in his or her diocese, while at the same time working in fellowship with other bishops to preserve the fellowship in the church as a whole. In some cases, the bishops are a part of a hierarchical structure with archbishops and patriarchs. An episcopal structure is an important element in the Orthodox churches, the Catholic Church, and the Anglican churches, but a system with bishops is found in other churches too (for example, in many Lutheran churches). In the Catholic Church, the bishop in Rome, the pope, is understood as the successor of Peter, and as such leader of the universal church. Other churches have not been willing to acknowledge such a claim to universal leadership.

In a *synodal* tradition, the fellowship and the oversight among the local communities are taken care of by elected councils and meetings (often called synods). Here it is the meetings and the councils in fellowship that take decisions, often on the basis of a democratic mandate from the congregations. Such a system is widespread in Reformed churches, but it is also found in Lutheran churches. Many churches with an episcopal structure have gradually also developed a synodal structure. This has led to the elaboration of church orders that include elements from a variety of traditions. This is true of many Anglican and Lutheran churches, including the Church of England and the Church of Norway.

Ecumenical conversations in recent decades have underlined the importance of a structure of oversight in the church (often called *episcope*, using the Greek term). The BEM document states that "every church needs this ministry of unity in some form in order to be the Church of God, the one body of Christ, a sign of the unity of all in the Kingdom."[6] The churches do not, however, agree about whether this service should be performed by a personal episcopal ministry, by elected councils, or by other means.

6. *Baptism, Eucharist and Ministry*, Ministry, par. 23.

8.3 MISSION AND MINISTRIES

The Ministries of the Church

Celebrating worship and carrying out the church's task in the world presuppose that some persons carry out specific tasks in the church and on behalf of the church. The New Testament speaks of various ministries in the communities, but not in such a way that we can identify any unambiguous common system. In addition to the apostles, we find terms such as "elders" (Greek *presbyteros*, from which the word "priest" is derived—Acts 14:23; 15:22; Tit 1:5–6), "deacons" (Greek *diakonos*—Rom 16:1; Phil 1:1; 1 Tim 3:8, 12), "overseers" or "bishops" (Greek *episkopos*—Phil 1:1; 1 Tim 3:2; Tit 1:7), "shepherds" (Latin *pastor*, which is also used in English—Eph 4:11; cf. 1 Pet 5:2), and "teachers" (1 Cor 12:28; Eph 4:11).

While such terms refer to various types of leadership, the New Testament also presupposes that all Christians have a service in the church. This perspective is expressed above all in Paul's exposition of the idea of the church as the body of Jesus in 1 Corinthians 12. The body is one, but consists of many members, he says. Applied to the church, this means that the individual Christians are the members, and the church the body: "Now you are the body of Christ and individually members of it" (1 Cor 12:27). The various members are an image of the various services in the church (or charisms, to use Paul's term). He gives various examples of these charisms (Rom 12:6–8; 1 Cor 12:4–11, 28; Eph 4:11), but these are not to be understood as complete lists of the gifts that the church needs at every time. The examples show that the ministries in the community include both structured leadership roles and more informal tasks.

As spiritual ministries—charisms—they express the reality that the Spirit works through the individual. From New Testament times onwards, this has been expressed in the case of particular ministries by the ordination of persons by means of prayer and the laying-on of hands (Acts 6:6; 1 Tim 4:14; 2 Tim 1:6). Such a ceremony of initiation to a certain ministry is practiced in most churches. Ordination gives the one who is ordained the church's authority to exercise his or her ministry, while the community prays for the "armament" of the Spirit (cf. Eph 6:11).

The ministries for which one is ordained vary from church to church. A threefold pattern with ordained ministries of priest, deacon, and bishop existed already in the early church, and this is still the pattern that prevails in Orthodoxy, Catholicism, and Anglicanism today. Within Lutheranism, ordination has traditionally been reserved to the ministry of pastor, but many Lutheran churches now ordain also to other ministries. Some Lutheran churches have drawn closer to a threefold pattern of ministry, while the Church of Norway ordains pastors, bishops, deacons, catechists, and cantors.

The Church—the Fellowship of Salvation

The relationship between ordained ministries and other church members has been understood and practiced in different ways in the various ecclesial traditions. While some traditions have been marked by a sharp distinction between clergy and laity, others have more strongly underlined the responsibility and maturity of all the believers. One important element in the distinction between the clergy and the laity was the attribution to the priestly ministry at an early date of elements drawn from the priestly ministry in the Old Testament. The priesthood in the Old Testament was primarily connected to the sacrifices in the sanctuary. The church's priestly ministry came to be understood in these categories thanks to a development in the understanding of the sacrifice of the Mass, where the priest was understood as the one who offered Jesus' sacrifice to the Father (see chapter 7). It was only a validly ordained priest who could offer this sacrifice.

The Reformers strongly criticized this understanding of the eucharist and of the priestly ministry. They pointed out that the church's priestly ministry and the sacrificial priesthood of the Old Testament are two different matters. When the New Testament draws on elements of the Old Testament priesthood, it applies them to all the Christians, not to a special group of ministers. This is the case, for example, in the First Letter of Peter, where the Christians are spoken of as "a holy priesthood" that offers "spiritual sacrifices" (1 Pet 2:5; cf. v. 9; Rev 1:6; 5:10; 20:6).

On the basis of such passages, the idea of "priesthood of all believers" was developed, in order to emphasize that all Christians have the same relationship to God and the same call to serve. According to Luther, baptism is the real ordination, which in principle puts all Christians on the same level. In a much cited passage, he writes:

> For whoever comes out of the water of baptism can boast that he is already a consecrated priest, bishop, and pope, although of course it is not seemly that just anybody should exercise such office. Because we are all priests of equal standing, no one must push himself forward and take it upon himself, without our consent and election, to do that for which we all have equal authority.[7]

Although all in principle possess the same rights, this does not exclude the necessity of having a structured ministry that acts on behalf of all. According to article 14 of the Augsburg Confession, "no one should teach publicly in the church or administer the sacraments unless properly called." The role that the Reformers ascribed to the Word and the sacraments in the mediation of salvation explains why pastoral ministry, understood as the proclamation of the Word and the administration of the sacraments, continued to be important in the Lutheran tradition. The importance of this ministry has often been justified by reference to article 5 of the Augsburg Confession. After speaking in the preceding article of the faith that justifies, the text states: "So that we may obtain this faith, the ministry of teaching the gospel and administering the sacraments was instituted."

---

7. Luther, *To the Christian Nobility*, 129.

Although the pastor or priest plays a central role in the church, he or she is not alone in carrying out the church's task. The lay movements in the church have emphasized that all Christians are called to service in the church with their charisms. The development in recent years of new groups of employed persons, both ordained and non-ordained, has also created a new awareness that the various services in the church belong together in a fellowship of service in which all Christians are called to share.

Sent to the World

The fact that the church is a fellowship of services has especial significance for its ability to perform the church's task in the world, whose members are sent out into the world from their gathering around the Word and the sacraments in public worship. A Christian leads most of his or her life out in the world, and the worship helps to see this life in the light of faith, as a service of God and of one's neighbor.

It is not only the individual Christian who is sent out. The church, as a fellowship, is likewise sent to the world, as we see not least when Jesus sends out the disciples and links this to the Father's sending of the Son to the world: "As the Father has sent me, so I send you" (John 20:21).

The Latin word for sending is *missio*, from which "mission" is derived. Recent theology has customarily used the concept of mission as a designation of the task in the world that is incumbent upon the whole church, not only upon a part of it. This perspective entails that one sees the church's primary task, not as self-maintenance or self-preservation, but as being an instrument for God's salvific action in the world. In this way, the church is a part of God's own mission (Latin: *missio dei*).

Since the church's mission is in continuity with the Father's sending of the Son, it is natural to understand the church's mission in the light of what Jesus himself did. In his public ministry, he proclaimed the gospel of God's kingdom and healed the sick (Matt 4:23); and he sent out the disciples to do the same (Matt 10:7-8). These two activities are expressions of God's saving work and signs of the kingdom of God that is to come, and they have been central in the church's history. The church has handed on the gospel, both through its public preaching and through the individual Christian's testimony; and the church has helped people in various forms of need, either through organized undertakings or through acts of love by the individual Christian. Although prayer for healing has always been a part of the church's activity, work for the sick, the poor, and persons in distress has generally been dominated by other methods. Historically speaking, the modern health service has its origin in the church's activity in care for the sick through nurses and doctors and hospitals. In the theological and ecclesial vocabulary, this aspect of the church's activity is often called *diakonia* (from the Greek word for "service"). For the church, diakonia is not merely a secondary appendix to the preaching of the gospel, but a part of the church's task with its own justification.

The Church—the Fellowship of Salvation

The fact that the church is sent to the world to bear testimony to the kingdom of God and to perform the works of the kingdom of God means that the church does not exist primarily for its own sake: it exists for the sake of the world. This does not mean that the church is unimportant. The church is important because it is God's instrument, and because God gives human beings salvation by making them members of the church. To belong to Jesus Christ, and to belong to the church which is Jesus' body, are two sides of the same coin.

The fact that the church is sent to the world also means that it is continuously *en route*. To be church is to live in the tension between "already now" and "not yet," between that which is already given through Jesus' first coming and that which is to be perfected when he comes again. The role played by hope in the church's faith is the theme of the next chapter.

9

Hope

9.1 THE QUESTION ABOUT THE FUTURE

What will happen in the future? This is a question people have asked in every generation. It can be asked out of sheer curiosity: What will the time that lies ahead bring? But very often, the question about the future is profoundly existential: What will the future bring for me, for those whom I love, for the world that I have come to know? The question about the future can involve the desire to hang onto something that is valuable, but it can equally well involve the longing for change: Will suffering and wickedness cease? Will the future be brighter than the present?

The question about the future can involve me personally, the group or society to which I belong, or the whole world. This question can involve the near future or things that lie much further ahead. With regard to the personal future of the individual, many are concerned about what comes after death. Threats from weapons of mass destruction and the ecological crisis lead many to ask questions about the future of the world and of the human race.

These are universal human questions, as we see from the fact that they have been a theme for the interpretation of life in every generation, a theme that finds expression in religions and worldviews. Archaeological discoveries show that one thing that distinguished the first human beings from their predecessors in the evolutionary chain was that they buried their dead, thereby expressing ideas about a continued existence after death.

Human ideas about the future display great variations throughout the course of history. One decisive factor is how one envisages the fate of the individual in relation to the future of the world. Does hope mean escaping from the world and living on in another form of existence, or does hope mean a better future for the world? Another question is the consequences that various ideas about the future have for what we choose to do in the present.

The vocabulary of theology usually calls this part of dogmatics *eschatology*, the doctrine of the last things (from the Greek *eschata* = the last things).

Hope That the World Will Be Saved

There is a close connection between religious ideas about the future and ideas about salvation (see chapter 6). Although salvation can also be perceived as something one can receive already here and now, ideas about salvation often contain a strong element of what is to happen in the future.

In the Christian faith, the understanding of the future is very important for the understanding of salvation. One essential element in a Christian interpretation of life is the expectation that the good will one day be victorious and the evil lose its power. In the biblical and Christian vocabulary, this is often connected to the concept of *hope*. According to Paul, we are saved "in hope" (Rom 8:24), and the list of the things that all Christian have in common includes "one hope" (Eph 4:4).

The link between salvation and hope does not mean that salvation belongs wholly to the future. As we have seen in many places in this book, Jesus' coming means that salvation is a reality that is already here and now present in the world, while at the same time it is not yet fully realized. This means that the experience of salvation here and now can be understood as a sign, a foretaste, or an anticipation of the definitive salvation.

Jesus' resurrection plays a special role in this context. This event is the anticipation of something that will happen to all human beings at the end of the world (1 Cor 15:20–24). And this means that hope is in a special way anchored in Jesus' resurrection: the Christian hope is not only a matter of pious expectations about something that is to occur at some future time, because it is anchored in what God has already done. Accordingly, the Christian hope can be called "a living hope through the resurrection of Jesus Christ from the dead" (1 Pet 1:3). The experience of the Holy Spirit being at work in people here and now, is seen by Paul as a sign that God has given "us his Spirit in our hearts as a first installment" (2 Cor 1:22; cf. 5:5). God can therefore be called "the God of hope" (Rom 15:13). Since hope rests on God's promise, it too can become an object of the Christian confession of faith (Heb 10:23). And this is why affirmations about the future also have their place in the Apostolic and the Nicene Creeds.

In earlier chapters in this book, the focus has been primarily on what it means to say that God's future salvation is anticipated here and now, or in other words, that "the kingdom of God has come near" (Mark 1:15). In this chapter, the theme will be the future towards which this anticipation points. How are we to understand the definitive salvation, the definitive fate of the world and of human beings, and the events leading up to this?

The future is an important theme in the Christian faith precisely because of the role that *history* plays. Since it is created, the world is not endless, but has its beginning in God's creative word. Since it is created, it is subject to the limitations of time. God's relationship to the world and his activity in relation to the world unfold in history, and this is the reason why God's actions in the past and in the future are important for the present. Just as the world and its history have a beginning, so too they have an end. In a biblical perspective, history is making its way towards "the end of the age" (Matt 13:49). However, the end of the world and of history is not the last word. When God terminates the course of the world, he does so not in order to annihilate the world, but in order to *recreate* it, and this is why the biblical narrative concludes with the idea of the new heaven and the new earth (Rev 21). The Second Letter of Peter expresses this Christian expectation as follows: "But, in accordance with his promise, we wait for new heavens and a new earth, where righteousness is at home" (3:13). Existence in the world to come is no longer marked by the transience that we know from the present world. On the contrary, it is marked by "eternal life" (Luk 18:30).

How Are We to Speak of a New Reality?

The idea of the re-creation of the world entails both continuity and breach: it is the *world* that is to become new, but at the same time, the world is to become *new*. This creates very specific challenges with regard to envisaging this reality and to how we can speak of it. Since it is a qualitatively different reality, the language we use to express our experiences in the present world is not truly appropriate here; nevertheless, we have no other language available. When we use it, therefore, we must be aware that we are not able to give direct and literal descriptions of a new reality. We must employ language in an indirect and metaphorical manner. In other words, we must take our starting point in phenomena and concepts from the reality that we know, while remaining conscious that the reality of which we are speaking shatters the limits of the reality we know.

We must also bear this in mind when we encounter biblical texts that deal with the new world and eternal life. These are to a large extent characterized by metaphors in which phenomena from known reality are used to describe what is to come. This applies in particular to the Revelation of John, a book that has been very important in forming ideas about the end of the world and the world to come. Here (for example) the coming kingdom of God is described as a city, the new Jerusalem, with streets of gold (Rev 21). Other passages can compare the kingdom of God to a feast where one sits at table, while being excluded from the kingdom of God is compared to being in a dark place of weeping and despair (Matt 8:11–12). This is metaphorical language, as is shown by the fact that the same place "outside" can also be described as characterized by unquenchable fire (Mark 9:48).

Our knowledge of what is to come is indirect and provisional, as Paul states when he compares our insight to looking into a mirror: "For now we see in a mirror, dimly, but then we will see face to face. Now I know only in part; then I will know fully, even as I have been fully known" (1 Cor 13:12). He makes a similar point when he compares the relationship between the bodily reality we know from this world and the reality of the resurrection in the new world to the relationship between the seed and the plant (1 Cor 15:36–44). The one who only has seen a seed can scarcely imagine what a flower looks like, and in the same way, our ideas about the coming world are extremely limited.

As in other questions, the basis for the discussion of these questions in dogmatics is to be found in the Bible. The New Testament understanding of the end of the world and the future kingdom of God is influenced by the Old Testament background, but also by Jewish apocalyptic thinking from the period after the last Old Testament texts had been written. However, the decisive factor for the New Testament ideas about the end of the world is the understanding of Jesus as the one who has brought the kingdom of God near. For the disciples, the ascension was not the last word in the story of Jesus, but rather the starting point for the expectation that he would one day return and establish his kingdom (see, for example, Acts 1:11; 2 Tim 4:1). This means that a Christian understanding of the end of the world and of history is not an isolated theme, but an integral part of faith in Jesus. The Christian hope entails a certainty that the God who has revealed himself in Jesus also has the future of the world in his hand.

Life after Death, or a Newly Created World?

While it builds on the biblical message, eschatology is a field where Christian thinking has also received impulses from many other sources, including Greek philosophy and various forms of popular religiosity. In many instances, such ideas have aided a necessary contextualization of the Christian message, but in other cases, they have been so influential that they have contributed to a distorted development of eschatology. This applies above all to the understanding of the importance of the physical in salvation. In the New Testament, this is expressed by means of the idea of the resurrection of the body. Greek thinking, however, envisaged the soul as something that lived on after death, independently of the body, and this idea gradually assumed a great importance in Christian thinking. Although the idea of the resurrection of the body on the last day was retained, the focus shifted largely to what happened immediately after death, and here people tended to think of a bodiless existence—in heaven, in purgatory, or in hell.

A central element in the modern theological discussion of eschatology has been the criticism of the influence of Greek thinking. A fundamental understanding of the human person as a bodily being has led to a criticism of the idea of a bodiless existence after death. Besides this, the biblical message of a newly created world has led to a criticism of the individualization of the Christian hope, which is rooted in the concern with the individual's existence after death. The critics have emphasized instead that the Christian hope does not consist in escaping from this world, but in sharing, through the resurrection of the body, in a life in a newly created world. In this perspective, the Christian hope is not only a hope for the individual, but for all of created reality. Salvation thus means, not escaping from the world and coming to heaven, but leading a life on a newly created earth (Rom 8:21; Rev 21:1–2). But while this reorientation in eschatology has won a large measure of agreement among professional theologians, many Christian milieus still cling to a more traditional eschatology centered on heaven, where salvation tends to be identified with "getting to heaven."

A renewed emphasis that the path to the definitive salvation goes via the resurrection of the body and consists in a life in a newly created world does not, however, eliminate the question of what happens after death. Theology often speaks of this as the "intermediate state," that which lies between the individual's death and the resurrection of the body on the last day. Here, there is a much wider range of views, and I return to this in section 9.3. First, we must look at how the future of the world and the end of history are understood.

9.2 WHAT IS TO HAPPEN AT THE END OF THE WORLD?

The Christian idea that history and the world are *en route* to an end has its roots above all in the Old Testament. While many of Israel's neighboring peoples had a cyclical understanding of time, in which existence consists of a recurring pattern of events, the Old Testament thinks in linear and historical terms. This means that God acts in relation to the people of Israel and to the world in a progressive series of events. This involves God's actions for liberation and salvation, but also for judgment, when human beings oppose God and his will. The liberation from Egypt and the settlement in the promised land occupied a special place among God's actions in relation to the people of Israel, and this event also became a model for the expectation of future events, not least for the hope of being brought back from the exile in Babylon (see, e.g., Isaiah 40–55).

Expectations about the Last Days in the Old Testament

While such events are thought of as ordinary historical events that are interpreted as expressions of God's intervention, the description in some texts of God's future actions to bring judgment and salvation breaks open the framework of an ordinary course of history. These are events with a definitive character that brings the existing order of things to an end and establishes a new order.

Hope

One example is the idea of the "day of the Lord." For the prophets, this was primarily a day on which God would settle accounts and hold judgment. The prophet Amos warned those who looked forward to this day: "Alas for you who desire the day of the Lord! Why do you want the day of the Lord? It is darkness, not light" (5:18; cf. Zeph 1:14–18). The prophet Joel affirms that this is a day of cosmic dimensions: "The sun shall be turned to darkness, and the moon to blood, before the great and terrible day of the Lord comes" (2:31). But in the midst of this prospect of judgment and destruction, there is also a hope of salvation: "Then everyone who calls on the name of the Lord will be saved" (Joel 2:32). The prophet Malachi links this hope to a prophetic figure who will be an instrument for this salvation: "Lo, I will send you the prophet Elijah before the great and terrible day of the Lord comes. He will turn the hearts of parents to their children and the hearts of children to their parents, so that I will not come and strike the land with a curse" (4:5–6).

Other texts emphasize more strongly the aspect of salvation in the events in the last days. This applies, for example, to the visions of a future state of salvation in the Book of Isaiah (2:1–5; 11:1–10; 65:17–25). In what is described as "new heavens and a new earth," joy will forever replace weeping and lament (65:17–19), and even the terrors of the natural world will disappear: "The wolf and the lamb shall feed together, the lion shall eat straw like the ox; but the serpent—its food shall be dust! They shall not hurt or destroy in all my holy mountain, says the Lord" (65:25; cf. 11:6–8). In this state, people will no longer wreak violence on each other. They will live in peace: "Nation shall not lift up sword against nation, neither shall they learn war any more" (2:4). And although the people of Israel plays a key role here, salvation is not restricted to them, but is for all the peoples who seek the Lord (2:3; 11:10). Both here and in several other passages, the future state is linked to one particular savior figure. In Isaiah 11, this is "the root of Jesse," a figure who, like King David, is the Lord's Anointed, the Messiah (see chapter 5).

In Judaism, in the period between the close of the Old Testament and the New Testament, ideas about the last days developed in what is often called apocalyptic literature. Detailed accounts of the historical development towards the end, in which the people of Israel would play a central role, were elaborated. We find the beginning of the apocalyptic literature already in the Old Testament, especially in the Book of Daniel, from chapter 7 onwards. Daniel's visions of a future political development, in a rich metaphorical langue, describe how various rulers and kingdoms will succeed each other until God finally establishes his dominion on earth. Here too, we encounter a figure who represents God and his power in a special way, and who will appear in the last times: "one like a son of man" (7:13*). This figure is also found in other apocalyptic writings, where he is identified with the Messiah.

One important element in the expectations about the last days in Daniel and in the apocalyptic literature is that not only those who are alive at the time will experience the establishing of God's kingdom: the dead too will rise up and receive their judgment: "Many of those who sleep in the dust of the earth shall awake, some to everlasting life, and some to shame and everlasting contempt" (Dan 12:2). We find in other Old Testament passages the idea that God can save people from death (Ps 116:8; Hos 13:14), and one text that points in the direction of the resurrection of the dead is Isaiah 26:19: "Your dead shall live, their corpses shall rise."

The Last Days according to the New Testament

Several New Testament passages show clearly that Jewish apocalyptic played an important role in the early Christian understanding of the last days. This applies, for example, to the Synoptic evangelists' presentation of Jesus' preaching about the end (Matt 24–25; Mark 13; Luke 21) and to the Revelation of John, which can be called a Christian apocalyptic text. However, the decisive element in the Christian understanding of the last days is not the apocalyptic ideas as such, but the encounter with the person of Jesus. It is in the attempt to understand who he was and what he wanted that the Christians drew on such ideas, where they were judged to be suitable.

One essential difference is that while apocalyptic sees the coming of the kingdom of God as something lying in the future, Jesus proclaims that the kingdom has drawn near already here and now. This does not mean that God's kingdom has come completely, but that it is close at hand and is at work, and that its reality is anticipated here and now. I have indicated the importance of this "already now, but not yet" idea at several points in this book. This means that Christian eschatology is concerned not only with the future, but also with the present.

When Jesus uses the term "Son of Man" of himself in the Gospels, this is probably an allusion to Daniel 7 and the apocalyptic literature. This concept is used of Jesus, although he does not appear as a powerful figure: on the contrary, he states that "Foxes have holes, and birds of the air have nests; but the Son of Man has nowhere to lay his head" (Matt 8:20).

Jesus' unique position is hidden, but only for the moment. When he returns one day, this will be in power and glory. In his trial before the council, Jesus indicates that his true identity will soon become visible: "From now on you will see the Son of Man seated at the right hand of Power and coming on the clouds of heaven" (Matt 26:64).

His return also plays a central role in his discourse about the last days, which is introduced by the disciples' question about "the sign of your coming and of the end of the age" (Matt 24:3). In his reply, Jesus depicts a period marked by false prophets, wars and conflicts, famine, and natural catastrophes. The last days will also be marked by the persecution of believers and the appearance of false prophets and false messiahs (Matt 24:4–26). When the real Jesus comes back, no one will be left in doubt that it is indeed he who comes: "For as the lightning comes from the east and flashes as far as the west, so will be the coming of the Son of Man" (Matt 24:27). His return is also accompanied by cosmic changes:

Hope

> Immediately after the suffering of those days the sun will be darkened, and the moon will not give its light; the stars will fall from heaven, and the powers of heaven will be shaken. Then the sign of the Son of Man will appear in heaven, and then all the tribes of the earth will mourn, and they will see the Son of Man coming on the clouds of heaven with power and great glory (Matt 24:29–30).

The idea of judgment is closely connected to his return. Jesus will appear as judge when he comes back: "For the Son of Man is to come with his angels in the glory of his Father, and then he will repay everyone for what has been done" (Matt 16:27; cf. 25:31–46).

Similar ideas about Jesus' return are found in other groups of New Testament writings. According to the Acts of the Apostles, after Jesus had been taken up to heaven, the disciples received the promise that he would return one day: "This Jesus, who has been taken up from you into heaven, will come in the same way as you saw him go into heaven" (1:11; cf. 3:21).

The New Testament Letters likewise speak in several passages of the expectation that Jesus will return. This is already expressed in what are probably the earliest texts in the New Testament, Paul's Letters to the Thessalonians. In 1 Thessalonians, Paul says that the resurrection of the dead will take place when Jesus returns: when he comes back, he will meet both those who are alive and those who have already died:

> For the Lord himself, with a cry of command, with the archangel's call and with the sound of God's trumpet, will descend from heaven, and the dead in Christ will rise first. Then we who are alive, who are left, will be caught up in the clouds together with them to meet the Lord in the air; and so we will be with the Lord forever (1 Thess 4:16–17).

Jesus' return is also a theme in the 2 Thessalonians (1:5—2:12). Paul warns against the idea that "the day of the Lord is already here" (2:2) and refutes this by spelling out what must happen before Jesus' return, not least the apostasy under the leadership of a figure who is called "the lawless one." When Jesus comes, judgment will be pronounced on the lawless one and on all who have not obeyed the gospel of Jesus. A similar figure is called "the antichrist" in the Letters of John (1 John 2:18, 22; 4:3; 2 John 1, 7).

The return of Jesus and judgment are presupposed as fundamental truths of the Christian faith in other passages in Paul's Letters too. In one of the latest Letters, 2 Timothy, the reference is explicit when an exhortation to Timothy begins as follows: "In the presence of God and of Christ Jesus, who is to judge the living and the dead, and in view of his appearing and his kingdom . . ." (4:1; cf. 1 Tim 6:14; Tit 2:13; 1 Pet 1:7, 13).

It is in the Revelation of John that we find the most ample account of a Christian hope for the end of time. The structure in its picture of the last days is not unlike what we find in Jesus' discourse about the last days in the Synoptic Gospels: after a period marked by war, catastrophes, and persecutions, Jesus will return, hold judgment, and establish his kingdom. In comparison to other New Testament writings, the description is much more detailed and is rich in metaphors. The events leading up to Jesus' return are described in a number of scenes from chapters 6 to 18, followed by the return (chapter 19), the judgment (chapter 20), and the vision of the new heaven and the new earth (chapters 21–22).

The Interpretation of the Millennium

One special element in the Revelation of John is the description of the "thousand years," or the "millennium" (from Latin *mille* = thousand) as it has often been called. According to chapter 20, Jesus will return after Satan is bound and the believers rise from the dead; they will rule the world together with Christ for one thousand years. After the end of the thousand years, Satan will be set free, but after a short struggle, he will meet his final end (20:1-10). Then all the dead will arise, and judgment will be held (20:11-15). After this come the new heaven and the new earth (chapter 21).

No other New Testament passage attests the idea of a thousand years' reign between Jesus' return and the final judgment and the ensuing new creation. Nor do we find anywhere else the idea that the resurrection of the dead will take place in two groups, although some have thought that it finds support in Paul (1 Cor 15:23). Nor does Jesus' discourse in the Synoptic Gospels assume that the end of the world will take place in various phases; it appears, on the contrary, that judgment takes place immediately after his return (Matt 25:31).

This understanding of the events in the last days seems also to be presupposed in the creeds of the early church. The second article of the Apostolic Creed says that after being seated at the right hand of God, Jesus "will come to judge the living and the dead." The Nicene Creed says that Jesus "is coming again in glory to judge the living and the dead" and that "we look for the resurrection of the dead and the life of the age to come."

In parallel to this relatively simple schema for the events of the last days, more comprehensive eschatological scenarios have also existed throughout the church's history. The millennium is usually an important component of these scenarios, and such understandings have often been called millennialism or chiliasm (from Greek *chilia* = thousand). The Orthodox, Catholic, and Lutheran traditions have normally rejected a literal understanding of the thousand years' reign. For example, article 17 of the Augsburg Confession begins by stating the traditional understanding of the end of the world, where the return of Jesus, the resurrection of all the dead, and the judgement are thought of as events that take place simultaneously. The article then goes on to take its distance vis-à-vis millennialist ideas, condemning "opinions, that before the resurrection of the dead the godly will take possession of the kingdom of the world, while the ungodly are suppressed everywhere." In the context of the Reformation period, this meant a distance not only vis-à-vis theological positions, but also in relation to those who would attempt to establish Christ's kingdom on earth on their own initiative, using political means.

The ideas about the millennium have varied enormously throughout church history. Some have seen it as a period that will literally last for one thousand years, while others have regarded this number as symbolic of a long period of time. Modern versions of belief in the millennium have tended to emphasize its character as a unique time for mission, when faith in Jesus will win many adherents. A literal reading of the Revelation of John, in which the return of Jesus takes place before the thousand years' reign and the judgment afterwards, is often called *premillennialism*. An alternative view is *postmillennialism*, where the second coming takes place after the thousand years' reign. It is often thought here that the church's work in preaching the gospel will ultimately lead to peace and justice in the world. The traditional understanding in the church is often called *amillenialism*, because it does not regard the thousand years' reign as a separate period in time. Appeal has often been made in this context to Augustine's interpretation, where he identifies the thousand years with the time of the church, that is, the time between the ascension of Jesus and his return.

Dispensationalism

Dispensationalism is an understanding of Christian eschatology that goes back to John Nelson Darby in the mid-nineteenth century which has become very influential in Protestant groups today. Dispensationalism is premillennialist, but it adds two very important new elements to the understanding of the last days.

First of all, the "rapture" is added as a separate event among the things that will happen in the last days. The rapture means that the believers are caught up from the earth to meet Jesus in heaven; it is argued that some texts about the return of Jesus provide support for this view (Matt 24:37–41; Luke 17:34–36; 1 Thess 4:17). The traditional interpretation has understood this as something happening at the same time as the second coming, but dispensationalism holds that it will take place beforehand, before a period with great tribulations afflicts those who are left behind (cf. the title of books and films: *Left Behind*). This is followed by Jesus' return and the thousand years' reign, before the last judgment.

The second element that characterizes dispensationalism is the role attributed to the people of Israel. According to Darby, God had one plan of salvation for the church and a completely different plan for the Jews. The rapture of the church means that the time of the people of Israel has come, when they will be gathered together in the land. With Christ as king in Jerusalem, they will be a blessing for all the peoples of the earth. The role that dispensationalism's scenario for the last days attributes to the Jews and to their land lies behind many forms of Christian Zionism, where political consequences for the evaluation of the situation in the Middle East are drawn from one particular understanding of the last days.

One problem with dispensationalism and similar detailed scenarios for the events of the last days is the way in which they use the Bible, combining different texts from the Old and the New Testaments like pieces in a jigsaw puzzle, without taking account of the metaphorical character of many texts. The problematic quality of such detailed scenarios can also be seen in the great differences between dispensationalist and non-dispensationalist versions. Dispensationalism also builds on the completely untenable idea that God has two separate plans of salvation for the church and for the Jewish people. This is in contrast to the New Testament idea of the church as a fellowship that unites both Jews and Gentiles in faith in Jesus (Eph 2:11–22).

When Does the End Come?

There is much to indicate that the first Christians expected Jesus' return in their own lifetimes. In 1 Thessalonians 4, Paul writes about some people's concern about what would happen to the Christians who had already died before Jesus came back. With a reference to the faith in the resurrection of the dead, Paul assures them that the dead will not be at any disadvantage compared to those who are still alive, and he even appeals to a word from Jesus himself: "For this we declare to you by the word of the Lord, that we who are alive, who are left until the coming of the Lord, will by no means precede those who have died" (4:15).

We find a similar understanding in the passage about the resurrection in 1 Corinthians 15, with the same assumption that Jesus will come back while Paul and some of his contemporaries are still alive: "Listen, I will tell you a mystery! We will not all die, but we will all be changed, in a moment, in the twinkling of an eye, at the last trumpet. For the trumpet will sound, and the dead will be raised imperishable, and we will be changed" (15:51–52). One saying of Jesus in the Synoptic Gospels can also be understood as affirming that some of the disciples would live until he returned: "Truly I tell you, there are some standing here who will not taste death before they see the Son of Man coming in his kingdom" (Matt 16:28; cf. Mark 9:1; Luke 9:27). The same applies to his saying: "Truly I tell you, this generation will not pass away until all these things have taken place" (Matt 24:34; Mark 13:30; cf. Luke 21:32).

The fact that the first Christian generation passed away before Jesus had returned may have caused disappointments, but it did not lead to the abandonment of hope in his second coming. The Second Letter of Peter explains the delay of his return as an expression of God's patience and of his wish that as many as possible shall receive a share in salvation: "The Lord is not slow about his promise, as some think of slowness, but is patient with you, not wanting any to perish but all to come to repentance" (3:9).

The importance of the belief in Jesus' second coming has varied strongly in the course of church history. At times, it has been a truth of the faith without any particular relevance, but at other times, it has been the object of intense expectation. Christians in periods marked by crises and persecutions have been especially interested in the second coming, partly because of the biblical affirmations that such events will occur before Jesus comes back (Matt 24:3–31). The expectation that Jesus would return soon has sometimes led to attempts to calculate when this would happen.

One example is the movement created by the American William Miller, which dated the second coming to 1843/44. Although the predictions failed to materialize, the expectation that it would happen soon lived on in various Adventist (from Latin *adventus* = coming) churches, including the Seventh Day Adventists. The Jehovah's Witnesses, who are known for their erroneous attempts to predict the date of the second coming, also have Adventist roots.

In addition to the fact that they have proven erroneous, such calculations are problematic because they directly contradict Jesus' statement that this date is known only to God: "But about that day or hour no one knows, neither the angels of heaven, nor the Son, but only the Father" (Matt 24:36; Mark 13:32; cf. Acts 1:7). A common characteristic of these calculations is their combination of details from different texts, without taking into account the symbolism that often attaches to numbers in the Bible.

Attempts to identify concrete events in one's own days with events in the last days that are spoken of in the Revelation of John or in other passages are similarly problematic. There have been many candidates for identification with the antichrist (or "the beast," as Revelation calls him); one example is Luther's identification of the pope with antichrist. On a completely different note, the biblical metaphors can help to create a depth in understanding of the events that the church encounters on its path through history—but without any requirement to understand these events as concrete predictions.

There may seem to be something of a tension in the biblical texts about the second coming. On the one hand, they point to signs that the end is drawing near, while on the other hand, they claim that only God knows when the end will come. In Matthew 24, the disciples are exhorted to interpret the signs of the time: "So also, when you see all these things, you know that he is near, at the very gates" (24:33), but the same discourse also states that only God knows "that day and hour" (24:36).

One obvious explanation for this is that the last days are understood not as one delimited period at some point in the future, but as a perspective on all the time between the ascension and Jesus' second coming (cf. 1 Cor 10:11). Such an interpretation also accords with Jesus' message that the kingdom of God has come near: through his first coming, God's definitive salvific action in relation to the world has begun, and it will be brought to completion when he comes again. In this perspective, the various signs that his return is drawing near are not to be used for calculations or speculations, but are a reminder that the second coming and the end of the world can occur at any time. This is also the point that Paul makes when he says that it is unnecessary to be concerned about "the times and the seasons," because "the day of the Lord will come like a thief in the night" (1 Thess 5:1–2; cf. 2 Pet 3:10).

Surprise and suddenness are an important motif in Jesus' sayings about his return and the end of the world (Matt 24:36—25:13; Mark 13:32–37; Luke 12:35–40). He too uses the image of the thief who breaks in when this is least expected, with the consequence that the householder must be vigilant at all times. When this is applied to Jesus' return, the message is that one must remain awake and always be ready: "Keep awake therefore, for you do not know on what day your Lord is coming" (Matt 24:42). The point is not only that one does not know when he will come back: but rather, that it will happen when one *least* expects it: "Therefore you also must be ready, for the Son of Man is coming at an unexpected hour" (Matt 24:44).

Since Jesus can come back when one least expects it, one must live every day as if it were the last day of one's life. However, the fact that *every* day can be one's last day signifies that the expectation of Jesus' return does not press the "pause button" on one's life (so to speak). According to Jesus, the best form of vigilance is to be busy doing what God has called one to do. This is precisely the point in the parable about the master who suddenly comes home: "Blessed is that slave whom his master will find at work when he arrives" (Matt 24:46). At the same time, the expectation of Jesus' return helps to put life here and now in a particular perspective: what happens in this world is not the last word. One day, he who is both the world's redeemer and the world's judge will come back.

While Jesus' identity is a matter of dispute at his first coming, it will be clear to everyone who he is, when he comes back: "Look! He is coming with the clouds; every eye will see him" (Rev 1:7; cf. Matt 24:30). This contrast is depicted in the Christ hymn in Philippians 2, where the story of Jesus from his birth to his death is described as the expression of his voluntary acceptance of a lower state. Through his resurrection and ascension, God "highly exalted him and gave him the name that is above every name" (v. 9). One day, this will be obvious to all: "so that at the name of Jesus every knee should bend, in heaven and on earth and under the earth, and every tongue should confess that Jesus Christ is Lord, to the glory of God the Father" (vv. 10–11). In the present age, the lordship of Jesus is a matter of faith, but one day, everyone will see it (Rev 1:7).

Belief in Jesus' return means that a Christian interpretation of life can never be limited to the personal life of the believer or to the internal concerns of the church. Belief in his return brings the Christian faith into a cosmic context. The Jesus whom the Christian faith confesses is not only the future of Christians: he is the future of the whole world. The definitive salvation that Jesus brings when he comes back is thus not only a salvation for the believers, but something that affects the whole of God's creation.

9.3 THE INTERMEDIATE STATE: WHAT HAPPENS AFTER DEATH?

Up this point, we have seen that the Christian hope is not only a hope for the salvation of the individual, but a hope that embraces the world and the whole of creation. Accordingly, the salvation for which the Christian faith hopes does not mean an escape from physical and bodily reality, but rather a life in a world that is created anew. And this means that in the encounter with death, the Christian hope is first and foremost hope for the resurrection of the body.

Since the resurrection of the dead will take place only when Jesus returns, this does not give a complete answer to the universal human question about what happens after death. Theologians have often called this the question about "the intermediate state," that which lies between the individual's death and the resurrection on the last day.

Where the Greek idea of the soul's immortality influences Christian thinking, death entails that the body dies, while the soul lives on in a bodiless state. As I pointed out at the beginning of the present chapter, this way of thinking has had a great influence on Christian thought, and the widespread understanding of salvation as "getting to heaven" shows that this idea is still very much alive. In a biblical perspective, the idea of such a bodiless existence of the soul is much more problematic. Since the human person is fundamentally a bodily being, salvation for the human person must also entail an existence in which the bodily dimension continues, albeit in an altered form. Since the human being is woven into the created order, his or her hope is not to escape from the world to a heavenly reality, but to lead a life in a world that is created anew.

Even where a Christian theology has envisaged salvation (or damnation) as something that happens immediately after death, it has not, of course, denied the idea of the resurrection of the dead on the last day. But since the focus has been on what comes immediately after death, this has often been a kind of "postscript" with no particular interest of its own. In addition, it has often been thought that the redeemed would live in heaven after the resurrection—not on earth.

The Intermediate State in the Bible

The Old Testament understanding of the human person as a bodily being does not mean that it excludes every idea of an existence after death, as we see in the idea of *the realm of the dead* (Hebrew: *sheol*) as the place where the dead dwell. This seems to have been understood as a shadowy existence to which all the dead come (Job 10:21–22; Ps 89:48). The development of the idea of the resurrection of the dead meant that the realm of the dead gradually came to be seen as a temporary dwelling place (Dan 12:2). Jewish thinking in the intertestamental period developed the idea of a differentiation in the fate of the dead: the good come to a heavenly paradise, while the wicked and the godless come to the realm of the dead, now understood as a place of punishment.

This understanding is reflected in some New Testament texts, such as Jesus' words to the robber on the cross: "Truly I tell you, today you will be with me in paradise" (Luke 23:43). The idea of two dwelling places after death is also found in the parable of the rich man and the poor Lazarus. After their deaths, the rich man is tormented in the realm of the dead, while the poor man rests in Abraham's bosom (Luke 16:19–31). One must, however, be cautious about inferring wide-reaching doctrinal consequences from the metaphorical element in a parable. In the discussion with the Sadducees about the resurrection, Jesus affirms that God is a God for the living, not for the dead, and that this means, in the case of the patriarchs, that "to him all of them are alive" (Luke 20:38). In its context, this is not primarily a statement about the intermediate state, but about the resurrection from the dead. But in order for God to be able to raise someone from the dead, that person must in some sense exist for God.

1 Peter 3:19 speaks of "the spirits in prison," to whom Jesus preached after his death. One can also read a reference to the intermediate state in the Revelation of John, which speaks of the souls of the martyrs under the altar in heaven (6:9–11) and of the great crowd in white garments (7:9–17).

The dwelling place of the dead was not a central theme for the New Testament writers, since they expected Jesus to come back soon. However, Paul is certain that even in death, God will protect him: "whether we live or whether we die, we are the Lord's" (Rom 14:8). Accordingly, to depart from this life means to "be with Christ" (Phil 1:23).

The passage in 2 Corinthians 4:16—5:10, where Paul speaks about being "away from the body and at home with Lord" (5:8), has often been read as a text about the intermediate state. But when he speaks in the same passage about being "clothed with our heavenly dwelling" (5:2), this need not refer to a bodiless existence in heaven. It can equally well refer to being clothed with the resurrection body. Paul writes elsewhere that the hope beyond death is precisely the resurrection: that "I may attain the resurrection from the dead" (Phil 3:11). It is here that the connection lies between what God did with Jesus and what he will do with us: "we know that the one who raised the Lord Jesus will raise us also with Jesus, and will bring us with you into his presence" (2 Cor 4:14).

What Becomes of the Dead?

Although the New Testament does not offer a clear picture of the intermediate state, fairly concrete ideas about what happens after death have arisen in the course of church history, and these ideas have been given the form of church teaching, to various degrees. Catholic theology presupposes that one receives a particular judgment immediately after death, either for salvation or for damnation. The souls of the damned go to hell, while the redeemed either go directly to heaven (the saints) or undergo a process of purification in purgatory. 1 Corinthians 3:15, where Paul speaks of being "saved, but only as through fire," has been seen as offering biblical support for purgatory. Appeal has also been made to 2 Maccabees 12:38–45, which relates how the Jews prayed and offered sacrifice for some of their dead (this text is regarded by Catholics as canonical, but not by Lutherans and other Protestants; cf. chapter 2.2). At the same time, also Catholics maintain that all the dead will rise again on the last day and receive their final judgment.

The importance of the Catholic doctrine on this point lies not least in its consequences for Christian praxis and spirituality. It is held that the believers can call on the saints in heaven and ask them for their intercession, and that the church can pray for the souls in purgatory and celebrate the Mass for them.

The invocation of the saints and the belief that one could help the dead in purgatory generated an important controversy during the Reformation. In the eyes of the Reformers, there was nothing in the Bible to support such ideas, which diverted the focus from the adoration of God himself. Luther did not understand the intermediate state as a conscious state in which people existed in one or other place. He saw death as a sleep, an unconscious state in which the dead person waited for the resurrection. This means that one has no conscious experience of the time that lies between the moment of death and the resurrection, and that it is meaningless either to invoke the dead or to pray for them.

The idea of the relativity of time has lent support in our own day to a similar perspective. The experience of time presupposes that one is alive, but in death, there is little sense in talking about time. This removes the need to speak of an intermediate state, since the individual goes directly from his or her death to the resurrection on the last day.

Despite the traditional disagreement between Catholic and Protestant theology about the dead and how one should relate to them, some Protestant theologians have proposed a reorientation in the understanding of the dead. When Luther had nothing more to say about the dead than that they are in a sleep-like state until the resurrection, his primary intention was to exclude the problematic ideas and practices that were the consequence of envisaging a conscious intermediate state. He had, however, no biblical evidence for his theory, since the biblical texts are mostly allusive and unclear on this question.

There is a price to be paid for Luther's position, namely, that the dead "depart" from us in a way that many find it hard to accept. In the Lutheran tradition, for example, it has not been customary to pray for the dead, and this has meant that the funeral ritual prays exclusively for the mourners, not for the deceased. A certain reorientation may for example be seen in the newest funeral ritual in the Church of Norway (2003), which says about the dead person that "we will surrender him/her into God's hands."[1]

---

1. Church of Norway, *Order for a Funeral*, 5.

One argument in favor of paying more attention to the dead than has been usual in the Lutheran tradition can be found in the understanding of the church as a fellowship that is not restricted in time and space, but embraces all those who will ultimately be gathered together in the perfected kingdom of God. None of these is at any time outside of God's care (Rom 14:8). We have no basis for saying anything certain about where the dead are, or what they do. All we can say is that we shall rise again on the last day. In other words, the dead have not already received the definitive salvation. When Revelation 6 speaks of the souls of the martyrs, the text displays the expectation that the coming judgment will create justice (6:10). Both for the living and for the dead, the judgment and the definitive salvation belong to the future, to which we look forward expectantly. Until that day comes, both the living and the dead wait in the hope of the coming of God's kingdom.

9.4 JUDGMENT

As we have seen, one central element in the New Testament images of the end of the world is the idea of God's judgment. This has its background in the Old Testament, where God is portrayed as one who summons individuals, the people of Israel, and other peoples to take responsibility for their actions, and who judges them. In many passages, God's judgment is identified with concrete events and circumstances, but the judgment gradually also becomes an important element in the picture of the eschatological "day of the LORD" (Isa 2:5–22).

In the New Testament picture of the judgment, it is Jesus who is the judge. He says in John 5: "The Father judges no one, but has given all judgment to the Son" (5:22), and that "he has given him authority to execute judgment, because he is the Son of Man" (5:27). In the parable of judgment in Matthew 25, the Son of Man is to sit on his throne in glory and judge the peoples. This parable contains an element found in many texts about the judgment, namely, the idea that it leads either to acquittal or to condemnation: "And these will go away into eternal punishment, but the righteous into eternal life" (25:46).

The creeds of the early church also presuppose the idea that Jesus' return entails judgment over both the living and the dead. The Nicene Creed states that Jesus "is coming again in glory to judge the living and the dead," and similar formulations are found in the Apostolic and the Athanasian Creeds. Article 17 of the Augsburg Confession likewise underlines the aspect of judgment in the second coming, when it states that "at the consummation of the world Christ will appear for judgement."

Judgment as Settling Accounts with Evil

The idea of judgment, and Jesus' role as the judge of the world, can at first sight seem problematic in relation to the idea that God loves the world and human beings, and that Jesus is sent in order that the world might be saved. It must, however, be pointed out that salvation in a biblical perspective means salvation from sin and evil. When God judges, therefore, this means that he settles accounts with everything that defies the good will of the Creator, everything that destroys human life and the world that he has created. In the judgment on the last day, accounts are settled definitively, once and for all. After the judgment, nothing evil will any longer be able to destroy God's world. Salvation from evil thus presupposes that what is evil will be judged.

The settling of accounts with evil also entails that those who have done evil will be held responsible for it. Evil is not an impersonal entity, but something that is performed by subjects who are capable of thinking and willing. In the judgment, the Creator summons the individual to take responsibility for his or her actions and choices.

The judgment thus becomes a part of the answer to what is called the problem of theodicy, that is, the question why a God who is almighty does nothing to abolish evil (on this, see chapter 4). The judgment means that God *does* something with evil, both by ensuring that it no longer exists, and by calling to account those who have done evil. In the judgment, justice will be done to all the victims of evil.

Why does this definitive settling of accounts with evil belong to the future? Why does it not happen at once? One reason is God's wish to save. The problem with evil is that no one is only a victim of evil: everyone also shares (in various ways and to various degrees) in responsibility for the fact that evil occurs. This is precisely the point in the understanding of the human being as a sinner whose sin also leads to guilt vis-à-vis God. Accordingly, salvation means, not only being saved from the evil that affects us, but also being saved from the evil that we ourselves commit (which includes the guilt we incur because of evil). This is why the forgiveness of sins is such a central part of a Christian understanding of salvation, and why salvation can also be understood as acquittal in the judgment, or as being saved from the judgment. This acquittal is based, not on one's lack of sin and guilt, but on the fact that one has received the forgiveness of one's sins through faith in Jesus. In the Gospel of John, Jesus says that the one who believes already "has eternal life, and does not come under judgment" (5:24), and that "those who believe in him are not condemned" (3:18). This means that the one who does not believe has no prospect of acquittal in the judgment, since each one must bear responsibility for his or her sin: "Those who do not believe are condemned already, because they have not believed in the name of the only Son of God" (John 3:18). Since the judgment is anticipated here and now through one's relationship to salvation in Jesus, one need have no fear of the definitive judgement. On the contrary, the believer "may have boldness on the day of judgment" (1 John 4:17).

Judgment in Accordance with Faith or Works?

There appear to be two different lines of thought in the New Testament about the basis for the judgment. On the one hand, some texts say that the judgment is decided by whether or not one believes in Jesus; on the other hand, some texts say that one will judged according to one's works. Sometimes, both perspectives are present in one and the same text, as in John 5, where it is first stated that it is faith in Jesus that decides the outcome of the judgment (5:24), and then that at the resurrection of the dead, "those who have done good" will come out from their graves "to the resurrection of life, and those who have done evil, to the resurrection of condemnation" (5:29). And Paul, who otherwise emphasizes that salvation comes through faith, not by works, writes that "all of us must appear before the judgment seat of Christ, so that each may receive recompense for what has been done in the body, whether good or evil" (2 Cor 5:10).

A one-sidedly forensic understanding of salvation and justification (see chapter 6.3) will tend to find the idea of judgment in accordance with works problematic, but it is not equally problematic for an understanding of salvation as something that is effective in the believer's life. In such a perspective, the works will express the effectiveness of faith in one's life. Understood in this way, the works are a fruit of faith, demonstrating that Christ dwells in a person. This idea is expressed in Jesus' saying about the tree and its fruits: "No good tree bears bad fruit, nor again does a bad tree bear good fruit; for each tree is known by its own fruit" (Luk 6:43–44). Another saying links fruitfulness to a person's relationship to Jesus: "Abide in me as I abide in you. Just as the branch cannot bear fruit by itself unless it abides in the vine, neither can you unless you abide in me" (John 15:4).

There is thus no necessary contradiction between the two lines of thought. When judgment is made in accordance with works, the works serve as a sign of how far the reality of salvation has taken effect in the individual's life. When a person is acquitted in such a judgment, this is not because of one's own merits, but because one's sins have been forgiven and God has been allowed to work through one.

Most of the texts dealing with judgment presuppose the possibility of two outcomes, salvation or damnation. For example, the parable of judgment in Matthew 25 concludes by stating that some "will go away into eternal punishment, but the righteous to eternal life" (25:46). This perspective is also expressed in the church's confessional texts, as in article 17 of the Augsburg Confession: "He will give eternal life and endless joy to the righteous and elect, but he will condemn the ungodly and the devils to endless torment."

This raises two sets of questions: first, what the two potential outcomes of the judgment entail for the individual; and secondly, how far damnation truly is the last word, or whether there will ultimately be a possibility of salvation for all.

The Definitive Salvation

Much has been said elsewhere in the present book, especially in chapter 6 on salvation, about what the definitive salvation entails. Here and now, salvation is received in a provisional and anticipatory manner, but then, salvation will be perfect and

Hope

definitive. This means that all wickedness and suffering are overcome, that death no longer exists, and that the human being lives in fellowship with God. Although the focus often lies on the individual and his or her salvation, it is important to underline that salvation in a biblical perspective is something collective and cosmic, something that entails a redeemed humankind and a world that is created anew. The definitive salvation concerns not only the world and its relationship to God, but also God himself. Paul writes that everything, including the Son, will be subjected to God:

> Then comes the end, when he hands over the kingdom to God the Father, after he has destroyed every ruler and every authority and power.... When all things are subjected to him, then the Son himself will also be subjected to the one who put all things in subjection under him, so that God may be all in all (1 Cor 15:24, 28).

This includes not only human beings, but also the whole of the created order, as Paul emphasizes in another passage when he says that redemption concerns the entire creation, which "will be set free from its bondage to decay and obtain the freedom of the glory of the children of God" (Rom 8:21).

As I mentioned at the beginning of this chapter, the Bible employs a strongly metaphorical language to speak of the perfected salvation. When phenomena from our world are used to describe the world to come, they are not to be interpreted directly and literally. In part, the texts point to phenomena that will no longer exist; and in part, to phenomena that will exist to an even greater degree. In the new world, there will no longer be destruction, death, grief, and pain, as the vision in the Revelation of John declares: "Death will be no more, mourning and crying and pain will be no more, for the first things have passed away" (21:4).

The continuity between the present world is seen in the fact that this is not a bodiless heavenly existence, but a transformed and renewed bodiliness on an earth that is created anew (1 Cor 15:35-51; Rev 21:1-2). The metaphor of the recreated world as a city ("the heavenly Jerusalem") also indicates that human fellowship will continue to be a part of the redeemed creation. This is also confirmed when Jesus speaks of the kingdom of God as a table fellowship (Luke 13:29). However, marriage and procreation will no longer be a reality (Matt 22:29-30).

One of the most fundamental elements in the picture of the new world is a new form of closeness between human beings and God. In the words of the Revelation of John: "See, the home of God is among mortals. He will dwell with them; they will be his peoples, and God himself will be with them" (21:3). In the world that is created anew, the human being is fully realized as the image of God, thanks to the immediate closeness to God himself: "What we do know is this: when he is revealed, we will be like him, for we will see him as he is" (1 John 3:2; cf. Rev 22:4).

While the New Testament texts describe the goal for God's salvific action in a world that is created anew, they also indicate a different fate for those who do not receive a share in salvation. In theological vocabulary, this is usually referred to as the idea of damnation.

The Possibility of Eternal Damnation

Jesus' own preaching, as it is recorded in the Gospels, already affirms that there are two possible outcomes of the encounter with God's judgment. Jesus tells his hearers about the two paths, the broad path "that leads to destruction" and the narrow path "that leads to life" and (Matt 7:13–14). He insists that there is little value in gaining the whole world, if one "forfeits one's life" (Matt 16:26*; Mark 8:36*) or "loses or forfeits one's own self" (Luke 9:25*). In the parable about judgment in Matthew's Gospel, damnation is linked to God's judgment, where the unrighteous "will go away into eternal punishment, but the righteous into eternal life" (25:46).

When the possibility of damnation is spoken of, we also find the concept of *hell*. The Greek word here is *gehenna*, which alludes to the Valley of Hinnom outside Jerusalem (Hebrew: *ge-hinnom*), a place that was used in the Old Testament period for sacrifice to idols, including the sacrifice of children (2 Chr 28:3; 33:6; Jer 7:31). The Valley of Hinnom thus became also the place for God's judgment and punishment of these wicked deeds (Jer 7:32; 19:6–7). In the intertestamental period, the concept was detached from its geographical localization and was seen as the place of God's punishment after the judgment on the last day. This is how Jesus too uses the concept, when he says that God is the one who "has authority to cast into hell" (Luke 12:5; cf. Matt 5:29; 18:9; Mark 9:45, 47). Jesus does not say much about what hell is like. All he says is that it is a place of eternal *fire* (Matt 18:8; 25:41; Mark 9:43). But it is clear that this is meant metaphorically, since Jesus can also use a completely opposite picture of hell, namely, being "thrown into the outer darkness" (Matt 8:12).

The idea of damnation must be understood first and foremost as a contrast to the message about salvation. When God gives human beings eternal life through Jesus, this is in order that they may escape damnation: "For God so loved the world that he gave his only Son, so that everyone who believes in him may not perish but may have eternal life" (John 3:16).

Many passages in the New Testament Letters express the idea of salvation and damnation as alternative possibilities for human beings (1 Cor 1:18; 2 Cor 2:15–16; 4:3–4; Phil 1:28; 2 Thess 2:10; Heb 10:39). Although the division between salvation and damnation takes effect already here and now, damnation in the true sense of the term is a result of God's judgment on the last day, as (for example) Paul puts it in 2 Thessalonians:

> . . . when the Lord Jesus is revealed from heaven with his mighty angels in flaming fire, inflicting vengeance on those who do not know God and on those who do not obey the gospel of our Lord Jesus. These will suffer the punishment

of eternal destruction, separated from the presence of the Lord and from the glory of his might, when he comes to be glorified by his saints and to be marveled at on that day among all who have believed (2 Thess 1:7–9).

The Revelation of John likewise describes the possibility of damnation as a contrast to the coming salvation. Its description of the new Jerusalem speaks of those who are not allowed to enter the city: "Outside are the dogs and sorcerers and fornicators and murderers and idolaters, and everyone who loves and practices falsehood" (22:15; cf. 21:27). Damnation is also called "the lake of fire" (Rev 19:20), where the devil and his helpers will end up, "and they will be tormented day and night forever and ever" (20:10). Death and the realm of the dead will also end up in the lake of fire, as well as all those whose names were not written in "the book of life" (Rev 20:14–15).

It is obvious that the texts' descriptions of the possibility of damnation are metaphorical attempts to describe the eschatological reality; but they have been understood in a highly literal manner in church history, while the popular and ecclesial imagination has further embroidered the biblical pictures. In this way, hell has often been understood as a subterranean torture chamber where the damned undergo unending physical torments. And the devil has often been thought of as a kind of prince of hell who presides over the torments. We find expressions of such an understanding both in Dante's *Divine Comedy* in the thirteenth century and in various folktales.

However, the idea of the devil as the prince of hell contradicts the New Testament understanding of damnation as an expression of God's judgment. The first on whom this judgment falls is the devil himself, and this is why Jesus speaks of "the eternal fire prepared for the devil and his angels" (Matt 25:41).

A literal interpretation of the various images used by the Bible to describe damnation is likewise theologically untenable. Since it is an expression of the eschatological judgment, damnation is not a direct continuation of the reality we know, the reality about which we can have concrete ideas. What we can say is that damnation is a contrast to salvation, and that to be damned means that one fails to realize the deepest destiny of the human being, namely, salvation. In damnation, the human being encounters God as the judge, as the one who withdraws his blessing. In Paul's words, it is "eternal destruction, separated from the presence of the Lord and from the glory of his might" (2 Thess 1:9).

Through the judgment, God puts an end once and for all to sin and wickedness. The possibility of damnation means that this judgment falls on a human being whose life is woven into evil and who refuses to accept salvation through faith in Jesus.

When damnation is spoken of as "eternal," this affirms its definitive character. The church's tradition has often understood this to mean that damnation is a state that lasts forever, as we see in article 17 of the Augsburg Confession, where it is said that the torment of the damned will be "endless." This position has been attacked by proponents of *annihilationism*, the theory that the damned simply cease to exist. This is the official teaching among the Adventists, but it has spokesmen in other churches too, such as John Stott, the Anglican theologian and leader of the Evangelical movement.

Annihilationists have appealed to the fact that several concepts that the Bible employs to speak of damnation literally mean being destroyed or ruined (e.g., in Luke 9:25), and that this indicates annihilation rather than a state that lasts forever. The image of fire in connection with damnation points in the same direction, since fire consumes, and what it burns ceases to exist (2 Pet 2:6; Rev 20:9). In addition to exegetical arguments of this kind, they hold that it is unreasonable to inflict a punishment that lasts forever as the penalty for sin that is committed in a finite lifetime.

The problem with annihilationism is that it too paints a somewhat concrete picture of what damnation entails (even if this deviates from the traditional picture). One can also ask whether it is compatible with the idea of the absoluteness and ineluctability of the judgment. If damnation is understood as annihilation, would not this imply that one can "be finished with" God's judgment, so to speak, and that a human being "settles the account" of one's sins by ceasing to exist?

Will All Be Saved at the End?

Another alternative to the traditional understanding of damnation is the *doctrine of the apokatastasis* (from Greek *apokatastasis panton* = the restoration of all things). In the New Testament, the phrase is used only once, in Acts 3:21—in a slightly different context. From Origen in the third century onwards, there have been some who claimed that damnation cannot be God's last word. At the last, all must be saved. Various versions of this position have won considerable support in modern theology. We find such an understanding in Schleiermacher at the beginning of the nineteenth century, and Barth's theology too gave an impulse in this direction, although Barth's respect for God's freedom made him refuse to assert that all *must* be saved.

It is above all Paul's affirmation that God will ultimately "be all in all" (1 Cor 15:28) that has been seen as providing biblical support for this idea. This text may appear hard to reconcile with the idea of eternal damnation, and it can seem difficult to unite the New Testament understanding of God as love with the idea that he will condemn some persons to eternal damnation. One can also ask how the definitive salvation can truly be perfect, if the redeemed live in the consciousness that other persons are damned.

One problem with the idea that all are saved at the last is that it risks not taking seriously the necessity of judgment. Would it be right of God to let victims and assailants meet each other in the perfected kingdom of God, if the assailants had never been willing to face up to what they had done? In order to avoid such a consequence, most proponents of the idea of *apokatastasis* would retain the idea of judgment, but they would claim that the judgment is not necessarily God's last word. Where they do envisage the possibility of damnation, this would at most be something transitory, until ultimately all are saved. Although there will indeed be a double outcome of the judgment, those who are condemned will get a new chance to let themselves be reshaped by the power of love. Alternatively, one can think that one will get such a chance after death, but before the final judgment. Ultimately, when face to face with God's love, no one will reject it.

One central objection to an *apokatastasis* doctrine is the weak biblical evidence. Most of the texts that say something about the judgment appear to be saying something completely different. One can also object that the assertion that everyone will be saved at the last contradicts human freedom; and that the explanations of how this will nevertheless happen are little more than speculative constructions.

But while it is not hard to point to decisive objections to the *apokatastasis* doctrine, one cannot resist the conclusion that it identifies challenging aspects of the notion of an eternal damnation. One can be disturbed by the idea that God really will not succeed in saving more than what may be a small number of the human beings whom he loves. And it is certainly untenable to attempt to come to terms with this by doubting whether God does genuinely want to save everyone—as is the case, for example, when Calvin teaches that God has predestined some persons to damnation (cf. chapter 6.4). On the contrary, the New Testament states that Jesus is an expiation for the sins of all the world, not only those of Christians (1 John 2:2), and that God "desires everyone to be saved and to come to the knowledge of the truth" (1 Tim 2:4). That some will ultimately be damned, despite God's desire to save all: this is a mystery in itself.

I believe, nevertheless, that there is no basis for asserting in a doctrinal form that all will be saved at the last. At the same time, we have no basis for asserting the opposite, namely, that God will ultimately *not* succeed in saving all. In keeping with the idea that God wants everyone to be saved, it is the church's task to hope and to pray for the salvation of all, while preaching the gospel through which people can be saved. But the church has no mandate to deny the possibility of damnation, and thereby deny the existential seriousness in Jesus' warning against "forfeiting one's life" (Matt 16:26*).

It is important to be critical of every tendency to give the impression that we ourselves know who will be saved and who will be damned. This breaches the biblical principle that "the judgment is God's" (Deut 1:17). In Jesus' preaching, the judgment contains an element of surprise. One should take the possibility of damnation as a warning against one's own certainty. It is not something one should use to classify others (Luke 13:23–30).

9.5 HOPE AS THE PERSPECTIVE FOR THE CHRISTIAN INTERPRETATION OF LIFE

It is easy for the doctrine about the last things to take on a somewhat speculative air. There are many questions about which one can speak only with caution. Nor is it easy to expound, within the framework of a dogmatic presentation, the metaphorical language that the Bible often employs in its message about the future. The future plays a very important role for the Christian interpretation of life, not as an object of speculation, but as the starting point for understanding life here and now. In a Christian perspective, hope is not a starting point for fleeing into dreams of a better future, but a perspective on the present day. The hope that the kingdom of God will one day be victorious gives us the faith that it is worth fighting for the good and against the evil. The faith that Jesus one day will return makes faith in Jesus here and now meaningful. The fact that God will one day judge the world means that all the judgments made by human beings have at most a relative validity. The definitive judgment is God's.

A Christian interpretation of life entails an understanding of life as fundamentally given by God, the Creator of heaven and earth. We are not creators of ourselves and of our lives: we receive everything from God's hand. Faith in a good God also entails that one understands evil, not as something that comes from God, but as something from which he wants to save the world through salvation in Jesus Christ. Through Jesus' resurrection, the reality of salvation is anticipated in our world, and through faith in Jesus, people can already now receive this salvation. The Christian hope entails a certainty that the God who has revealed himself in Jesus also has the world's future in his hand.

Glossary

Adoptionism/adoptionists: a theological current in the early church that claimed that Jesus was not God's Son from all eternity, but that he acquired this status at a later point in time.

Anabaptists: movements belonging to the Radical Reformation in the sixteenth century and their successors.

Anglican: the name of churches with roots in the sixteenth-century Reformation in England.

Anthropomorphic image of God: an understanding of God in which God is formed in the image of the human being.

Apocalyptic: the name of currents that believe that the world's end is near at hand, and that have concrete ideas about the events that lead up to this.

Apostolic succession: the unbroken chain of bishops who follow one another, from the apostles onwards.

Arianism/Arians: a theological current in the early church originating with Arius' teaching that Jesus was not God's Son from all eternity, but was a divine creature who came into being before everything else was created.

Arminian: designates theological positions in the tradition from Arminius.

Atheism/atheist: the idea that there is no God.

Atonement, doctrine of: theological interpretation of the significance of Jesus' death.

Baptists: the name of churches that practice "believers' baptism" and have their origin in movements in the sixteenth and seventeenth centuries.

Calvinist: designates theological positions that stand in the tradition from Calvin.

Canon: in a theological context, the name for the collection of the biblical writings (the biblical canon) (from Greek *kanon* = guideline).

Catholic: a designation of the church's general and universal character; used as a self-designation by the Roman Catholic Church.

Charism: a spiritual gift or a service in the church, bestowed by the Spirit.

Glossary

Charismatic: a theological and ecclesial current that emphasizes the experience of the Spirit and the gifts of the Spirit.

Chiliasm: a way of thinking about the last days that has its starting point in the idea of the thousand years' reign (Rev 20).

Christology: the doctrine about Jesus Christ.

Congregationalist: a church order in which the local congregations are completely independent in relation to each other.

Council: a church assembly.

Deism: belief in a God who has created the world, but who does not intervene actively in history.

Descriptive: giving an account of how things are (the antithesis of "normative").

Deuteronomist historical books: a name given to Deuteronomy, Joshua, Judges, and the books of Samuel and the Kings in the Old Testament.

Dispensationalism: a way of understanding salvation history and the last days that has its origin in John Nelson Darby.

Donatism/Donatists: a current in the church in North Africa in the fourth century that claimed that sacraments administered by a priest who leads an unworthy life are invalid.

Dualism/dualist: a way of thinking that understands reality on the basis of two basic principles (unlike, e.g., monism).

Early church: a term covering the Christian church from the beginning until the start of the Middle Ages, ca. 500.

Eastern church: a designation for that part of Christendom that goes back to the church in the Eastern Roman Empire, with Greek as its language. It separated from the Western church in the Great Schism of 1054. This concept is often used today to speak of the Orthodox churches.

Ecclesiology: the doctrine about the church.

Economic Trinity: The Trinity, as it is in its working in the world (in contradistinction to the immanent Trinity).

Ecumenical: that which is common to the churches, and that which concerns unity between the churches.

Enthusiasts: a polemical name for the radical wing of the Reformation in the sixteenth century.

Episcopal: church orders with a system that includes bishops.

Episcopal succession: see "Apostolic succession."

Eschatology: the doctrine of the last things (the last days).

Glossary

Evangelical: (1) that which is in agreement with the gospel. This is a self-designation of Lutheran, Reformed, and other Protestant churches.

(2) the name of a group of conservative Protestant churches and theologians, especially in the United States and Great Britain.

Faith and Order: The commission for theology and church order in the World Council of Churches.

Feminist theology: theology that takes its starting point in women's experience and uses a feminine perspective.

General revelation: God reveals himself and his will through nature and the human conscience.

Gnostic: a name given to various currents in classical antiquity that emphasized spiritual knowledge (Greek: *gnosis*) and stressed the antithesis between the spiritual and the material.

Hamartiology: the doctrine about sin.

Image of God: the idea that the human being is created in the image of God and has similarities to God (Gen 1:27).

Immanence/immanent: these words can have a variety of meanings. As the antithesis of transcendence/transcendent, they signify that which is within the world of human experience.

Immanent Trinity: the Trinity, as it is in the internal relationship between the divine persons (in contradistinction to the economic Trinity).

Kenosis: the idea that Jesus renounced ("emptied himself of," from Greek *ekenosen*, "emptied") his divine status and characteristics when he was born as a human being (Phil 2:7).

Laity, layperson: terms often used in the church of those who are not priests or ordained ministers.

Liberation theology: a theology that takes its starting point in the experiences of oppressed persons and groups.

Lutheran: the name of the churches that have their roots in Luther's Reformation in sixteenth-century Germany.

Manichaeism: a religious movement with its roots in Iran in the third century AD. It emphasized the antithesis between spirit and matter, and regarded good and evil as two fundamental principles in existence that are locked in a mutual struggle.

Metaphor: a word or expression that is used as an image or in a transposed sense.

Methodist: an ecclesial tradition with its roots in the movement founded by John Wesley.

Millennialism: a way of thinking about the last days with its starting point in the idea of the thousand years' reign (Rev 20).

Ministry: in a theological context, the name of ecclesial services such as those of priest, bishop, etc.

Modalism/modalists: a theological current in the early church that regarded the persons in the Trinity as three modes (Latin: *modus*) in which the one God acts in relation to the world.

Monism/monist: a way of understanding reality on the basis of one fundamental principle (as opposed, e.g., to dualism).

Monophysitism/Monophysites: a theological current in the early church that claimed that Jesus had only one nature.

Naturalism/naturalistic: an understanding of reality with its starting point in the concrete reality that is perceptible to the senses.

Natural law: the idea that there exist universal norms, and that these can be recognized by all human beings.

Natural theology: affirmations about God that are based on what we can experience.

Nestorianism/Nestorians: a theological current in the early church that emphasized the distinction between the human and divine natures of Jesus.

Normative: statements that express how something ought to be (the antithesis of "descriptive").

Ontology: the doctrine about that which exists; the doctrine about how things are.

Ordination: the commissioning or consecration for specific ecclesial ministries (e.g., pastor or priest).

Oriental Orthodox churches: a collective term for churches that did not accept the doctrine of two natures (Council of Chalcedon, 451), e.g., the Coptic, Ethiopic Orthodox, and Armenian Apostolic churches.

Orthodox: holding the correct doctrine; used as a self-designation by the Orthodox churches.

Pelagianism: a theological position originating in Pelagius.

Pentecostal: belonging to, or referring to, the Pentecostal movement.

Platonic: a way of thinking that goes back to the philosopher Plato, often marked by the antithesis between spirit and matter.

Pneumatology: the doctrine about the Spirit.

Pre-existence: in a theological context, this usually refers to the idea that Jesus existed as the Son of God before he was conceived and born as a human being.

Glossary

Protestant: a collective term for churches that are not Catholic or Orthodox, and that mostly stand in the tradition from the sixteenth-century Reformation.

Reformation (adjective): ways of thinking or principles that go back to the sixteenth-century Reformation.

Reformed: a designation of the churches that have their roots in the Swiss Reformation in the sixteenth century.

Revelation: something that was hidden becomes visible.

Secular: having to do with the world; that which is not marked by religion and the church.

Secularization: a process whereby the church and religion lose influence.

Semipelagianism: a diluted version of Pelagianism that emphasized the human being's ability to adhere to grace.

Septuagint: a translation of the Old Testament into Greek, from ca. the second century BC.

Soteriology: the doctrine about salvation.

Special revelation: God's revelation through the history of the people of Israel and through Jesus Christ.

Supersessionism: a theology that holds that the church has replaced the people of Israel as God's people.

Synodal: a church order in which the church is governed by elected councils and assemblies.

Synoptic Gospels: a collective term for the Gospels of Matthew, Mark, and Luke.

Theodicy: the attempt to explain how a good God can allow wickedness and suffering.

Theology: the doctrine about God; this term is used more narrowly about the doctrine of God, and more broadly about Christian doctrine in general.

Transcendence/transcendent: that which lies outside the world of human experience.

Trinitarian: that which has to do with the triune God.

United churches: European churches that are a result of unions between Lutheran and Reformed churches.

Western church: that part of Christendom that goes back to the church in the Western Roman Empire, with Latin as its language. It separated from the Eastern church in the Great Schism of 1054. This concept includes today both the Catholic Church and Protestant churches.

Zwinglian: a designation of theological positions in the tradition from Zwingli.

Bibliography

Agreement between Reformation Churches in Europe (*The Leuenberg Agreement*). 1973. http://www.leuenberg.net/leuenberg-agreement.

Anselm of Canterbury. *Cur Deus Homo*. Translated by Janet Fairweather. In *Anselm of Canterbury: The Major Works*, edited by Brian Davies and Gillian R. Evans, 260–356. Oxford World's Classics. Oxford: Oxford University Press, 2008.

———. *Proslogion* [English and Latin]. Translated with an introduction and philosophical commentary by M. J. Charlesworth. Notre Dame: University of Notre Dame Press, 1979.

Augustine. *Epistulae*. Patrologiae Cursus Completus, Series Latina 33. Edited by J.-P. Migne. Paris 1865.

———. *In Iohannis Evangelium Tractatus*. Corpus Christianorum, Series Latina 36. Turnhout: Brepolis, 1954.

———. *Quaestiones in Heptateuchum*. Corpus Christianorum, Series Latina 33. Turnholt: Brepols, 1958.

Aulén, Gustaf. *Christus Victor: An Historical Study of the Three Main Types of the Idea of the Atonement*. Translated by A. G. Hebert. London: SPCK, 1931.

Baptism, Eucharist and Ministry. Faith and Order Paper 111. Geneva: World Council of Churches, 1982. https://www.oikoumene.org/en/resources/documents/commissions/faith-and-order/i-unity-the-church-and-its-mission/baptism-eucharist-and-ministry-faith-and-order-paper-no-111-the-lima-text.

Barth, Karl. *Church Dogmatics*. Vol. 1, *The Doctrine of the Word of God*, part 1. Translated by G. T. Thomson. Edinburgh: T. & T. Clark, 1975.

Church of Norway. *The Order for a Funeral*. 2003, rev. 2004. https://kirken.no/globalassets/kirken.no/om-troen/liturgier-oversatt/funeral_2003.pdf.

———. *The Order of Baptism When Placed within the Principal Service*. 2011. https://kirken.no/globalassets/kirken.no/om-troen/liturgier-oversatt/baptism_within_principal_service.pdf.

———. *The Order of the Principal Service*. 2011. https://kirken.no/globalassets/kirken.no/om-troen/liturgier-oversatt/the-order-of-the-principal-service.pdf.

The Church towards a Common Vision. Faith and Order Paper 214. Geneva: World Council of Churches, 2013. https://www.oikoumene.org/en/resources/documents/commissions/faith-and-order/i-unity-the-church-and-its-mission/the-church-towards-a-common-vision.

Constitution and Rules of the World Council of Churches. 2013. WCC_Constitution_and_Rules_Amended_Busan_2013_EN.pdf.

Cyprian. *Epistulae*. Corpus Christianorm, Series Latina 3C. Turnholti: Brepols, 1996.

Bibliography

Daly, Mary. *Beyond God the Father: Towards a Philosophy of Women's Liberation*. Boston: Beacon, 1973.

Denzinger, Henricus, and Adolfus Schönmetzer, editors. *Enchiridion Symbolorum*. 36th ed. Barcelona: Herder, 1976.

The Didache, or Teaching of the Twelve Apostles. In *The Apostolic Fathers*, vol. 1, translated by Kirsopp Lake. Loeb Classical Library 24. Cambridge, MA: Harvard University Press, 1977.

Gravem, Peder. "Livstolkning." *Prismet* 47/6 (1996) 235–74, 284.

Hägglund, Bengt. *History of Theology*. Translated by Gene J. Lund. 4th ed. St. Louis: Concordia, 2007.

Jenson, Robert. *Systematic Theology*. Vol. 1, *The Triune God*. Oxford: Oxford University Press, 1997.

Joint Declaration on the Doctrine of Justification. The Lutheran World Federation and the Roman Catholic Church, 1999. https://www.lutheranworld.org/sites/default/files/Joint%20Declaration%20on%20the%20Doctrine%20of%20Justification.pdf.

Kolb, Robert, and Timothy J. Wengert, editors. *The Book of Concord: The Confessions of the Evangelical Lutheran Church*. Minneapolis: Fortress, 2000.

Kristiansen, Staale Johannes, and Svein Rise, editors. *Key Theological Thinkers: From Modern to Postmodern*. Farnham: Ashgate, 2013.

Luther, Martin. *Lecture on Romans*. In *Luther's Works*, edited by Helmut T. Lehmann, vol. 25. St. Louis: Concordia, 1972.

———. *De Servo Arbitrio* ("The Bondage of the Will"). In *Luther's Works*, edited by Helmut T. Lehmann, vol. 33. Philadelphia: Fortress, 1972.

———. *To the Christian Nobility of the German Nation concerning the Reform of the Christian Estate*. In *Luther's Works*, edited by Helmut T. Lehmann, vol. 44. Philadelphia: Fortress, 1966.

———. *Die Übersetzung des Apocryphenteils des Alten Testaments*. In: *Luthers Werke, Deutsche Bibel*, vol. 12. Weimar: Hermann Bohlers Nachfolger, 1961.

One Baptism: Towards Mutual Recognition. Faith and Order Paper 210. Geneva: World Council of Churches, 2011. https://www.oikoumene.org/en/resources/documents/commissions/faith-and-order/ii-worship-and-baptism/one-baptism-towards-mutual-recognition.

Pascal, Blaise. "Mémorial." November 23, 1654. https://www.vofoundation.org/faith-and-science/memorial-blaise-pascal/.

The Porvoo Common Statement. London: Council for Christian Unity of the General Synod of the Church of England, 1993. http://www.porvoocommunion.org/porvoo_communion/statement/the-statement-in-english/.

Rahner, Karl. *The Trinity*. New York: Crossroad Herder, 1997.

Second Vatican Council. *Dogmatic Constitution on the Church* (*Lumen gentium*). 1964. http://www.vatican.va/archive/hist_councils/ii_vatican_council/documents/vat-ii_const_19641121_lumen-gentium_en.html.

Tertullian. *De Praescriptione Haereticorum*. Corpus Christianorum, Series Latina 2. Turnhout: Brepolis, 1954.

Vincent of Lérins. *Commonitorium*. Corpus Christiana, Series Latina 64. Turnholti: Brepols, 1985.

Name Index

Aalen, Leiv (1906-83), Norwegian Lutheran theologian, 47
Aalen, Sverre (1909-80), Norwegian Lutheran theologian, 121
Abelard, Peter (1079-1142), French theologian and philosopher, 142, 145
Anselm of Canterbury (ca. 1033-1109), Italian philosopher, theologian, and archbishop, 34, 141-43, 145, 150
Apollinaris (d. 390), bishop of Laodicea in Syria, 127-28
Aristotle (384-322 BC), Greek philosopher, 213
Arius (256-336), priest in Alexandria in Egypt, 65, 126, 265
Arminius, Jacobus (1560-1609), Dutch Reformed theologian, 179, 265
Athanasius (ca. 296-373), theologian and bishop of Alexandria in Egypt, 66, 126
Augustine (354-430), theologian and bishop of Hippo in North Africa, 34, 42-43, 68-69, 107-11, 132, 170, 177-79, 192, 194-96, 207, 249
Aulén, Gustaf (1879-1977), Swedish Lutheran theologian and bishop, 141-43, 145

Barth, Karl (1886-1968), Swiss Reformed theologian, 3-4, 6, 22, 27, 33, 35-37, 70, 99, 180, 194, 262
Basil of Caesarea (ca. 330- ca. 379), theologian and bishop in Cappadocia, 68
Basilides (ca. 85- ca. 145), gnostic teacher in Alexandria, Egypt, 146
Brunner, Emil (1889-1966), Swish Reformed theologian, 99
Bultmann, Rudolf (1884-1976), German Lutheran theologian, 119, 149

Calvin, John (1509-64), Francophone Swiss theologian and church Reformer, 22, 80, 111, 179-80, 214-16, 263, 265

Daly, Mary (1928-2010), American Catholic feminist theologian and philosopher, 74
Dante Alighieri (1265-1321), Italian poet and philosopher, 261
Darby, John Nelson (1800-82), British preacher, founder of dispensationalism, 249, 266
Darwin, Charles (1809-82), British natural scientist, 94-95
Dawkins, Richard (1941-), British biologist and critic of religion, 96

Erasmus of Rotterdam (1466-1536), Dutch theologian and Renaissance humanist, 178

Flacius, Matthias (1520-75), Lutheran theologian, originally from Croatia, worked in Germany, 110

Gravem, Peder (1945-), Norwegian Lutheran theologian and scholar of religion, 8-10
Gregory of Nazianzus (ca. 329-90), bishop and theologian in Cappadocia, 68
Gregory of Nyssa (ca. 335-ca. 394), bishop and theologian in Cappadocia, 68

Hallesby, Ole (1879-1961), Norwegian Lutheran theologian and leader of the Norwegian Home Mission, 133
Hedenius, Ingemar (1908-82), Swedish philosopher and critic of religion, 5

Irenaeus (ca. 135-ca. 200), theologian and bishop of Lyons, 50, 156

Jerome (347-420), theologian and biblical translator, 42
Justin Martyr (ca. 100-65), Christian theologian and philosopher, worked in Rome, 34

Name Index

Jüngel, Eberhard (1934–), German Lutheran theologian, 36–37

Kant, Immanuel (1724–1804), German philosopher, 101

Leibniz, Gottfried Wilhelm (1646–1716), German philosopher and mathematician, 114
Lessing, Gotthold Ephraim (1729–81), German author and philosopher, 35
Lindbeck, George A. (1923–2018), American Lutheran theologian, 6, 72
Luther, Martin (1483–1546), German theologian and church Reformer, 22, 27, 33, 35, 42, 44–46, 50–51, 54, 83–84, 87, 99, 109–10, 142–44, 152, 166–67, 169–73, 175, 178–79, 187–88, 194–96, 201–2, 205, 209–10, 212–15, 219, 237, 251, 255, 267
Løgstrup, Knud Ejler (1905–81), Danish Lutheran theologian and philosopher, 32

Marcion (ca. 85–ca. 160), church leader, worked in Rome and other places, 77, 86, 123
Melanchthon, Philipp (1497–1560), German theologian and church Reformer, 82, 144, 170, 172, 179, 195, 217
Miller, William (1783–1849), American Baptist preacher, 251
Moltmann, Jürgen (1926–), German Reformed theologian, 145

Nestorius (ca. 386–ca. 450), theologian and patriarch of Constantinople, 127
Nome, John (1904–80), Norwegian Lutheran theologian and philosopher, 6

Origen (ca. 185–ca. 254), Christian theologian from Alexandria, 262

Pannenberg, Wolfhart (1928–2014), German Lutheran theologian, 7, 9, 36–37, 113, 119–20, 131
Pascal, Blaise (1623–62), French Catholic philosopher and mathematician, 59–60

Pelagius (ca 350–ca. 420), British-born Christian preacher and theologian, 107–9, 177, 268

Rahner, Karl (1904–84), Austrian Catholic theologian, 71
Reimarus, Hermann Samuel (1694–1768), German philosopher and classical scholar, 118

Schleiermacher, Friedrich Daniel Ernst (1768–1834), German Reformed theologian and philosopher, 3, 262
Schweitzer, Albert (1875–1965), German-French Lutheran theologian, philosopher, and physician, 119
Smith, Joseph (1805–44), American religious leader, founder of the Church of Jesus Christ of Latter-day Saints (Mormons), 30
Stott, John (1921–2011), British Anglican theologian and church leader, 262
Strauss, David Friedrich (1808–74), German Protestant theologian and philosopher, 118–19

Tertullian, Quintus Septimius Florens (ca. 155–ca. 240), theologian and author, worked in North Africa, 34
Theophilus of Antioch (d. ca. 183), theologian and bishop of Antioch, 88
Thomas Aquinas (1225–74), Italian theologian and philosopher, 34–35, 59, 213

Vincent of Lérins (d. ca. 445), monk and theologian in Gaul, 52

Wesley, John (1703–91), Anglican priest and founder of Methodism, 22, 55, 179, 186, 267
Wingren, Gustaf (1910–2000), Swedish Lutheran theologian, 32

Zwingli, Huldreich (1484–1531), Swiss theologian and church Reformer, 214, 269

Scripture Index

OLD TESTAMENT

Genesis

1–11	29
1–2	86
1:1—2:3	48, 98
1:1	93
1:2	86, 163
1:3	88, 193
1:8	96
1:26–29	104
1:26–27	98
1:26	73
1:27	73, 98, 102, 267
1:28	98, 99
1:2	63, 68
2:4–25	48, 98
2:7	98, 103, 104, 164
2:17	112
2:18	98, 101
2:19–20	98
2:21–24	98
2:24	102
3	112
3:1	107
3:3	112
3:5	107, 112
3:11–13	107
3:19	103, 104
6:5	107
8:21	107
9:1–7	100
12	29
12:1–3	79
12:3	78, 224
16:7–11	64
17:10–14	206

Exodus

1–15	157
3:2	64
3:6	60
3:14	60
3:15	60
12–13	211
12	139
15:13	78
20:1–17	108
20:3	63, 84
20:6	79
20:12	102
20:14	102
24:11	211

Leviticus

7:12–15	139
15	198
16	139
16:19	139
16:20–22	140
17:11	139
19:2	182
19:18	108

Numbers

14:18	81
15:22–29	139
24:2	163

Deuteronomy

1:17	263
4:25–31	157
5:6–21	108
5:7	63
6:4	63
6:5	84, 108
7:6	81
7:8	80
14:2	176, 224
20:16–18	77
26:5–10	38
27:9	224

Deuteronomy (continued)

30:15–20	30
32:4	79
32:6	64

Joshua

6:21	77

Judges

3:10	163
6:11–24	64
6:34	163

1 Samuel

10:1	122
10:10	163
10:24	177
16:1	177
16:13	122, 163

2 Samuel

7:14	124

1 Kings

8:27	96
8:32	168

2 Kings

2:23–24	77
17:20	177

2 Chronicles

24:20	48
28:3	260
33:6	260

Job

10:21–22	253
25:4	168
27:3	164
33:4	86, 163

Psalms

1	167
1:2	93
2:7	64, 124
6	93
7:1	157
7:8–9	168
7:11	168
8	86
9:8	168
11:4	96
14:1	61
15:3–4	48
22	82
28:9	157
33:9	88
36:9	104
47:8	94
59:1–2	57
68:3	168
68:20	158
69:35–36	157
78	38
89:48	253
104	86, 87
104:30	63, 68, 86, 163, 164
105–106	157
110:1	152
115	96
116:5	168
116:8	246
135	91
136	86, 91, 92
139	87
143:2	168
148	86, 88

Proverbs

8	64

Isaiah

2:1–5	245
2:2–4	158, 224
2:3–4	245
2:5–22	256
6	81
6:1–4	97
6:3	81
6:7	81
9:7	122
11:1–10	245
11:2	163
11:4	168
11:10	245
14:1	30
25:6	211
26:19	246
38:4	38
40	86
40–55	244
42:5–6	224
42:6	224
43:1–7	157

Scripture Index

45:5	58	**Zephaniah**	
45:22	158	1:14–18	245
49:6	158, 224		
49:15	74	**Malachi**	
53	140	4:5–6	245
53:5	144		
54:7–8	30		
55:7	168	**DEUTEROCANONICAL BOOKS**	
55:10–11	193	**2 Maccabees**	
61:1	163	7:28	88
61:10	168	12:38–45	255
61:11	224		
65:17–25	158, 245	**NEW TESTAMENT**	
66:13	74	**Matthew**	
Jeremiah		1:1–17	131
1:2	38	1:18	131
1:12	64	1:20	163
7:31	260	1:21	117, 158
7:32	260	1:22–23	123
19:6–7	260	3:1–12	121, 199
31:9	124	3:11	164
Ezekiel		3:13–17	121, 199
11:5	63	3:16	164, 208
18:5–9	167	3:17	64, 124
37:14	163	4:1–11	134
Daniel		4:1	164
7	246	4:3	124
7:13–14	120	4:6	124
7:13	245	4:23	238
12:2	246, 253	5:1–12	135
		5:9	125
		5:16	28
Hosea		5:17–42	135
11:1	124	5:17	42
13:8	74	5:20	168
13:14	246	5:21–30	108
		5:29	260
Joel		5:43–48	100, 135
2:28–29	163	5:44	108
2:31–32	245	6:8–9	125
		6:9	64, 96
Amos		6:10	93, 96, 228
5:18	245	6:11	92
		6:12	185
		6:13	106
Jonah		6:25–34	87
2:9	158	6:26	91
		6:33	168
Micah		7:7	92
3:8	163	7:13–14	260
		8:5–13	225
		8:11–12	242

Matthew (continued)

8:11	136, 211, 216, 219
8:12	260
8:20	246
9:1–8	121
9:10–13	211
10:5–6	225
10:7–8	238
11:4–5	121
11:25–27	64, 125
11:27	125
12:1–14	135
12:28	164
12:37	168
13:41–43	168
13:49	93, 242
13:55–56	132
14:13–21	91
14:22–33	91
14:23	64, 125
14:33	124
15:19	108
15:24	225
16:13–20	122
16:18	225
16:21–23	136
16:24	189
16:26	260, 263
16:27	247
16:28	250
17:22–23	136
18:1–5	206
18:8	260
18:9	260
18:20	151, 234
19:4–6	102
19:16–19	108
20:17–19	136
20:28	138, 140
22:29–30	259
22:34–40	82
22:37	84
24–25	246
23:1–36	135
23:28	168
23:35	48
23:37	74
24:3–31	251
24:3	246
24:4–27	246
24:13	181
24:29–30	247
24:30	153, 252
24:33	251
24:34	250
24:36—25:13	252
24:36	251
24:37–41	249
24:42	252
24:44	252
24:46	252
25:31–46	247
25:31	248
25:34–40	168
25:41	260, 261
25:46	256, 258, 260
26–28	137
26:26–29	211
26:26–28	140
26:27	213
26:28	159, 218
26:29	136, 212, 216
26:39	126, 134
26:42	126, 134
26:64	246
27:54	124
27:57–59	146
28	147, 201
28:11–15	148
28:18–20	176
28:18	152, 153
28:19–20	199, 203
28:19	65, 200, 227
28:20	151

Mark

1:2–8	121, 199
1:4–5	159
1:9–11	121
1:10	134
1:11	64, 124
1:12–13	134
1:12	134
1:15	94, 121, 150, 159, 241
1:23–28	114
1:40–42	91
1:44	120
2:1–12	91, 121
2:5–7	64
2:5	159, 205
2:7	121
2:16	136
3:11	124
4:1–20	193
5:35–43	91, 136
6:3	132
7:36	120
8:27–30	122
8:31–33	136

Scripture Index

8:36	260	9:18–21	122
9:1	250	9:22	136
9:30–32	136	9:25	260, 262
9:43	260	9:27	250
9:45	260	9:30–32	136
9:47	260	9:44–45	136
10:13–16	206	10:16	38
10:30	94	10:21	134
10:32–34	136	10:25–37	100, 108
10:45	138, 140, 143	10:25–36	103
12:30–31	108	10:27	108
12:29	63	12:5	260
13	246	12:35–40	252
13:26	153	13:10–17	159
13:30	250	13:23–30	263
13:32–37	252	13:29	216, 219, 259
13:32	134, 251	16:19–31	254
14–16	137	17:34–36	249
14:22–25	211	18:14	168
14:22–24	140	18:30	160, 242
14:25	212	18:31–34	136
14:36	134	18:31	137
15:42–47	146	19:9	158
16	147	20:38	254
16:16	200, 201	21	246
16:19	151	21:27	153
		21:32	250
Luke		22–24	137
1:1–4	39, 118	22:14–20	211
1:15	163	22:16	216
1:17	164	22:18	212
1:26–38	97	22:19–20	140
1:34	131	22:19	212, 216
1:35	68, 131, 163, 164	22:20	206, 217
1:46–47	103	22:42	134
2:9–14	97	22:69	152
2:19	93	23:43	254
2:34–35	136	23:50–56	146
2:41–52	130	24	147
3:1–20	121	24:25–26	137
3:1–18	199	24:31	148
3:21–22	121	24:37–40	148
3:22 64	124	24:41–43	148
3:23–38	131	24:47	159
3:38	133	24:50–52	151
4:1–13	134		
4:1	134	**John**	
4:16–21	159	1:1–14	64
4:41	124	1:1–2	64
5:17–26	121	1:1	64, 124
5:32	159	1:3	68, 86, 129
6:43–44	258	1:4	159
7:11–17	91, 136	1:6–8	121
7:18–23	135	1:10	152
7:22	121	1:11	129, 181

Scripture Index

John (continued)

1:12–13	182
1:12	64, 125, 176
1:14	30, 64, 124, 130, 131, 152
1:15	121
1:18	64, 124
1:19–34	199
1:19–28	121
1:29	140
1:32–34	121
2:1–11	91
2:11	136
2:22	122
3:3–8	164
3:5	159, 200
3:8	164, 190
3:13	151
3:14	150
3:15–16	94
3:16	68, 124, 138, 176, 228, 260
3:17–18	30, 176
3:18	124, 257
3:22	199
3:35	78
3:36	160
4:1–26	225
4:1–2	199
4:24	65, 165
4:42	158
5:20	78
5:21	159
5:22	256
5:24	135, 257, 258
5:27	256
5:29	258
6:15	123
6:52–58	211
6:54	218
6:56	218
6:62	151
6:63	164
8:1–11	135
8:28	150
8:36	159
8:44	115
10:18	138
10:30	65
10:33	64, 125
11:25	159
11:38–44	91, 136
12:16	122
12:32	150
14:6	17, 158, 159, 160
14:9	134
14:10	65
14:11	125
14:14	64, 92, 125
14:26	65, 153, 165
14:31	78
15:4	258
15:7	92
15:16	177
15:26	153
16:7	65, 153, 165
16:8	165
16:13	31, 165
16:14–15	165
16:14	153
17	64, 125, 231
17:18	228
17:21	231
18–21	137
19:38–42	146
20–21	147
20:17	151
20:19	148
20:21	238
20:23	195
20:27	148
20:28	64, 125

Acts of the Apostles

1:1–11	151
1:1–5	147
1:2	134
1:3	148
1:4–5	153
1:7	251
1:8	38, 162, 164, 176
1:10	31
1:11	153, 243, 247
2	153
2:14–36	38
2:16–21	163
2:22–36	130
2:33	152, 209
2:37	38
2:38	163, 199, 200, 209
2:41	176, 193, 199, 203, 225
2:42	212, 234
2:43	91
3:15–19	138
3:19	159
3:21	247, 262
4:8	190
4:12	158, 226
4:31	190
5:31	152
6:2	38

Scripture Index

6:6	236	3:25	138, 140
7:55	190	3:28	169, 187
7:56	152	3:30	63
8:12	193	4:5	169
8:14–17	209	4:25	150
8:16	200	5:8	140
8:26–39	201	5:9	158
8:36–38	203	5:12–21	111, 133
8:39	208	5:12	112, 112
9:18	203	5:17	112
10:34–43	130	6:1–11	189, 200
10:38	164	6:3–4	208
10:44–48	209	6:3	200
10:44	193	6:4	200
10:45–46	190	6:13–14	184
10:45	209	6:14	187
11:18	225	6:18	184
13:9	190	6:19	182
14:2	176	6:23	144
14:23	236	7:6	187
15	225	7:19–25	185, 186
15:22	236	8	177
16:15	204	8:1	173
16:33	204	8:3	64
17:23	60	8:4	188
17:24–28	86	8:9	190
17:27	28	8:13	184
17:31	150	8:14–17	125
18:8	204	8:14	65, 165, 189
19:1–7	190, 199	8:15–16	191
19:5–6	209	8:15	164
19:5	200	8:18–23	105, 113
19:6	190	8:19–22	228
20:7	212	8:21	162, 244, 259
22:16	200	8:24	241
28:24	176	8:26–27	191
		8:28	115
		8:29–30	177
Romans		8:29	99, 125, 189
1:1	177	8:32	138
1:2	80, 123	8:34	152
1:4	62, 134, 149, 150, 164	9–11	177
1:7	81, 182	9:18	177
1:16	39, 158, 193, 226	10:14	176
1:19–23	28	10:17	193
1:19–20	58	11:1	226
1:25	160	11:16–29	226, 227
1:26–27	102	12:3–8	190
2:4	81	12:4–5	229
2:14–15	28	12:6–8	236
2:15	32	13:1–7	103, 110
3:19	169	13:8–10	108
3:20	169	13:8	188
3:21–22	169	14:8	254, 256
3:22–23	169	15:6	61
3:24	169		

Romans (continued)

15:13	241
16:1	236
16:15	182

1 Corinthians

1:2	64, 125
1:3	125
1:16	204
1:17–31	83
1:18	137, 260
2:4	164
2:10–11	165
2:12	165
3:16	164, 229
5:7	140
6:9–10	102
6:19	189
7:32–35	103
8:6	64, 68, 125
10:11	251
10:17	219
11:20–34	212
11:23–25	140, 211
11:24–25	216
11:27	220
11:29	215
12–14	190
12:1	164
12:3	53, 125, 153, 164, 189
12:4–11	236
12:4–6	65
12:10	190
12:27	229, 236
12:28	236
13:5	78
13:9	17
13:12	17, 243
14:1	164
15	103, 148
15:1–2	39
15:3–5	53, 147
15:3–4	42
15:3	38, 41
15:5–7	118
15:6–7	147
15:7	38
15:17	149
15:20–24	150, 241
15:20–23	31, 159
15:20	148
15:23	153, 248
15:24	123, 259
15:25–27	152
15:28	94, 160, 259, 262
15:35–51	259
15:36–44	243
15:36–38	148
15:42–44	149
15:45	133
15:51–52	250
15:56	112
16:16	123

2 Corinthians

1:20	80
1:22	241
2:15–16	260
3:6	86, 164, 206
4:3–4	260
4:4	99, 129
4:14	254
4:16—5:10	254
5:5	241
5:10	258
5:14	140
5:17	160, 173, 182
5:19	138, 176, 228
5:20	176
5:21	134, 140
6:16	229
7:1	183
10:15	183
13:13	65

Galatians

1:4	138, 159
1:19	132
2:16	169
2:20	173
2:21	168, 200
3:26–27	201
3:26	125
3:28	102, 220
4:4–5	125
4:4	64, 125, 131
4:6	65, 165
4:19	189
5:3–4	169
5:16–17	183
5:16	164, 190
5:19–21	183
5:22–23	183, 188
5:22	189
6:2	188
6:14	137

Ephesians

1:1	182
1:4	177
1:10	156
1:20–21	152
1:23	229
2:1–2	159
2:4–5	159
2:8	175
2:11–22	226, 250
2:19	226
2:20–22	229
2:20	233
2:22	164
3:6	229
3:14–15	73
3:16	164
4:3	231
4:4–6	207, 231
4:4	229, 241
4:6	125
4:11	236
4:12	229
4:22–24	183, 184
4:24	99
4:32	185
5:2	138, 140
5:18	190, 191
5:21—6:9	102
5:23	229
5:30	229
6:1	204
6:11	236
6:12	113
6:17	193

Philippians

1:1	236
1:23	254
1:28	260
2	152, 252
2:6–11	53, 130, 133
2:7	181, 267
2:8	138
2:10–11	151
2:10	64, 125, 227
2:11	118, 125
3:11	254
3:20	158
4:8	28
4:10	151

Colossians

1:13	159
1:15	99, 129
1:16	68, 86
1:18	229
1:20	153
1:24	229
2:11–12	204
2:12	200
2:14	141
2:15	141
2:19	229
3:10	99
3:12	177
3:13	185
3:15	229
3:18—4:1	102
3:20	204

1 Thessalonians

4:15–17	153
4:15	250
4:16–17	247
4:17	249
5:1–2	252
5:10	140
5:17	191
5:19	191
5:23	186

2 Thessalonians

1:5—2:12	247
1:7–9	261
1:9	261
2:10	260

1 Timothy

2:4	160, 178, 263
2:6	138, 140
3:2	236
3:8	236
3:12	236
3:16	130
4:14	236
6:15	94
6:16	104

2 Timothy

1:6	236
1:7	164
3:16	49
4:1	243

Titus

1:5–6	236

Titus (continued)

1:7	236
2:14	138, 140
3:5–6	209
3:5	159, 200

Hebrews

1:1–2	29, 77, 123
1:3	99, 129, 152
1:13	152
3:7–8	181
4:12	193
4:14—10:18	104
4:15	134
7:25	152
7:26–27	134
7:27	140, 217
9:14	134
9:15	206
9:24	152
10:23	241
10:39	260
13:15	217
15:13	241

James

1:25	188
2:12	188
5:16	185

1 Peter

1:1	225
1:3	150, 159, 241
1:10–11	123, 163
1:15	182
1:23	159
2:1	220
2:5	237
2:9–10	225
2:9	81, 237
2:12	28
2:22	134
2:24	140
3:1–7	102
3:18–20	146
3:19	254
3:21	200
3:22	151
4:6	146
4:10	190
5:2	236

2 Peter

1:16	153
2:4	114
2:6	262
3:9	250
3:10	252
3:13	80, 162, 242
3:18	183

1 John

1:1–3	118
1:1	38
1:5	17
1:8–9	184
2:1	152
2:2	140, 263
2:15	228
2:18	247
2:22	247
2:23–24	160
3:2	31, 259
3:5	134
3:8	113
3:9	184
3:10	185
3:16	140
4:3	247
4:7	79
4:8	78
4:9–10	83
4:9	124
4:10	138, 140
4:14	158
4:16	78
4:17	257
5:1	122

2 John

1:7	247
1:13	247

Jude

6	114

Revelation

1:6	237
1:7	153, 252
4:11	88
5:8–14	125
5:10	237
5:12	140
6:9–11	254
6:10	256

Scripture Index

7:9–17	254	20:14–15	261
7:9	227	21	223, 242
7:11–12	97	21:1–2	244, 259
19:9	216, 219	21:3	259
19:10	97, 125	21:4	136, 259
19:20	261	21:27	261
20–21	248	22:4	259
20	266, 268	22:8–9	63, 125
20:6	237	22:13	154
20:9	262	22:15	261
20:10	261		

www.ingramcontent.com/pod-product-compliance
Lightning Source LLC
Chambersburg PA
CBHW081417230426
43668CB00016B/2261